MW00354258

Sex Crime, Offenders, and Society

Sex Crime, Offenders, and Society

A Critical Look at Sexual Offending and Policy

Christina Mancini

<small>VIRGINIA COMMONWEALTH UNIVERSITY</small>

CAROLINA ACADEMIC PRESS

Durham, North Carolina

Copyright © 2014
Christina Mancini
All Rights Reserved

Library of Congress Cataloging-in-Publication Data

Mancini, Christina.
  Sex crime, offenders, and society : a critical look at sexual offending and policy /
Christina Mancini.
      pages cm
  Includes bibliographical references and index.
  ISBN 978-1-61163-375-7 (alk. paper)
  1. Sex crimes--United States. 2. Sex offenders--United States. 3. Offenses against the
person--United States. I. Title.

  HV6561.M36 2014
  364.15'3--dc23

                                2013038164

Carolina Academic Press
700 Kent Street
Durham, North Carolina 27701
Telephone (919) 489-7486
Fax (919) 493-5668
www.cap-press.com

Printed in the United States of America
2019 Printing

Contents

Part II

Societal Responses to Sexual Offending

Part III

Sex Crime Policy and Reform

Preface

In contemporary American society sex crimes represent the "worst of the worst" offenses—particularly those committed against vulnerable victims such as children. At the same time, society's definition of "sex crime" has expanded and changed in recent decades. For example, a wide range of sex offenders fit under this broad umbrella—from those who commit statutory rape offenses and non-contact sex crimes to those who sexually assault and murder victims. Thus, substantial variation is evident across this broad category. All too often though, discussions about sex offending and sexual violence in the U.S. have been reduced to pithy arguments. To illustrate, there is the impression among the public and, to a large extent, policymakers, that all sex offenders are essentially homogenous—committing similar types of crimes and doing so because of an underlying mental illness. This view, in turn, has translated into a one-size-fits-all, "get tough" policy response, primarily one that has emphasized longer prison sentences and a host of post-incarceration sanctions. Accordingly, over the last two decades, sex crime legislation has become a "growth industry"—with varied responses designed to curtail sexual offending currently in place across the nation. In short, public discussions and debates have increasingly emphasized sex offender management as a crime prevention tool, but have done so too simplistically—without taking into account the substantial heterogeneity across sex offenders and sex crime.

The end result? Some scholars have claimed that such laws built around a flawed logic of sexual offending are not likely to reduce sex crime. If indeed true, the varied efforts to prevent sex crime—undoubtedly well-intended—could very well be in vain. This book argues that moving beyond simplistic views about sex crime is critical toward fully appreciating the complexity of sexual offending and, most importantly, informing our efforts to prevent it. In turn, such an approach has the potential to lead to policies rooted in empirical evidence and not on perceived notions about sex crime and sexual victimization. The overarching goal of the text is to introduce readers to a broad overview of research and policy issues concerning sex offenders and sex crime reform. This focus has become a critical one in current criminological and criminal justice scholarship. A growing body of literature has been devoted toward understanding the nature and extent of sex crime, its causes, and public and policy responses to sex offending. Yet, relatively few scholarly texts which summarize and review this large knowledge base currently exist. This text seeks to fill this void by examining three critical dimensions of sex crime scholarship which are covered in twelve chapters. Part one discusses the nature and extent of sexual offending and prominent explanations of sex crime. In contrast, part two describes societal responses to sex offenders. The third and final focus of the text examines sex crime policy and reform in the U.S. These broad domains are further described below.

The first theme, "The Nature and Extent of Sex Offending and Prominent Theoretical Explanations," which encompasses four chapters, reviews what is known about sexual offending and sex crime. Chapter 1 provides an introduction to sex crime and current controversies surrounding prominent sex crime laws. Chapter 2 reviews methods to measure sexual offenses and victimization. Chapter 3 traces recent sex crime patterns and trends in the U.S. Chapter 4 applies theoretical perspectives relevant to understanding the etiology of sex offending.

The text then moves into the second substantive domain, "Societal Responses to Sexual Offending," which includes three chapters. This focus is particularly relevant toward a broader understanding of sexual offenders and sex crime policy given that public opinion, and more generally, societal impressions, have played a significant role in the creation of sex crime laws. Here, Chapter 5 evaluates prominent misperceptions of sex crime, offenders, and policy. Chapter 6 moves toward investigating public opinion about sexual offending and sex crime legislation. In contrast, Chapter 7 traces the historical development of societal efforts to respond to sexual offending in the U.S.

The final focus of the text, "Sex Crime Policy and Reform," analyzes prominent laws and policies developed in recent decades to punish and control sex offenders. It includes the remaining five chapters. Chapter 8 assesses the logic and effectiveness of sex crime legislation. Chapter 9 moves toward reviewing methods to determine sex offender recidivism and treatment issues. In comparison, Chapter 10 examines variability in the enactment of sex crime laws nationally, and also variation within the content of sex crime reforms. Chapter 11 reviews current legal challenges to sex crime legislation. Finally, Chapter 12 concludes the text with an emphasis on the future of sex crime policy in America.

There are several talented and kind individuals who have greatly assisted with the writing process. First and foremost, I thank the Publisher of Carolina Academic Press (CAP), Keith Sipe, for the opportunity to undertake this project. The entire staff at CAP has been exceptionally professional and friendly. Beth Hall, Acquisitions Editor at CAP, was a pleasure to work with from the start. She has served as an exceptional resource for both substantive and administrative direction. I also thank Karen Ehrmann, Senior Permissions Editor at Sage Publications, who assisted with granting copyright permissions for a chapter in the text.

Special thanks also go to many professionals and experts for their research assistance. I acknowledge Michael Dineen at Cornell University for sharing his expertise with securing data tracking child sexual abuse trends. David Finkelhor, Lisa Jones, and Sherry Hamby at the University of New Hampshire Crimes against Children Research Center were incredibly generous in responding to my many questions, and with providing great insight into understanding the extent of sexual abuse in the U.S. Grant Duwe (Minnesota Department of Corrections) kindly provided his recent research evaluating innovative sex offender reentry projects, and he too deserves my thanks.

I also extend my sincere appreciation to Jill Levenson (Lynn University) for her advice early in the manuscript process. It goes without saying that my mentor, Dan Mears (Florida State University), deserves outstanding recognition (and frankly, a medal) for his continued guidance, mentorship, and patience shown to me throughout my career. I value his friendship and appreciate his continued support. Gordon Bazemore (Florida Atlantic University) is also someone who has served as an exceptional mentor and has encouraged me to explore this project from the start. Audrey DePass, senior secretary of the School of Criminology and Criminal Justice at Florida Atlantic University, endured many hours of hearing about this endeavor and she too deserves my appreciation for all of her support and help. I extend my thanks to all of my former colleagues in the School of Criminology and Criminal Justice at Florida Atlantic University for their encouragement in undertaking this research. Moreover, my new colleagues in the L. Douglas Wilder School of Government and Public Affairs at Virginia Commonwealth University have been exceedingly supportive of my scholarship. I thank them all for welcoming me into the School and for the kindness they have shown me.

I also recognize the efforts of former graduate student friends and colleagues. Ryan Shields (Johns Hopkins University) reviewed several drafts of chapters and lent his expertise in a number of places. Justin Pickett (SUNY-Albany) served as a great sounding board for bouncing off ideas in the initial development of the text.

My students also deserve recognition. Liron Stav, former undergraduate student at Florida Atlantic University, assisted with developing a list of U.S. Supreme Court cases focused on sex crime policy. Justin Smith, a graduate student whom I supervised at Florida Atlantic University during my tenure there, had keen insight into methods that would best assist students with understanding material from the text. More generally, I thank my students, former and current, for inspiring and challenging me to pursue this line of research.

Most importantly, I thank my family: my mother, Christine Mancini, sister, Danielle Guess, Aunt Carol and Uncle Dick, my in-laws, Betty and Paul Seiden, and my brother-in-law, Jeremy Seiden. My grandmother, "Nanny," as she is affectionately called, has played a pivotal role in my life. She has shown that despite adversity, one can always find a way to fulfill his or her goals. She has done so with grace and humility throughout her life. I thank her for instilling in me a drive to pursue my goals in life despite the challenges that I may encounter along the way. My husband, Jesse Seiden, has shown unwavering support and encouragement for all of my scholarly pursuits. He has served as an exceptional partner for the last decade or so. Words are far too inadequate to express my love for him.

Introductory Note

Few crimes evoke greater disgust, anger, and alarm than sex offenses. As a testament to the seriousness of sex crime, a large body of research has been devoted toward understanding its nature and extent, its causes, and public and policy responses to prevent it. The author argues that despite this knowledge base, current discussions and debates about sex crime and the appropriate policies to address it are far too simplistic, and rarely draw on this empirical body of work. That is, they tend to emphasize that all sex offenders are alike—despite the vast heterogeneity within this broad category. Moreover, many prominent efforts to effectively reduce sex crime are underpinned by misperceptions about the reality of sex offending. From her assessment what is needed for a more accurate view of sex offending in America is a critical look at the following: the nature, extent, and causes of sexual offending, societal reactions to sexual deviance, and the various policy responses developed to prevent sex offending. Moving beyond superficial perceptions is a necessary first step toward comprehending the complexity of a most serious and detrimental crime, and importantly, informing our efforts to better address it. Given the book's emphasis on research and policy, it appeals to a broad audience. Criminology and criminal justice undergraduates and graduates, scholars, and practitioners will find the text's focus, organization, and analysis particularly helpful for their academic pursuits.

Christina Mancini is an Assistant Professor at Virginia Commonwealth University's L. Douglas Wilder School of Government and Public Affairs. She received her doctoral degree from Florida State University's College of Criminology and Criminal Justice in 2009. Dr. Mancini has published close to 20 studies in the areas of sexual offending, sex crime policy, violent victimization, public opinion, and criminological theory. These works have appeared in highly ranked journals such as *Criminology, Crime & Delinquency, Journal of Research in Crime and Delinquency, Journal of Criminal Justice*, and other crime and policy journals. She is currently involved in several studies related to sex crime, criminal justice policy, race, offending, and public opinion. She serves as an editorial advisory board member for the *Journal of Criminal Justice* and *Sociology and Criminology*.

Part I

The Nature and Extent of Sex Offending and Prominent Theoretical Explanations

Chapter 1

Sex Crimes and Offenders

Chapter Introduction

Throughout the 1990s and continuing today, the federal government and states have enacted an array of new sex crime laws in an effort to reduce sexual victimization. With state legislators on average passing in excess of fifty new sex offender laws in any given year (Zilney & Zilney, 2009) the extent of legislative action directed toward sexual offenders highlights the increased concern about sexual violence. Given this focus, this chapter serves to present context for understanding the complex issues surrounding sex crime, offenders, and policy. It first seeks to introduce readers to the wide range of offenses which fall under the general umbrella of "sex crime," and the caveats that arise from these classifications. In addition, it provides an overview of the prominent typologies of sex offenders that have been identified by research.

In its most general terms, the federal government defines a sex crime as "a criminal offense that has an element involving a sexual act or sexual contact with another" (Office of Justice Programs, 2012, p. 17). This definition of course is a broad one. Specifically, an extensive range of sex crimes exists. These categories include rape/sexual battery offenses (such as forced sexual intercourse), sexual assault (e.g., unwanted touching or sexually threatening behavior), child sexual abuse, incest offenses, indecent exposure or public indecency crimes, and statutory rape offenses. With the advent of the Internet, greater attention has been directed toward criminalizing online offenses such as the manufacturing, distributing, and accessing of child pornography. Most recently, "sexting" or sending sexually explicit text messages and pictures in some cases has been outlawed by states.

Below, we turn toward these broad offense categories. Comprehension of them will provide context for the chapter's next section—examining typologies of sex offenders. While definitions of individual sex offenses vary from state to state (an issue we will discuss later in the chapter and text), the following discussion centers on their general descriptions.

An Overview of Sex Crimes

Rape/sexual battery offenses. Although states vary in the language of their legal statutes, rape and sexual battery offenses are typically sex crimes involving oral, anal, or vaginal penetration of a non-consenting person. Notably, prior to the 1970s, most rape statutes across the nation were sex-specific (Belknap, 2007) and did not apply to offenses committed by husband perpetrators (Finkelhor & Yllo, 1985). That is, under the technical application of these prior laws, only women could be victimized by men. Additionally, many of these laws set forth a martial exception—thus, married women could not be legally raped by their spouses. Since then, states have recognized the need for broader laws and have revised their sex crime legislation accordingly. Thus, as this general definition describes, men, women, or transgendered individuals would be protected under this statute. Additionally, these laws have been revised to reflect that sex crimes can be perpetrated by anyone—including spouses.

Sexual assault. In recognition that sex crimes include diverse offenses with different criminal elements, some states have enacted sexual assault laws (Lippman, 2010). These laws typically prohibit a wide range of criminal behavior that fall short of penetration related crimes (in contrast to sexual battery offenses). To illustrate, a sexual assault would involve the unwanted touching of another or sexually threatening behavior (e.g., threatening to commit a sex act against a non-consenting person).

Child sexual abuse. Although any of the above offenses could technically be applied to children (as they are, by legal definition, non-consenting persons), states have created additional provisions to protect child victims of sex crime. For example, in Florida, "lewd and lascivious acts against minors" fall under child sexual abuse statutes and include offenses such as showing children pornography, committing a sexual act in front of a child, or encouraging or coercing a child to commit a sex act (Florida Department of Children and Families, 2011).

Incest offenses. In the U.S., incest-related crimes have been prohibited since colonial times. These offenses involve sexual relationships between family members (Groth, 1982). Incest between adults and juveniles under the age of consent is considered a form of child sexual abuse. Incest can take any form from parental perpetrated abuse to sibling incest.

Indecent exposure/public indecency crimes. The prior crime classifications above are related in that they typically involve physical contact with a victim. In contrast, indecent exposure offenses are more often characterized as non-contact or "hands-off" sex crimes. To illustrate, such an offense might involve a person who appears nude in public or "flashes" his or her genitals or body parts to others. Thus, under this example, the victim has little physical contact with the offender. Despite this difference, these offenses are still considered serious sex crimes. For example, most states require those persons with prior indecent exposure convictions to register as convicted sex offenders (Levenson, Letourneau, Armstrong, & Zgoba, 2010).

Statutory rape. Statutory rape or consent laws prohibit sexual relationships between adults and juveniles who have not yet reached the age of majority. These offenses are distinct from sexual battery or assault because they would not be criminalized if all participants were above the age of consent. There are limits on the reach of these laws, however. For example, some states allow for individuals under the age of majority to marry with parental permission. As a result, statutory rape offenses do not apply to legally married couples where one spouse is an adult and the other is under the age of majority (Cocca, 2004). At the same time, some states have revised these laws to reflect gender-neutral legislation (Loewy, 2005). Thus, modern statutes make no distinction between male and female statutory rape offenders.

Internet and technology-related offenses. A final classification of sex crimes involves offenses facilitated by the Internet or technology. For example, most states have implemented laws that prohibit the manufacturing, distributing or accessing/downloading of child pornography such as videos or images (Mears, Mancini, Gertz, & Bratton, 2008). Relatedly, states have begun to criminalize the sending of child pornography or sexually explicit text messages via cell phones—an act colloquially characterized as "sexting." Under the law, adults who receive pornographic images of juveniles via cell phone can be charged under existing child pornography legislation (X. Zhang, 2010). At the same time, senders or producers of the images (even if they are minors) may also be charged with violating pornography laws (Humbach, 2010).

Special Legal Issues in Classifying Sex Crimes

Before moving on toward discussing sex offender typologies, some caveats about these offense categories are in order. In particular, four legal issues make generalizing across these offenses a more difficult endeavor.

Inherent Difficulty in Generalizing Offenses across States

First, it should be noted that the above offense descriptions are general ones that may or may not be uniform across states. That is, research has documented that significant variation in sex crime legislation exists (Mancini, Barnes, & Mears, 2013). For example, in some states, sexual assault laws would prohibit acts listed in other states' sexual battery statutes, and vice versa. Still other states have broad "forcible rape" laws that cover a broad range of sex crimes, and not merely ones involving penetration-related offenses. In short, some states have adopted distinct "versions" of other laws in different states. We move now to three other considerations that make generalizing about these laws more complicated.

Significant Variation in the Design of Sex Crime Statutes

Beyond detecting variation in the types of measures enacted by states, prior work has identified variability in the content of certain sex crime laws. This issue is one that has implications for the generalizability of sex crime laws nationally and one we will revisit later in the text. For now, however, this issue can be briefly summarized. Under that backdrop, statutory rape legislation is illustrative. As Cocca (2004) explained in her review of statutory rape laws nationally, all fifty states have implemented statutes prohibiting sexual contact among minors. However, these laws are not uniform. Some states have significantly younger ages of majority (e.g., 15 years old) compared to others. Whereas other states such as Tennessee require that an individual be 18 years or older to legally consent to sexual acts. This difference is notable because it indicates that what would be a crime in one state (e.g., a 15-year-old in Tennessee having a sexual relationship with someone significantly older) would be legally permissible in another.

Additionally, as Cocca's (2004) research illustrates, states further differ in the age-span or age-differential provisions of these laws. These provisions typically mandate that one partner be a certain number of years older than the younger partner for a crime to have occurred. For instance, Nevada retains one of the broadest age ranges of all the states at six years. Its age of consent is also relatively younger, in comparison to some other states which have incorporated higher ages of consent (e.g., Arizona and California). Accordingly, a 15-year-old could legally consent to sexual acts in Nevada with a partner up to age 21. Similar to Nevada, New Hampshire mandates that individuals be at least

16 years of age to consent to sex. However, it does not provide for an age differential exception. That is, a 15-year-old could not legally consent to sex with a peer who was slightly older in that state.

Decriminalization Efforts Vary across States

Some states have begun to decriminalize or reduce the penalties associated with certain sex crime laws. In turn, this effort has resulted in greater difficulty generalizing across states. For instance, Georgia recently enacted a new "sweetheart" exception in response to controversy about its statutory rape law. The exemption is designed to reduce the punishment for statutory rape convictions in instances where the victim and offender are close in age. As scholars contend, the change was motivated in part by concern about the unintended effects of statutory rape laws (Christopher & Christopher, 2012). Illustrative of this concern is the case of Genarlow Wilson. Wilson, a 17-year-old high school student living in Georgia had by all accounts a consensual sexual relationship with his 15 year old girlfriend in 2003. A videotape documenting the sexual relationship between Wilson and his girlfriend surfaced soon thereafter and was presented to local prosecutors. In 2005, under the existing Georgia statute, Wilson was charged with and ultimately convicted of committing child sexual abuse. He received a ten-year sentence and upon his release from prison would have been required to register as a convicted sex offender in the state (Stevenson, Sorenson, Smith, Sekely, & Dzwairo, 2009). In 2007, the Georgia Supreme Court reviewed the case and found the sentence to be disproportionate (*Wilson v. State*, 2007). Shortly thereafter, Wilson was released from prison. In response to the controversy surrounding the sentence, Georgia legislators recently amended the law under which Wilson was convicted to include an exception to the minimum sentence for cases where the victim is between 13 and 16 years old and the offender is 18 or younger (Rodriguez, 2010).

Notably, the federal government has followed Georgia's lead in decriminalizing certain offenses. For example, the Sex Offender Registration and Notification Act (SORNA), a provision of the Adam Walsh Child Protection and Safety Act (2006), includes a clause that does not require states to implement registry procedures for statutory rape offenders (particularly when "consensual" sexual activity occurs between a victim who is at least 13 years old and an offender who is not more than four years older than the victim). Thus, the exemption allows for states to reduce post-incarceration sanctions for such offenders. Notably, however, states *may* incorporate such penalties—SORNA, however, does not require it as a provision of federal law.

A different decriminalization debate has ensued among states. It centers around the extension of child pornography laws to penalize "sexting" offenses. As discussed earlier, acts of sending sexually explicit texts or images can fall under existing child pornography statutes if children are involved in the creation, distribution, or sending of the images. The law applies even to the minors who may have created or sent the images. For example, a 15-year-old girl who sends a naked photo of herself to a boyfriend could be charged with creation and distribution of child pornography—which in many states constitute felony charges and typically require that those convicted register as convicted sex offenders (Hinduja & Patchin, 2012).

This broad application of the law has sparked new debates about the purview of sex crime legislation. Should sex crime law apply to incidents of sexting—particularly among teens who have voluntarily sent the images to other teens? In recognition of the debate, some states have relaxed their child pornography laws. For example, some states have reduced the penalties for sexting-related convictions or have implemented diversion programs for youth convicted of sexting offenses. Still other states, such as Vermont, have enacted — according to Wolak and Finkelhor (2011, p. 9) — the "most sweeping reform ... exempting minors from prosecution for child pornography provided that the sender voluntarily transmitted an image of him or herself." Despite this push for decriminalizing certain provisions of sex crime laws, it should be emphasized that not all states have followed Vermont's lead. That is, as Wolak and Finkelhor (2011, p. 9) emphasize, some states have retained a "get tough" stance against sexting for three reasons:

> First, they believe such statutes and the prosecution of youth under them are important to send a message to young people about the dangers involved, even if the dangers are primarily to the youth themselves. [Second,] they also tend to be concerned that the production and circulation of these images will abet sex criminality if they get into the wrong hands and [third, and finally they] undermine efforts to combat the widespread availability of and trafficking in child pornography.

Laws Subject to Judicial Challenge

A fourth and final issue is that these laws are not without legal challenge. Thus, judicial review of them can affect their existence and implementation. This is an issue that we will more fully explore later in the text. For now, it is relevant to highlight that court decisions can directly affect crime laws. For instance, the U.S. Supreme Court ruled on a child pornography law in 2002 (*Ashcroft v. Free Speech Coalition*). Specifically, it considered whether the Child Pornography Prevention Act of 1996 (CPPA), which bans computer-generated images of children engaging in sex acts, violates the First Amendment right to free speech. Thus, under the CPPA, individuals who used computer software to simulate children engaging in sex acts could face felony child pornography charges. At the same time, those who distributed the media or accessed it could be charged with criminal offenses. The Court ruled that Act was overly broad and restrictive, and therefore was unconstitutional. As the *Ashcroft v. Free Speech Coalition* (2002) decision illustrates, even once enacted, laws face judicial challenge. In turn, these decisions can affect whether legislation is upheld, modified, or repealed.

Now that we have reviewed the diverse types of sexual offenses and the legal considerations in generalizing about them, we turn toward examining specific sex offender typologies. The proceeding discussion will provide readers with a comprehensive review of different offender "types" that research has identified.

Sex Offender Typologies

As evidenced by the preceding discussion, significant heterogeneity exists within sexual offending. Scholars have acknowledged this diversity and have developed sex offender typologies to better understand nuances in sexual offending. In addition, these classification systems per Chaffin, Letourneau, and Silovsky (2002, p. 220) "may be geared to [other purposes], including determining appropriate interventions, identifying different etiological patterns, or predicting risk for recidivism." Accordingly, these typologies can be helpful in understanding the heterogeneity — or differences — in patterns of sexual offending. Notably, these classifications have been clinically or empirically derived, and some have been developed by law enforcement. That is, clinicians — such as psychologists — have relied on their direct experience with offenders—or "educated guesses" (Chaffin et al., 2002, p. 220) to develop offender sub-types. Alternatively, other classification schemes have been empirically developed (meaning prior research has found statistical support for their use). Still others have been developed by law enforcement based on their practitioner and field experience with sex offenders. Despite scholarship in this area, scholars caution that the need for refined classification systems is evident, and that not all offenders "fit" neatly into these predefined categories (Terry & Tallon, 2004). With these limitations in mind, we move toward understanding classification systems. Our first focus is on child molester typologies. Our second focus is on rapist typologies. The third emphasis is on juvenile sex offender classification systems. The fourth centers on understanding female sex offenders, and the fifth and last—on "cyber" sex offenders. Before proceeding, one note bears emphasis. The classification systems discussed below are not exhaustive of the ones that exist. However, the following typologies are representative of the major ones identified in the literature. The suggested reading guide provides additional citations about other classification schemes.

Child Molesters

Several typologies have been designed to better understand offenses that involve child victims. Although "child molester" is a broad term described in the extant research, such an offender can commit other offenses—beyond molestation crimes—against children. The following three typologies are the prominent classification schemes found in the criminological literature.

Groth and Birnbaum's (1978) Typology. Sex offender typologies consider several factors related to the offender, victim, and offense. For example, one of the earliest classification systems—a clinically derived one—was developed by Groth and Birnbaum in 1978. It focused on identifying unique characteristics of child molesters. Their pioneering work indicated that such offenders could be categorized as being either "fixated" or "regressed" offenders. Fixated offenders tend to have a preoccupation with children—both socially and sexually. These offenders often experience more satisfying relationships with children than with similarly aged peers. Research indicates they are highly likely to exhibit "grooming" behavior, a process whereby offenders gradually entice children to engage in sexual activity (Hensley & Edwards, 2001), typically by gaining the trust of the victims and their families.

In contrast, regressed offenders normally prefer having sexual relationships with adults. However, their increased propensity to victimize children is typically triggered in response to experiencing a negative life event, such as relationship difficulty or loss of employment. As a result their offenses against children have been seen by some scholars as a coping mechanism to deal with stressful experiences. Additionally, research has identified the role of opportunity in understanding this typology. Many regressed offenders victimize children who are easily accessible—such as young relatives or children with whom they have normal contact.

Research has been generally supportive of Groth and Birnbaum's (1978) classification system. Moreover, their work has assisted in understanding the heterogeneity in offending among different child molester groups. For example, in assessing the dangerousness of these types, research generally indicates that the fixated offenders—primarily due to their fascination with children—are at particularly greater risk of recidivism. Because much of their sexual deviancy goes undetected, they may commit numerous offenses before they are first apprehended by law enforcement (Terry & Tallon, 2004). Additionally, those fixated offenders with a male victim preference are considered particularly more likely to reoffend (Marques, Day, & Nelson, 1994; Marques, Nelson, Alarcon, & Day, 1994). In short, as Terry and Tallon explain (2004, p. 24), "it is the strongly fixated offenders who have the most victims and the highest rate of recidivism ... that should consequently be considered the highest risk to the community." Despite these generally supportive findings, some scholars believe this typology is too simplistic. For example, Simon, Sales, Kazniac, and Kahn (1992) argue that Groth and Birnbaum's (1978) typology overlooks the intricate relationship between levels of fixation and child molestation. Below, additional and more complex typologies are discussed.

Knight and Prentky's (1990) Massachusetts Treatment Center: Child Molester Typology, Version 3 (MTC: CM) Classification System. Several years later, Knight and Prentky (1990) extended Groth and Birnbaum's (1978) typology by creating an empirically-derived multidimensional classification system that focused on the degree of fixation and also, the amount of contact offenders had with children (i.e., high versus low). In particular, their system focused on two axes. Axis I evaluates the extent to which offenders are fixated with children. Additionally, it assesses their level of social competence (e.g., levels of self-confidence, assertiveness, interpersonal skills). Four sub-types fall under this axis:

- high fixation/high social competence
- high fixation/low social competence
- low fixation/high social competence
- low fixation/low social competence

In contrast, Axis II measures the amount of contact an offender has with children. It makes a distinction between high and low levels of contact by considering the intent of offenders who experience high contact with children. Is the high contact motivated by interpersonal or narcissistic goals? For example, offenders who experience high contact that is motivated by interpersonal goals (meeting social, emotional, or sexual needs) are, per the researchers, attempting to establish a meaningful "relationship" with children. In contrast, among high contact offenders a narcissistic goal would involve satisfying purely sexual needs (i.e., the offender is motivated primarily by sexual gratification, rather than the desire to cultivate a relationship with the victim). Thus, two "high contact" sub-types are possible:

- high contact/interpersonal need
- high contact/narcissistic need

Knight and Prentky (1990) consider contact to be a defining variable differentiating child molester "types." Thus, high contact and low contact offenders are qualitatively distinct in that their motivation and intent to sexually offend depend on separate factors. As a result, low contact offenders are further divided into four sub-types first based on the extent to which they caused physical injury to their victims (low or high). Then, these groups are sub-divided again based on whether the offenders are considered to have sadistic or non-sadistic personality traits. Such a classification scheme results in four additional typologies:

- low contact/low physical injury/non-sadistic
- low contact/low physical injury/sadistic
- low contact/high physical injury/non-sadistic
- low contact/high physical injury/sadistic

Since it was developed, the MTC: CM3 typology has been subject to evaluation. Results indicate that it has shown acceptable reliability—that is, other studies have generally found support for Knight and Prentky's (1990) sub-typologies (Looman, Gauthier, & Boer, 2001; see also, Terry & Tallon, 2004). Additionally, separate studies testing this framework report that offenders who fall under the high-fixation/low-social-competence group (identified in Axis I) have the highest levels of sexual deviance (and thus, likely greater odds to reoffend). Axis II findings are less clear, but some general results bear mention. First, no statistically significant differences in sexual recidivism were reported among the Axis II sub-types. Thus, Axis II groups appear to have similar odds of sexual reoffending. One caveat from this general finding was that sadistic offenders committed a greater number of violent offenses. Not least, certain types of "preferential" child molesters (in the high fixation and high contact categories) were found to be more likely to exhibit deviant arousal and to have greater numbers of victims (factors related to increased sexual recidivism; for a review see Terry & Tallon, 2004).

The Federal Bureau of Investigation (FBI) Typologies (Lanning, 2001). The FBI began to extend the work of prior research in the 1980s and developed a series of child molester typologies. These typologies were derived from practitioner and law enforcement observations (see e.g., Lanning, 2001, p. 31). Below, we discuss the most recent version developed in 2001. It considers a motivation continuum and distinguishes between "situational" and "preferential" offenders.

At the first end of the continuum are the more "situational" child molesters. Per the typology, situational offenders may not have a child victim preference. However, situational offenders tend to target victims based primarily on availability and opportunity. Thus, if child victims are available and opportunities to victimize them exist, a situational (and regressed) offender will often turn to committing child molestation offenses. The FBI typology also considers other offender characteristics in their framework. For example, it identifies the following characteristics of situational offenders: less intelligence, lower socioeconomic status, diagnosed with personality disorders (e.g., antisocial personality), has varied criminal background, prefers violent pornography, and is impulsive.

Within this situational category at least three major patterns of behavior are evident: "regressed," "morally indiscriminate," and "inadequate" patterns. The regressed offender typically has poor coping skills. Thus, when confronted with a difficult life event (e.g., quarreling with spouse), this group will often turn toward abusing children to cope, or as a substitute for an adult relationship. In contrast, the morally indiscriminate child molester does not necessarily prefer children for sexual relationships, however, may turn to them to fulfill their own interests (e.g., sexual or for power/control). This sub-type is described by the FBI (Lanning, 2001) as a "user or abuser" of others—indicating that for this particular offender, "the sexual victimization of children is simply part of a general pattern of abuse in his life" (p. 26). The final sub-category includes what the FBI has designated as "inadequate" offenders. This grouping refers to offenders who may be mentally ill, insecure, or socially inept. Often, such inadequate offenders have poor relationships with other adults. Generally, they view children as their only viable sexual outlet.

The further end of the FBI continuum includes offenders aligned more closely with the "preferential" classification. In contrast to situational offenders, preferential offenders often prefer victimizing children, usually having a specific victim type (e.g., certain hair color, body build). The typology also outlines additional traits of preferential offenders: greater intelligence, higher socioeconomic status, diagnosed with paraphilia or abnormal sexual disorder (e.g., pedophilia), tends to have specific history of offending (e.g., may have committed prior sex crimes involving children), prefers "theme" pornography (e.g., child pornography), and is compulsive. This category can be further sub-divided: seductive, introverted, sadistic, and diverse. The seductive offender tends to see the abuse as consensual. They may "court" their victims, treating them as if they were similarly aged romantic partners (e.g., by being very attentive, buying their victims gifts). In contrast, the introverted offender is attracted to children, but lacks the social skills to "court" them (as in the above sub-type). Accordingly, this offender typically engages in a minimal amount of verbal communication with victims and usually molests strangers—often very young children. He may often seek out situations where he would have access to children (e.g., traveling to a foreign country for child prostitutes, marrying a woman with small children). The FBI (Lanning, 2001) describes the sadistic group as aggressive offenders who are sexually aroused by inflicting violence. Often, they will target stranger victims. Because of their reliance on physical violence, they are considered particularly dangerous. The final classification includes diverse offenders. Per Lanning, the driving motivation for this offender is sexual experimentation. The main criteria for including children may be that they are new or less threatening sexual targets.

The FBI (Lanning, 2001) typology—while possessing some of the hallmarks of the earlier systems—is considered a more flexible framework. Thus, under this classification system, "a preferential sex offender can have some of the motives and behavior patterns of a situational sex offender and vice versa. It is a matter of degree" (p. 25). For example, consider the following scenario: For a situational child molester, "sex with children may range from a 'once-in-a-lifetime' act to a long-term pattern of behavior. The more long-term the pattern, the further down the continuum he may move ... exhibit[ing] more and more of the behavior patterns of the preferential-type offender." Research has been supportive of this general framework, particularly its focus on a continuum of motivation, rather than a dichotomy of one—as found in Groth and Birnbaum's (1978) work. For example, Simon et al. (1992) argued that their analysis indicates that fixation with children occurs along a broad range (thus, fixation is continuous and not dichotomous). So, some offenders may have high levels of fixation (prefer exclusive contact with children), some medium levels (prefer neither high nor low levels of contact), and still some may have none at all (prefer exclusive contact with adults). What might predict whether those on the "medium" and "low" dimensions of fixation offend is the presence of various other factors (e.g., marital discord, availability of minor victim). More generally, the FBI's conception of situational versus preferential offenders accords with the other typologies that we have discussed (such as the MTC: CM3 typology). Table 1.1 provides a summary of child molester typologies.

Rapists

Research along this line has also examined the characteristics of rapists. In contrast to the earlier typologies, most of this work has focused on male offenders who have committed sex crimes against adult women. In particular, several typologies have been developed by researchers. The three discussed below are representative of the prominent classification systems that currently exist.

Groth's (1979) typology. Once again, Groth's (1979) research contributes greatly to this literature. In particular, his work, based on clinical observations, identified three types of rapists. The first classification—the "anger" rapist—describes an offender who typically experiences difficulty interacting with others and in turn displaces this hostility by sexually offending. These offenses typically involve significant physical violence, force, and victim humiliation. Rather than being carefully planned, these crimes are thought to occur spontaneously and are often triggered by interpersonal conflict, such as an argument involving the offender.

The second rapist sub-type identified by prior research is the "power" rapist. This type emphasizes that rape is expressive of an offender's need to dominate or control victims. These offenses are typically committed by men who feel sexually inadequate or perceive

Table 1.1. Child Molester Typologies

Typology	Distinguishing Characteristics
Groth and Birnbaum's (1978) Child Molester Typology	*Fixated vs. regressed dichotomy* *Fixated offenders* a) abuse because of an innate and persistent attraction to children and fascination with childhood, and b) often see their crimes as consensual "relationships" *Regressed offenders* a) prefer adult sexual and interpersonal relationships, and b) typically offend after experiencing stressors or negative life events (e.g., argument with spouse, loss of job)
Knight and Prentky's (1990) MTC: CM, Version 3	*Focuses on two axes* *Axis 1* a) measures the degree of fixation offenders have with children, and b) offenders' level of social competence (e.g., self-confidence, assertiveness) *Axis 2* a) measures the amount of contact offenders have with children, b) the meaning of the contact (e.g., does it fulfill purely sexual or social needs?), and c) amount and type of injury involved in the contact (e.g., verbal threats, use of physical force)
FBI Typologies (2001)	*Considers motivation along a continuum; distinguishes between situational and preferential offenders* *Situational offenders* a) target victims based on availability, not necessarily preference, and b) fall into three categories: regressed, morally indiscriminate, and inadequate *Preferential offenders* a) prefer victimizing children, b) have a victim "type" (e.g., female, long hair), and c) are further sub-divided into four categories: seductive, introverted, sadistic, and diverse

threats to their masculinity. Sexual assault, then, is viewed as a tool through which offenders can assert their dominance over women. On average, victims are unlikely to be physically harmed by these rapists since the offender's primary motivation driving the offense is the need to feel in control, rather than the need to express anger or hostility (as in the first classification). Some prior investigations reveal these offenses involve significantly more planning than anger rapes.

The final category is comprised of "sadistic rapists," or offenders who are sexually aroused by inflicting pain on victims. These offenders are the rarest among this particular typology of rapists. Because they receive sexual gratification from physically harming and torturing victims, they are considered to be on the most extreme and violent end of the rape spectrum. Sadistic rapes often involve premeditation and careful selection of victims—who often share some type of distinct physical characteristic (e.g., small build, long hair).

Efforts to assess the validity of Groth's (1979) typology have generally been mixed. Part of the issue, according to scholars, has been that these types are rarely mutually exclusive. Accordingly, in any given sample, a majority of rapists could be classified as fitting both the anger and power sub-types (Lisak, 2011). In assessing which typology likely poses the greatest risk to society, Groth (1979) endorses the view that the sadistic offender—given his propensity to inflict violence and torture on victims—could be classified as the most dangerous and predatory rapist sub-type. The next rapist typology expands on this earlier work.

Knight and Prentky's (1990) Massachusetts Treatment Center: Rapist Typology, Version 3 (MTC: R3). Knight and Prentky (1990) extended Groth's (1979) focus by developing an empirically-derived multi-dimensional typology that included four distinct motivations to sexually offend. These rapist groupings were described as follows: "opportunistic rapist," "pervasively angry rapist," "sexual gratification rapist," and not least, the "vindictive rapist." Within each sub-type, additional factors were considered for a final classification system of nine types.

The opportunistic rapist tends to commits impulsive sex crimes. Typically, contextual or situational factors (e.g., encountering a victim during the commission of another offense, such as a burglary, a chance encounter with a woman at a party) affect the likelihood of offense. Within the opportunistic category, Knight and Prentky (1990) further classify offenders on the basis of social competence (e.g., levels of assertiveness, interpersonal and communication skills). This classification scheme results in two groups:

- opportunistic/high social competence (Type 1)
- opportunistic/low social competence (Type 2)

In contrast, the primary motivation for the pervasively angry rapist (Type 3) is presumed to be "global and undifferentiated anger" that pervades virtually all aspects of the offender's life (Knight, 1999, p. 312). On average, these offenders inflict physical violence and aggression in the commission of their sex crimes. Notably, this classification accords with Groth's (1979) earlier conception of the anger rapist. Given that generalized anger motivates offending among this group, only one classification system ("the pervasively angry rapist") is outlined by Knight and Prentky (1990).

The next and third broad category includes sexually motivated offenders. Per Knight and Prentky (1990), these offenders are compelled to commit rape primarily to fulfill sexual needs. Typically, these offenders exhibit a high degree of sexual preoccupation (e.g., sexual fantasizing, using pornography). This grouping is further sub-divided on the basis of whether their sexual preoccupation is due to the fusion of sexuality and violence (sadism) or expressive of dominance needs/inadequacy (social competence). Thus, within this category, there are four sub-types:

- sadistic/overt (Type 4)
- sadistic/muted (Type 5)
- non-sadistic/high social competence (Type 6)
- non-sadistic/low social competence (Type 7)

The final general umbrella category includes vindictive offenders. These offenders can be characterized as being motivated by misogynistic anger. It follows that these offenders are distinct from the pervasively angry rapists in that the former's hostility is not generalized, but rather, directed primarily at women. Per Knight and Prentky (1990), these offenders can be further divided on the basis of their levels of social competence. In particular, two sub-categories were developed by the researchers:

- vindictive/low social competence (Type 8)
- vindictive/moderate social competence (Type 9)

The MTC: R3 classification system has been applied to other samples. Results indicate that it is a reliable method for identifying nuances in rapist motivation (Knight, 1999; McCabe & Wauchope, 2005; Reid, Wilson, & Boer, 2010). Although it has generally been recognized as a sophisticated taxonomic system for studying rapists and for understanding their motivations to offend, it is, as one of the developers of the system mentioned still in need of "fine-tuning" (Knight, 1999, p. 326).

Hazelwood and Warren's (2000) Impulsive vs. Ritualistic Rapist Typology. Hazelwood and Warren (2000) developed a rapist typology based on their law enforcement experiences, and also, from their review of extant research. Their classification divides male rapists into two distinct groups: the "impulsive offender" and the "ritualistic offender."

Broadly, the impulsive offender is a "common type of sexual offender who is generally the least successful at evading identification and apprehension" (p. 269). Put differently, this offender—as the classification describes—devotes little planning to his sex crimes. This grouping of offenders is believed to be a "criminally unsophisticated and reactive offender" (p. 270), with a diverse and generally antisocial pattern of prior criminal behavior; however, rarely do these offenses indicate a sex offense specialization. This type of offender is motivated by a sense of entitlement, as well as anger and control. Physical force is typically used by impulsive offenders because they "often lack criminal skills to control a person without resorting to violence" (p. 271). This level of force is often excessive, perhaps because it is expressive of underlying anger and hostility toward women.

In contrast, the ritualistic offender is less typical among rapists. Comparatively, he is considered more successful than the impulsive group at evading detection. In line with the impulsive offender, the ritualistic offender is thought to be motivated by power, anger, or a combination of power-anger intentions. In virtually every case, the ritualistic offender, in direct contrast to the impulsive offender demonstrates paraphilic behavior. That is, "recurrent, intense sexually arousing fantasies, sexual urges, or behaviors that often involve non-human objects, the suffering or humiliation of oneself or one's partner, children, or non-consenting persons" (American Psychiatric Association, 2000). Additionally, and perhaps related to the specific paraphilia, the ritualistic offender's crimes revolve around persistent fantasy. Thus, he will go to great lengths to "recreate a situation from his fantasies" (p. 274). Accordingly, his crimes typically will involve targeting specific victims (e.g., women with shoulder-length hair) and similar contexts (e.g., may have a pattern of committing offenses near a body of water). The amount of physical violence used by these offenders is dependent on their respective fantasies. To wit, per Hazelwood and Warren (2000, p. 277), "fantasies provide the conscious, repetitious template for offenses" committed by ritualistic offenders. For example, in cases where fantasies involve inflicting physical violence on victims (as in the case of an offender motivated by sadism), offenses will involve significantly more victim injury. Notably, fantasies may involve seemingly non-violent aspects or themes. For instance, the researchers describe an offender who used virtually no physical force, but during the course of his crimes requested that victims address him as a boyfriend or lover.

Hazelwood and Warren's (2000) dichotomy of impulsive versus ritualistic offenders has enjoyed general support from other studies. For example, Goodwill and Alison (2007, p. 283) in their study of offender profiling, concluded that their findings "leave little doubt that situational and contextual factors have a very significant impact on various offense behaviors and victim choice." That is, their study was generally supportive of Hazelwood and Warren's (2000) dichotomous conception of rapists—the impulsive, spontaneous sex offenders, versus the ritualistic and methodical rapists. Notably, however, this study relied on a relatively small sample of sex offenders (n=85). More specifically, other work has found support for impulsive sub-types of rapists particularly among juvenile sex offender populations (Myers, 2002). Even so, future work is needed that more directly and with larger and diverse samples tests Hazelwood and Warren's impulsive-ritualistic typology. Table 1.2 describes the classification systems that we have just discussed.

Table 1.2. Rapist Typologies

Typology	Distinguishing Characteristics
Groth's (1979) Rapist Typology	*Three types of rape—anger, power, sadistic* *Anger rapes* a) expressive of hostility or anger, b) impulsive and triggered by interpersonal conflict, and c) involve physical force and victim humiliation *Power rapes* a) rape is expressive of need to control victim, b) involve less physical force as primary motivation is to dominate victim rather than express hostility or anger, and c) involve more planning than anger rapes *Sadistic rapes* a) rare sub-type, b) receive sexual gratification by inflicting pain on victims, and c) involve significant premeditation in selecting victims (e.g., sadistic offenders often prefer a certain "type" of victim)
Knight and Prentky's (1990) MTC: R3	*Focuses on nine sub-types:* a) Opportunistic/high social competence (Type 1) b) Opportunistic/low social competence (Type 2) c) Pervasively angry (Type 3) d) Sadistic/overt (Type 4) e) Sadistic/muted (Type 5) f) Non-sadistic/high social competence (Type 6) g) Non-sadistic/low social competence (Type 7) h) vindictive/low social competence (Type 8) i) vindictive/moderate social competence (Type 9)
Hazelwood and Warren's (2000) Impulsive vs. Ritualistic Typology	*Distinguishes between impulsive versus ritualistic offenders:* *Impulsive offenders* a) spontaneous in offending, b) motivated by sense of entitlement, and c) more likely to be apprehended *Ritualistic offenders* a) follow a "script," motivated by recurring fantasies, b) selective about victim and crime location, and c) significantly more difficult to apprehend

Juvenile Sex Offenders

The two prior typologies—the child molester and rapist classifications—apply to adult offenders. However, scholarship has advanced to include special classifications of juvenile sex offenders (hereafter, JSOs). Given the increased scholarly interest, several typologies have been created. Below, we turn to three typologies examined in the sex offender literature.

O'Brien and Bera's (1986) Typology. One of the first JSO classification systems was developed by O'Brien and Bera (1986). Specifically, they relied on their clinical experience with male sex offenders when generating their typology. This early work outlines seven distinct categories of JSOs—the "naïve experimenter," "under-socialized child molester," "pseudo-socialized child molester," "sexual aggressive," "sexual compulsive," "disturbed impulsive," and the "group-influenced." Each of these sub-types is discussed below.

The naïve experimenter per O'Brien and Bera (1986) is motivated to sexually offend by general curiosity. On average, this specific sub-type is younger and socially competent (i.e., has few obvious social or family problems). Three other characteristics are notable. Typically, the naïve experimenter has a limited number of victims, uses little force during the course of his offending, and takes advantage of situational opportunities to offend, rather than devoting significant time planning the offense.

In contrast, the under-socialized JSO is defined as primarily antisocial—that is, per the researchers, as an "isolated and socially inadequate" individual (p. 2). This sub-type prefers to abuse younger children and often uses force, violence, or threats to obtain victim compliance. Notably, this JSO does not appear to target a particular sex and will often have abused multiple victims of either gender. O'Brien and Bera (1986) indicate that many of these problematic behaviors can be traced to deviant sexual arousal—where offending allows the offender to meet unmet social and intimacy needs—among this sub-type.

The third sub-category of offenders identified by the researchers is the pseudo-socialized child molesters. Unlike the earlier group of JSO child molesters, this sub-type does not appear to be outwardly antisocial. Indeed, such JSOs are often described as intelligent, charming, and confident. However, this initial appearance is deceiving as such individuals can quickly exhibit antisocial tendencies and manipulative behavior. The pseudo-socialized child molester group is characterized as having little regard for their victims—who may be of either sex. Generally JSOs falling under this category are motivated to offend to satisfy sexual and physical needs. As a result, this group is described as displaying narcissistic behavior—often portraying their offenses as consensual acts with willing victims.

A fourth group—the sexual aggressive JSO—shares similar personality traits to the pseudo-socialized child molester. At first glance, offenders under this sub-category appear outwardly pleasant and charming. However, this disposition per O'Brien and Bera (1986) is a façade that allows for greater manipulation of others and "conning." In contrast to the pseudo-socialized child molester group, however, the sexual aggressive typically comes from a disorganized and dysfunctional family system. Additionally, he has a much broader range of victims—that is, no clear age or gender preferences are evident. Because this offender may link sexual arousal with physical aggression he is thought to be at risk of persistent and violent offending.

O'Brien and Bera (1986) identified a fifth group of JSOs—the sexual compulsive. This particular offender exhibits sexually ritualistic or addictive behaviors (e.g., repetitively masturbating, acting out sexually). On average, offenders who fit this sub-type can be characterized as "hands-off" or non-contact offenders. For example, they are inclined to engage in voyeuristic (e.g., "peeping" in homes) and exhibitionist (e.g., indecent exposure) behavior rather than offenses involving direct victim contact or violence. Having said that, over time offenders may become desensitized to these non-contact acts. Thus, these offenses have the potential to escalate to contact offenses although these are typically limited to froutteriusm-related offenses (i.e., the non-consensual rubbing against or touching of an individual for sexual gratification).

A sixth group described in O'Brien and Bera's (1986) typology is the disturbed impulsive JSO. The researchers depict this group of JSOs as having little impulse control and exhibiting antisocial tendencies (e.g., social isolation, poor interpersonal relationships). As a result, these offenders typically act out in an unpredictable manner. Offending patterns may range from single acts of sexual deviancy to multiple, bizarre, and ritualistic sex offenses. Not least, the disturbed impulsive JSO appears to commit offenses across a range of victim populations (e.g., children and adults).

The final classification defined by the researchers includes the group influenced offender. To a large extent, this designation fits the classic "peer pressured" offender whose deviancy is limited to the context of a peer group. O'Brien and Bera (1986) indicate that this particular JSO is not a particularly persistent offender, on average committing only a small number of sex crimes, and always, as part of a group. It is further believed that these offenders act out to gain peer approval or attention.

The O'Brien and Bera (1986) typology has been described as having high face validity (that is, on a general level, it appears to present a reasonable and logical grouping of offenders). However, it is not a classification system that has been subjected to systematic empirical investigation (Righthand & Welch, 2001). Having said this, some indirect support for O'Brien and Bera's sub-types exist. For example, Knight and Prentky's (1993) typology (a more fully developed version of this particular classification system is discussed next) identified similar sub-types as proposed by O'Brien and Bera (1986). Little clear distinction has been made however as to which of the seven types constitute the greatest harm to society—that is, which offenders appear most dangerous. Evident from this model, however, is the substantial heterogeneity that exists within the JSO population.

Prentky, B. Harris, Frizzell, and Righthand's Typology derived from the Juvenile Sex Offender Assessment Protocol (J-SOAP, 2000). Another prominent system was developed by Prentky and colleagues (2000). Their work examined the characteristics of juvenile sex offenders (e.g., offense history, quality of peer relationships, evidence of empathy) referred to a mental health facility and then determined whether specific groupings of offenders were evident (n=96). The J-SOAP outlines six broad categories of JSOs. The first group includes JSOs who fit under the "child molester" classification. These JSOs exclusively target young victims (on average, 11 years or younger). The second group consists of what the researchers termed, "rapists." These offenders tend to commit crimes against older victims (at least age 12 or older) compared to the child molester category. Thus, a smaller age gap exists between these JSOs and their victims. A third classification was defined as the "sexually reactive child." Offenders under this category typically target same-age peers; this grouping consists of relatively young offenders (on average offenders are unlikely to be over the age of 12). Also identified by this scholarship is a fourth category, "fondler." These offenders commit primarily non-penetrative sex acts (e.g., fondling, caressing). Similar to the rapist category, their victims tend to be around the same age (12 or older) and are less likely to be significantly younger than the offender. Another grouping includes "paraphilic" offenders. JSOs in this category have committed "non-contact" sex crimes (e.g., indecent exposure, making sexually obscene phone calls). No clear pattern exists regarding offender preference for younger or older victims. A final classification—the "unclassifiable" group consists of offenders who do not fit in any of the above groupings. Notably, the J-SOAP typology (2000) has been revised several times since its initial development. However, the broad categories or offender classifications outlined by Prentky et al.'s (2000) work have been found to be fairly reliable groupings (Prentky & Righthand, 2003; Worling, 2004). We move now to a classification system that extends Prentky et al.'s (2000) work. It considers personality functioning in developing its specific typology of juvenile sex offenders.

Worling's Typology (2001). Worling's (2001) work focused on developing empirically derived personality-based subgroups of adolescent male sex offenders (n=112). In particular, the California Psychological Inventory (CPI) was used to assess the different personality types of offenders. Cluster analysis indicated that four specific sub-types were evident: "antisocial/impulsive," "unusual/isolated," "overcontrolled/reserved," and "confident/ aggressive."

The first classification includes the antisocial/impulsive sex offenders. According to Worling (2001) this group comprises the largest proportion of offenders (48 percent) in his typology. The antisocial/impulsive offenders tend to have higher scores on pathology indicators. Put differently, in Worling's (2001) study, these offenders were more likely to have a rebellious attitude, to report being unhappy and anxious. Per Worling (2001), these offenders have a "propensity for rule violation ... [thus] their sexual offending may, at least initially, be more a result of this factor than deviant sexual arousal per se" (p. 162). Along with a third sub-type (the "confident/aggressive" group), the antisocial/impulsive offender appears most at risk of assaulting intrafamilial victims (e.g., siblings). Additionally, this group (as well as the next sub-type we will discuss — unusual/isolated offenders) had the greatest odds of general and sexual recidivism in a six-year follow-up. Not least, study results indicate that the antisocial/impulsive offender had a high prevalence of childhood abuse.

In contrast, the second grouping is comprised of the unusual/isolated sex offenders. These offenders account for a relatively smaller proportion of offenders (14 percent) in Worling's (2001) typology. In line with the earlier sub-type, the antisocial/impulsive group, these offenders also scored highly on pathology indicators. In particular, they shared negative personality traits (e.g., Worling classified them as being "undependable," "isolated," and "confused"). More generally, as Worling (2001, p. 163) describes, these offenders possess "awkward personality features." And, as noted above, the unusual/isolated offenders were significantly more likely to reoffend in a follow-up period.

The overcontrolled/reserved classification is distinct from these two prior sub-types. Generally, offenders within this group are not considered to be antisocial. Rather, they tend to endorse pro-social attitudes, and are responsible and reliable. At the same time, they are generally reserved and emotionally "overcontrolled" — rarely expressing their feelings to others. As a result, the overcontrolled/reserved juvenile offender may "initiate offending behaviors, in part as a result of their shy and rigid interpersonal orientation, which may result in limited access to intimate personal relationships" (Worling, 2001, p. 162).

In direct contrast, offenders in the last grouping, the confident/aggressive classification, per Worling (2001, p. 163), "can be described as friendly, confident, and optimistic." Thus, they are considered to have a "much healthier interpersonal presentation" than the other sub-types (p. 163). Having said this, certain features of this personality type might contribute to sexual offending. That is, these offenders, while having a generally positive attitude may also be aggressive and narcissistic. Thus, their propensity to offend may in part be affected by these personality traits.

Worling's (2001) typology has not been directly applied to another sample of juvenile sex offenders. However, some work indicates his conception of antisocial personality types is valid. For example, in a meta-analysis, Hanson and Morton-Bourgon (2005) found that antisocial orientation (central to two of Worling's sub-types) was a strong predictor of violent recidivism and sexual recidivism. Findings from a separate review of 13 studies conducted by Dreznick (2003) indicate broad support for Worling's (2001) contention that some adolescent sex offenders are socially incompetent (e.g., they have difficulty engaging others in conversation, maintaining friendships, and being friendly or sociable). For example, with the exception of the confident/aggressive classification posited by Worling (2001), social incompetence is seen as contributing to sexual deviance to some degree among three other groups: antisocial/impulsive unusual/isolated, overcontrolled/reserved types. Other reviews indicate more tempered support of Worling's (2001) broad classification scheme. For example, in a rigorous and recent meta-analysis of 59 studies, Seto and Lalumière (2010) found that only social isolation (suggesting support for the unusual/isolated sub-type) was a significant predictor of offending among juvenile males. Even so the extent to which Worling's (2001) overall classification system is valid remains an open question as virtually no scholarship has tested his specific hypotheses regarding these four adolescent sex offender sub-types. Table 1.3 provides a general outline of the different JSO typologies we have discussed.

Table 1.3. Juvenile Sex Offender (JSO) Typologies

Typology	Distinguishing Characteristics
O'Brien and Bera's (1986) Typology	*Seven categories of JSOs:* a) naïve experimenter (sexual curiosity primary motivation for offending), b) under-socialized child molester (offending allows offender to meet unmet social needs), c) pseudo-socialized child molester (appears adequately socialized, but is also manipulative and narcissistic), d) sexual aggressive (sexual arousal linked with physical aggression), e) sexual compulsive (commits primarily non-contact crimes, such as voyeurism), f) disturbed impulsive (antisocial and unpredictable), and g) group-influenced (offend to gain peer approval)
Prentky et al.'s (2000) Typology (derived from J-SOAP)	*Six classifications of JSOs:* a) child molesters (offend against younger children), b) rapists (commit offenses against older victims), c) sexually reactive child (young offenders who victimize similarly aged peers), d) fondler (commits non-penetrative offenses like fondling), e) paraphilic offenders (commits non-contact crimes such as indecent exposure), and f) the unclassifiable JSOs (offenders who do not neatly fit into any of the other five categories)
Worling's (2001) Typology	*Developed personality-based JSO sub-types:* a) antisocial/impulsive offenders (have a propensity for rule violation), b) unusual/isolated offenders (possess antisocial tendencies, "undependable," socially isolated), c) overcontrolled/reserved offenders (endorse pro-social attitudes, but are reserved and guarded, may initiate offending behaviors because of their shy personality), and d) confident/aggressive offenders (friendly and confident, but also considered narcissistic and aggressive)

Female Sex Offenders

Beyond these classification systems, researchers have begun to separately examine female sex offenders. Some scholars contend that female sex offenders have not been given sufficient empirical attention (Mathews, Matthews, & Speltz, 1989; Vandiver & Kercher, 2004). Additionally, some emphasize that while women commit substantially fewer sex crimes compared to men, they comprise a "not insignificant" proportion of offenders (Chaffin et al., 2002, p. 219)—and thus are worthy of study. These research gaps have led to greater investigation of female sex offenders. The discussion below highlights three prominent female sex offender typologies.

Mathews et al.'s (1989) Typology. One of the first typologies of female offenders was developed by Mathews and colleagues (1989). The researchers relied on their clinical judgment in assessing offender sub-types among sixteen women. Their work identified three major categories: the "male-coerced" offender, the "predisposed" offender, and the "teacher/lover" offender.

The first offender sub-type identified by the researchers includes the male-coerced offender. Offenders under this category share a few distinct characteristics. First, these offenders tend to be passive and dependent on others for emotional and social support.

Second, they appear susceptible to others' influence. Hence, most of their offenses are committed in conjunction with a male co-offender — often a romantic partner. Many male-coerced offenders victimize their children.

In contrast, the predisposed female sex offenders often have prior histories of having had experienced sexual abuse or incest as children. Mathews et al. (1989) also observed that psychological problems and deviant sexual fantasies were characteristic of this offender population in their study. These offenders tend to act alone and often target their children or other young relatives.

A final classification included the teacher/lover offenders. As the designation implies, this set of offenders primarily victimize students or other adolescents with whom they have regular contact. At the time of their crimes, the teacher/lover offenders often report experiencing difficulties with peer relationships; thus their offenses may be reflective of a regression to adolescence. Mathews et al.'s (1989) research indicates that these women often rationalize their offending as providing sexual mentoring to their adolescent victims.

The Mathews et al. (1989) study is considered a seminal work in the sexual offending literature. Having said that, flaws are evident. First, the study relied on a very small sample — one that is not necessarily generalizable to the larger population of female sex offenders. Second, the Mathews et al. (1989) typology was not statistically generated, but rather conceptualized based on clinical observations. Notably, the work of Syed and Williams (1996) and Vandiver and Kercher (2004) — the typologies we now turn to — extended this focus. The Syed and Williams (1996) study was one of the first to validate Mathews et al.'s (1989) typology; the Vandiver and Kercher (2004) study relied on a much larger sample and used complex statistical analysis to identify clusters or groups of broad sex offender categories. Both studies are notable for refining Mathews et al.'s (1989) earlier typology. At the same time, both provide indirect support for some of Mathews et al.'s (1989) main category-types.

Syed and Williams' (1996) Typology. Seeking to test Mathews et al.'s (1989) framework, Syed and Williams (1996) relied on a sample of incarcerated Canadian women (n=11). Their work was largely descriptive and based on their clinical observations. All of the women had been convicted of at least one sex offense. In line with Mathews et al.'s (1989) work, the authors identified two similar categories: the "teacher/lover" offender and "male-coerced or accompanied" offender. However, an additional profile was identified: the anger as motivation offender. Below, Syed and Williams' (1996) typology is summarized.

Their first classification — the "teacher/lover" group refers to offenders who have committed sex offenses against a minor victim — typically an adolescent male. Often, these offenders do not perceive their actions as criminal. Rather, they rationalize their behavior as proffering a beneficial, educative effect for the victim. In Syed and Williams' (1996) study, this group comprised a small proportion of offenders (9 percent).

The next grouping includes offenders who committed their crimes with male co-offenders (n=9). In contrast to Mathews et al. (1989) Syed and Williams (1996) make a distinction between male-coerced or male-accompanied offenders. The former represents a female offender who commits sex crimes because of fear of the male accomplice or force by him. In contrast, for the latter category, the male-accompanied group, there is no evidence force or threats were used to coerce these women to offend. Thus, these female offenders appear, per the researchers, to be more complicit in the crimes than male-coerced offenders. The coerced (36 percent) and male-accompanied (46 percent) categories constitute the two largest groups of female offenders.

A final group is comprised of women who do not fit into either of these two sub-categories. This group is designated as the "anger as motivation" offenders. Rather, these crimes appear to be motivated by anger, frustration, or hostility. These offenses are typically violent. Notably, these offenders, per the authors "appear more similar in typology to sexually assaultive men who are motivated by anger." In Syed and Williams (1996) study, only one offender fit this sub-type.

Syed and Williams' (1996) general framework has been supported by prior work. However, some tests indicate that it should be further refined. For example, Nathan and Ward (2002) while finding general support for the male-coerced vs. male-accompanied distinction also identified a third sub-type, "male-accompanied, rejected/revengeful" offender. Thus, such offenders are motivated to offend by a sense of retribution. Notably, no cases in the Syed and Williams (1996) sample fit this typology. There were other inconsistencies. For instance, unlike previous work, Syed and Williams' (1996) study did not identify a "predisposed" group of women (i.e., those who had been sexually abused prior to committing offenses). Thus, this finding goes against previously proposed typologies and extant research centered on female sex offenders (see, e.g., Mathews et al., 1987; for a review, see Vandiver, 2006).

Vandiver and Kercher's (2004) Typology. Vandiver and Kercher (2004) extended this prior work by relying on a larger sample of female sex offenders to develop an empirically derived typology. Specifically, they relied on the Texas sex offender registry database to collect their data. Ultimately, they identified 417 female sex offenders. In particular, their analysis resulted in six categories of female sexual offenders.

The first category includes the "heterosexual nurturers." Offenders under this classification typically victimize young males (average victim age of 12 years old). This population had an average age of 30—on par with typical ages of the offenders in the other classifications outlined by Vandiver and Kercher (2004). Notably, these offenders are presumed to be relatively less criminal compared to offenders falling into the other groupings. In the study, they were the second least likely of all of the sub-types to be rearrested for a sex crime. Additionally, the heterosexual nurturer group constituted the largest offender category. Per the researchers, this class of offenders is comparable to Mathews et al.'s conception of the "teacher-lover" group.

Distinct from this group is Vandiver and Kercher's (2004) second category—noncriminal homosexual offenders. These women have a clear victim gender preference. An overwhelming majority of them (96 percent) had committed offenses against young girls and women (average victim age of 13 years old). Similar to the heterosexual nurturers, the offenders in this group were relatively less criminal, having committed the fewest offenses of all of the sub-types, and the lowest average number of prior arrests.

A third classification—the female sexual predator—constitutes the most persistent and criminal offender type identified by Vandiver and Kercher's (2004) research. For example, in their study, these offenders were most likely to have been re-arrested for another offense. In addition, they tended to have a high average number of offenses in comparison to the other groupings of offenders, and were at a younger age at the time of their arrest (mean age=29). This sub-type has an obvious victim preference. A majority of victims were male; they also tended to be younger (average age=11) than the victims of the two previously mentioned offender groupings—heterosexual nurturers and noncriminal homosexual offenders.

Vandiver and Kercher's (2004) fourth grouping, young adult child exploiters, comprised women who had committed sex crimes against children. As their designation implies, this category included the youngest population of offenders (average age=28) and their victims tended to be significantly younger (average age=7) compared to the other offender types. No pattern emerged however concerning victim sex preference in this group. Thus offenders who had victimized males and females were equally represented in this particular category.

A fifth classification includes homosexual criminals. Per the researchers these offenders was significantly more criminal compared to the offenders included in the other classifications. In particular, findings indicate that these women were more likely to reoffend and had the highest average number of total arrests (mean=10) of all offenders. Thus, these offenders are the most likely group to come in contact with law enforcement. Victims were older (average age=32) and primarily female (73 percent). This group is also distinct in that many of their sexual offenses involve "forcing behaviors"—including forcing other females into prostitution. As a result, Vandiver and Kercher (2004, p. 133) surmise that for this particular group economic gain is a primary motivator for offending. A mean offender age was not provided for this small number of women (n=22); however, the researchers revealed that this was a relatively older group of offenders (see e.g., p. 133).

The remaining category—aggressive homosexual criminals—comprised the smallest group of offenders in Vandiver's and Kercher's (2004) typology. In particular, this group had the highest odds of committing sexual assault. They preferred older (average age=31) and female victims. These offenders were also significantly older at time of arrest than other offender types (average age not given).

Limited research has attempted to validate Vandiver and Kercer's (2004) typology. One study conducted by Sandler and Freeman (2007) found mixed support for the typology using a sample of female offenders in New York. For example, two of Vandiver and Kercher's (2004) clusters ("heterosexual nurturers" and "young adult child exploiters") were similar to clusters identified by Sandler and Freeman (2007) (they defined these categories as "criminally-limited hebephiles" and "young adult child molesters," respectively). However, Sandler and Freeman's study (2007) revealed little support for Vandiver and Kercher's (2004) "homosexual" categories. That is, four of Vandiver and Kercher's (2004) six clusters indicate a "definite preference" for one victim gender over the other (thus, labeled, "heterosexual" or "homosexual"), but only one of Sandler and Freeman's (2007, p. 86) clusters showed a strong gender preference among female sex offenders. More generally, however, Sandler and Freeman (2007) concluded that despite these differences "our results support prior work with female sex offenders [such as the work of Vandiver and Kercher, 2004] that indicates the importance [of examining] victim and offender ages ... when deciding into which group a specific offender falls" (p. 87).

In assessing which typologies are most likely to present a risk to society or to reoffend, results from both studies apply. For example, Sandler and Freeman's (2007) "high-risk chronic offender" typology—which includes persistent and criminally involved offenders—is similar to Vandiver and Kercher's (2004) conceptions of high risk offenders (particularly, the "female predator" and "aggressive homosexual criminal" offenders).

A separate strand of research has examined juvenile female sex offenders. Recall that we discussed juvenile sex offender typologies earlier. However, the development of these typologies relied exclusively on male samples. We turn now to one of the only typologies that would apply to adolescent female sex offenders.

Mathews, Hunter, and Vuz (1997). Mathews et al. (1997) are among a small handful of researchers to have proposed a classification system for this offender population (n=67). They examined the characteristics of female sex offenders to those of male sex offenders. In particular, their focus was on developing a typology of young female sex offenders. A general finding from this descriptive study (relying on clinical observations) was that female sex offenders experienced substantially greater levels of prior sexual abuse and maltreatment; in turn, this factor is believed to play a role in subsequent offending among this population. Thus, this characteristic is a defining feature in developing their typologies (p. 192). Mathews et al.'s (1997) work can be summarized as finding three general types of offenders: adolescent females who engaged in offending within the context of baby-sitting, girls who appeared to be "sexually reactive," and those who committed more extensive and repetitive sexual offending.

The first classification refers to offenders who commit offenses during their baby-sitting duties. Per the researchers, this category includes a "small, but distinct subgroup" (approximately 17 percent) of female sex offenders (p. 195). A defining feature of this category is that it includes primarily less criminal, situational offenders. That is, youth who fit under this sub-type have substantially greater opportunities to commit offenses during their normal course of contact (e.g., through baby-sitting) with young victims; however, they engage in relatively fewer acts of abuse than other types. Most often, the victims are not related to the offenders. Additionally, these offenders rarely have histories of having had experienced prior sexual abuse or maltreatment. Mathews et al. (1997) claim that these offenses are motivated primarily by sexual curiosity, rather than for other reasons (e.g., to gain power or control over victims).

Another grouping identified by Mathews et al.'s (1997) research includes "sexually reactive" girls; this group comprised a larger proportion of offenders (approximately one-third) in the study than the previous type. On average, sexually reactive offenders have prior histories of sexual victimization. Notably, however, the typical extent of maltreatment and physical abuse is believed to be "mild to moderate" for this population (p. 196). Hence, it is believed that prior sexual abuse "triggers" subsequent sexual offending among sexually reactive female offenders. The researchers note, for example, that a majority of offenders began to sexually offend shortly after experiencing sexual victimization. Moreover, their offenses often mirrored the earlier acts of abuse they had previously experienced. In comparison to the "extensive and repetitive" offenders (discussed below) this population is thought to be fairly resilient. For example, Mathews et al. (1997, p. 196) observed that such offenders, on average, "[possess] adequate social skills and [exhibit] a number of personality strengths."

A final classification consists of extensive and repetitive offenders. This population made up half of the study sample. Characteristic of this sub-classification is a prior history of severe maltreatment and sexual abuse, including parental incest. Generally, this group is the least well-adjusted of all offender types. For example, in Mathews et al.'s (1997) study, a majority of offenders had been previously diagnosed with disorders such as depression and post-traumatic stress disorder (PTSD). In comparison to the two other sub-types, offenders under this classification are more likely to be involved in a variety of impulsive delinquent behaviors (e.g., drug and alcohol use, lying, running away, engaging in unprotected sex).

There have been few empirical attempts to validate the specific sub-types outlined in the Mathews et al. (1997) typology of juvenile female sex offenders. However, in a review Vick, McRoy, and Matthews (2002, p. 6) observed that "some overlap" exists in the typologies outlined by Mathews et al. (1997) and others (e.g., Faller, 1987; Turner & Turner, 1994).

More generally, a primary finding from the Mathews et al. (1997) study — that juvenile girls experienced substantially higher levels of maltreatment and sexual abuse compared to male offenders — has been consistently supported by other research (Araji, 1997; Gray, Busconi, Houchens, & Pithers, 1997; Miccio-Fonseca, 2000). Table 1.4 summarizes the female sex offender typologies that we have already discussed.

Cyber Sex Offenders

A fairly new focus in criminology has been on studying cyber-related sex crimes. Recall that these offenses are distinct sex crimes because of their reliance on technological advances — such as the Internet. For example, cyber offenders may use the Internet or online

Table 1.4. Female Sex Offender Typologies

Typology	Distinguishing Characteristics
Mathews et al.'s (1989) Typology	*Included three sub-categories of offenders:* a) male-coerced (typically dependent on others for emotional and social support, commits sex offenses with a male co-offender), b) predisposed (have history of prior sexual victimization), and c) teacher-lover (rationalize sex offending as providing an "education" to young adolescents, typically males)
Syed and Williams' (1996) Typology	*Identified three sex offender sub-types:* a) teacher-lover (targets primarily male adolescents, tending to believe offenses benefit victims), b) male-coerced (commits offenses with male co-offender, typically out of fear of male partner, takes a passive role in offending) or male-accompanied (commits offenses with male co-offender, takes an active role in offending, and c) anger as motivation (offenses motivated by hostility and frustration)
Vandiver and Kercher's (2004) Typology	*Developed six category classification system:* a) heterosexual nurturers (victimize young males, commit fewer offenses), b) noncriminal homosexual offenders (prefer victimizing young girls and women), c) female sexual predators (target younger male victims, significant criminal history), d) young adult child exploiters (younger women who target child and adolescent victims), e) homosexual criminals (victimize females in similar age range, significantly more criminal, may have history of forcing other women into prostitution), and f) aggressive homosexual criminals (significantly older female offenders who target same-age peers, have the highest likelihood of committing serious sex crimes)
Mathews et al.'s (1997) Female Adolescent Sex Offender Typology	*Developed classification system with three offending sub-types:* a) adolescent females who engaged in offending during baby-sitting duties (situational offenders; this group is considered to be "experimental" and curious about sexuality), b) sexually reactive offenders (offending follows previous "mild to moderate" sexual victimization), and c) extensive and repetitive sex offenders (have long history of deviance and delinquency, have experienced severe physical and sexual abuse prior to offending)

communications to target victims, to distribute or access child pornography, or to send sexually suggestive messages or content to juveniles. In particular, we will discuss three prominent classification systems. The first is centered on general classifications of cyber sex offenders developed by McLaughlin (2000).

McLaughlin (2000). Relying on his practitioner observations as a law enforcement officer and an analysis of arrests (n=200), McLaughlin outlined four broad categories of cyber offenders: "collectors," "travelers," "manufacturers," and "chatters." McLaughlin (2000) notes that his analysis is limited to "fixated" or "preferential" male child molesters. Recall from our earlier discussion about child molester typologies that fixated/preferential offenders tend to have more extensive histories of committing sex offenses against children compared to other child molester sub-type (e.g., regressed). These offenders also report experiencing more fulfilling relationships with children. For those reasons, McLaughlin's (2000) analysis focuses on this high-risk sub-group.

In particular, his first conceptualization refers to the "collector" cyber offender. This category comprises the largest group of cyber offenders (n=143). Under this classification, a typical offender collects pornographic images of children. Additionally, these images may be "traded" with other interested parties. Often, a specific "look" is desired by these offenders. That is, they typically focus on amassing photos depicting children with certain physical characteristics (e.g., specific age or hair color). Despite involvement in these crimes, offenders in this category are presumed to be non-contact offenders and relatively law-abiding. For example, a majority of offenders in McLaughlin's (2000) analysis did not have prior contact with law enforcement and virtually none had known illegal contact with children. These offenders are often employed in occupations where they may work closely with children or young people (e.g., as teachers, youth counselors, professors).

A second sub-type includes "travelers." This group accounts for one-fourth of the cyber sex offenders identified by McLaughlin (2000). Here, offenders are presumed to share similar characteristics as collectors. Thus, they collect images and pictures and typically have no history of having committed prior offenses. However, unlike collectors, travelers amplify their offending by making arrangements to meet with victims. Grooming behaviors are evident among this group. That is, they often engage in online conversation to gain rapport before suggesting that a meeting occur. For example, most often (half of the time in McLaughlin's study) offenders began online conversation by first falsely representing themselves as teenagers. A majority of offenders also sent self-photographs, often nude photos. McLaughlin (2000) reported that a wide range of occupations of travelers (e.g., military officer, attorney, athletic director, priest, college professor) exists.

A third classification recognized by McLaughlin's (2000) work — the manufacturers — comprise a much smaller proportion of cyber sex offenders. In McLaughlin's (2000) study, for instance, only eight offenders, or four percent of the total sample, fit within this grouping. These offenders not only collect pornographic images of children but they also distribute them on the Internet or among other interested parties. McLaughlin (2000) observed that many of the men in his sample had photographed their prior victims. Not least, upon their arrests, half of the distributors also had harbored runaway children. It does not appear that these offenses were committed for financial gain. For instance, only one offender in this grouping had received any financial compensation as a result of the distribution, and it was a fairly modest sum ($1,000).

By far, the smallest group — the chatters — included just one offender in the study. McLaughlin (2000) explained that these offenders prefer exclusive online contact with children (e.g., engaging in sexually explicit online conversations, "cyber sex"). However, they seldom send explicitly sexual photographs of themselves or ask for lewd photos of the children they engage in online conversation. Rarely do they attempt to meet the child in person.

There have been few empirical tests of McLaughlin's (2000) typology of cyber sex offenders. However, at least one study exists that tested McLaughlin's classification system in a different sample of cyber sex offenders. Alexy, Burgess, and Baker (2005) relied on McLaughlin's (2000) framework in their study on online sex offenders. Specifically, during a six-year period, print and electronic media coverage was surveyed to analyze the portrayal of Internet offenders. From here, the researchers systematically analyzed the coverage for specific information about each case (e.g., whether the offender traveled to visit the victim). In all, they identified 225 cases. They found some indirect support for three of McLaughlin's (2000) classifications. For example, Alexy et al. (2005) discovered a "traders" grouping. These offenders collect and or trade child pornography. This conception accords with McLaughlin's "collectors" category. Approximately 60 percent of Alexy et al.'s (2005) sample fell into this category. Similarly, collectors comprised 72 percent of McLaughlin's (2000) sample. The Alexy et al. (2005) study is also notable for having identified a category of "traveler" sex offenders. Here again, their findings accord with McLaughlin's (2000). In particular, in the Alexy et al. (2005) study, 22 percent of offenders fell into the traveler category. In line with this number, McLaughlin (2000) estimated that 24 percent of offenders in his sample were travelers. Notably, however, there were differences between the two studies. For example, Alexy et al. (2005) developed a third typology—"combination collectors-travelers." McLaughlin's (2000) work however had no such category. In addition, Alexy et al. (2005) did not identify two other sub-types found in McLaughlin's (2000) typology—"distributors" and "chatters." Despite these divergent findings, both studies highlight the heterogeneity in the motivations and modus operandi of cyber sex offenders.

Wolak and Finkelhor (2011). Other work exists that has attempted to provide context for a better understanding of online sex offending. For example, in 2011, Wolak and Finkelhor outlined a "sexting" typology. Recall that sexting refers to "sexual communications with content that includes both pictures and text messages sent using cell phones and other electronic media" (p. 2). Their typology was broadly divided into two categories— "aggravated" and "experimental" sexting.

Their first conception, the aggravated category, includes acts that involve "additional criminal or abuse elements beyond the creation, sending, or possession of youth-produced sexual images" (p. 2). This general classification can be further divided into "adult-involved aggravated cases" and "youth only aggravated cases." The former sub-type—adult-involved cases—are those offenses where adults solicited the sexual images from juveniles, other instances of minors producing and sending images to adults, or other illegal adult involvement. Illustrative of this sub-type is the following example: an adult male requests that a minor send him sexually suggestive photos. In contrast, the latter category under this general umbrella—"youth only cases" involves exclusively minors—both in the creation and sending of images or sexually explicit messages. It is further distilled into cases with "intent to harm" and "reckless misuse." Thus, these sub-categories distinguish between levels of culpability. "Intent to harm" acts refer to situations where a clear motivation to inflict emotional distress and embarrassment by the distribution of received "sexts" is evident. For example, Wolak and Finkelhor (2011) offer the following example to illustrate these offenses: A 16-year-old female accidently uploads a nude photograph of herself on a social networking site. She quickly deletes it. However, a male classmate has downloaded the image and threatens to send it to others if she does not send him other nude photos. In contrast, the remaining sub-classification, "reckless acts," refers to instances where youth offenders were simply acting carelessly and either created sexual images of other minors without their consent or sent the images to others without the knowledge or permission of the pictured minor. To illustrate, the authors mention a case involving a 16-year-old male who sent a picture of his penis to a female peer. She in turn shared it—without the permission of the sender—with several other classmates.

Wolak and Finkelhor (2011) distinguish between these acts and those with an "experimental" element to them. Thus, "experimental incidents," the authors' second classification refers to the "creation and sending of youth-produced sexual images, with no adult involvement, and no apparent intent to harm or reckless misuse" (p. 5). This category is further sub-divided into three groupings: "experimental incidents, romantic," "experimental incidents, sexual attraction seeking," and "experimental incidents, other." Romantic experimental incidents might include the creation and sending of sexually explicit messages/images in the context of a relationship between two minors. Wolak and Finkelhor

(2011) offer the following scenario as an illustration: A 12-year-old girl and her 14-year-old boyfriend created and sent sexual photos to each other. The young girl's parents discovered the photos and reported the incidents to law enforcement.

A separate category includes acts that Wolak and Finkelhor (2011) designate as "sexual attention seeking." In contrast to the earlier sub-type, this latter category includes cases where images were created and sent not to romantic partners, but to acquaintances or other individuals. Per the researchers, the "intent was to interest someone in a relationship" (p. 5). Thus, as an example, these incidents might involve a 16-year-old female who sends unsolicited naked photos of herself to a classmate that she would like to date.

A final classification can be summarized as "other" incidents. According to Wolak and Finkelhor (2011, p. 6), "a small number of cases did not appear to have aggravating elements like adult involvement, malicious motives, or reckless misuse." Additionally, they did not appear to occur in the context of romantic relationships or to fit the author's definition of sexual attention seeking behavior. The researchers share the following case to illustrate these outside cases: An 11-year-old female takes pictures of her breasts and saves them on her cell phone. Her grandparents discover the photos. Believing they are of another minor, they report the images to law enforcement.

Given the novelty of Wolak and Finkelhor's (2011) typology, it has not yet been subjected to empirical testing. Having said that, it is one of the only classification systems to center directly on "sexting" offenses as opposed to other types of sex crimes. The most important

Table 1.5. Cyber Sex Offender Typologies

Typology	Distinguishing Characteristics
McLaughlin's (2000) Typology	*Classifications consist of four sub-categories:* a) collectors (collect and "trade" pornographic images of children via the Internet), b) travelers (also collect and trade child pornography, but often amplify offending to include physically meeting with child victims), c) manufacturers (create and distribute child pornography on the Internet or among other interested offenders), and d) chatters (prefer exclusive online contact with children, rather than physical contact, rarely request lewd photos, but will engage in sexually explicit conversations online)
Wolak and Finkelhor's (2011) Sexting Typology	*Identified two broad "sexting" categories:* *Aggravated* a) involve criminal element beyond the creation and distribution of sexually explicit images, and b) can be further sub-divided into adult-involved aggravated cases (involves an adult offender) and two other types: youth-only aggravated cases (involves only minors) with intent to harm, youth-only aggravated cases (involves only minors) with reckless misuse (i.e., no clear intent to harm or cause injury or emotional distress to others) *Experimental* a) acts that involve minors only with no intent to harm or reckless misuse; presumed to be "experimental" behaviors among minors, and b) can be further sub-divided into three groupings: experimental incidents, romantic; experimental incidents, sexual attraction seeking; and experimental incidents, other

implication of the study per the authors lies in the finding of heterogeneity among sexting acts, as evident by their concluding remarks (p. 7): "youth-produced images are made and disseminated under a wide range of circumstances." Thus, future studies will want to work toward identifying whether Wolak and Finkelhor's (2011) typology extends to other populations, or whether it can be extended or modified. Table 1.5 reviews cyber sex offender classifications.

Chapter Summary

The broad term "sex crime" includes many diverse types of offenses (rape, sexual assault, child sexual abuse, incest, indecent exposure, statutory rape, and Internet and technology-related crimes). A variety of issues make generalizing about sex crime laws more difficult: variability in the enactment of certain reforms, variation in the design of statutes, state-level efforts to decriminalize certain sex offenses, and judicial review of policy.

In recognition of the substantial heterogeneity or diversity across sexual offending categories, researchers have developed sex offender typologies. These typologies have been developed based on offender "type." That is, classification systems exist for the following offender groupings: child molesters, rapists, juvenile sex offenders, female sex offenders, and cyber sex offenders. Each system posits different conceptions of sex offender subtypes. Having said that, evaluation of the diverse typologies indicates a prominent theme—that is, wide heterogeneity across sexual offenders exists.

Additional readings which cover these issues in greater depth are suggested below. The next chapter explains how criminologists measure sex crime.

Additional Suggested Readings

Abel, G. G., & Rouleau, J. L. (1990). Male sex offenders. In M. E. Thase, B. A. Edelstein, & M. Hersen (Eds.), *Handbook of outpatient treatment of adults*, (pp. 271–290). New York: Plenum.

Almond, L., Canter, D., & Salfati, C. G. (2006). Youths who sexually harm: A multivariate model of characteristics. *Journal of Sexual Aggression, 12*, 97–114.

Boyd, N. J., Hagan, M., & Cho, M. E. (2000). Characteristics of adolescent sex offenders: A review of the research. *Aggression and Violent Behavior, 5*, 137–146.

Byrne, J., & Roberts, A. (2007). New directions in offender typology design, development, and implementation: Can we balance risk, treatment and control? *Aggression and Violent Behavior, 12*, 483–492.

Caldwell, M. F., Skeem, J., Salekin, R., & Van Rybroek, G. (2006). Treatment response of adolescent offenders with psychopath-like features. *Criminal Justice and Behavior, 33*, 571–596.

Crimes Against Children Research Center. (2000). *Child sexual abuse*. Durham, NH: Author.

Elliott, I. A., Beech, A. R., & Mandeville-Norden, R. (in press). The psychological profiles of Internet, contact, and mixed Internet/contact sex offenders. *Sexual Abuse: A Journal of Research and Treatment*.

Harris, A. J., & Lobanov-Rostovsky, C. (2010). Implementing the Adam Walsh Act's sex offender registration and notification provisions: A survey of the states. *Criminal Justice Policy Review, 21,* 202–222.

Jenkins, P. (2001). *Beyond tolerance: Child pornography on the Internet.* New York: New York University Press.

Lawson, L. (2008). Female sex offenders' relationship experiences. *Violence and Victims, 23,* 331–343.

Letourneau, E. J., Schoenwald, S. K., & Sheidow, A. J. (2004). Children and adolescents with sexual behavior problems. *Child Maltreatment: Journal of the American Professional Society on the Abuse of Children, 9,* 49–61.

Malesky, L. A. (2007). Predatory online behavior: Modus operandi of convicted sex offenders in identifying potential victims and contacting minors over the Internet. *Journal of Child Sexual Abuse, 16,* 23–32.

Strickland, S. M. (2008). Female sex offenders: Exploring issues of personality, trauma, and cognitive distortions. *Journal of Interpersonal Violence, 23,* 474–489.

Wijkman, M., Bijleveld, C., & Hendriks, J. (2010). Women don't do such things! Characteristics of female sex offenders and offender types. *Sexual Abuse: A Journal of Research and Treatment, 22,* 135–156.

Chapter 2

Measuring Sex Crime

Chapter Introduction

To this point, we have discussed types of sex crime and typologies of sex offenders. A related focus centers on the measurement of sex offenses. The goal of this chapter is to understand the various methods for measuring sex crime. To be clear, different indicators of offending exist. Two primary methods involve official and unofficial data collection. Official data collection refers to instances where actual records of offending exists. For example, police records (Uniform Crime Reports, UCR; National Incident Based Reporting System, NIBRS data) are considered official crime data. Note, however, that such estimates account for only those offenses where an actual crime has been reported to law enforcement. What about non-reported offenses? For example, research indicates that crimes involving sexual violence are significantly less likely to be reported to law enforcement compared to other serious offenses (Bachman, 1998; Fisher & Cullen, 2000). Thus, official estimates of sex crime are believed to reflect only a small fraction of actual sexual offending. The answer lies in "unofficial" methods. For instance, to better account for the "dark figure of crime," the federal government has developed the National Crime Victimization Survey (NCVS)—which regularly monitors criminal victimization in the U.S. More broadly, this unofficial approach involves conducting victimization surveys to better capture the extent of unreported offenses. To illustrate, several specialized victimization surveys have been developed: the National Women's Survey/National Women's Survey-Replication (NWS, NWS-R), National Violence Against Women Survey (NVAWS), National College Women Sexual Victimization (NCWSV) study, National Intimate Partner and Sexual Violence Survey (NISVS), and National Survey of Children's Exposure to Violence (NatSCEV).

These methods are discussed below. A clear understanding of them will help highlight the strengths of each approach, and also the difficulty in measuring sex crime and sexual victimization. In particular, this chapter provides a description of official data collection, unofficial data collection, and also, the strengths and limitations of each approach.

Official Data Collection

Uniform Crime Reports (UCR)

History. The UCR system was first implemented in the U.S in the late 1920s. It was one of the first federal programs that provided national statistics on serious and violent offenses. Upon its initial implementation, the UCR Program did not cover a majority of police jurisdictions. That is, its first publication included statistics for 400 cities throughout

43 states, covering approximately 20 percent of the total U.S. population (FBI, 2004). Initially, the International Association of Chiefs of Police (IACP) managed the Program. Soon after in 1930, the FBI began to oversee the UCR. Today, the UCR covers an overwhelmingly large majority of jurisdictions. On any given year, more than 17,000 law enforcement agencies participate in the Program. Thus, UCR coverage is extended to more than 295 million United States residents, or approximately 96 percent of the total population (FBI, 2004).

Description. The UCR system divides offenses into two groups, Part I and Part II crimes. Part I offenses include eight "index" or serious offenses: "criminal homicide," "forcible rape," "robbery," "aggravated assault," "burglary," "larceny-theft," "motor vehicle theft," and "arson." Historically, the UCR has defined forcible rape in narrow terms. According to current UCR definitions, forcible rape involves "the carnal knowledge of a female forcibly and against her will." Attempts or assaults to commit rape by force or threat of force are also considered forcible rape offenses. Other sex offenses, such as statutory rape crimes or molestation offenses are not included under this category. More specifically, under this restricted definition, rapes committed against male victims would not fall under the FBI's current forcible rape classification. Recognizing the limitations of such a definition, in December 2011, the UCR Program devised a more valid classification. The new definition is "penetration, no matter how slight, of the vagina or anus with any body part or object, or oral penetration by a sex organ of another *person*, without the consent of the victim" (emphasis added). This revised measure however, will not be reflected in reported crime data until after January 2013 (FBI, 2012). Thus, it is unknown how this definitional change will affect future UCR statistics.

For Part I offenses, participating law enforcement agencies submit monthly reports that detail information on the number of offenses that are reported to them. To illustrate, in any given month, an agency might report that it arrested 20 individuals for homicide offenses, 100 for forcible rape offenses, and so on. The UCR also includes information for those index (Part 1) offenses cleared by arrest or exceptional means. Put differently, clearance rates refer to offenses that fit the following three criteria: 1) individual has been arrested, 2) s/he has been charged with the commission of the offense, and 3) s/he has been turned over to the court for prosecution (whether following arrest, court summons, or police notice). Agencies may also clear offenses through "exceptional means." In this instance, four criteria must be met. Law enforcement must have: 1) identified the offender, 2) gathered enough evidence to support an arrest, make a charge, and turn over the offender to the court for prosecution, 3) identified the offender's exact location so that the suspect could be taken into custody immediately, and 4) encountered an unforeseen circumstance outside the control of law enforcement that prevents the agency from arresting, charging, and prosecuting the offender (FBI, 2010a). To illustrate, crimes cleared by exceptional means might include the following: cases where the offender has died (e.g., suicide or justifiably killed by police or citizen), instances where the victim refuses to cooperate with the prosecution after the offender has been identified, or cases where a denial of extradition occurs—typically where the offender has committed an offense in another jurisdiction and is being prosecuted for that crime. Not least, for Part 1 offenses, law enforcement agencies report limited aggregated data (i.e., age, sex, and race) for persons arrested for each of the offense categories. However, beyond this information, little is known about the offense (e.g., its location, time committed), victim (e.g., male or female, child or adult), or other aspects of the incident (e.g., whether multiple perpetrators were involved, how law enforcement detected the offense).

In contrast, law enforcement agencies provide only arrest data for Part II offenses. No information is provided about cleared offenses or the age, sex, and race of persons arrested for each of the crimes. Part II offenses include 21 crimes such as "forgery," "other assaults-simple," and "sex offenses." For example, the sex offense category would include sexually-related crimes that fall short of "carnal knowledge of a female." Thus, penetrative sex offenses committed against male victims historically have fallen under Part 2 of the UCR in the sex offenses category and not under the forcible rape category in Part 1 of the UCR. Note however with the recent change in the UCR's forcible rape definition (anticipated to take effect in 2013) these offenses (cases where males have been victims of penetrative sex crimes) will now be cataloged under the UCR's Part 1 offenses (forcible rape).

Strengths. The UCR Program clearly proffers many advantages when measuring crime. First, it provides a longstanding data source on crimes that have occurred nationally for several decades. This consistent longitudinal measurement of crime allows researchers to track crime trends, and test theories about the factors that may contribute to increases and declines in offending (e.g., economic recessions, shifts in demographics). Additionally, it may also lead to "evidence-based" policy as it can assist criminal justice actors with crime prevention and the allocation of law enforcement resources. For example, say UCR reports indicate an increase in homicide rates nationally over a three-year period. Policymakers can use such information to assess whether legislative changes are warranted, or whether new criminal justice polices should be developed and implemented.

Second, the UCR Program covers an overwhelmingly large proportion of the population. Although reporting to the Program is not required by federal law, thirty-eight states mandate that law enforcement agencies regularly submit UCR records to the FBI (Barnett-Ryan, 2007). Additionally, other states encourage participation among its agencies. Current estimates indicate that UCR coverage extends to 96 percent of the population. Thus, only a tiny segment of the population is not covered by the UCR (FBI, 2010b).

Third, UCR records represent official offenses and are subject to verification by the FBI. Put differently, UCR records represent incidents that have been investigated by law enforcement. On one level "probable cause" exists — as evidenced by an arrest — to believe a crime has actually been committed. At the same time, both internal and external audits would be able to verify the information about offenses submitted by law enforcement agencies.

Fourth, while crime definitions often vary from state to state, the UCR system attempts to provide reporting processes that result in standardization of offense categories. The Program requires that law enforcement agencies submit reports that follow the FBI's definition of crime offenses, rather than their state's specific statutes (FBI, 2004). For example, in documenting criminal homicides, local agencies are required to follow the UCR's definition: "The willful (nonnegligent) killing of one human being by another." Per the UCR Program "any death caused by injuries received in a fight, argument, quarrel, assault, or commission of a crime is classified by the FBI as 'Murder and Nonnegligent Manslaughter.'" States are cautioned to not include other offenses such as traffic-related fatalities or fetal deaths regardless if these offenses fall within state homicide statutes (FBI, 2004).

Weaknesses. Notwithstanding these advantages, several weaknesses of the Program have been identified. One of the strongest criticisms levied by criminologists is that the UCR represents a non-exhaustive measure of crime. Under this view, the UCR is seen as an incomplete indicator of crime since it only "counts" those offenses that come to the attention of law enforcement. More specifically, researchers have found that certain serious and violent offenses are significantly less likely to be reported to police. Several extant studies indicate that sex crimes — forcible batteries and other sexually related offenses — are rarely reported to law enforcement. To illustrate, federal statistics indicate only one-third of sex offenses are reported to law enforcement in any given year (Hart & Rennison, 2003; Langton, Berzofsky, Krebs, & Smiley-McDonald, 2012). Notably, this low reporting average is unique to sexual offenses. That is, it is substantially lower than reporting estimates for other violent non-sex offenses. For example, close to 60 percent of all robberies (59 percent) and aggravated assaults (56 percent) are reported to law enforcement annually (Hart & Rennison, 2003; Langton et al., 2012). Thus, on average, these violent offenses are reported at significantly higher rates than those for sex offenses.

What factors prevent the reporting of sex crimes to law enforcement? In recent decades substantially greater empirical attention has been directed toward addressing this very question. Scholars have identified five factors associated with reduced reporting: 1) victims may fear retaliation from offenders, 2) victims may blame themselves for the offense, 3) victims may be fearful of rape stigma, 4) victims may prefer to keep the matter private, and 5) law enforcement practices may have prevented accurate reporting of sex offenses.

Prior research has documented that victims of crime who experience fear of retaliation are often deterred from reporting sex offenses. For example, national statistics indicate that 12 percent of non-reporting sex crime victims cited "fear of reprisal" as their primary reason for not reporting (Hart & Rennison, 2003; see also Bachman, 1993; Hattem, 2000). Victim blame may also affect reporting patterns. For example, some studies suggest that victims often blame themselves for their victimizations (Du Mont, Miller, & Myhr, 2003). In turn, "self-blame" is associated with reduced reporting among victims of sex crime (Stewart, Dobbin, & Gatowski, 1996; Wiehe & Richards, 1995). Some investigations have also revealed that concern about rape stigma—or being labeled a "rape victim"—might also attribute to reduced reporting among victims (Bachman, 1993, 1998; Fisher, Cullen, & Turner, 2000; Neville & Pugh, 1997; Roberts & Grossman, 1994). Other studies indicate that some victims may prefer to keep the matter private. For example, Hart and Rennison (2003, p. 7) in a national study of victimization and reporting practices from 1992–2000 found that nearly 25 percent of rape victims who did not report the offense claimed they did so because they viewed the offense as a "private/personal matter." Not least, traditional policing practices may have had an effect on reporting patterns. Baumer and his colleagues (2003, p. 843) summarized the institutional barriers to reporting in the early 1970s:

> The legal statutes in most states included a relatively narrow definition of rape, required that the incident be reported promptly and be corroborated by a third party, and required that the victim demonstrate that she physically resisted the attack. Moreover, the rules of evidence in many jurisdictions permitted the in-troduction at trial of information about the victim's character, reputation, and prior behavior, which often were used by defense attorneys in efforts to discredit the victim's testimony (citations omitted).

Notably, various rape reforms (e.g., the implementation of sex crime victim advocacy centers, enactment of rape shield laws) were instituted in the 1980s and 1990s to encourage greater reporting among victims of sexual violence. However, it does not appear that rape reforms have completely mitigated the effect of these earlier policing policies, as their legacy may to some extent, still adversely affect the reporting of sex crime. For example, Clay-Warner and Burt (2005) tested the impact of recent rape reforms on sex crime reporting. In particular, their examination of data pre-reform and post-reform suggest that "rape type" predicts the likelihood of reporting to law enforcement. Put differently, despite an increase in the overall likelihood of a rape being reported, "aggravated rapes" or stereotypical offenses (assaults where the victim and assailant are unknown to each other, there are multiple offenders, or "violence is explicit, as evidenced by use of weapons and victim injury," p. 151) continue to be more likely to be reported than "simple rapes" (rapes that do not involve aggravated factors as in the prior classification). Thus, the re-searchers conclude that the reforms have only been "partially successful" at changing reporting behavior (p. 167). This situation, in turn, per scholars, suggests "an unfinished agenda for rape law reform" (Clay-Warner & Burt, 2005, p. 173).

Collectively, this body of research indicates that the reporting of sexually related offenses has substantially increased since 1973 (Baumer, 2004). This figure lends some credence to the view that rape reforms—or more generally, cultural shifts in views about sex crime—have been partly effective in encouraging sex crime victims to report crimes committed against them to a greater extent than in prior decades. Even so, a fundamental limitation of the UCR that is still relevant today is that it significantly underestimates the extent of sexually related offenses that occur nationally.

A separate weakness of the UCR involves the hierarchy rule in the measurement of criminal incidents that involve multiple offenses. In particular, the rule mandates that in "multiple-offense situations" (cases where several offenses are committed at the same time and place) only the most "serious" offense will officially count for crime reporting purposes. The general ranking (most serious to least) is as follows: homicide, rape, robbery, aggravated assault, burglary, larceny, and motor vehicle theft. For example, in a case where a person is arrested for forcible rape and homicide offenses which occurred concomitantly, only the latter arrest "counts." That is, the UCR in this case would not record the forcible rape offense. Notably, one exception involves arson. This category is unaffected by the hierarchy rule; in cases where arsons co-occur with another offense, both crimes would be recorded by the UCR system (FBI, 2004). Because only homicide offenses "trump" sexual battery crimes, the hierarchy rule does not affect the recording of forcible rape offenses to the extent that it would other crime categories (e.g., burglary offenses). Yet, it may still affect the accuracy of rape estimates. For example, prior research suggests that rapes that occur with other offenses (e.g., robbery offenses) constitute an important subset of rape cases as they "appear to comprise more serious and aggravated victimizations when compared to solo-occurring rapes ... and perhaps as a result, victims of co-occurring rapes are more likely to report their rape to police than are victims of solo-occurring rapes, and police are more likely to clear these cases" (Addington & Rennison, 2008, pp. 221–222). However, the hierarchy rule prevents these offenses from being disaggregated from solo forcible rape offenses. Thus, researchers are precluded from analyzing solo rape offenses separately from rape offenses that co-occur with other crimes.

A third criticism levied against the UCR centers on its measurement of "forcible rape" offenses. The FBI defines forcible rape as "the carnal knowledge of a female forcibly and against her will." The UCR Handbook (2004, p. 19) further elaborates on this definition: "Carnal knowledge is defined by Black's Law Dictionary, 6th ed. as 'the act of a man having sexual bodily connections with a woman; sexual intercourse.' There is carnal knowledge if there is the slightest penetration of the sexual organ of the female (vagina) by the sexual organ of the male (penis)." Clearly, this represents a limited definition of sex crime; concomitantly, it is gender-specific. Under this logic, only females who have been forced to submit to vaginal intercourse can technically be "raped." Put differently, sexual battery (or penetrative) offenses involving male victims would not fit within this narrow scope of rape.

These limitations have been recognized by FBI. As mentioned earlier, in 2011 the UCR Program implemented steps to revise its nearly 80-year-old definition of "forcible rape." The new "rape" definition (which omits "forcible" in its title) is: "Penetration, no matter how slight, of the vagina or anus with any body part or object, or oral penetration by a sex organ of another person, without the consent of the victim." These changes are notable for three reasons. First, the new definition is gender neutral. Under this classification, sexual battery offenses against persons of any gender (including transgendered individuals) would fall under "rape" offenses in the UCR. Second, the new category removes "forcible" from its title. Thus, this broader definition would include cases where offenders sexually batter victims who are unconscious or intoxicated. Third, the revised classification covers a broader range of penetrative sex crimes (beyond penile-vaginal penetration). This new change is expected to be implemented in the UCR Program by 2013. However, as of now,

Table 2.1. Official Data Collection, UCR

Summary	Strengths	Weaknesses
• Oldest official data source in the U.S. • Participating agencies report arrest records to FBI • Provides summary statistics of police reports nationally • Includes information on clearance rates for select crimes	• Longitudinal data • Wide coverage • Subject to verification • Standardized estimates of serious crime	• Does not measure unreported crimes • Hierarchy rule • Relies on outdated definition of rape • Omits important information for sex crime research

it is unknown what impact the change will have on the recording of sex offenses. Additionally, it is unclear the extent to which the earlier estimates of "forcible rape" will be comparable to the future statistics relying on the new definition.

As a related criticism, crime researchers have emphasized that UCR reports often lack critical information about the victim, offender, and criminal event. Typically, the UCR provides aggregate information about police reports. For Index 1 offenses, it also reports on clearance rates and general characteristics of criminal arrests (the age, sex, race of offenders). Beyond that information, however, few other details are recorded. This omission adversely affects sex crime research. For example, as discussed earlier, wide heterogeneity exists within sexual offenses. Often, researchers code sex offenses (e.g., as "indecent exposure crimes" or "child sexual abuse offenses") based on specific information about criminal events. In studying child sexual abuse cases, researchers often need to know the age of the victim to properly assess if an offense in fact would fit under this general umbrella. The gender of the victim might also be relevant to their investigations. However, UCR reports do not provide disaggregated information about individual cases. Although some aggregate information about offenders is given for Index 1 crimes (demographics), little else is known. For example, sex crime researchers often focus on the victim-offender relationship (e.g., stranger, acquaintance, family member). The UCR system provides virtually no information about this critical variable. Understanding the crime context (e.g., location, time of day) is also a prominent focus in theories and research about sexual offending. Such details, however, are largely absent in UCR reports. Table 2.1 provides a summary of the UCR.

National Incident-Based Reporting System (NIBRS)

History. In the late 1970s, law enforcement officials and crime researchers voiced their concerns about the limitations of the UCR. In recognizing the flaws in this reporting system, the FBI began working toward implementing a new crime reporting system. The new system, NIBRS, would provide greater information about criminal events. Pilot testing for the recently created NIBRS system began in South Carolina in 1987. The new system was approved for general use by certified jurisdictions at a national UCR conference in 1988 (FBI, 2000).

Description. Because NIBRS provides additional data about individual criminal events, it holds a distinct advantage over the UCR. For example, rather than submitting aggregate counts of arrests for select offenses (under the traditional UCR system), in following NIBRS, participating law enforcement agencies submit detailed information for individual (select) offenses. Information is provided about offenders such as their age, sex, race, ethnicity, and suspected drug or alcohol use. NIBRS also records data about the victim (e.g., age, sex, race, type of injury, relationship to offender). Additionally, it provides specific details about the offense (e.g., location, date/time, whether a weapon or force was used during the commission of the crime). A second improvement involves the range of crimes NIBRS covers. In all, NIBRS collects data on each incident and arrest within 22 offense categories (comprised of 46 specific crimes called "Group A" offenses). In addition to the Group A offenses, there are 11 Group B offenses for which only arrest data are collected. Group A offenses include violent, interpersonal, and property offenses (e.g., "homicide offenses," "sex offenses — forcible," "sex offenses — non-forcible," "robbery," "embezzlement"). Group B crimes — for which only limited data are provided — can best be described as "miscellaneous" arrests (FBI, 2004). For example, arrests for "writing bad checks," "disorderly conduct," and "peeping Tom" crimes are included here. Not least, under NIBRS, the hierarchy rule is removed. Accordingly, for multiple-offense events, arrests for all crimes are recorded by NIBRS (Rantala, 2000).

Strengths. The strengths of NIBRS are obvious. First, the system provides invaluable data about criminal events. For example, NIBRS data details information about the arrestee, victim, and criminal event. This information is critical for sex crime research. Researchers often draw on these variables to study the predictors of sexual offending, and also for categorizing sex offenses. For example, NIBRS includes variables about the offense, such as the time of day it occurred, and also other characteristics about its location (e.g., school, home). In turn, such data can allow for a direct test of whether these variables are associated with sexual offending. At the same time, NIBRS data allow for a determination of whether an offense constitutes "child sexual abuse," "sexual battery," or a "stranger" offense. Notably, the previously discussed UCR data does not include such information, and so, would not permit for disaggregation of sex offenses.

Second, NIBRS provides information about a broad range of offenses. This advantage permits criminologists to better understand crimes that fall beyond index crimes. For instance, NIBRS includes detailed information about a broad range of sexually-related crimes. In turn, this extended focus permits a greater examination of the various types of sex offenses that exist (beyond simply, "forcible rape" offenses), such as sexual assault offenses, offenses involving children, child pornography offenses, and other types of sex crime (see e.g., Finkelhor & Ormrod, 2004).

Third, and finally, under NIBRS the hierarchy rule which traditionally has limited information about criminal events where multiple crimes are committed, does not apply. Thus, substantially greater information, particularly where multiple offenses co-occur within one criminal event, is included under NIBRS. To illustrate, for a single incident involving child pornography offenses, and actual contact offenses (e.g., sexual abuse of a child), information about all of these crimes would be recorded. As a result, this approach permits for a greater examination of sex crime cases that involve multiple criminal elements.

Weaknesses. NIBRS clearly offers advancements over the traditional UCR system. At the same time, it is not without its limitations. The most prominent criticism of NIBRS involves its limited generalizability. Notably, the system is costly to implement and requires a significant amount of resources (Faggiani, Kubu, & Rantala, 2005). These barriers in part are implicated as precluding the national implementation of NIBRS. In contrast to the UCR which covers 96 percent of the American population, only a minority of agencies submit to the NIBRS database. The most recently available statistics indicate that NIBRS currently covers 29 percent of the population, representing 27 percent of the nation's reported crime, and 43 percent of law enforcement agencies (Justice Research and Statistics Association, 2012). Alternatively, this indicates that most of the population is not covered by NIBRS. More specifically, some scholars have emphasized that the reporting agencies

Table 2.2. Official Data Collection, NIBRS

Summary	Strengths	Weaknesses
• Implemented in 1988 • Sought to address flaws in UCR • Participating agencies provide arrest and incident information (e.g., age of offender, victim sex, location of crime) for select offenses • Removes hierarchy rule	• Rich data source (includes important information about the offender, crime, and victim) • Provides information about broad range of crimes • More accurate recording of multiple element offenses	• Limited generalizability • Relies on official records of crime

are not representative to the larger population. For example, Finkelhor and Ormrod (2000, p. 2) in a study analyzing NIBRS data on kidnapping offenses noted:

> Conclusions drawn from these [NIBRS] data must be used with caution. Although the [crime] patterns and associations discovered are real, they apply only to the jurisdictions reporting and are not necessarily representative of national patterns and dynamics of crime. Also, NIBRS relies on local law enforcement agencies to collect data, and it is not clear how systematic agencies are in their recording of [crime].

As a result, the extent to which NIBRS data reflect national estimates is unknown.

Additionally, NIBRS relies on official police records, or crimes known to law enforcement. Accordingly, the same criticisms levied against the UCR in this regard, are applicable to NIBRS. To summarize, official crime data are limited because a significant proportion of offenses, which represent the "dark figure of crime," are never reported to law enforcement. Notably, research indicates one of the most underreported offense categories involve sexually related crimes. This is a notable finding to highlight because it suggests that official methods in measuring sex crime are inherently flawed. Thus, any official count of sexually related offenses (even NIBRS which captures significantly greater information about individual incidents of sex crime) should be interpreted with caution. More generally, it suggests that another method—perhaps one that is better able to tap into the "dark figure of (sex) crime"—would more accurately measure the nature and extent of sexual offending in the U.S. We move now to a qualitatively distinct data collection technique that directly addresses this concern. Table 2.2 briefly reviews NIBRS.

Unofficial Data Collection

National Crime Victimization Survey (NCVS)

History. The recognition that official data vastly underestimate crime particularly for violent and interpersonal offenses surfaced as early as the 1970s. During this time, research conducted by the National Opinion Research Center and the federal government detected that many offenses were never reported to law enforcement. In response, the "National Crime Survey" (later named the "National Crime Victimization Survey; NCVS") was implemented in 1973. Currently, the U.S. Census Bureau oversees the administration of the NCVS (U.S. Census Bureau, 2012).

Description. The NCVS represents one of the only national efforts to measure crime through the use of victimization surveys. In contrast to the UCR or NIBRS, the NCVS relies on responses from victimization surveys to estimate the nature and extent of crime in the U.S. Each year, data are obtained from a nationally representative sample of 76,000 households comprising 135,300 Americans. The NCVS depends on participation from three types of respondents: "household respondents," "individual respondents" (age 12 and older in the household), and "proxy" respondents. A "knowledgeable adult" answers specific questions about the household. Individual respondents (12 and older) also participate in the survey and are asked the full range of NCVS questions. Proxy respondents answer questions that pertain to members of the household who are not able to participate because of mental impairment or for some other reason (U.S. Census Bureau, 2003). For these three groups, the NCVS provides information on victimization frequency, characteristics of the offense, and other aspects of the crime (e.g., whether the victim reported the offense to law enforcement).

The survey measures a range of criminal victimizations among Americans 12 and older: rape, sexual assault, robbery, assault, theft, household burglary, and motor vehicle theft. The U.S. Census Bureau uses sophisticated methods in drawing representative samples of Americans to participate—garnering on average a 95 percent response rate. The NCVS uses a panel study design. Accordingly, samples are interviewed at six-month intervals for a period of three years (for a total of seven interviews). After that time, a new sample is identified, and the same process follows. Generally, interviews have been conducted in a hybrid format. The first and fifth interviews are face-to-face, and the rest are conducted by telephone (Bureau of Justice Statistics, 2012; Truman & Planty, 2012). Notably, the NCVS also administers "special" supplementary victimization surveys to select populations—such as school-aged youth—but these are not conducted on a regular basis.

Strengths. As a crime indicator, the NCVS holds many advantages over official data collection. First, because it relies on victim accounts' of crime, it taps into the extent of unreported offenses. Put differently, the survey inquires about *any* criminal victimization experience—even those not reported to law enforcement.

Second, the survey design allows for important information about the victim, offender, and context in which the crime occurred to be documented. For example, the NCVS records information about the victim (e.g., age, sex, race, ethnicity, marital status). It also asks victims to recall important details about the crime (e.g., the time it occurred, its location). Not least, the survey also inquires about the offender (e.g., whether the offender appeared intoxicated, used a weapon during the crime).

A third strength of the survey is that it permits for a better understanding of the dark figure of crime. In that regard, two NCVS measures bear emphasis. The first asks respondents whether the crime was reported to law enforcement. If respondents answer "no," a follow-up question—what was the "most important reason for not reporting"—is asked. If respondents answer affirmatively, they are then probed about their primary reason for reporting the offense (e.g., "to prevent future violence," "to punish offender," "collect insurance"). This focus allows for a clearer understanding about the underreporting of crime, and also, what factors influence reporting. Such information is valuable for criminologists and policymakers. If the factors that deter (or encourage) reporting could be identified, policies and procedures could be designed to better capture the "dark figure of crime."

Weaknesses. Although the NCVS has been heralded as an improvement toward measuring unreported offenses, it is not without its limitations. One glaring shortcoming is that it relies on victim accounts' of crime. Faulty memory recall could thus affect the accuracy of reports. A victim may not accurately recall specific details of the offense. In addition, the problem of telescoping exists. Telescoping refers to the phenomenon where respondents mistake when a criminal incident occurred. There are two types. Forward telescoping includes the misspecification of events having taken place at a time that was more recent than when they actually occurred. Backward telescoping includes reporting events as having taken place at a time that was less recent than when they actually occurred. For retrospective survey designs such as the NCVS, forward telescoping is of special concern because of the possibility of over-reporting events during the survey's reference period (typically, in six-month intervals). For example, forward telescoping occurs if a respondent is asked about victimization experiences within the last six months and erroneously reports information about a crime that occurred nine months ago.

A second limitation centers on the NCVS's traditional definition of sexual victimization. Prior to a redesign in the 1990s, the NCVS indirectly inquired about prior sexual battery. That is, respondents were vaguely asked to report "attacks" that they had experienced in the past. Moreover, the earlier NCVS definition was limited as it was not able to detect sexual assaults other than rape. Notably, with input from criminologists, the NCVS revised its sexual victimization measure in 1993. These changes are summarized by Bachman and Saltzman (1995, p. 1):

> Questions were added to let respondents know that the interviewer is interested in a broad spectrum of incidents, not just those involving weapons, severe violence, or violence perpetrated by strangers. New methods of cuing respondents about potential experiences with victimizations increased the range of incident types that are being reported to interviewers. And behavior-specific wording has replaced criminal justice terminology to make the questions more understandable.

Even so, while this change represents an improvement in the NCVS, the earlier estimates of sexual victimization cannot be directly compared to later estimates after the redesign. In turn, this discrepancy limits our understanding of trends in sexual victimization over time.

Moreover, the NCVS is limited in the measurement of sex crimes committed against children 11 years old and younger. That is, the NCVS limits interviews to respondents who are 12 or older. This situation is problematic for accurate estimates of sexual victimizations involving children (Finkelhor & Jones, 2004, p. 8). Notably, these offenses account for a substantial percentage of all sexually related offenses (Greenfeld, 1997). Thus, the NCVS is unable to document the nature and extent of child sexual abuse in cases where victims are younger than 12.

In addition, there is the potential that the interview approach could produce response bias. For example, the NCVS administers its survey using in-person and telephone interviewing (U.S. Census Bureau, 2003). In each instance, respondents have contact with interviewers who read the questions and record responses. Given this method, there is the potential for respondents to not report sexually violent offenses. For example, prior survey research has revealed that sensitive information is most reliably obtained when respondents have no contact with other individuals (e.g., self-administered questionnaires; Tourangeau & Yan, 2007). Table 2.3 highlights the important aspects of the NCVS.

National Women's Study (NWS) and National Women's Study-Replication (NWS-R)

History. Although the NCVS provides data on sexual victimization, it is limited in some respects. In particular, it does not provide a systematic account of rape experiences.

Table 2.3. Unofficial Data Collection, NCVS

Summary	Strengths	Weaknesses
• Conducted since 1973 and overseen by the U.S. Census Bureau • Interviews respondents 12 and older using a panel design (mostly telephone interviews) • Asks about victimization experiences in 6-month period • Inquires about whether crime was reported to law enforcement	• Better captures "dark figure of crime" compared to official methods • Records details about criminal offense and victim • Can estimate the extent of non-reporting • Inquires about reasons for not reporting	• Relies on victim recall of offenses and dates (i.e., faulty recall and telescoping might occur) • Prior to a redesign in 1993 vaguely measured sexual victimization • No data on crime victims younger than 12 • Potential for interviewer bias

To illustrate, because it focuses on crime that has occurred in six-month intervals, it does not measure the lifetime prevalence of sexual assault. Recognizing this limitation and others, in 1989, the federal government, specifically, the National Institute of Drug Abuse, commissioned a special survey that would focus on women's sexual victimization experiences over the life course. The National Women's Study (NWS) provided the first nationally representative systematic examination about women's rape and sexual abuse experiences in the U.S. It used a longitudinal survey design and was administered over a three-year period in 1989–1991 (NWS; Kilpatrick, Edmunds, & Seymour, 1992) and then again in 2006 (NWS-R; Kilpatrick, Resnick, Ruggiero, Conoscenti, & McCauley, 2007).

Description. The NWS sought to address three research questions: How much rape is there in the United States? What are the characteristics of rape? How have victims been affected by the rape experience? The earlier surveys (conducted in 1989–1991) focused on a broad definition of rape: "an event that occurred without the woman's consent, involved the use of force or threat of force, and involved sexual penetration of the victim's vagina, mouth, or rectum" (Kilpatrick et al., 1992, p.1). Notably, the latter survey instrument was revised in 2006 to include drug and alcohol facilitated rapes. In addition, this more recent study included a sample of college women to better understand their sexual assault experiences.

To ensure that the sample of women chosen to participate in the sample represented the larger population, the 1989–1991 NWS relied on a large national probability sample of 4,008 women (age 18 or older), 2,008 of whom represented a cross section of all adult women and 2,000 of whom were an oversample of younger women between the ages of 18 and 34. The logic for relying on an oversample of young women derives from prior research findings indicating that this age group faces the highest risk of sexual assault (see generally, Belknap, 2007). The survey was conducted by telephone. Most of the women who were contacted agreed to participate in the study (response rape=85 percent). The survey had three waves of data collection—the initial survey (1989), a first follow-up (Wave 2), and a two-year follow-up (Wave 3). Several findings are notable (Kilpatrick et al., 1992):

- Approximately 1 in 8 (12.1 million) American women have been raped at least once in their lifetime.
- Sexual assault is a "tragedy of youth" (p. 3)—61 percent of rape victims were under the age of 18 when the assault occurred.

- Most women who were raped experienced only one assault (56 percent); however, a significant proportion also experienced multiple rape victimizations (39 percent).
- Seventy-eight percent of rape victims were assaulted by a known perpetrator.
- Most victims (70 percent) did not sustain physical injury.
- A majority of victims reported being "fearful of serious injury or death" during the rape.
- Nearly one-third of rape victims met criteria for posttraumatic stress disorder (PTSD), compared to 5 percent of non-victims.
- Only 16 percent of victimized women had reported their rape to law enforcement.
- Fifty percent of raped women reported that they would be "a lot more likely to report" the offense if there was a law prohibiting news media from disclosing their names and addresses (note: this study was conducted prior to the national emergence of rape shield laws).
- NWS forcible rape estimates were 5.3 times larger than UCR and NCVS estimates.

Notably, after the Wave 3 data collection, the NWS survey was not administered again until the mid-2000s (NWS-R). During this time, the survey instrument was revised to better account for "hidden" rapes and "hidden" rape victims. For example, prior to the change, little research had been conducted that looked specifically at drug and alcohol facilitated sexual offenses. At the same time, researchers and policymakers became increasingly concerned about the extent of sexual violence on college campuses (Fisher et al., 2000). Accordingly, the new NWS-R instrument included questions about incapacitated (alcohol facilitated) and drug-facilitated rapes. Additionally, it included a sub-sample of college women.

In particular, the 2006 NWS-R sample included 5,000 U.S. women aged 18–86. Of these, 3,000 comprised a national sample representing all U.S. women and 2,000 comprised a national sample representing women currently attending U.S. colleges and universities (response rate=78.6 percent; Dean Kilpatrick, personal communication, November, 21, 2012). The findings from this latter wave of the survey generally correspond to those findings in the earlier study, with some caveats:

- For the general sample, the NWS-R uncovered substantially more rapes because it used a broader definition of rape.
  - About 20 million out of 112 million women (18 percent) in the U.S. have ever been raped during their lifetime. Notably, this estimate includes 18 million women who have been forcibly raped, and 3 million women who have experienced incapacitated rape, and nearly 3 million women who have experienced drug-facilitated rape.[1]
  - For the college sub-sample, nearly 673,000 women (12 percent of the college population) have ever been raped. This includes an estimated half-million college women who have been forcibly raped, and over 200,000 who have experienced incapacitated rape, and about 160,000 who have reported drug-facilitated rape.[1]
- Criteria for PTSD within the past year were met by 9 percent and 12 percent of women in the general and college samples, respectively. In the general sample, this includes approximately 23 percent of rape victims versus 6 percent of non-victims. In the college sample, this includes 34 percent of rape victims versus 9 percent of non-victims.
- Reporting rates for the general sample (16 percent) and the college sample (12 percent) remain low and correspond to the earlier NWS estimates.

---

1. These percentages add up to more than 100 percent because a significant proportion of rape incidents involved more than one of these three elements (Kilpatrick et al., 2007).

Strengths. The NWS and NWS-R improve upon earlier victimization research. Thus, the primary strength of this study lies in the fact that it represents one of the first systematic examinations of rape and sexual assault among women in the U.S. The survey inquired about various aspects of sexual victimization—such as when the victimization occurred, characteristics of offenders, and reporting characteristics. The latter redesign (NWS-R) was better able to tap into the extent of sex crimes previously unexamined. Moreover, the later version examined "hidden" rape victims (i.e., college students), and so, was able to compare and contrast their sexual victimization experiences to non-college rape victims. Not least, the NWS and NWS-R inquired about the consequences of sexual victimization and the extent of reporting.

Weaknesses. Three flaws are evident in the NWS and NWS-R. First, the survey focuses exclusively on women. Of course, the intent of the study, as the name of it implies, is to do just that. Certainly, it makes ample sense to direct empirical attention to a group who disproportionately experiences sexual victimization and abuse (i.e., women). Having said that, male sexual victimization experiences remain an empirical "black box." More alarming in this regard is emerging evidence that males, particularly young boys, experience substantial sexual abuse and victimization (for a review see Tewksbury, 2007). This is all the more so disconcerting as males are even less likely to report these offenses than female victims (Weiss, 2010). Thus, the extent to which male sexual victimization experiences compare with female victimization is largely unknown as significantly less empirical attention (including that of the NWS and NWS-R) has been directed to the former.

A second limitation involves the inconsistent administration of the survey. Initially, the survey was administered in three waves from 1989–1991. After that period, respondents were not consistently interviewed. Indeed, the redesign of the survey did not occur until 15 years later (in 2006). Since then, it does not appear that the survey has been administered again. This limitation is potentially problematic because the data do not permit for consistent tracking of trends in sexual victimization—including the nature and extent of sexual violence, and the reporting and consequences of it.

Third and finally, the same criticism of the NCVS can be recapitulated here. Put differently, study findings might be biased because of the reliance on victims' memories and telephone interviewers. Since the study queries about offenses that may have occurred years ago, there is concern victims may not accurately recall details about the offense. At the same time, because of the direct interaction with another person, victims may be reluctant to report sensitive details about their victimization experiences. Table 2.4 summarizes the NWS and NWS-R.

National Violence against Women Survey (NVAWS)

History. In 1995, shortly after the initial administration of the NWS, the Centers for Disease Control (CDC) and the National Institute of Justice (NIJ) funded a separate national study—the National Violence against Women Survey (NVAWS; Tjaden & Thoennes, 2000)— to better understand the nature and extent of sexual victimization and physical violence in the U.S. Two differences between the NVAWS and the NWS bear emphasis. First, the former broadened the scope of victimization—focusing not just on sexual assaults, but also on related offenses (e.g., physical violence, stalking). Second, the NVAWS included males in its sample to better understand how their victimizations compared to women's experiences.

Description. The NVAWS relied on a nationally representative sample of 8,000 females and 8,000 males ages 18 and over. The survey was a random-digit dial telephone-based interview (response rate=72 percent). In contrast to the NWS-R, the NVAWS did not

Table 2.4. Unofficial Data Collection, NWS/NWS-R

Summary	Strengths	Weaknesses
• National telephone-based survey initially administered over a three-year period in 1989–1991; additional wave conducted in 2006 (NWS-R) • Analyzed the extent of sexual battery (penetrative) offenses, characteristics of offenses, and effects of rape on victims • Latter wave also focused on sample of college women and alcohol/drug facilitated rapes	• Represents one of the first systematic examinations of sexual victimization • NWS-R tapped into extent of sex offenses previously unexamined • NWS-R focused on college sample in addition to general population sample of women • Both surveys measured the consequences of sexual victimization (e.g., health effects)	• Study sampled only females • Inconsistent administration of the survey • Possibility for recall and memory errors • Potential for interviewer bias

include assessments for alcohol or drug facilitated sexual assault. In particular, it centered on addressing five research gaps. First, the study sought to measure the extent of physical violence experienced by respondents. A second goal of the study was to measure intimate partner violence (physical and sexual). A third focus was on assessing the extent of stalking victimization among men and women. Fourth, the study assessed the extent of forcible rape experiences among the American population. A final and related emphasis was on examining characteristics and consequences of these victimization experiences. Put differently, respondents who disclosed that they had been victimized were then asked additional follow-up questions about the victimization, including injuries they sustained and their use of medical services.

Several findings from the NVAWS are notable. First, physical assault was experienced by a significant proportion of the sample: approximately 52 percent of women and 66 percent of men admitted that they were physically assaulted as a child by an adult caretaker and/or as an adult by any type of attacker. Annually, an estimated 1.9 million women and 3.2 million men are physically assaulted in the United States.

In contrast, intimate partner violence was highly gendered. Women (22 percent) reported a substantially higher prevalence of intimate partner physical violence compared to men (7 percent). Alternatively, this finding suggests that on average, approximately 1.3 million women and 835,000 men are physically assaulted by an intimate partner annually in the United States. Notably, the survey uncovered a smaller prevalence of intimate partner abuse involving sexual assault. In particular, it found that 8 percent of surveyed women and 0.3 percent of surveyed men were raped by a current or former intimate partner at some time in their life.

Stalking victimization also varied by gender. On average, 8 percent of women and 2 percent of men in the NVAWS reported ever being stalked. This estimate equates to approximately 1 million female and 371,000 male stalking victims in the U.S. for any given year.

Three findings bear emphasis when focusing on sexual victimization. First, in line with other studies (e.g., the NCVS), the NVAWS found that sexual victimization (completed or attempted sexual battery) was significantly more prevalent among females (18 percent) compared to males (3 percent). This estimate suggests that approximately 302,091 women and 92,748 men are forcibly raped each year in the U.S. Second, many of the sampled women and men reported being raped at a young age. Of the women surveyed who admitted being sexually assaulted, more than half (54 percent) were younger than age 18 when they experienced their first attempted or completed rape. This pattern is also evident among males. An overwhelming majority of male rape victims (71 percent) experienced the assault prior to age 18. Third, and finally, the extent of sexual victimization varies by race and ethnicity. For example, American Indian/Alaska Native women were significantly more likely than White women, African-American women, or mixed-race women to report they were raped. In addition, mixed-race women were significantly more likely than White women to report they were raped. Notably, this effect did not extend to male victims of rape. That is, no significant racial or ethnic differences were observed for the male sample of victims.

Recall that a final focus of the NVAWS centered on examining additional characteristics and consequences of victimization (i.e., the extent of injury, whether the victim received medical care). In particular, the study found that the risk of injury increases among female rape and physical assault victims when the perpetrator is a current or former intimate partner. Women who were sexually or physically assaulted by a current or former spouse, partner, boyfriend, or date were significantly more likely than women who were raped or physically assaulted by other types of perpetrators to report being physically injured during their most recent rape or physical assault. Additionally, approximately one-third of injured female rape (36 percent) and physical assault victims (30 percent) received medical treatment (e.g., paramedic care, emergency room treatment, dental care, or physical therapy) for their most recent victimization.

Strengths. The NVAWS is one of only a small handful of studies to examine sexual victimization experiences. Thus, it has many strengths; four of which are discussed below. First, it inquired about a wide range of victimization experiences. That is, it focused on measuring sexual victimization and related crimes, such as stalking. This is an important advance over other surveys as these "analogous" offenses (e.g., intimate partner abuse, stalking) are linked to sexual assault and rape (see Tjaden & Thoennes, 2000, p. 25). Thus, focusing on a wide range of related experiences can assist with efforts to more systematically understand sexual victimization.

Second, it measured rape using a range of indicators (see below). Along this line, the study examined males' sexual victimization and violence experiences. In contrast, the NWS and NWS-R focused exclusively on females. The NVAWS also considered the gendered nature of sexual victimization and asked questions according to respondent sex (Tjaden & Thoennes, 2000, p. 4):

- [Female respondents only were asked:] Has a man or boy ever made you have sex by using force or threatening to harm you or someone close to you? Just so there is no mistake, by sex we mean putting a penis in your vagina.
- Has anyone, male or female, ever made you have oral sex by using force or threat of force? Just so there is no mistake, by oral sex we mean that a man or boy put his penis in your mouth or someone, male or female, penetrated your vagina or anus with their mouth.
- Has anyone ever made you have anal sex by using force or threat of harm? Just so there is no mistake, by anal sex we mean that a man or boy put his penis in your anus.
- Has anyone, male or female, ever put fingers or objects in your vagina or anus against your will or by using force or threats?
- Has anyone, male or female, ever attempted to make you have vaginal, oral, or anal sex against your will but intercourse or penetration did not occur?

Table 2.5. Unofficial Data Collection, NVAWS

Summary	Strengths	Weaknesses
• Administered shortly after the NWS in 1995 • Examined a broad range of victimizations (i.e., rape and related assaults—such as physical violence, intimate partner abuse, and stalking) • Included a male sample	• Represents one of the first examinations of sexual victimization and related offenses • Measured sexual victimization using various indicators • Analyzed lifetime prevalence of victimization • Included follow-up questions about post-victimization experiences	• Cross-sectional study • Did not include indicators of non-penetrative sexual victimization • Unable to identify factors contributing to sex crime trends • Respondents may not accurately recall aspects of the victimization • Potential for interviewer bias

Third, the NVAWS inquired about lifetime prevalence of sexual victimization. Notably, this emphasis represents an advance over extant victimization surveys. For example, the NCVS inquires about victimization that has occurred over a specified time (i.e., six months). Thus, it is unable to document prevalence trends in sexual victimization.

Fourth and finally, the NVAWS included follow-up questions about the aftermath of victimization. Specifically, its focus on measuring the extent of physical injuries and medical care received by victims improves upon prior research by documenting how victimization affects Americans after the offense. Per the authors of the study, such a focus also has the potential to provide critical insight to the medical community when treating crime victims.

Weaknesses. The NVAWS has drawbacks. First, the study relied on a cross-sectional design. Put differently, in contrast to a prospective, longitudinal study the NVAWS did not follow respondents over time (say, from childhood to adulthood), but rather used retrospective data to calculate the prevalence of victimization. Thus, responses elicited from the survey about victimizations that may have occurred several years ago are potentially subject to recall bias.

Second, the survey did not inquire about non-penetrative sex offenses. For example, the indicators of sexual victimization tapped into crimes involving penetration of the victim (i.e., vaginal, anal, or oral). To be clear, several other types of victimization exist. In particular, the study was unable to detect sexual victimization beyond rape—such as sexual assault (e.g., molestation offenses).

Third, while the NVAWS greatly contributed to our understanding of sexual victimization, it was unable to assess what factors might be contributing to certain trends. To illustrate, a striking observation per Tjaden and Thoennes (2000) centered on the finding that prevalence of experiencing violence—particularly sexual victimization—varies significantly by ethnicity and race. As a result, additional studies—ideally ones that include a range of theoretically important variables—"are needed to determine why the prevalence of rape, physical assault, and stalking varies significantly among women and men of different racial and ethnic backgrounds" (Tjaden & Thoennes, 2000, p. 60). Finally, the same criticism of other victimization surveys applies here. Specifically, NVAWS results are potentially biased given the survey method. Table 2.5 provides an outline of the NVAWS.

National College Women Sexual Victimization (NCWSV) Study

History. Beginning in the early 1990s, the federal government instituted legislation that required public universities and colleges to prepare and distribute crime statistic reports, particularly for violent offenses, and to also develop and publish campus policies regarding the awareness and prevention of sexual assaults. Per experts, this attention, in part, was "prompted by the rising fear that college campuses are not ivory towers but, instead, have become hot spots for criminal activity" (Fisher et al., 2000, p. 1). To illustrate, in 2000, the NIJ provided funding for a large-scale study—the National College Women Sexual Victimization (NCWSV) study—that examined sexual victimization experiences among college students in the U.S.

Description. The study sought to address several gaps in prior research examining sexual victimization. In particular, it relied on a nationally representative sample of college women. At the time, few studies examining a national sample of college students existed. For example, the earlier NWS and NVAWS focused on a wide range of women, but not necessarily those attending colleges or universities. In addition, the NCWSV study examined a range of sexual victimizations (e.g., sexual assault, rape), and related offenses, including stalking. It also included cues and behaviorally specific questions to ensure respondents were aware of what was being asked. For example, prior to asking screen questions about forced sexual acts, the survey included a short introduction that emphasized the realities of sexual victimization (Fisher et al., 2000, p. 6):

> Women may experience a wide range of unwanted sexual experiences in college. Women do not always report unwanted sexual experiences to the police or discuss them with family and friends. The person making the advances is not always a stranger, but can be a friend, boyfriend, fellow student, professor, teaching assistant, supervisor, coworker, somebody you meet off campus, or even a family member. The experience could occur anywhere: on or off campus, in your residence, in your place of employment, or in a public place. You could be awake, or you could be asleep, unconscious, drunk, or otherwise incapacitated. Please keep this in mind as you answer the questions.

Along this line, the study also employed a quasi-experimental design to assess whether question wording impacts responses. This focus distinguishes the NCWSV study from other studies such as the previously discussed NVAWS (which examined only penetrative sex crimes). It also differs from the earlier NWS survey which focused on a comparatively limited set of sexual victimizations than the NWS-R. Additionally, the NCWSV study examined how the risk of being sexually victimized was affected by a variety of factors, including demographic characteristics, lifestyle traits, prior victimization experiences, and the characteristics of the college or university attended. Prior to the NCWSV study, there was little systematic examination of the variables that might affect sexual victimization.

In particular, study results are based on a telephone survey of a randomly selected sample of women (n=4,446) attending American colleges or universities during the fall semester of 1996. As evidenced by the study's high response rate (86 percent), an overwhelming majority of women selected to participate in the study did so. The NCWSV study asked "screener" questions about various types of victimization: sexual battery offenses, sexual assault victimization, sexual coercion, and stalking.

The survey inquired about rape/sexual battery offenses similar to the NWS and NVAWS. For example, it asked students about crimes involving non-consensual penetrative acts committed against them: "Since school began in fall 1996, has anyone made you have sexual intercourse by using force or threatening to harm you or someone close to you? Just so there is no mistake, by intercourse I mean putting a penis in your vagina."

Additionally, it queried about non-penetrative sexual assaults. To illustrate, the survey asked: "Not counting the types of sexual contact already mentioned, have you experienced any unwanted or uninvited touching of a sexual nature since school began in fall 1996? This includes forced kissing, touching of private parts, grabbing, fondling, and rubbing up against you in a sexual way, even if it is over your clothes."

The survey also included measures of sexual coercion and related acts. For example, the NCWSV study asked, "Since school began in fall 1996, has anyone made or tried to make you have sexual intercourse or sexual contact when you did not want to by making threats of nonphysical punishment, such as lowering a grade, being demoted or fired from a job, damaging your reputation, or being excluded from a group for failure to comply with requests for any type of sexual activity?"

In measuring stalking victimization, the survey inquired, "Since school began in fall 1996, has anyone—from a stranger to an ex-boyfriend—repeatedly followed you, watched you, phoned, written, e-mailed, or communicated with you in other ways that seemed obsessive and made you afraid or concerned for your safety?" In each instance—where respondents answered affirmatively to any of the above screener questions—they were then probed for further details about the assault.

Responses to these questions indicate that approximately 3 percent of college women will experience a completed and/or attempted rape. At first glance, this statistic appears to indicate that rape is relatively rare on campus. Alternatively, it suggests that a vast majority of women—nearly 97 percent—enrolled in colleges and universities will not be victimized. What this estimate obscures is that the study measured victimization over a relatively short incident period (approximately seven months). Put differently, per Fisher and her colleagues (2000, p. 10), when "the victimization figure is calculated for a 1-year period, the data suggest that nearly 5 percent of college women are victimized in any given calendar year ... over the course of a college career ... the percentage of completed or attempted rape victimization among women in higher educational institutions might climb to between one-fifth and one-quarter."

For other types of sexual offenses, threats of sexual victimization occurred less often than other forms of sexual victimization (i.e., actual contact offenses). For example, the victimization percentages for "other" sexual assaults ranged from 0.18 percent ("threat of contact with force or threat of force") to 3 percent ("attempted sexual contact without force") in the sample.

Substantially more respondents reported being stalked since the start of the school year. Approximately 13 percent of the sample admitted that they were stalked in the last year. Fisher et al. (2000) observed that this estimate is significantly greater than the figure obtained in the NVAWS conducted by Tjaden and Thoennes (2000). Notably, they attribute this difference to measurement and the sample. For example, the NCWSV study used a broad measurement of stalking, defining (Fisher et al., 2000, p. 27) it as a "woman experiencing repeated, obsessive, and frightening behavior that made her afraid or concerned for her safety." This is notable because other stalking measures such as the ones used by Tjaden and Thoennes (2000) were more restrictive. Additionally, the NVAWS focused on a wide cross-section of the population, whereas Fisher et al. (2000) examined only college students—per the authors, "it may be that the social domain of college places women in situations and in contact with a range of men that increase the chances of being stalked" (p. 27).

The NCWSV study also examined how question wording might impact responses. That is, at the same time the NCWSV study was being conducted, a special version of the NCVS—one that focused on college student experiences was administered to a national sample of students. The two surveys were virtually identical, except for one critical difference. The NCWSV study relied on the screener questions and follow-up probes mentioned earlier, while the NCVS used its standard measure of sexual victimization. Results from this quasi-experiment indicate that in comparison to the survey items used by the NCVS, the NCWSV study methodology that employed behaviorally specific screen questions in combination with follow-up questions yielded substantially higher estimates of completed, attempted, and threatened rape. In short, these findings suggest future studies rely on nuanced measures of sexual victimization.

As a final focus, the NCWSV study also examined risk factors for sexual victimization. In particular, four characteristics appeared to significantly increase various types of victimization—residing on campus, being unmarried, frequently using alcohol to the point of becoming drunk, and experiencing prior sexual victimization.

Strengths. The NCWSV study improved upon a very limited body of extant research examining female college students' sexual victimization experiences. Specifically, it illuminated three gray areas in sex crime research. For example, prior to the NCWSV study little was known about the extent of sex assaults and related crimes (beyond rape) on college campuses. The study's methodology allowed for a detection of these offenses. At the same time, it provided a direct test of how question wording can significantly influence responses to victimization prompts. Put differently, the quasi-experimental results (comparing the NCVS and NCWSV study methodologies) provide empirical evidence that relying on behavioral specific indicators and important follow-ups are valid methods to tap into sexual victimization. A third strength lies in the study's multivariate analysis of risk factors for sexual assault. Prior to this study, relatively few studies had identified factors that might contribute to sexual victimization of college women using a nationally representative sample of students. For all of these reasons, the NCWSV study is considered a seminal work in understanding college students' sexual victimization experiences.

Weaknesses. Having said that, there are limitations to the NCWSV study. For example, similar to the NWS and NWS-R, the NCWSV survey examined only females' experiences. Certainly, there are compelling arguments to be made that such a focus is warranted given the disproportionate risk of sexual victimization that women face in comparison to men. At the same time, perhaps college males also experience a range of sexual victimization experiences. Anecdotally, there have been incidents where males were victims of sexual assault as part of hazing rituals in college (see e.g., Kirby & Wintrup, 2002). However, the extent to which these and other sexual victimizations compare with females' experiences is unknown as virtually no national studies that have systematically compared and contrasted these experiences exist.

Another limiting factor involves the study's reference period. Fisher and her colleagues (2000) investigated college women's sexual victimization experiences over a seven month period. There is concern that this reference period is too short and not necessarily indicative of long-term victimization trends, as evidenced by Fisher et al.'s (2000, p. 10) comments, "Projecting results beyond this reference period is problematic for a number of reasons, such as assuming that the risk of victimization is the same during summer months and remains stable over a person's time in college." In short, while illuminating NCWSV study figures do not necessarily extend to longer time periods (i.e., over a typical college career).

More generally, the same criticism of victimization surveys can be again summarized here. That is, the reliance on victims' recall and telephone interviewers might bias estimates. Table 2.6 provides an overview of the NCWSV study.

Table 2.6. Unofficial Data Collection, NCWSV Study

Summary	Strengths	Weaknesses
• Administration motivated by increased concern about campus crime in the 1990s • Relied on national sample of women enrolled in colleges and universities • Examined broad range of sexual victimization • Also measured stalking offenses • Relied on behaviorally specific questions and cues	• Represents one of the first systematic examinations of sexual victimization and related behaviors in a national college sample of women • Was able to demonstrate that question wording significantly affects detection of sexual victimization • Identified statistically significant risk factors for experiencing victimization	• Survey did not include males • Relatively short reference period • Survey method potentially biases results

National Intimate Partner and Sexual Violence Survey (NISVS)

History. In 2010, a multi-agency effort was launched to better document sexual victimization and its consequences. Specifically, the National Center for Injury Prevention and Control (part of the CDC), along with funding from the NIJ and the Department of Defense, conducted a nation-wide victimization survey—the National Intimate Partner and Sexual Violence Survey (NISVS; Black et al., 2011)—that measured sexual violence, stalking, and intimate partner abuse. It is anticipated that the study will be conducted on an annual basis. So far, only data for the first administration of the survey, in 2010, have been released by the government.

Description. Although the NISVS acknowledged that prior research—such as the NWS, NWS-R, and NCWSV study—has greatly expanded the sex crime literature, it also noted that flaws exist in this body of work. In particular, there has been an absence of consistent tracking and monitoring of sexual victimization. Moreover, while national studies exist, it is often difficult to compare and contrast results because of the varying methodologies and samples used in these prior studies. Not least, substantially less is also known about how forms of violence impact specific populations in the U.S., or the related emphasis on the extent to which rape, stalking, or violence by a romantic or sexual partner are experienced in childhood and adolescence. To address these research gaps, the NISVS focused on three areas: the prevalence and characteristics of sexual violence, stalking, and intimate partner violence, groups most likely to experience these forms of violence, and not least, health consequences of victimization.

For 2010 (the first year data collection began, and the only wave thus far to be made available by the government), the NISVS obtained completed interviews (response rate=31 percent) from 16,507 adults (9,086 females and 7,421 males). The survey was administered using a random-digit dial telephone method.

Several findings from this study bear emphasis. First, similar to other estimates, the study indicates that violence is experienced at alarming rates among the general public. About 18 percent of women and 1 percent of men reported having been raped (i.e., completed forced penetration, attempted forced penetration, or alcohol/drug facilitated completed penetration) at some time in their lives. The study also measured sexual coercion (i.e., unwanted sexual penetration after being pressured in a nonphysical way), and unwanted sexual contact (sex offense not involving penetration). Here, about 13 percent of women and 6 percent of men reported having had experienced sexual coercion at some point in their lives. Substantially more women (27 percent) and men (12 percent) in the survey experienced unwanted sexual contact. In line with findings from the NWS, NISVS results indicate that sexual victimization is indeed "a tragedy of youth" (Kilpatrick et al., 1992, p. 3). For instance, approximately 42 percent of female victims reported experiencing their first completed rape before the age of 18. Nearly one-quarter of male victims of completed rapes experienced their first rape when they were 10 years old or younger. In most instances, women and men were assaulted by intimates and acquaintances. Stranger assaults were rare for females (8 percent of cases) and males (15 percent of cases). Stalking offenses were also measured by the NISVS. Here, 16 percent of women and 5 percent of men reported being stalked at some point during their lifetime to the degree that they felt "very fearful or believed that they or someone close to them would be harmed or killed" (Black et al., 2011, p. 2). NISVS also inquired about intimate partner violence. Approximately 36 percent of women and 29 percent of men admitted that they have experienced rape, physical violence, and/or stalking by an intimate partner in their lifetime.

A second notable finding is that demographic variation exists in victimization risk, particularly for sexually violent and stalking experiences. For instance, in line with other studies, the NISVS found that American Indian/Alaska Native women and women who identified as multiracial experienced the highest lifetime prevalence of sexual assault — 27 and 34 percent, respectively. The statistics for White and African American women were comparable — 19 and 22 percent reported being raped at some point in their lifetime, respectively. Hispanic women had the lowest overall risk of experiencing rape over the life course (14 percent). This general trend exists for other forms of violent victimization experiences of females — such as other types of sexual violence (e.g., unwanted touching) and stalking.

Notably, rape statistics for males, disaggregated by race and ethnicity could not be reliably reported because of the small frequency of males who reported being rape victims in the survey. However, statistics for other types of unwanted sexual contact of males indicate a similar racial and ethnic trend as for females. For instance, nearly one-third of multiracial (32 percent) men in the U.S. had these experiences during their lifetime. Between one-fifth and one-quarter of African American (23 percent), White (22 percent), Hispanic (26 percent), and American Indian /Alaska Native (20 percent) men experienced sexual violence other than rape in their lives. Stalking victimization statistics for males, disaggregated by race and ethnicity, are not available due to the small baseline number of males who admitted being stalked in the past.

A final focus of the survey centered on measuring the health consequences of victimization. In short, results from the NISVS indicate that victims experience a range of health issues, compared to non-victims. For instance, women and men who experienced rape or stalking victimization and those who experienced physical violence from an intimate partner were significantly more likely to report having frequent headaches, chronic body pain, difficulty sleeping, activity limitations, and generally poor physical and mental health than women and men who did not experience these types of violence. Because the study was cross-sectional in nature (i.e., it collected data at only one point in time), it is not possible to determine if a violent victimization caused related health problems. Having said that, "there may be a number of potential mechanisms by which violence is related to health over one's lifetime ... some health conditions may result directly from a physical injury ... or from the adoption of health-risk coping behaviors such as smoking and the harmful use of alcohol or drugs" (Black et al., 2011, p. 61, citations omitted). The NISVS is designed to be administered on an annual basis. Thus, the potential exists in the future to better determine the direction of this relationship.

Strengths. The NISVS directly addresses the flaws of prior research, and so in this way, contributes to current efforts to better document and understand sexual violence and related victimization. To illustrate, it provides national data on the prevalence of violent victimization, and on the specific groups who are disproportionately affected by crime. Of course, other studies have addressed these areas. However, the NISVS provides the most recent national statistics on these offenses. Additionally, the survey's focus on the health consequences of experiencing violent victimization represents an advance in current efforts to better comprehend the effects of experiencing violence. Not least, the survey is slated to be administered on an annual basis (Black et al., 2011). This longitudinal design will ensure that trends and patterns in experiencing violent victimization will be better tracked and monitored.

Weaknesses. Although the NISVS represents one of the most recent and innovative victimization surveys, it has a few weaknesses. One concern involves its relatively low response rate of 31 percent. Alternatively, this estimate indicates that 69 percent of initial respondents chosen to be in the sample did not participate in the study. Recall that the response rates for the previously mentioned victimization survey are much higher (e.g., approximately 95 and 86 percent for the NCVS and NCWSV study, respectively). To be clear, response rates, especially for telephone surveys have been on the decline in recent years (Pew Research Center, 2012). Thus, the NISVS's relatively low response rate is not unusual to telephone-based surveys. Nonetheless, there is still concern from a methodological standpoint that the "non-responders" are qualitatively distinct from those individuals who actually participated in the study. This remains a critical issue for survey research, and in particular, for victimization surveys that rely on a telephone method to contact participants.

Relatedly, there is the potential that recall and interviewer bias exists. In line with other victimization surveys, the NISVS survey design depends on respondent recall of events to accurately tally the extent of victimization. Thus, the potential exists for faulty memory errors to influence estimates. Additionally, the NISVS administers its survey using telephone interviewing. In each instance, respondents have actual contact with interviewers who administer the survey. As discussed earlier, there is the concern that this method reduces the extent of victimization reporting (Tourangeau & Yan, 2007). Survey methods have recently evolved to address this critical issue. For example, telephone-audio computer-assisted self-interviewing (T-ACASI) removes the human element in phone interviews. In a T-ACASI survey, an actual interviewer screens and recruits respondents, and explains the purpose of the study. However, after that point, respondents have no further interaction with the interviewer. They simply record their responses to sensitive questions (Currivan, Nyman, Turner, & Biener, 2004; Turner et al., 2002). What this suggests is that more sophisticated methods exist to accurately record sensitive information. Given that the NISVS is scheduled to be consistently conducted on an annual basis, it may be that this innovative method is used at some point during the survey's administration. Table 2.7 summarizes the NISVS and highlights its strengths and weaknesses.

Table 2.7. Unofficial Data Collection, NISVS

Summary	Strengths	Weaknesses
• First wave of survey administered in 2010 • Designed to be conducted on a regular basis • Examined prevalence and characteristics of sexual violence, stalking, and intimate partner violence; groups most likely to experience violence; and, the health effects of violence	• Provides most recent national statistics on sexual victimization and other forms of violence • Slated to be administered on an annual basis—a design that may better capture long-term trends in sexual violence	• Relatively low response rate • Faulty memory may affect respondents' accounts of victimization • Potential bias in survey method—interviewer effects might influence results

National Survey of Children's Exposure to Violence (NatSCEV)

History. The victimization surveys previously discussed focused exclusively on adults or as is the case with the NCVS, individuals 12 and older. How is sexual victimization of children measured? The answer to this question is that much less empirical attention has been directed toward studying victimization experiences among this group. To address this research gap, in 2007 the federal government provided funding for one of the only national systematic studies of childhood victimization. The survey named the "National Survey of Children's Exposure to Violence" (NatSCEV; Finkelhor, Turner, Ormrod, Hamby, & Kracke, 2009), was administered in 2008 and 2011. In line with the NISVS, it is designed to be conducted on a consistent basis.

Description. The survey limited responses to American children ages 1 month/2 years old to 17 years old (the age range varies slightly by wave). It examined violence across several domains: "conventional crime," "child maltreatment," "victimization by peers and siblings," "sexual victimization," "witnessing and indirect victimization," "school violence and threats," and "Internet victimization." In particular, NatSCEV measured prior year (i.e., incidence) and lifetime exposure to violence (i.e., prevalence). Similar to other victimization surveys, the NatSCEV used random digit dialing to develop a nationally representative sample of children. Both waves garnered large sample sizes and adequate response rates (n=4,549, response rate=54 percent for the first wave; n=4,503, response rate=40 percent for the second wave). Additionally, the general survey design relied on an oversampling method to ensure adequate minority representation. Parents or caregivers provided demographic information (e.g., race, household income). Children age 10 and older in the households were interviewed. For children age 9 or younger, a "proxy" respondent, or a caregiver knowledgeable of the children's daily routine and experience, was interviewed.

A discussion of notable highlights from the 2008 NatSCEV follow (for complete statistics for all of the 48 types of victimizations, see Finkelhor, Turner et al., 2009). Overall, findings indicate American children are exposed to a substantial amount of violence. Approximately six in ten of the surveyed children were exposed to violence within the last year, either directly (i.e., having had experienced an actual victimization) or indirectly (i.e., witnessing violence against someone else). Close to half of the children in the sample were assaulted at least once in the prior year. Twenty-five percent were prior victims of property offenses (robbery, vandalism, or theft). Nearly 10 percent of the sample experienced non-sexual child maltreatment (e.g., physical abuse, neglect).

Sexual victimization was measured using a range of indicators; the survey examined rape and attempted rape offenses, sexual assault offenses, indecent exposure crimes, sexual harassment, and statutory rape offenses. Overall, approximately 6 percent of children had been sexually victimized in the last year, and 10 percent had experienced a sexual assault over their lifetimes. Rape offenses (attempted and completed) accounted for approximately 1.1 percent and 2.4 percent of the sample in the past year and for lifetime prevalence, respectively. Other findings revealed the following about sexual assaults: by a known adult (0.3 percent past year, 1.2 percent lifetime), an adult stranger (0.3 percent past year, 0.5 percent lifetime), or a peer (1.3 percent past year, 2.7 percent lifetime). For indecent exposure offenses by an adult, 0.4 percent of the sample reported past year victimization and less than one (0.6) percent reported prior victimization during their lifetime. Peers were much more likely than adults to commit these offenses. For instance, 2.2 percent of the sample reported a peer had "flashed" them in the past year, and nearly 4 percent reported lifetime victimization. Sexual harassment percentages were not disaggregated by perpetrator type (e.g., peer). Here, approximately 3 percent of children reported being sexually harassed in the prior year, whereas 4 percent reported lifetime victimization. Statutory sexual offenses were relatively rare, with 0.1 percent of the sample reporting such victimization in the past year, and 0.4 percent reporting lifetime victimization. Additionally, survey results indicate that adolescents ages 14 to 17 were the most likely age group to be sexually victimized compared to other age groups. Indeed, nearly one in six (16.3 percent) was sexually victimized in the prior year and more than 25 percent had been victimized during their lifetimes. Notably, 2011 NatSCEV findings (the most recent wave of the survey) indicate that overall sex crime victimization trends among children have remained relatively stable in the U.S. (Finkelhor, Turner, Shattuck, & Hamby, in press).

Strengths. The NatSCEV expands on prior efforts to accurately document the extent of violence afflicting American youth. As a result, it has a number of strengths. First, it focuses exclusively on youth. With the exception of the NCVS, prior victimization surveys have measured sexual violence only among respondents 18 years and older. Additionally, while the NCVS represents wider coverage, it too is limited in that it examines only older children's (12 years and up) victimization experiences. Second, the NatSCEV also measures a range of victimizations—including actual victimization experiences and exposure to violence. Moreover, the survey included several indicators of sexual victimization—rape, sexual assault offenses, indecent exposure/"flashing" offenses, sexual harassment, and statutory rape offenses. Third, the NatSCEV's survey design allows it to calculate prior year (incident) and lifetime offenses. This approach has the added benefit of better understanding sexual victimization over the life course. Finally, in line with the NISVS, the NatSCEV is scheduled to be conducted on a consistent basis (Finkelhor, Turner, & Hamby, 2011). This longitudinal design will better allow researchers to monitor trends and patterns in childhood victimization experiences.

Weaknesses. The NatSCEV is not without its weaknesses. One limitation involves the use of a "proxy" or stand-in respondent for children age 9 and younger. It may be that caregivers are unaware of the child's victimization experiences. Relatedly, in the case where caregivers are abusers, it is unlikely that they would report their offenses to interviewers. Under this logic, the survey may underestimate the extent of victimization. Not least, the same criticisms of survey research apply to the NatSCEV. Put differently, recall bias—especially where children are the respondents—and interviewer effects might impact the accuracy of reporting. Table 2.8 highlights the major aspects of the NatSCEV.

Table 2.8. Unofficial Data Collection, NatSCEV

Summary	Strengths	Weaknesses
• Survey first administered in 2008 and again in 2011 • Scheduled to be administered on a regular basis • Examined prior year and lifetime prevalence of victimization among American children 17 and younger	• One of the only national recent studies to examine victimization among children • Included several indicators of sexual victimization • Measured one year incidence and lifetime prevalence of victimization • Designed to be a longitudinal study	• Use of proxy respondent for children 9 and younger may underestimate victimization • Potential for recall bias to affect responses • Survey results may be affected by interviewer bias

Chapter Summary

To conclude, two broad approaches toward measuring sex crime exist in the U.S. Official data collection is dependent on police records of crime. UCR and NIBRS estimates comprise official crime data. These methods have a number of strengths (e.g., wide coverage, long-standing data collections, subject to verification). At the same time, a fundamental flaw of the official data approach is that it measures only reported offenses. Recognizing that official methods do not account for the "dark figure of crime," unofficial crime collection methods (victimization surveys) have been established. In the U.S., the federal government regularly conducts the NCVS. More recently, specialized surveys designed to measure sexual victimization have been designed and implemented nationally. These include the NWS/NWS-R, NVAWS, NCWSV study, NISVS, and NatSCEV. Although survey methods hold a critical advantage over official data collection, they are not without their limitations. To illustrate, such methods depend on the recall and honesty of respondents to record details about sexual victimization. In turn, this reliance means that unofficial estimates of sex crime cannot be verified. More generally, survey design (e.g., the types of questions asked, the survey method) may also impact the accuracy of estimates. In short, official and unofficial methods complement one another as each approach brings with it weaknesses that the other addresses.

The reading list below provides additional citations to other research examining sex crime measurement. The following chapter reviews patterns and trends of sex crime in the U.S. over the last two decades.

Additional Suggested Readings

Fisher, B. S., Daigle, L. E., Cullen, F. T., & Turner, M. G. (2003). Reporting sexual victimization to the police and others results from a national-level study of college women. *Criminal Justice and Behavior, 30*, 6–38.

Fluke, J. D., Yuan, Y. Y., & Edwards, M. (1999). Recurrence of maltreatment: An application of the National Child Abuse and Neglect Data System (NCANDS). *Child Abuse & Neglect, 23*, 633–650.

Kilpatrick, D. G. (2004). What is violence against women? Defining and measuring the problem. *Journal of Interpersonal Violence, 19,* 1209–1234.

Koss, M. P. (2010). The under detection of rape: Methodological choices influence incidence estimates. *Journal of Social Issues, 48,* 61–75.

Miethe, T. D., Olson, J., & Mitchell, O. (2006). Specialization and persistence in the arrest histories of sex offenders: A comparative analysis of alternative measures and offense types. *Journal of Research in Crime and Delinquency, 43,* 204–229.

Rand, M. R., & Rennison, C. M. (2005). Bigger is not necessarily better: An analysis of violence against women estimates from the National Crime Victimization Survey and the National Violence against Women Survey. *Journal of Quantitative Criminology, 21,* 267–291.

Weinrott, M. R., & Saylor, M. (1991). Self-report of crimes committed by sex offenders. *Journal of Interpersonal Violence, 6,* 286–300.

Chapter 3

Sex Crime Patterns and Trends

Chapter Introduction

One might assume that reports of sex crime have dramatically increased in recent years given the unprecedented proliferation of sex crime legislation beginning in the mid-1990s. Indeed, legislators and policymakers have emphasized an escalation in sexual violence when discussing the need for "get tough" sex crime laws (Sample & Kadleck, 2008). However, to what extent are these views consistent with actual statistics tracking sexual offending over time? The goal of Chapter 3 is to address this question by analyzing recent patterns and trends in sexual offending nationally. In so doing, it provides further context for understanding sexual violence in the U.S. It proceeds as follows. First, it examines the extent of sexual offending using data sources that have consistently tracked sex crime over time. In particular, national crime patterns and trends examining general sexual offending and victimization are examined using UCR data, NCVS data, and survey data of adult women. Additionally, data sources measuring the extent of child sexual abuse are highlighted. Second, the chapter outlines factors theorized to be associated with these patterns and trends.

Data Examining General Sexual Offending and Victimization

As previously emphasized in Chapter 2, in measuring sex crime one can rely on several indicators. For example, UCR data provide information on "official" offenses, or those crimes reported to law enforcement. In contrast, the NCVS and other crime victimization surveys rely on victim accounts for measuring reported and unreported offenses. Below patterns and trends of these data are reviewed. Overall, these data sources are best suited for measuring general sex offending trends. The UCR, for example, does not provide specific information about sex offenses by age or other characteristics of victims. Additionally, the NCVS is limited in that it does not provide offense data involving young children.

UCR Data

One avenue into investigating crime patterns and trends involves analyzing "official" or record data. Recall that the FBI regularly compiles UCR reports submitted by an overwhelming percentage of police jurisdictions nationally. UCR data have a number of or measuring crime. For example, these data are helpful for understanding the ffenses reported to law enforcement on a national scope. At the same time, they record" data or information that is subject to verification. To be sure, they are discussed in Chapter 2, a main shortcoming of UCR records is that they include only those offenses reported to police. Because sexually related crimes are notoriously un-derreported, UCR records are incomplete estimates of sexual violence nationally. Even so, we likely can trust the overall patterns and trends of these data as there is little evidence that the reporting average of rape has declined. If anything, the criminal justice system has mounted several campaigns to increase reporting of sexually violent crimes. Additionally, efforts to improve law enforcement treatment of rape victims have been implemented nationally. As a result, the overall reporting of rape appears to have increased compared to prior years. Indeed, Clay-Warner and Burt (2005) demonstrate that sexual offenses committed after 1990 were significantly more likely to be reported to police than those offenses committed in earlier decades (see more recently, Lonsway & Archambault, 2012). What this indicates then is that although the accuracy of sex offense rates reported by the UCR may be "off" for any given year—thus, reflecting the "dark figure of crime"—the overall trend in reports is less affected. This is because the underreporting rate is unlikely to change dramatically for any given year. Put differently, there is little reason to believe that the rate of underreporting is less as time goes on. Thus, if a decline in reports of rape were to be detected, we could confidently assume it is not due to a decrease in reporting over time (i.e., a methodological factor), but rather, may reflect a genuine decline.

Figure 3.1 (below) depicts forcible rape rate trends (per 100,000 individuals) using UCR data from 1976 to 2010. Looking long-term over a 34-year period, inspection of the figure suggests relative stability of rape rates. That is, in 1976, approximately 27 rapes per 100,000 persons were reported. In 2010, 34 years later, that number barely increased to 28 rapes per 100,000 people.

Focusing on short-term trends, a different pattern is evident, however. To illustrate from 1976 to 1980, the rape rate increased from 26.6 rapes per year to almost 37 rapes in 1980. Throughout that decade, rape rates steadily increased. However, a dramatic shift is evident from 1992 and the proceeding years. That is, throughout the early 1990s, the rape rate consistently declined nationally. As Nash (1999, p. 45) has observed, this era marks the beginning of unprecedented legislation to manage and punish the "predatory sex offender." Even so, despite this particularly intense period of policymaking the forcible

Figure 3.1. Forcible Rape Rates per UCR Data, 1976–2010

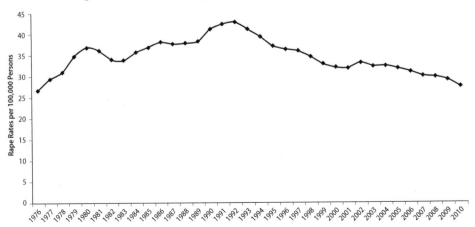

rape rate declined by nearly 26 percent. From each year forward, with few exceptions, the rape rate continued to decline. More precisely, from the peak year of reports (1992) to the most current year for which data are available (2010), the forcible rape rate diminished by approximately 40 percent. Thus, this pattern indicates a significant decline in forcible rapes reported to law enforcement in recent decades. To be sure, UCR statistics provide information only on reported sex offenses. Next, NCVS estimates of sexual victimization—which account for the "dark figure of crime"—are discussed.

NCVS Data

As discussed earlier (Chapter 2), in the 1970s the federal government created the NCVS to administer to a national sample of Americans on a consistent basis. The impetus for the survey's development stemmed from concern that many offenses were unreported to law enforcement. Chapter 2 provides greater detail about the NCVS. For now, important highlights about the NCVS will be reviewed.

The NCVS uses a survey approach to estimate the extent of crime. In particular, it queries Americans about their prior criminal victimization experiences. As a result, it has clear strengths over official methods in tapping into the "dark figure of crime." For instance, extant studies reveal that only a small proportion of sex offenses are ever reported to police (Lonsway & Archambault, 2012). Thus, the NCVS may be particularly valuable for measuring sexual victimization given that it is among the most underreported offenses in the U.S. But, the NCVS is far from a perfect measure. To illustrate, the NCVS relies on the honesty of respondents. In contrast to the UCR, reports of criminal victimization obtained by the NCVS are not subject to verification through official records. A separate issue involves the recall or accuracy of experiences described by crime victims. That is, respondents are typically asked to recall events that occurred six months prior to the interview. Accordingly, such an approach indicates that some respondents may be unable to remember certain details of the crime. One final limitation is that interviews are only administered to individuals age 12 and older. As a result, the NCVS does not provide information about crimes involving very young victims.

Despite these shortcomings, estimates from the NCVS greatly assist with tracking the extent of sexual offending over time. Figure 3.2 (below) for instance shows the rate of

Figure 3.2. Rape/Sexual Assault Rates per NCVS Data, 1993–2011

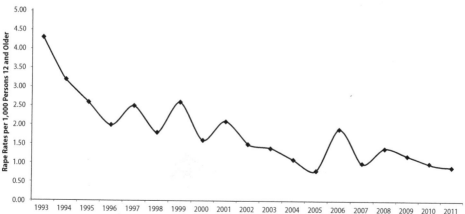

tion for individuals age 12 and older from 1993–2011. Data collected
omitted because they are not necessarily comparable to estimates from
ifically, the NCVS underwent a substantial redesign in 1992 (Bachman
)5). The new version includes revised survey items designed to tap into
tion. The first administration of the newly revised version began in 1993.
ensure estimates are comparable across years, only trend data from 1993
to 2011 are shown. Inspection of the figure indicates a significant decline in reports of
sexual victimization in line with UCR trends. In particular, rape rates diminished
dramatically from 4.3 to 0.9 sexual victimizations per 1,000 persons. This difference
represents a 79 percent reduction in reports of rape and sexual assault from 1993 to 2011
(the year for which the most recent data are available). Specifically, reports of sex crime
began to decline markedly in the mid-1990s. For example from 1993 to 2000, rape rates
involving those 12 and older decreased by more than 62 percent (from 4.3 to 1.6). Notwithstanding some peaks in reporting, rape rates consistently decreased every year thereafter.
In short, findings from the NCVS are on par with those results from the UCR indicating
a substantial decline in reports of sex offending. The following discussion highlights
estimates of sexual victimization found in other national surveys.

Other National Surveys of Adult Women

As discussed in Chapter 2 beyond the NCVS criminologists can look toward other victimization surveys that have been conducted nationally to understand the extent of sex
crime in the U.S. Beginning in the late 1980s and early 1990s, the federal government
commissioned specialized surveys designed to better measure sexual victimization of adult
women. Figure 3.3 (below) depicts estimates of lifetime (i.e., prevalence) and annual (i.e.,
incidence) percentages of sexual victimization among adult women across three time
periods and surveys: 1989–90 (NWS), 1998 (NVAWS), 2005 (NWS-R), and 2010 (NISVS;
for a review of these surveys refer to Chapter 2). These are shown in an effort to highlight
estimates gleaned from specialized victimization surveys of adult women. Unlike the
patterns shown in earlier figures, inspection of this figure indicates an increase in the
percent of women reporting ever being the victim of a sex crime over time. For instance,
in the first time period (NWS, 1989–90) 12.5 percent of American women reported that
they have ever been sexually assaulted or raped. Data collected in later years indicate a
consistent increase in lifetime prevalence percentage (e.g., 18.5 percent of women reported
lifetime victimization per the NISVS).

However, no clear trend exists when analyzing annual or incidence estimates of sexual
victimization. For instance, annual prevalence estimates are higher in 2010 than in the
NWS study (1.1 percent versus 0.7 percent, respectively). Having said that, this pattern
is not consistent over time. In 1998, for example, the annual incidence of sexual assault
(0.3 percent) was lower than in 1989–90 (0.7 percent).

What do these estimates reveal about sexual victimization? First, although the lifetime
prevalence percentages appear to increase across time, it is not clear if these estimates
indicate a genuine decline or are due to methodological differences across studies. To
illustrate, studies differ in the questions posed to respondents to measure sexual
victimization. Indeed, it may be that the latter studies (indicating an increase in lifetime
prevalence of sexual victimization) are merely more sensitive than the earlier surveys in
capturing sexual victimization experiences. Second, the annual percentages of sexual victimization do not indicate a clear trend over time. Thus, it is not at all clear that these
estimates suggest a significant increase in sexual victimization annually. Additionally,

Figure 3.3. Extent of Sexual Victimization of Adult Women from Different Surveys

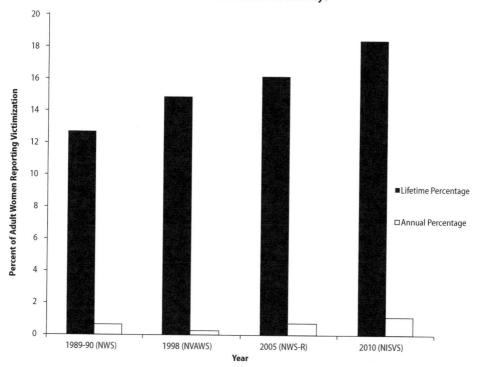

with few exceptions these studies have not been conducted over significant periods of time. That is, they are mostly cross-sectional, having measured the sexual victimization experiences of women at a single time point, and not on a consistent, yearly basis using the same survey items. Thus, relying on these four estimates to calculate the actual extent of sexual victimization of women across time has its limitations. Comparing these estimates, however, is advantageous for understanding sex crime patterns and trends for other reasons. First, collectively, these results demonstrate that regardless of the trend in the extent of sex crime, a non-trivial percentage of American women report being sexual assault victims. That is, if these estimates are averaged across studies, nearly 15 percent of women reported lifetime prevalence of victimization, and approximately one percent were victims of rape or sexual assault for any prior year. If these estimates were to be extrapolated to women in the larger population (see e.g., U.S Census Bureau, 2013), nearly 1.6 million women will be victims of sexual violence annually and approximately 23.5 million women will experience a sex crime at some point in their lives. Concomitantly, these estimates can contribute to a greater understanding of how question wording and survey methodology can impact responses. Regardless, these surveys (in addition to UCR and the NCVS) are limited because they have been unable to measure sexual victimization among young children. In the discussion that follows, data sources specific to tracking patterns and trends of child sexual abuse are analyzed.

Figure 3.4. Cases of Child Sexual Abuse Claims, 1990–2011

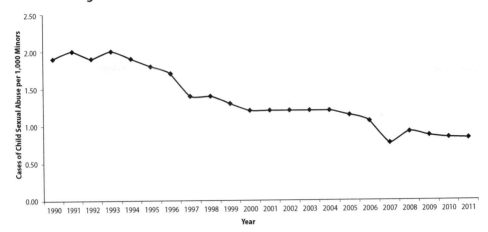

Child Sexual Abuse Statistics

The data sources previously discussed are limited in understanding the extent of child sexual victimization. The UCR for instance does not provide disaggregated information about arrests involving child victims. In contrast, the NCVS only counts victimization involving individuals age 12 and older. Not least, the other victimization surveys discussed (NWS, NVAWS, NWS-R, and NISVS) have not been consistently administered and have focused generally on adult female experiences. Accordingly, other data sources must be analyzed to track patterns and trends for child sexual abuse. Below, two specific measures are discussed.

National Child Abuse and Neglect Data System (NCANDS)

In line with the UCR, NCANDS data represent "official" cases of sexual abuse allegations. However, the latter data system tracks only reports of victimization involving children reported to state child protective agencies. Specifically, it aggregates state-level data involving reports of physical abuse, sexual abuse, and neglect of children (Finkelhor & Jones, 2012). Given this focus, a clear strength of such data is that it provides information about sex offenses involving young children. Recall that the UCR does not provide disaggregated information of crime reports based on victim age. Having said that, the UCR most certainly includes offenses reported to NCANDS where cases have been substantiated. Even so, the NCANDS is a comprehensive data source that allows specific allegations involving children to be consistently tracked and monitored. This is not to say that the NCANDS is a perfect measure of child sexual abuse. It still represents "official" data, and thus, is subject to similar criticisms as other official data sources regarding underreported offenses.

With this caveat in mind, Figure 3.4 shows substantiated reports of child sexual abuse over the last two decades (1990–2011). In line with measures of adult sexual victimization, inspection of NCANDS data over time indicates a significant reduction in reports of child

Figure 3.5. Reports of Child Sexual Victimization from Survey Data

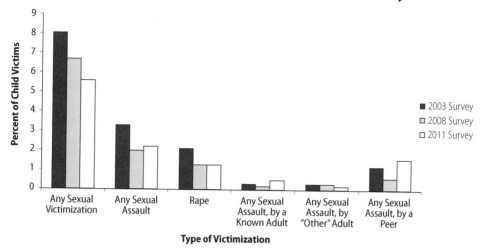

sexual abuse. In particular, rates of alleged child sexual victimization declined from 1.9 offenses to 0.8 offenses per 1,000 children. In turn, this change represents an approximate 56 percent decline in child sexual abuse rates over a 22-year period. Specifically, a steep decline is evident throughout the 1990s. To illustrate, the child sexual abuse rate diminished by nearly one-third during this decade. For each year thereafter, the general pattern indicates consistent decreases in sexual victimization involving children. Consistent with the trend observed in the 1990s, rates of child sexual abuse diminished by 31 percent during the 2000s. Overall, NCANDS statistics indicate that sexual victimization allegations reported to states have significantly declined over the last two decades.

NatSCEV

Along with the NCANDS, the NatSCEV (discussed in Chapter 2) provides another indicator of the extent of child sexual abuse. Given that this data source was already reviewed, for now it is will be briefly summarized. In contrast to the NCANDS, the NatSCEV is a victimization survey administered to youth and their caretakers. It is designed to measure the extent of physical abuse, child sexual victimization, and also indirect victimization (e.g., witnessing intimate partner abuse, abuse of peer). The NatSCEV relies on a telephone method to contact respondents and their caretakers. Compared to the NCVS, it taps into victimization experiences of very young children. Accordingly, the NatSCEV improves upon survey research by targeting children. However, it is also limited as it is subject to the same biases (e.g., recall errors, relies on respondent honesty) as other criminal victimization surveys.

Although it is designed to be administered on a regular basis, data currently exist for only two years (2008 and 2011). However, one earlier study conducted in 2003 used nearly identical survey items as the NatSCEV (Finkelhor, Turner, Ormrod, & Hamby, 2010). Because the two surveys used instruments that were comparable, we can directly compare their results. Thus, three data points (2003, 2008, and 2011) are illustrated in Figure 3.5. The figure shows the percent of children who reported being victims of sexual victimization annually for these three years. Additionally, it shows the yearly percentages of sexual assaults (e.g., molestation), rapes (i.e., penetrative offenses), and sexual assaults by perpetrator.

Overall, inspection of the figure indicates a substantial decline in all three offense categories from 2003 to 2008: "any sexual victimization," "sexual assault," and "rape" (which includes completed and attempted rapes). To illustrate, the total sexual victimization percentage decreased from 8 percent in 2003 to 6.7 percent in 2008. This difference per Finkelhor and his colleagues (2010) reflects a marginally significant change (p-value=0.06). The percent of victims reporting prior sexual assaults was significantly less in 2008 than in 2003 (2 percent versus 3.3 percent, p-value<0.001). Rape offenses also declined from 2.1 percent in 2003 to 1.3 percent in 2008, representing a statistically significant decline (p-value=0.02). The remaining categories breakdown sexual assault percentages by offender type. Offenses committed by known adults decreased from 2003 to 2008, but only slightly, and not significantly so (from 0.3 in 2003 to 0.2 in 2008; p-value=0.45). Sexual assaults committed by "other" adult perpetrators remained constant from 2003 to 2008. In contrast, peer-perpetrated sex crimes significantly decreased over the five-year period (from 1.2 percent to 0.6 percent, respectively; p-value=0.01).

What about changes in sexual victimization trends from 2008 to 2011? The answer is that findings from the latter wave of the NatSCEV show relative stability in trends—no substantial increases or decreases were evident when comparing trends across these three years. That is, although some changes are illustrated in Figure 3.5 (e.g., "any sexual victimization" decreased from 6.7 to 5.6 percent), these small fluctuations were not statistically significant (Finkelhor et al., in press).

Collectively, in line with results from other data sources, these findings from the NatSCEV and an earlier related survey indicate a significant decline in sex offenses from 2003 to 2008. However, when comparing more recent trends (2008–2011), a pattern of stability in sex offenses exists. Even so, comparing 2003 survey results to 2011 estimates shows a significant decline in most sex offenses across this eight-year period.

Examining Potential Factors Related to the Decline in Sexual Offenses

Across several independent data sources, reports of sexual offending and victimization have substantially decreased in the U.S. over the last two decades. This pattern is evident for both crimes involving adults and those against children. A natural follow-up question then is, what factors have contributed to the national decline in sex crime? Some of the prominent arguments regarding this trend are discussed below. To be clear, not all of these factors have been systematically examined as a cause in the decline of sex offenses nationwide. Indeed, it is difficult to precisely isolate potential contributors to crime generally. However, the factors discussed below are ones that have been highlighted in recent discussions and debates about sexual offending trends.

The Implementation of Sex Offender Restrictions in the 1990s

At first glance, it would appear that the prominent shift in sex crime legislation in the mid-1990s spurred the reduction of sex offenses. For instance, over the last two decades, the federal government and states have enacted a range of post-incarceration sanctions for sex offenders. These laws aim to increase monitoring and surveillance of convicted sex offenders in the community. However, determining the effects of the myriad of laws enacted during this time is difficult given the nearly simultaneous implementation of them, as well as the variation within specific reforms (e.g., registry laws versus residence restrictions). More detailed discussions about these research caveats are discussed in Chapter 10. For now, however, three findings are notable to highlight for discussions and debates about the impact of sex crime laws on sex offending rates. First, research suggests that the decline in sex offenses occurred prior to the systematic implementation of sex offender laws such as registries and community notification policies (Zgoba, Witt, Dalessandro, & Veysey, 2008). And so, the enactment of sex crime legislation does not stand out as an especially compelling factor in explaining the onset of the sex crime decline. Second, recent evaluations indicate that registry laws—one of the most widely implemented laws nationally—have inconsistent and largely null effects on sex crime prevention (Vásquez, Maddan, & Walker, 2008). Third, in contrast to their intent, most reforms do not appear to reduce recidivist sex crimes. Specifically, of the small number of evaluations that demonstrate a significant positive effect of sex crime laws (e.g., Letourneau, Levenson, Bandyopadhyay, Armstrong, & Sinha, 2010; Socia, 2012) most show evidence of a general deterrent effect, reducing first-time offenses, as opposed to a specific deterrent effect among convicted offenders.

To be sure, this is not to suggest that sex offender laws are uniformly ineffective in reducing sex crime. On balance, what extant findings do indicate is that most reforms occurred after the onset of a substantial decline in sex offenses. As a result, it is not at all clear that such reforms are causally linked with trends showing a reduction of sex offenses in the last two decades. Having said that however, it may be that some reforms have further contributed to the consistent decline in offenses. Additionally, for whatever reason, sex crime laws—when positive effects are observed—appear more effective at promoting general deterrence than encouraging specific deterrence. Accordingly, this provides some evidence that sex offender reforms have not been implemented to work as intended. That is, nearly all were designed with the goal of reducing reoffending among convicted sex offenders. However, of the small handful of evaluations that indicate positive effects— nearly all have uncovered general deterrent, as opposed to specific deterrent effects. Thus, greater attention is needed to the timing of the implementation of these reforms as well as to the variation within such measures to more strongly demonstrate the impact of sex crime laws on rates of offending. Again as elaborated on in Chapter 10 these are important methodological considerations that make it difficult to fully assess the effect of sex crime laws.

Incapacitation Effects

Along with the implementation of post-incarceration sanctions, the federal government and states have also enacted more stringent sentences for convicted sex offenders over the last two decades. Although there was an increased reliance on incarceration for nearly all offenders during this time period (Blumstein & Wallman, 2006), incarceration trends suggest that sex offenders were disproportionately targeted by these new policies. For example, one federal study conducted by Greenfeld (1997) examined incarceration rates from 1980 to 1994. His analysis revealed that the number of imprisoned sex offenders grew by more than 7 percent per year over this 14 year period—faster than any other category of violent crime. In 1994, nearly one in ten state inmates incarcerated nationally was serving a sentence for a sex crime conviction (Greenfeld, 1997).

This estimate has slightly increased over the last decade. To illustrate, a later federal study concluded that about 12 percent of all incarcerated offenders were serving a sentence for a sex crime conviction in 2010 (the most recent year for which data are available; Carson & Sabol, 2012). Few national studies have disaggregated prison admissions by specific sex offense conviction (e.g., sex crime against child versus adult). However, one study revealed that prison admissions of sex offenders who have victimized children dramatically increased from 19,000 to over 63,000 between 1986 to 1997 (Finkelhor & Ormrod, 2001).

It follows that these incapacitation effects may have contributed to a decrease in violent crime, including sex offenses. Even so, incarceration can only affect crimes where the offense has been reported to law enforcement, and where the charge results in a felony conviction. At the same time, not all offenders—even those known to law enforcement—are ultimately convicted and incarcerated. Thus, it is unclear how incarceration would impact non-reported crimes or offenses that do not result in a prison conviction. Juxtaposed against these observations, Finkelhor and Jones' (2006, p. 700, citations omitted) conclusion in a review of prior research is illustrative of the nuances in incarceration effects:

> A problem with the incarceration theory is that some classes of child molesters, like incestuous abusers, are much less likely to be incarcerated than others ... [trends] suggest intrafamily abuse has declined as much as other child molesting if not more. Adolescent perpetrators are also a group who comprise as much as a third of all sexual abusers ... they are less likely than adults to be incarcerated, even though such incarcerations have also increased ... incarceration may have possibly resulted in a general deterrent effect on all offenders. But then the effects of incarceration become difficult to distinguish from some of the other theories, which also posit mechanisms that would generally deter [sex] offending. In any case, if incarceration is a key mechanism, it should have its biggest effect on the classes of individuals most likely to be incarcerated. So even in the case of sexual abuse, other factors must be at work, and incarceration does not explain why the declines have been so across-the-board.

Efforts to Increase Reporting

Some scholars argue that other factors such as recent efforts to increase reporting of sex offenses are responsible for the steep decline in sex offending. To illustrate, Clay-Warner and Burt (2005) traced efforts to increase reporting of sex offenses against females to law enforcement in the 1990s. Their analysis indicates that on average women were more inclined to report sex offenses during the 1990s as opposed to prior decades. This change potentially reflects the impact of criminal justice efforts to increase reporting. In turn, this finding implies that the generally greater reporting of sex offenses in recent decades has led to greater accountability of offenders, and thus, reductions in sex crime over time.

Many efforts to increase disclosure of child sexual victimization have also been recently implemented across the U.S. For instance, hotlines, mandated reporting practices, and other similar policies have all emerged during a time of steady declines in child sexual abuse (see generally, Alvarez, Donohue, Kenny, Cavanagh, & Romero, 2005). In turn, per Finkelhor, Ormrod, and colleagues (2011), such campaigns may have had some impact on the reporting of child sexual abuse. Their study demonstrates that in 50 percent of sexual abuse cases in 2008—a time period when most states have implemented some form of these practices—child sexual victimization had been reported to an authority, compared with only 25 percent in 1992, when fewer such interventions existed.

In short, policy changes such as the ones discussed above may have contributed to a greater frequency of reporting among sex crime victims during the last twenty years. As a result, increased identification and apprehension of sex offenders potentially followed, resulting in fewer sex crimes over the last two decades.

Recognition of Victims' Rights

Several notable policies emphasizing victims' rights emerged in the criminal justice system during the 1980s and 1990s. "Rape shield" laws and laws that exempt sex crime victims from the normal statutes of limitations for certain sex offenses are illustrative of these reforms. Rape shield laws prohibit certain practices that were theorized to discourage victims of sex crime to come forward with their allegations. For instance, prior to rape shield legislation media outlets were permitted to publicize the names of sex crime victims. Additionally, under rape shield reforms, the victim's prior sexual history as an indicator of promiscuity is not allowed to be discussed in criminal proceedings unless it is an issue that it is directly relevant to the criminal allegations. Thus, defendants are no longer permitted to allege that victims share culpability in the offense due to their prior sexual relationships or manner of dress. Nearly all states have enacted some form of a rape shield statute (McMahon Howard, 2011).

These laws may have impacted sex crime rates in two ways. First, they have potentially encouraged increased reporting of sex offenses among victims. In line with an earlier point, increased reporting has led to greater apprehension and punishment of sex offenders. Second, rape shield laws may have generated a larger number of criminal convictions for sexual offenses as defendants could no longer present as evidence of their innocence, non-relevant facts about the victim, such as their prior sexual history.

Related to such efforts have been laws that permit longer time periods for victims to report sex crime committed against them. Over the last two decades, most states have implemented statutes of limitations exceptions for sex offenses involving children (National Center for Prosecution of Child Abuse, 2012). These laws recognize that victims, particularly young individuals, may not initially report a sex offense due to fear of retribution or because they did not recognize the abuse as criminal or wrong. And so given this situation, victims should be permitted to bring forth allegations beyond the normal statutes of limitations for such offenses (Jen, 2004). In turn, these legal changes may have been partly responsible for the increased apprehension and punishment of sex offenders who would otherwise go undetected by law enforcement. As a result, such laws may have brought about greater identification, apprehension, and prosecution of sex offenders, resulting in incapacitation effects and ultimately reducing the extent of sex crime.

Greater Educational Efforts

Related to campaigns to increase reporting, there has also been a dramatic shift in educational efforts to recognize sexual abuse over the last twenty years. For example, such interventions include programs such as child maltreatment prevention (Lindsey, 2004) and school-based sexual abuse awareness programs (Finkelhor & Dziuba-Leatherman, 1995). Such efforts have been shown to increase children's knowledge about sexual victimization. For example, Gibson and Leitenberg (2000) revealed that college students exposed to child sexual abuse awareness programs as children had reduced odds of experiencing sexual victimization as adolescents or adults. Additionally, their results indicate wide prevalence of educational efforts as nearly two-thirds of the sample had participated in a "good touch, bad touch" type of program as children. Similar findings emerged in a study of high school students (Ko & Cosden, 2001). That is, in Ko and Cosden's (2001) investigation, students who completed a sexual abuse awareness program (a majority of the sample) were significantly less likely to report a sexual abuse incident than high-school students who were not exposed to a prevention program. It follows, although research has yet to clearly demonstrate, that such efforts may have increased the detection of sexual abuse on a national scale, and thus, reduced opportunities for sexual victimization to occur. Put differently, because potential victims and their caregivers presumably have become more aware of potential threats against them than in earlier decades, greater efforts have been taken to prevent sexual victimization.

At the same time, efforts to educate and protect women from sexual assault have also emerged during the last two decades in which sex crime began to dramatically decline. Illustrative of this movement has been the creation of self-defense and rape awareness programs for women. Specifically, such interventions serve to "educate [women] about how they can effectively respond to potential assaults to decrease the negative consequences of rape," in turn, such training "may enhance rape prevention strategies and provide women with the skills to effectively fight back against future assaults" (Brecklin & Ullman, 2005, p. 757). Indeed, evaluations of these programs indicate they may have the potential to reduce the completion of sex offenses. For instance, in Brecklin and Ullman's (2005) study of college women who completed a self-defense program to prevent rape, women with training who experienced an attempted rape were more likely to indicate that their resistance stopped the offender or made him less aggressive than women without training. Other evaluations indicate positive impacts of defense training, finding for instance that it increases assertiveness, reduces fear, and increases physical competence (for a review see Brecklin, 2007; McDaniel, 1993).

Educational programs geared to adults, particularly college students, also exist. In contrast to the programs developed for children, these programs go beyond "good touch, bad touch" and aim to educate adults about a range of issues related to sexual victimization. To illustrate, such programs purport to educate participants about the extent of sexual victimization, the prevalence of sex crime in the U.S., factors related to victimization, types of victim-offender relationships, and to dispel "rape myths" or misperceptions about sexual victimization (Lonsway et al., 2009).

Relatedly, several agencies have been created to provide education and support for those concerned about sexual victimization. For example, the mission of the Center for Sex Offender Management (CSOM; http://www.csom.org), a federally funded agency, is to educate the public about sex offenders. It includes information about sex crime legislation, sex crime trends and patterns, crime prevention, and other resources. A non-federally funded but large non-profit organization, the Rape, Abuse, and Incest National Network (RAINN; http://www.rainn.org), created in 1994, aims to provide programs to prevent sexual assault and assist sex crime victims. It offers a range of services including online counseling for victims, hotlines, educational information about sex crime, and counseling referrals. Per their website, RAINN has also produced several public service campaigns featuring celebrity spokespeople.

Collectively, these educational efforts may have reduced sex offending along two dimensions. First, exposure to the reality of sex offending has potentially provided those at greatest risk of victimization with techniques to prevent sex crime. Second, these efforts may have encouraged increased reporting and generated greater awareness and detection of offending.

Chapter Summary

Findings across several data sources—the UCR, NCVS, victimization surveys of adult women, NCANDS data, and surveys examining child victimization—paint a similar portrait of recent sex crime patterns and trends. Namely, nearly all indicate a significant decline in reports of sex offenses committed against adults and children in the U.S. over the last few decades, with the most recent data suggesting relative stability in trends, particularly for offenses committed against children. Accordingly then, little evidence exists to suggest a substantial increase in sexual offending over the last twenty years. It is difficult to pinpoint the precise factor or factors driving the downward trend in sex offenses involving children and adult victims. To be clear, this pattern is on par with general crime rates across the U.S. That is, violent crime has substantially declined nationally over the last 20 or so years (Blumstein & Wallman, 2006). Criminologists have proposed several factors that may be associated with this pattern. The chapter reviewed five specific factors—post-incarceration sanctions for sex offenders, increased reliance on incarceration, greater reporting, sex crime victims' rights movement, and increased educational efforts—that may be related to the drop in sex crime. Even so, as Finkelhor (2004, p. 10) explains, "the answer [as to why sex crime has declined], if it can be determined, is not likely to be a simple one ... in all likelihood, multiple factors were involved in the trend."

The additional suggested reading section lists a sampling of other scholarship that has examined the crime drop in the U.S. Chapter 4 outlines prominent theoretical perspectives relevant toward understanding sexual offending.

Additional Suggested Reading

Baumer, E. P., & Wolff, K. (in press). Evaluating the contemporary crime drop(s) in America, New York City, and many other places. *Justice Quarterly*.

Gruber, A. (2009). Rape, feminism, and the war on crime. *Washington Law Review, 84,* 581–660.

Levitt, S. D. (2004). Understanding why crime fell in the 1990s: Four factors that explain the decline and six that do not. *Journal of Economic Perspectives, 18,* 163–190.

Mishra, S., & Lalumière, M. (2009). Is the crime drop of the 1990s in Canada and the USA associated with a general decline in risky and health-related behavior? *Social Science & Medicine, 68,* 39–48.

Chapter 4

Prominent Theoretical Explanations

Chapter Introduction

One of the most intriguing aspects in the study of sex crime involves understanding the motivation or propensity to commit sex offenses. Researchers and professionals who work with sex offenders are often asked, "Why do they do it?" Theories of etiology—or, simply, offending—attempt to address this fundamental question. The answer, however, is not a simple one as many theoretical perspectives, some competing, currently exist. The goal of this chapter is to introduce readers to the various theories centered on explaining sex offending. Moreover, comprehension of these perspectives has other implications. For instance, some of these perspectives drive sex crime management and policy—a later focus of our text. This chapter reviews three prominent theoretical explanations of sexual offending: the biological perspective, social learning theories, and the feminist perspective. To be clear, although numerous other theories exist, the goal of this chapter is to highlight those prominent perspectives emphasized in current criminological literature. Accordingly, our focus is limited to criminological perspectives that appear to directly apply to sexual offending. A supplementary reading list is presented at the end of the chapter that directs interested readers to comprehensive theory texts and other theoretical work.

Biological Perspective

Per experts, the biological perspective posits that offenders "may develop physical and mental traits at birth or soon after that affect their social functioning over the life course and influence their behavior choices" (Siegel, 2010, p. 130). Broadly, this theory emphasizes the effect of biological characteristics on offending. Thus, it centers on explaining crime as a function of the effects of biological processes. Relevant to discussions about sex crime is the theory's emphasis on androgens in sexual offending and, also, brain functioning.

Hormone Production

We will begin with a discussion centered on the first focus—sex hormones. In particular, testosterone has been implicated as a catalyst in increasing sexual aggression among males. Per experts, testosterone has "a diverse set of effects upon and throughout development: in utero, in childhood, and into adulthood" (Studer, Aylwin, & Reddon, 2005, p.172). In adolescent males, for instance, testosterone surges are responsible for normal adult growth, including increased body hair, deepened voice, and sexual development. Testosterone production continues throughout the life course and is responsible for maintaining distinctly "male" characteristics (e.g., facial hair, muscular physique). Thus, for most men, testosterone is a vital hormone that regulates normal bodily functioning (Yildirim & Derksen, 2012). However, some men have disorders that prevent normal androgen regulation. That is, they have elevated levels of testosterone in their bodies. While testosterone imbalance is believed to be a relatively rare occurrence among adult males, it is thought to increase aggression and sexual drive. Thus, one hypothesis that flows from this general observation is that sex offenders may be predisposed to possessing larger quantities of testosterone than non-offending males (Studer et al., 2005).

Notably, results from empirical studies examining the relationship between testosterone and sexual aggression have been mixed. That is, some studies have found a significant and positive result of increased testosterone levels on sexual aggression (Rada, Laws, & Kellner, 1976; Studer et al., 2005). Even so, others have reported a statistically significant negative relationship between testosterone and male sexual offending and aggression (Seim & Dwyer, 1988). Still other investigations have revealed no statistically significant effect (Aromaki, Lindman, & Eriksson, 2002). Other work has revealed the importance of separately studying different "types" of sex offenders. For example, Bain and colleagues (1988) examined a sample of pedophiles (offenders with a child victim preference) and found that they had reduced levels of testosterone compared to non-offender controls. Findings from a study conducted by Giotakos, Markianos, Vaidakis, and Christodoulou (2003) further indicate that offender "type" matters. In particular, the researchers found that incarcerated rapists (n=57) had substantially higher levels of testosterone compared to a group of non-criminal males (n=25).

These divergent findings have led experts to conclude, "both sexually violent offenders and pedophiles may differ in testosterone levels from controls, but in opposite directions" (Blanchard, Cantor, & Robichaud, 2006, p. 93). Even so, the available studies do not offer a clear interpretation of how testosterone influences sexual offending. Methodological issues are largely attributed to these disparate findings. For example, the measurement of testosterone levels has not been consistent across studies. Instead, it has been measured through serum, blood, or saliva. Some studies measured testosterone production at only one point in the day, despite the fact that prior research indicates that levels fluctuate, sometimes widely, throughout the day. Still other studies have relied on primarily small samples without adequate controls (Blanchard et al., 2006).

Notably, biological theory with an emphasis on sexual aggression has recently evolved to include the study of other hormones in explaining the etiology of sexual offending such as cortisol and androstenedione. However, per Blanchard and colleagues (2006) in a review, this is a relatively nascent state of research as studies are "too few and the findings too mixed to draw even tentative conclusions" (p. 93).

This is not to say that anti-androgen treatment for sex offenders is completely ineffective. On the contrary, it is considered to be one of the more effective treatment options that have been developed to treat sex offenders. To illustrate, one large-scale meta-analysis conducted by Lösel and Schmucker (2005) examined findings from prior sex offender treatment studies (n=69) comparing treated and untreated offenders. Hormonal treatment and surgical castration were determined to be two of the most effective interventions for reducing sexual reoffending among treated males compared to other types of treatment efforts (see also, Schmucker & Lösel, 2008). Even so, it is clear that a much larger and sophisticated research base is needed to come to firm conclusions about how such interventions, and specifically, sex hormones affect sexual offending.

Notwithstanding this debate, some states have developed laws which mandate chemical castration for convicted sex offenders (Beauregard & Lieb, 2011). Often, these measures are reserved for repeat or sexually violent offenders. These efforts include distributing medroxyprogesterone acetate (MPA), a drug designed to control the production of testosterone, to convicted sex offenders. Other states allow eligible offenders to choose chemical castration rather than other types of punishments (Mancini et al., 2013). A smaller handful of states permit offenders to elect surgical castration—that is, removal of the testes—instead of the reversible chemical castration treatment (Scott & Holmberg, 2003). This policy is discussed further in forthcoming chapters.

Neurophysiological Functioning

Additionally, biological-based theories hold that neurophysiological conditions—often acquired as early as the prenatal stages or through birth defects—affect decision-making and impulse control. In turn, reduced neurophysiological or brain functioning might positively impact offending propensity. This sub-theory is particularly useful in understanding sex crime. Recall our earlier discussion of offender typologies. For example, prior research finds that some sex offenders have reduced impulse control and tend to commit sex crimes spontaneously, often with little planning or premeditation (Hazelwood & Warren, 2000; Knight & Prentky, 2000; O'Brien & Bera, 1986; Worling, 2001). Accordingly, then these deficits may indirectly affect offending among certain offender types.

In particular, the origins of sexually deviant behavior may derive from abnormal brain development "leading to problems in neurological function, specifically problems in neurobiology around the levels or operation of the neurotransmitters such as serotonin, norepinephrine, and dopamine" (Ward & Beech, 2006, p. 52). Each of these neurotransmitters stimulates a different response in the brain. For example, serotonin is involved in arousal, attention, and general mood. In contrast, norepinephrine affects alertness, drive, and motivation. Not least, dopamine regulates the pleasure and reward process. Ward and Beech (2006, p. 52) explain that "for some individuals the motivation/emotional system can be compromised by [these] dysfunctional neurotransmitter mechanisms ... [in turn] lower[ing] the threshold for sexually aggressive behavior by increasing the strength, salience, and duration of sexual goals, and desires, and additionally by weakening the action selection and control systems." These deficits are believed to affect the frontal and/or temporal lobes of the brain. Put differently, neurophysiological conditions—primarily those that adversely affect the regulation of the aforementioned neurotransmitters in specific areas of the brain—might "override" an offender's ability to control intense sexual urges and impulses.

Research examining brain function in sex offenders has relied primarily on four methodological techniques. The first involves measuring brain functioning using battery tests. For example, the Halstead-Reitan battery consists of several tests that are designed to evaluate brain and nervous system functioning (Langevin, Wortzman, Wright, & Handy, 1989). The second method relies on IQ test scores to assess offender brain functioning. These standardized tests are generally regarded as an accurate measure of intelligence (Cantor, Blanchard, Robichaud, & Christensen, 2005). A third method documents "nonright handedness" (hereafter, NRH) which per experts is indicative of "perturbations in prenatal neurodevelopment" (Blanchard et al., 2006, p. 80). A final and more recent development involves measuring brain functioning using brain imaging technology (Aigner et al., 2000). The research that has relied on these methods is discussed below.

Beginning in the 1980s, researchers began to assess the brain functioning of sex offenders using battery tests. The two most prominent ones include the Halstead-Reitan and the

Luria Nebraska tests. In short, these inventories, administered by trained practitioners, tap into a wide range of neurological functions, including visual, auditory, and tactual input, verbal communication, and the ability to analyze information, and make judgments (Archer, Buffington-Vollum, Stredny, & Handel, 2006). A composite score is then generated which indicates either mental impairment or not. Results from these studies have been inconclusive. For example, some early research indicated that nearly 90 percent of sex offenders had inadequate brain functioning (Yeudall & Fromm-Auch, 1979). Later studies, however, could not replicate these findings (Blanchard et al., 2006). One other study examined pedophiles and their performance on a battery test. Results indicated a general pattern by which pedophiles evinced higher levels of impairment than non-sex offender controls (Langevin et al., 1989). However, subsequent studies were not able to reproduce these findings (for a review see, Blanchard et al., 2006). Similar inconsistent results have emerged when studying sex offenders who have assaulted adults (Hucker et al., 1988; Langevin, Ben-Aron, Wright, Marchese, & Handy, 1988).

In a review, Blanchard and colleagues (2006, p. 85) concluded that "neuropsychologists have generally concluded that the batteries reliably distinguish persons with organic brain impairment from persons with intact brains, but 1) the batteries do not distinguish between brain impairment from psychiatric disorders [e.g., schizophrenia] as successfully, 2) many of the findings have failed to replicate the results when attempted by researchers other than the batteries developers, and 3) neither battery has been shown to reliably localize brain dysfunction." Put differently, while these batteries were initially helpful in understanding how brain functioning might affect sexual deviance this area has produced largely inconsistent findings. In recognizing this disparity, researchers have begun to explore other ways to tap into the effects of brain dysfunction among sex offenders.

A second methodological technique involves measuring the IQ of offenders to assess whether their levels of intelligence are comparable to non-sex offender controls. If sex offenders on average have lower IQ scores than non-sex offender controls, support would be found for the hypothesis that sex offenders possess underlying cognitive and neuro-physiological problems which might contribute to their offending. Psychologists have developed several versions of these tests since their initial emergence in the early 1900s. While several versions of the IQ test currently exist, they are all geared to tap into the latent construct of intelligence.

Significant empirical attention has been directed toward examining the IQ of sex offenders. The earliest study on sex offender IQ was published in the 1930s (Frank, 1931). This focus has spanned nearly eight decades. Cantor, Blanchard et al. (2005) conducted one of the largest reviews of this body of research. Using a meta-analytic technique, the authors examined 75 studies (comprising 236 independent samples and representing 25,146 individuals). They found little evidence that sex offenders score significantly lower on IQ tests than normal (average IQ score was close to 95). However, some notable differences emerged when comparing sex offenders' mean IQ to that of non-sex offenders. Their review can be summarized as follows: adult males who commit sex offenses and males who commit non-sex offenses on average have lower IQ scores compared to non-offending males, adult males who commit sex offenses against adults have comparable IQ scores to males who commit non-sex crimes, adult males who commit sex crimes against children have significantly lower IQ scores than males who commit sex offenses against adults, males who commit non-sex offenses, and males who commit no offenses. In short, Cantor, Blanchard et al.'s (2005) review suggests that on average sex offenders who abuse children possess significantly greater odds of having lower IQs than other sex offender types and controls. Notably, Langevin (2009, p. 31) in a review of extant literature comes to a similar conclusion, as observed by his observation — "the majority of sex offenders' IQs will fall within the normal range, but the distribution will be skewed toward the lower end of normal." Additionally, it could also be said that heterogeneity exists— with the average IQ score being largely dependent on offender "type."

Although this body of research has greatly illuminated the link between IQ and sexual offending, future studies are needed to examine a range of issues not yet addressed. For example, virtually no study has examined other aspects of offender heterogeneity (beyond victim age) and IQ. That is, little work has examined IQ differences among pedophiles who prefer abusing male versus female children. Along this line, virtually no work has assessed whether IQ differences are apparent between intrafamilial (incest offenders) and extrafamilial sex offenders (those who victimize acquaintances or strangers, but not family members).

A third method generated by researchers to tap into brain functioning relies on measuring NRH. On its face, this might appear to be an odd approach to measure brain dysfunction. However, non-right hand dominance has been associated with abnormal brain functioning and organization. In particular, as Langevin (2009) explained, "if there are more non-right-handed individuals among sex offenders, it suggests their brains may be organized in a different way and [it may] be associated with the development of their paraphilia" (p. 31). As this observation implies, NRH is not *causally* related to sexual offending. Rather, it may be symptomatic of underlying neurophysiological deficits, which have "prevented the development of more typical intellectual and sexual characteristics" (Cantor, Klassen et al., 2005, p. 448).

A limited number of studies have measured NRH prevalence in the sex offender population. To illustrate, one of the largest studies (n=8,000) was conducted by Bogaert (2001). Using data collected from the Kinsey Institute for Sex and Reproduction in Indiana, he found that sex offenders and non-sex offenders had substantially higher likelihoods of being non-right-handed (assessed based on asking respondents which hand they write with) compared to the general male population. However, educational difficulties mediated this effect among sex offenders with an adult victim preference and non-sex offenders. Notably, however, even with the addition of the education variable, the NRH effect persisted in the sample of pedophiles. Put differently, for the sex offender group who prefers victimizing adults and general offenders, "some NRH (or the brain abnormalities it may represent) may cause educational difficulties, which ultimately affect criminality (e.g. by 'acting out')" (Bogaert, 2001, p. 468). In contrast, a different mechanism is evident among the pedophiliac group. Per Bogaert (2001, p. 468), these disparate results "may indicate that elevated NRH in pedophiles reflects CNS [central nervous system] abnormalities that, in part, directly affects their *sexual* preference systems" (emphasis added). Thus, NRH in pedophiles may be symptomatic of underlying neurological conditions that adversely shape sexual development. This effect, however, does not extend to other types of sex offenders. Cantor, Klassen et al. (2005) reported similar results in their study of 404 sex offenders who had victimized either children or adults. Overall, their findings indicate that pedophiles had a higher prevalence of NRH compared to offenders who had victimized an adult in the past (see also, Blanchard et al., 2007). Notably, however, the Cantor, Klassen et al. (2005) study found no differences between men erotically interested in male versus female children. While these studies provide general support for the notion that NRH is more typical among pedophiliac offenders, compared to controls (i.e., non-pedophiliac sex offenders, general offenders, and non-offending males) other scholars caution that these are tentative results not supported by earlier studies (see e.g., Langevin, 2009 for a review). Accordingly per some scholars, NRH may play a "very minor role" in the etiology of sex offending (Langevin, 2009, p. 32). Additionally, it bears emphasizing that NRH is not a causal factor in predicting sexual offending. Thus, additional scholarly attention is needed to more fully understand how brain abnormalities which partially manifest themselves as NRH impact the propensity to commit sexual offenses, particularly among pedophiles.

A final method for assessing neurophysiological functioning in sex offenders involves brain imaging technology. This area remains highly exploratory. Most research in this arena has relied on the use of computerized tomography (CT) scans rather than the more fine-grained (and preferred) method of magnetic resonance imaging (MRI) to detect structure abnormalities (particularly in the temporal lobes of the brain). The strength of these scans is that they can provide visual indicators of brain dysfunction—which might suggest neuropsychological deficits. Early research in this area revealed broad support for the contention that brain abnormalities among sex offenders, particularly pedophiliac offenders are more prevalent compared to the general population (Hendricks et al., 1988; Hucker et al., 1986, 1988). However, these works have been critiqued by other researchers. For example, Blanchard et al. (2006) in a review reported that of the eleven published studies using CT imaging technology, eight were conducted by the same researchers and used overlapping samples of participants/offenders, and controls, indicating potential problems with the validity of these studies. Barring these methodological issues inherent in prior studies, more recent work indicates that brain functioning may be an important variable to consider in understanding the etiology of sex crime. For instance, Schiltz and colleagues (2007) using MRI technology found that pedophilic perpetrators, in comparison to non-offending controls, showed structural impairments of brain regions critical for sexual development. These effects persisted even with the addition of theoretically important controls such as education and age (similar results were reported by Mendez, Chow, Ringman, Twitchell, & Hinkin, 2000).

Other investigations have focused on analyzing irregularities in brain functioning as opposed to structure using position emission tomography (PET) or regional cerebral blood flow (rCBF) measures. Put simply, these methods allow researchers to assess abnormal brain activity in subjects. Overall, two of the three studies in this area provide tentative support for the notion that sex offenders—particularly those who target child victims—show evidence of abnormal brain functioning compared to controls (see e.g., Hendricks et al., 1988; for a review see Blanchard et al., 2006). Given the novelty of this area, scholars caution that greater empirical investigation is in order. In particular, three areas should be addressed: future studies should a) better address heterogeneity in sex offending (i.e., include larger groups of different offender "types"), b) more closely examine the structures of the brain putatively involved in sex offending using refined methods such as MRI technology, and c) rely on larger samples with comparable control groups. Table 4.1 provides an overview of the biological perspective.

Social Learning Theories

In contrast to the biological perspectives we have just discussed, social learning theories emphasize that sociological factors, rather than innate physical or mental traits, influence behavior. In particular, this perspective holds that offenders "learn" to commit sex offenses from cues in the larger society. These are prominent perspectives in explaining sex crime and they form the basis for current criminal justice initiatives. For example, attempts to control convicted sex offender access to sexually related materials stem from a social learning perspective. That is, as a typical condition of probation or parole, convicted sex offenders are often prohibited from possessing pornographic movies or magazines (even those depicting "mainstream" pornography; see e.g., Mancini, Reckdenwald, & Beauregard, 2012). Moreover, the increased penalties for accessing child pornography—even virtual,

Table 4.1. Biological Perspective Overview

Theoretical Focus	Argument and Summary
Hormone Production	*Argument*: Hormones may increase the propensity to sexually offend. Testosterone in particular may be linked to increased sexual aggression. *Summary*: Research has produced mixed findings, due primarily to methodological differences among studies. Some indication of variation of effects among offender types. Rapists on average have higher levels of testosterone and child molesters have lower amounts. Thus, testosterone may be linked to increased sexual aggression, but the precise process is still not clearly understood.
Neurophysiological Functioning	*Argument*: Sex offenders may have brain deficits or poor neurophysiological functioning resulting in impulsivity and increased sexual aggression. *Summary*: In studying neurophysiological functioning, criminologists have relied on four methods: battery tests, IQ test scores, "non-right handedness," and brain imaging technology. Overall, some research indicates that brain functioning may play a role (albeit, a small one) in sexual offending. However, heterogeneity exists in this relationship—it is largely dependent on offender "type." On average, offenders with a child victim preference, compared to other offenders, show a greater manifestation of poor neurophysiological functioning.

computer-generated images in some instances—derive in part from concern that such material might lead to actual, contact sex offenses against children (Bourke & Hernandez, 2009). There is also the concomitant hypothesis that prior sexual victimization may "teach" offenders how to commit sex offenses; thus, prior sexual victimization may perpetuate such behavior as victims mature into adults. In particular, our focus is on two broad social learning theories: differential association theory and neutralization or "drift" theory. Each of these perspectives is further discussed below.

Differential Association

The concept of differential association, developed by Edwin Sutherland in 1947, refers to the belief that individuals learn the techniques, values, and attitudes conducive to crime from interacting with criminal others. In particular, Sutherland (1947, pp. 75–77) outlined nine principles:

1) Criminal behavior is learned.
2) Criminal behavior is learned in interaction with other persons in a process of communication.
3) The principal part of the learning of criminal behavior occurs within intimate personal groups.
4) When criminal behavior is learned, the learning includes techniques of committing the crime, which are sometimes very complicated, sometimes simple, and the specific direction of motives, drives, rationalizations, and attitudes.
5) The specific direction of motives and drives is learned from definitions of the legal codes as favorable or unfavorable.

6) A person becomes delinquent because of an excess of definitions favorable to violation of law over definitions unfavorable to violation of the law.
7) Differential associations may vary in frequency, duration, priority, and intensity.
8) The process of learning criminal behavior by association with criminal and anti-criminal patterns involves all of the mechanisms that are involved in any other learning.
9) While criminal behavior is an expression of general needs and values, it is not explained by those needs and values, since non-criminal behavior is an expression of the same needs and values.

Thus, criminality is predicted by the differential or excess associations one has with criminal others. Essentially, differential association can be thought of as a product between the ratio of "pro-crime" attitudes to "anti-crime" attitudes. Thus, the propensity to offend is amplified when one holds an abundance of greater "pro-crime" values or definitions favorable to crime, rather than prosocial (or anti-crime) values or attitudes. Typically, these values and attitudes are acquired through interactions with criminal agents. Although Sutherland's (1947) theory emphasizes interpersonal relationships (such as those with peers), with the advent of technological advances, the theory has been extended to account for the effects of other social influences—such as the media and Internet. In short, under this logic individuals are presumed to be "blank slates" and become criminal only after interaction with criminogenic influences (e.g., deviant peers or siblings, violent media). Additionally, the amount, intensity, and significance of the interaction are critical in predicting differential involvement in crime (that is, the theory allows for an explanation of why not everyone who interacts with a criminal agent becomes criminal).

In line with differential association theory, scholars have tested whether peer influence impacts sexual offending. Peers may be particularly salient in shaping attitudes about sexuality especially among youths. Some scholars point to statistics examining sex crime that involves multiple perpetrators as indicative of indirect support for the notion that sexually aggressive behavior might be formed as part of peer association. For example, national statistics indicate that on average 9 percent of sex offenses involve multiple perpetrators (Greenfeld, 1997). On college campuses, that figure increases to approximately 25 percent of completed and attempted rapes (Neumann, 2006). Findings from other studies that have more directly focused on peer influence and sexual offending also suggest a link. For instance, some early work has detected a link between male peer support and sexually aggressive attitudes toward women (Alder, 1985; Kanin, 1967). Other work indicates that the social networks of sex offenders may be offense specific. For instance, Hanson and Scott (1996) examined the peer groups of 126 charged/convicted sex offenders (disaggregated by particular offense and currently incarcerated or receiving treatment in a specialized facility) to those among nonsexual offenders (n=57) and community controls with no prior history of sexual offending (n=85) and community controls with a prior self-reported history of sexual offending (but no official convictions; n=49). Their results indicate that peer association differs based on offender type. That is, child molesters knew more child molesters on average than did the other groups of sex offenders and community controls. Conversely, convicted rapists were the most likely group to report knowing other sexually aggressive people. Nonsexual offenders reported knowing almost as many sexually aggressive men as did the convicted rapists. Notably, however, the nonsexual criminals did not report knowing a disproportionate number of child sexual abusers. This result may be an artifact of the prison subculture—in which, per Hanson and Scott (1996, p. 256), "it is more acceptable to disclose sexual aggression against women than against children."

Other work along this line has found that the endorsement of pro-rape attitudes is associated with peer influence, particularly among college males. This research stems in part from the observation that women face a substantial risk of sexual victimization while attending college (Fisher, Daigle, Cullen, & Turner, 2000). Thus, researchers have devoted greater attention toward understanding these offenses. For example, Schwartz, DeKeseredy, Tait, and Alvi (2001) in a study of Canadian college students (n=1, 307) found that male peer support in encouraging sexually abusive behavior toward females (measured using a scale; e.g., respondents indicated whether their male friends made comments such as, "your dates or girlfriends should have sex with you when you want") was the most powerful predictor of self-reported sexual offending in the models. That is, receiving such "advice" was a stronger predictor of having committed sexual violence than having used drugs or alcohol prior to the crime in the study.

In recognizing that certain subcultures may be more susceptible to peer influence, some of this empirical work has focused on fraternity affiliation. Put differently, this emphasis derives from the observation that fraternities, by definition, are important sources of male peer support. For example, Schwartz and Nogrady (1996) studied a sample of male college students in fraternities and controls (college males not affiliated with fraternities) from a large Midwestern university (n=119). They found strong evidence that male peer support for the victimization of women exists. Thus, men who believed their friends were supportive of exploiting women, and who further report their friends have sexually exploited women in the past, were significantly more likely to self-report sexually aggressive behavior (e.g., used force to coerce a partner to submit to sex in the past). In particular, greater male peer support for sexually aggressive behavior toward women was related to extensive alcohol use. Additionally, the effect of peer support in shaping sexually aggressive attitudes toward women was found among college males regardless of fraternity status. Other studies have found similar results, with some caveats. For example, Humphrey and Kahn (2000) reported that while in general males from fraternities versus males not affiliated with fraternities were similar, particular characteristics of fraternities affected the influence of peer support on sexually aggressive attitudes. That is, males from "high-risk" fraternities (measured by asking the general student body how likely it was that women faced the risk of sexual assault when attending fraternity functions/parties) were particularly susceptible to peer influence in forming sexually aggressive attitudes toward women, compared to non-fraternity affiliated males and males from "low-risk" fraternities. Not least, in a meta-analysis of 29 studies examining fraternity affiliation and athletic participation, potentially influential male peer groups, Murnen and Kohlman (2007) found that both peer associations were correlated with increased self-reported sexual aggression; albeit, such experience exerted a relatively weak statistically significant effect on behavior. Further, the researchers caution that their research does not establish causality—as none of the included studies were experimental—making it difficult to "determine the nature of the associations revealed in the analyses" (p. 154).

Studies focused on social learning theory have also tested whether prior sexual victimization impacts later offending. Per differential association, a victim of a sex crime might learn pro-sex crime values and techniques of the offense and go on to commit offenses. Under this "victim to victimizer" (Garland & Dougher, 1990) logic, the abuse experience itself may serve to "teach" victims how to offend in the future. Of course, there are many variables that might moderate this relationship—that is, interfere with the "learning" process. Again, recall that differential association posits that crime occurs only when "pro-crime" attitudes prevail over "anti-crime" values. Thus, for example, sexually abused youth who receive counseling and treatment (which proffer "anti-crime" values) might better understand that the abuse committed against them was wrong and criminal.

Thus, as this example exemplifies, many processes might intervene to affect the "victim to victimizer" progression.

Generally, a very large body of research focused on the "cycle of violence" indicates broad support for the notion that previous maltreatment (physical, sexual, emotional) may affect the propensity to offend later in life (see e.g., Widom, 1989; Paolucci, Genuis, & Violato, 2001 in a review). Additionally, studies have found some support for the specific contention that sexual victimization may be linked to subsequent offending (for a review, see Seto & Lalumière, 2010). In one of the first tests of this sexual victimization-sex offending hypothesis, Burton and colleagues (1997) relied on clinicians' responses to a questionnaire about their patients (sexually aggressive youths). In total, data were collected on 287 individuals. The authors reported significant correlations between the presence of prior sexual victimization and the number of people the children went on to sexually abuse. Thus, those youth with a prior history of sexual victimization had a greater number of victims/offenses than those sexually aggressive youth with no prior history of abuse. In a separate study, Burton, Miller, and Shill (2002) examined differences in offense patterns between adolescent sexually victimized nonsexual offending delinquents (i.e., individuals with a history of previous sexual victimization, but no sexual offenses) and adolescent sexually victimized sexual offending delinquents (i.e., individuals with a history of previous sexual victimization, and sexual offenses). Burton et al. (2002) found that sexually victimized youths who went on to commit sex offenses (the latter group) had a significantly longer duration of sexual victimization, more forceful sexual victimization experience, and closer relationship with their perpetrator compared to the adolescent sexually victimized nonsexual offending delinquents (see for similar results, Cooper, Murphy, & Haynes, 1996). In line with Sutherland's (1947) propositions, this particular abuse experience—with its greater intensity and duration—may have had a more influential impact on the victim, who in turn went on to sexually offend.

In contrast, Skuse et al. (1998) found no significant impact of characteristics of sexual abuse victimization on subsequent offending in a group of previously sexually abused youth. However, they did find that exposure to "family violence" (witnessing abuse of a parent or sibling) moderated this relationship. Accordingly, sexually abused youth who also had witnessed abuse had increased odds of offending, compared to sexually abused youth who had witnessed no family violence. While this finding is somewhat at odds with the larger body of work detecting a specific effect of sexual abuse, particularly more severe victimization, it indicates broad support for the cycle of violence perspective, and more generally differential association theory.

A different strand of this research has considered how pornographic media impacts sexual offending. That is, under differential association logic, some scholars believe that pornography—even "mainstream" pornography might serve to teach individuals how to sexually offend, or to degrade or humiliate sexual partners. Illustrative of this perspective is Flood's (2010, pp. 394–395) observation in a review, "Pornography is a poor educator … most pornography is sexist, and some is based on and eroticizes violence."

There are two contradictory findings that this body of work has uncovered concerning how pornography exposure might impact offending. We will begin with imitation effects. Some scholars claim that pornography depicts women and children as sexual objects. In turn, it has been theorized that pornography exposure fuels sexually aggressive attitudes toward certain groups. For instance, some research indicates that pornography may serve as a "training manual" for assaulting women (Bauserman, 1996; see Hald, Malamuth, & Yuen, 2010 for a review). These social learning effects of pornography—whereby offenders recreate scenes from pornographic movies or magazines—have been discovered in some studies (Kingston, Fedoroff, Firestone, Curry, & Bradford, 2008; Russell, 1993). For example, research testing the effect of exposure in laboratory settings indicates support for imitation effects, particularly for males shown pornography depicting violent scenes (Donnerstein, 1984; for a review, see Harrington & Neilson, 2009). The generalizability of these findings has been critiqued by some scholars. For example, Weitzer (2009, in a review) questions the external validity of such methods noting that, "experimental studies may have little resonance in the real world given the artificiality of the viewing conditions in a lab" (p. 215).

Other work has detected cathartic effects of pornography exposure—whereby exposure reduces sexual aggression. For instance, some early research indicates null or cathartic effects. Thus, in these studies, exposure to pornography was not only benign, but actually beneficial by reducing the extent of sexual violence (Ben-Veniste, 1971; Howard, Liptzin, & Reifler, 1973; Kutchinsky, 1973). For example, Ben-Veniste (1971) in a macro-level study relayed that the decriminalization of pornography and the subsequent increased consumption of pornographic material in Denmark in the 1960s were associated with significant declines in sexual assaults in the country. More contemporary work examining macro-level trends indicate a similar pattern in other areas. To illustrate, D'Amato (2006) suggested that the increasingly wide availability of pornography in the U.S. during the last twenty years has contributed to a decline in reported sex offenses. Other consumption study findings lend indirect support to the null/cathartic logic. For example, some work indicates that offenders are as likely as non-offenders (non-offending males in the community) to admit to using pornography (for a meta-analysis see, Allen, D'Alessio, & Emmers-Sommer, 2000).

Still other work indicates that timing of pornography exposure is critical to its effects. In a recent study, Mancini and her colleagues (2012) found the greatest support for differential association theory when examining adolescent pornography exposure. Put differently, offenders with prior exposure to pornography as teens, compared to offenders without such exposure, were significantly more likely to humiliate victims. In contrast, adulthood exposure exerted no statistically significant effect on victim physical injury or the extent of degradation. Immediate prior use (to the offense) actually reduced victim harm, indicating a cathartic effect of pornography exposure. Thus, the researchers' findings here indicate that pornography exposure differentially impacts an offenders' propensity to harm victims. Their findings are congruent with the contention that adolescence is a critical time toward understanding differential association effects (Akers, 1985; Sutherland, 1947).

The above summary of research focused mainly on "legal" types pornographic media. It bears emphasizing that some types are illegal. For instance, as discussed earlier, the federal government and states have enacted laws that severely punish offenders convicted of accessing child pornography (Wolak, Finkelhor, & Mitchell, 2005). What has research revealed about the effects of exposure to this specific type of pornography? The answer is unclear. To be certain, there exist subcultures of individuals who download, share, and trade child pornography. For example, Jenkins (2001, p. 102) identified certain enclaves of individuals ("child porn enthusiasts") who visit child pornography websites, download pornographic images of children, and participate in child pornography message boards. However, whether such viewing leads to actual, contact sexual offending is debated. To illustrate, some scholars claim that no evidence of a causal link between child pornography viewing and sexual offending exists. In a review of child pornography studies, Jenkins (2001, p. 128) concluded that "statistics establish no causal link between child porn materials and actual behavior." Moreover, other studies suggest "only a modest association of general pornography crimes with child victimization" (Finkelhor & Ormrod, 2004, pp. 6–7). For example, in a majority (92 percent) of the child exploitation pornography offenses in the U.S. from 1997–2000, law enforcement was unable to link the offender with an identifiable victim (Finkelhor & Ormrod, 2004). Some studies have attempted to more directly unpack this relationship. For example, in 2009, Bourke and Hernandez (n=155) studied incarcerated sex offenders serving time in a federal prison. They found that offenders with a prior child pornography offense were more likely than those who had no such record to have committed a "hands-on" sex offense. However, the authors cautioned that it would be "presumptuous" to attribute a causal relationship between child pornography viewing and contact sexual offending (p. 189). Indeed, the majority of offenders in the study reported viewing child pornography only *after* having committed a contact sex offense (e.g., child molestation; similar results are reported in Seto, Hanson, & Babchishin, 2011, p. 136).

In concluding this section, a few observations follow. From a differential association standpoint, the frequency of pornography exposure, the context under which it occurs (e.g., watching it alone or in a group setting), and the significance of the viewing to the individual are additional factors that might affect the impact of exposure. Relatedly, as is the case with child pornography research, it is difficult to assess the causal effect of pornography viewing. Although some research indicates a correlation between pornography viewing and sexual aggression, the "chicken or the egg" issue arises. Does pornography viewing lead to greater sexual aggression? Or, are sexually aggressive people more strongly attracted to pornography? That is a question that is still debated among scholars. Future directions for research would be to design studies that more directly address this question and account for pornography effects across the life course.

Neutralization/Drift

Another relevant social learning theory in understanding the etiology of sexual offending includes the "neutralization" or "drift" theory. It was developed by criminologists Gresham Sykes and David Matza in 1957. Broadly, the theory posits that offenders are not unilaterally deviant. Rather, they "drift" out of conformity (and into offending) by employing specific rationalizations. In particular, the theorists outlined four observations from their work with juvenile delinquents (Sykes & Matza, 1957, pp. 664–665):

- Most delinquents genuinely feel guilt or shame over their actions.
- Many delinquents respect and admire honest and law-abiding individuals.
- Delinquents frequently make judgments about "appropriate victims."
- Delinquents are not completely immune to conformity.

Under this logic, delinquents are not fundamentally distinct from non-delinquents. By definition however the former group commits crime, whereas the latter group does not. What accounts for this disparity? Central to Sykes and Matza's (1957) theory is the role of neutralizations that allow offenders to "drift" into illegitimate behavior, as captured by this premise (pp. 666–667): "disapproval flowing from internalized norms and conforming others in the social environment is neutralized, turned back, or deflected in advance ... social controls that serve to check or inhibit deviant motivational patterns are rendered inoperative, and the individual is free to engage in delinquency ..." Specifically, they identified five justifications:

- denial of responsibility
- denial of injury
- denial of victim

- condemnation of the condemners
- appeal to higher loyalties

How might neutralization theory apply toward understanding sexual offending? One avenue of research has examined how cognitive distortions—which, per Abel et al. (1989, p. 137), "refer to an individual's internal processes, including the justifications, perceptions, and judgments used by the sex offender to rationalize his behavior"—affect subsequent sexual offending. Other related research has uncovered "rape myths"—faulty beliefs or overgeneralizations about sex crime prevalent in larger society—which correspond to many of the neutralizations outlined by Sykes and Matza (1957). In turn, the endorsement of such myths, particularly among males, is correlated with increased sexual aggression toward women. At first glance, these broad definitions seem difficult to differentiate. However, scholars have distinguished them using the following principles (Howitt & Sheldon, 2007, p. 470–471):

> Cognitive distortions ... reflect the distorted experiences of the offender. Since the cognitions reflect the distorted experiences of the offender, they pre-exist offending but at the same time are closely linked to the offending behavior ... thus, for example, cognitive distortions which emphasize that children are sexual beings may simply be a reflection of the fact that as a child the offender was sexualized and sexually active.
> [In contrast] rape myths, according to feminist writings, are common throughout society and constitute normal male (and female) thinking. For example, rape myths are incorporated institutionally into the criminal justice system. In contrast, cognitive distortions are regarded as deviations from, or distortions of, normal thinking.

More specifically, cognitive distortions "refer to self-statements made by offenders that allow them to deny, minimize, justify, or rationalize their behavior" (Murphy, 1990, p. 332). Under this logic, cognitive distortions are not posited to be the direct cause of deviance, but rather refer to the processes that offenders use to justify and maintain their behavior. Thus, unlike rape myths—which, per theorists, "activate" sexually aggressive behavior—cognitive distortions are not theorized to be causally related to the onset of sexual offending. However, they have been implicated in the maintenance of such behavior. That is, cognitive distortions represent "post-hoc" rationalizations—and, in this way are similar to Sykes and Matza's (1957) neutralization conceptions—that allow the offender to avoid feelings of guilt, shame, or regret about the offense. In turn, these disinhibitors (absence of guilt, shame, empathy for the victim) are believed to contribute to further offending. In essence then, cognitive distortions—while not theorized to be directly implicated in the onset of sex crime—are relevant to neutralization theory and important to study, as they lead to the increased incidence of further sexual deviance.

A large body of research has examined cognitive distortions in sex offenders. Several types of distortions have been identified. Generally, researchers have found that offender type is relevant to the specific cognitive distortion. For example, studies examining child molesters find that their cognitions center on flawed beliefs about acceptable sexual contact with children. To illustrate, they are more likely to believe that children are similar to adults in mental and sexual development, children are interested in having sexual relationships with adults, and sexual abuse confers benefits to victims—increased attention, love, and "sexual" education (Stermac & Segal, 1989). Moreover, such offenders often misinterpret social cues. That is, they may mistake a child's kindness as indicative of sexual interest. Or, they might misconstrue normal childhood actions as sexually provocative behavior (e.g., a child asks to be "tucked in" before bedtime, but the offender views this request as a sexual invitation). Notably, one study conducted by Hayashino, Wurtele, and Klebe (1995), found that variation within the child molester category exists. Using a cognition scale they found extrafamilial child molesters (compared to incest offenders, rapists, other nonsexual offenders, and controls) showed a strong endorsement of faulty sex beliefs (similar to the ones mentioned above). More specifically, Ward and Keenan (1999, p. 833) synthesizing prior research have identified five core types of cognitive distortions in child sexual offenders: "Children as sexual objects" (belief that children are capable of initiating and enjoying sex), "Entitlement" (belief that some people are superior to others and are deserving of using others to meet needs), "Dangerous world" (belief that the world is threatening, that people are inherently evil; such beliefs in turn can lead to attacks on others), "Uncontrollability" (belief in fatalism; namely, that "the world is uncontrollable and that events just happen to people"), and finally, "Nature of harm" (belief that some sexual crimes proffer positive effects for victims). Notably, emerging research has validated these broad classifications of cognitive distortions (Marziano, Ward, Beech, & Pattison, 2006).

In contrast, incest offenders—specifically, father-daughter incest offenders—tend to hold flawed beliefs about normal father-daughter relationships. For instance, in a study conducted by Hanson and colleagues several findings are notable: offenders reported that their daughters initiated the incident, most of the fathers felt entitled to have sex with their daughters, some equated sex with love, and many misinterpreted their victims' responses as being indicative of acquiescence (Hanson, Gizzarelli, & Scott, 1994). Notably, the same study assessed the victims' (daughters of the offenders) perceptions as well. On average, victims' accounts of the abuse differed dramatically from those of the offenders. Thus, this body of work indicates that these types of cognitive distortions are specific to incest offenders.

Rapists of adult women, on the other hand, tend to hold negative views about women generally. Moreover, there is evidence that rapists are more apt to minimize their responsibility in committing the offense, compared to other offenders who also experience cognitive distortions. For example, offenders who have victimized children (the earlier group) tend to see the act as consensual, and acceptable, and thus, not criminal or deviant. On the other hand, rapists may accept that an offense has occurred, but they attribute much of the blame to the victim, tending to believe that the offense would not have transpired if the victim had behaved differently (e.g., "if she had not flirted with me, this would never have happened"). More generally, research has found that convicted rapists are more likely to attribute less guilt to other accused rapists when compared to other offenders (Marolla & Scully, 1986), providing indirect support for the notion that rapists perceive victims to be integral, but not offenders, to the commission of the crime.

Within this broad framework, some studies have focused on guilt as a specific cognitive distortion found among sex offenders. For example, Wilson, Abel, Coyne, and Rouleau (1991) reported that the more guilty sex offenders feel about their crimes, the less deviant acts they commit in the future. Ward, Hudson, and Johnston (1997) explained in a review that, "Guilt is linked to causal attributions of control, which, in turn, is thought to increase motivation to avoid negative outcomes ... it is possible that the way offenders manage guilt, its intensity, and its link with self-evaluation more generally, can mediate offending behavior" (p. 497). Thus, the absence of guilt among sex offenders represents a critical cognitive distortion that in turn facilitates future offending. That is, offenders whose thinking is distorted in this manner (i.e., they attribute no guilt to their actions) are at a greater likelihood of committing further offenses.

While scholars have generally agreed that sex offenders—regardless of their offending patterns—show flaws in cognition (Ward & Beech, 2006), critiques of this literature exist. For example, much of the extant work in this area has focused exclusively on certain populations. Males have been the focus for most studies examining cognitive distortions with only a small handful of studies focused on female sex offenders (see e.g., Beech, Parrett, Ward, & Fish, 2009). Thus, this preliminary work indicates that cognitive distortions might manifest themselves differently among this population. For this reason, scholars urge further investigation in this area. Additionally, while there is consensus that distortions—albeit, while not considered to be causally linked to the onset of sexual deviancy—play a role in sexual offending, little is known about their origins. That is, do cognitive distortions arise from socialization processes (e.g., interactions with delinquent peers or parents)? Or, are they related to faulty neurological deficits (as biological-based theories would posit)? Moreover, how these distortions interact with other disinhibitors—such as drug and alcohol use or peer influence—is not fully understood. This is a critical area to emphasize for future studies. If the development and maintenance of thinking errors are better understood, treatment interventions for offenders could be better designed to reduce sexual deviance.

In contrast to criminologists and psychologists who have focused on examining cognitive distortions in the etiology of sexual offending, other scholars have emphasized the role of rape myths. Brownmiller (1975) was one of the first to put forth the theory that rape myths legitimize sexual violence against women in American society. In particular, rape myths are "attitudes and generally false beliefs about rape that are widely and persistently held, and that serve to deny and justify male sexual aggression against women" (Lonsway & Fitzgerald, 1994, p. 133, in a review). Such myths are posited to be widely prevalent in society and can be seen as flowing from three specific techniques of neutralization: denial of responsibility, denial of injury, and denial of victim. Below a rape myth example is given for each specific neutralization (these specific examples can be found in Lonsway & Fitzgerald, 1994):

> Denial of responsibility: "Many women have an unconscious desire to be raped."
> Denial of injury: "Rape reports are generally false."
> Denial of victim: "Only certain bad women are raped."

Perhaps spurred by Brownmiller's (1975) initial observation about rape myths, in the 1980s and 1990s scholars began to develop rape myth scales (typically measuring how strongly respondents ascribed to such myths as those listed above) to further research their effects on sexual behavior. Overall, this research has revealed a significant and positive effect of rape myth acceptance and self-reported sexual aggression toward women. Notably, this effect persists in studies examining college students (Burt, 1980; Koss, Leonard, Beezley, & Oros, 1985; Muehlenhard & Linton, 1987; Reilly, Lott, Caldwell, & DeLuca, 1992) and community samples (Feild, 1978; Murphy, Coleman, & Haynes, 1986). A more recent meta-analysis synthesizing results from 37 extant studies focused on rape myth endorsement and sexual aggression confirmed this general finding. In particular, Suarez and Gadalla (2010) found rape myth endorsement to be the strongest predictor of self-reported sexual violence among males.

Despite these findings, limitations in this body of research need to be addressed. For example, scholars have emphasized that most studies finding statistically significant effects of rape myth acceptance on sexual violence are correlational. That is, they have not been able to tease out whether myth endorsement causally affects the propensity to offend, and of the small handful of studies that has been able to do so methodologically, virtually no statistically significant effect of rape myth endorsement (more generally, rape myth justifications) on contributing to subsequent offending has been discovered (for an exception using an experimental design and a college population see, Bohner et al., 1998). For example, some third factor might cause both strong endorsement of rape myths and increased propensity to sexually offend. This issue was recognized by Maruna and Mann (2006, p. 160):

> The argument that excuses precede and lead to offending (as opposed to just following it) has almost no empirical support and it is difficult to imagine a research design that could conclusively demonstrate this link. Certainly, some of the more innovative attempts to establish this chronology retrospectively and longitudinally have been unable to identify any strong link between the acceptance of rationalizations at Time One and criminal behavior measured at Time Two (citations omitted).

As another matter for future research, rape myth scales might need to be revised to reflect societal changes in attitudes about victims and rape. For example, recent comments made by U.S. Congressional Representative Todd Akin that "legitimate rapes" rarely result in pregnancy because the body can "shut that whole thing down" (Eligon & Schwirtz, 2012), imply two unsupported assertions about the reality of sexual offending. First, embedded in his claim is the belief that some rapes are genuine, "true" offenses and others, in contrast, are not, and so do not constitute crimes. Thus, this assertion falls in line with various other rape myths that deny the existence of rape victims. Second, his observation also implies that the biology of "true" victims — that is, "legitimate" rape victims — differs dramatically from the biology of "illegitimate" rape victims. Notably, meta-analyses in leading medical journals have found no empirical support for his specific claim about biological mechanisms that might interfere with conception during acts of rape (Belluck, 2012). Although Rep. Akin's views are not necessarily representative to general American beliefs, there is some evidence that he is not alone in his endorsement of this myth (see e.g., Belluck, 2012). In short, his comments and others like them illustrate that contemporary attitudes toward sexual offending do not always reflect reality, and that despite best efforts to minimize the endorsement of such views myth acceptance persists among certain populations (see e.g., Rozee & Koss, 2001). For these reasons, greater empirical attention to rape myths, including understanding their content and origins, and their effects on sexual offending, particularly among males, is warranted.

We move now to feminist theories about sexual victimization. Although there is some overlap between social learning theories (particularly, our discussion about rape myth endorsement) and feminist theories, these are distinct bodies of literature, and so, they will be discussed separately. An overview of social learning theories is presented in Table 4.2.

Feminist Perspective

The feminist perspective emphasizes that historical and structural factors have contributed to sexual offending. In particular, feminist scholars have pointed to specific observations about the nature and prevalence of sex crime. For example, they have observed that sex crime victims — particularly victims of sexual battery — are overwhelmingly female. They also note that the perpetrators of such crimes are typically male. Accordingly, under a feminist lens, these situations reflect larger societal trends. Feminist scholars, for instance,

Table 4.2. Social Learning Perspective Overview

Theoretical Focus	Argument and Summary
Differential Association	*Argument*: Criminality is predicted by the differential or excess associations one has with criminal others. *Summary*: Research has been supportive of this general tenet. On average, peer support for sexual violence, prior abuse (negative effect may be mitigated by other factors, such as treatment or counseling for the abuse), and pornography use (in adolescence) have been associated with increased sexual aggression. However, a main criticism of this broad body of literature involves causality—the "chicken or the egg" issue. For example, might a third factor—perhaps a biological trait—be causally related to these factors and sexual offending?
Neutralization or Drift	*Argument*: Offenders are typically law-abiding, but drift into criminality by employing rationalizations. *Summary*: This work has generally focused on cognitive distortions and the endorsement of rape myths (as these directly correspond to three neutralizations—denial of responsibility, denial of injury, and denial of victim). Research examining cognitive distortions has found that offender "type" matters in assessing the extent of faulty thinking. However, this work has been criticized for not providing a clear explanation of how distortions develop, and also their effects among certain populations (e.g., female sex offenders). While other studies have found a link between myth endorsement and sexual aggression, a glaring limitation of this body of research is that it has not been able to assess whether rape myth endorsement causally affects offending. Among those few studies that have, no statistically significant effect of rape myth endorsement has been detected.

might explain sexual offending stemming from "gendered power relations" (Mardorossian, 2002, p. 743). Under this perspective, sexual violence is linked with a male-dominated social structure and, also the processes that reinforce gender-specific roles for men and women (e.g., the expectation that males are naturally sexually aggressive).

Alternatively, some theorists explain that sex crimes, particularly against young women originate from a rape culture—one where the sexual objectification of women and children in larger society is typical (e.g., sexualized images of young women that appear on television, in music videos, and in pornographic material). In short, the feminist perspective emphasizes that "men assault women (both sexually and physically) because they have opportunities and support for doing so, or because doing so is an extension of men's violence in general, or because men gain 'masculinity points' for such displays" (Mustaine & Tewksbury, 2002, p. 91). Below, we turn toward understanding two specific concepts from feminist theory—"patriarchy" and "rape culture"—that apply toward our understanding of sexual offending.

Patriarchy

A central concept of feminist theory revolves around the notion of patriarchy. Per experts, patriarchy refers to the "social, legal, and political climate that values male dominance and hierarchy, [the belief that] women's nature is biologically, not culturally determined, and [the recognition that criminal justice] laws are from men's standpoint consistent with men's experiences" (Belknap, 2007, p. 10). Thus, patriarchy defines one's social standing in American culture. As a result, women and young girls—historically marginalized groups—are at particular risk of experiencing sexual violence because the larger social structure encourages and, and at the same time, reinforces sexual victimization.

Empirical examination of patriarchy and sexual offending has mainly focused on examining gender variation in sexual victimization and offending, entitlement attitudes, and acceptance of sexual victimization against women. For example, research generally shows that sexual victimization is highly gendered. National statistics indicate that male perpetrators commit 99 percent of forcible rapes (i.e., penetrative sex crimes/sexual battery) and 90 percent of "other" sex offenses (e.g., sexual assault, child pornography offenses, lewd and lascivious acts; see Greenfeld, 1997). Victims of sex offenses tend to be female (Fisher & Cullen, 2000). Feminist scholars have drawn on these statistics to support the notion that patriarchy (as indicated by primarily male offenders and female victims) is linked to sexual victimization.

Relatedly, it has been theorized that patriarchy results in male entitlement (Hill & Fisher, 2001), and more generally attitudes accepting of sexual victimization. Scholars have defined male entitlement as a phenomenon by which men feel deserving of certain privileges (e.g., sex); more specifically, the concept stresses male dominance—"general masculine entitlement derive[s] from male power and privilege in patriarchal society and reflect[s] a belief that men's needs or desires take precedence over women's needs" (Bouffard, 2010, p. 871). In one of the only empirical investigations examining the impact of sexual entitlement (n=325), Bouffard (2010) reported that among male college students, the endorsement of "pro-entitlement" views (e.g., believing that "a woman should submit to her husband's decisions," "women enjoy being submissive during sex," "the husband has a right to sex if he pays all of the bills") was a distinguishing factor between sexually aggressive and non-sexually aggressive men. Put differently, in Bouffard's (2010) study, men who felt entitled to sex or who viewed women as being inferior to men scored significantly higher on indicators of sexual aggression. More specifically, Schwartz and DeKeseredy (1997) coined the term "courtship patriarchy" to refer to the "unwritten rules" pertaining to dating and martial relationships. Thus, within systems of courtship patriarchy, attitudes legitimizing violence against women are evident. In particular, the concept stresses that in typical relationships, there is an expectation that sexual favors will follow dates funded by men (e.g., expensive dinner, movies). In cases where women refuse to follow through with sexual expectations, violence is considered an acceptable response by males. Feminist scholars posit that these attitudes are pervasive in society especially in college settings (Schwartz & DeKeseredy, 1997).

In understanding how patriarchal values impact sexual offending, feminist scholars have also identified the effect of "pro-offending" or "victim-blaming" attitudes. As we have already discussed, "rape myths" are attitudes—pervasive in society—that typically "excuse" offender behavior, and instead place blame for the offense on victims (e.g., "a woman wearing a short skirt deserves to be raped"). However, while the social learning perspective would explain the endorsement of such views as originating from learning processes (i.e., learning the techniques to rationalize sexual violence), the feminist theory posits a different process. Per feminist scholars, rape myths derive from, and are reinforced by "society's acceptance of patriarchy and male dominance" (Suarez & Gadalla, 2010, p. 2013). Thus, rape myths originate from the larger power structure and are "normative" in general society.

Notably, research examining these myths—specifically regarding how they might affect sexual aggression has already been reviewed. What bears emphasis here is that feminist scholars believe the endorsement of rape myths has additional consequences—in particular, it results in the underreporting of sexual violence. For example, a broad observation cited by feminist scholars is that only a small fraction of all sex crimes that occur in the U.S. are subsequently reported to law enforcement (Fisher & Cullen, 2000). Other work finds that victims of rape and sexual assault routinely "blame" themselves for their victimization. In turn, victim blame is linked with reduced reporting of the offense (Schwartz & DeKeseredy, 1997). Moreover, some women whose victimization experiences fit the legal definition of "rape" do not conceptualize themselves as rape victims—a class of women Koss (1985, p. 195) has referred to as "unacknowledged rape victims." Given the apparent level of underreporting of sex crime, feminist scholars are skeptical that official data (arrest reports, conviction records) accurately reflect the extent of sexual victimization. Instead, they rely on victimization survey data (whereby populations are asked to report their victimization experiences). Additionally, feminist researchers have developed scales which are designed to measure a wide variety sexual victimization experiences (e.g., sexual assaults, forced intercourse offenses, threats of sexual violence, completed versus attempted offenses; for a review see Fisher & Cullen, 2000).

Although victimization surveys are now widely acknowledged to be more valid indicators than official reports of sex crime, these approaches—and more broadly, the feminist perspective—have been criticized by other researchers. To illustrate, Neil Gilbert has questioned the validity of some sexual victimization survey measures. Specifically, he pointed to two discrepancies in research conducted by Mary Koss and her colleagues. First, he emphasized the statistic indicating that 73 percent of victims who fit Koss' definition of a rape victim did not in fact believe they were raped. Additionally, he also noted that 42 percent of this "unacknowledged" rape victim group reported that they again had consensual sex with the man who "supposedly raped them" (Gilbert, 1997, p. 236). These statistics lead Gilbert to question whether in fact Koss and her colleagues have inflated the actual extent of sexual victimization. That is, if victims do not perceive the acts committed against them as offenses, perhaps Koss et al.'s research is tapping into behavior that is not in fact criminal (see also, Roiphe, 1993). In turn, Gilbert has concluded that "radical feminists have distorted the definition of rape and created a bogus epidemic [of sexual violence against women]" (as quoted in Hendrix, 1991). Thus, competing views about the extent of sexual victimization in American society exist.

Despite these arguments, it has been acknowledged that measuring sexual victimization is an incredibly difficult task. That is, unlike other types of offenses (e.g., homicide, burglary), the measurement of sexual victimization includes a great deal of measurement error as what constitutes sexual violence is open to interpretation. This view is further illustrated by Fisher and Cullen (2000, p. 376) in a review: "discerning how much force has been used, or the extent to which consent has not been given, is a daunting methodological task; objective behaviors may be open to diverse interpretations or 'constructions of reality' by the people involved in an incident and by researchers seeking to measure what has occurred." Even so, the problem of sexual violence—whether the extent of it is at epidemic proportions or not—is one Americans see as a priority crime issue to address (Mancini et al., 2013; Mears et al., 2008). Thus, future research will ideally work toward developing better measures of sexual victimization and assessing, on an annual or longitudinal basis, the nature and extent of sex crime in the U.S.

Rape Culture

A separate strand of feminist thought has centered on examining "rape culture" or a society where "the objectification of, and violent and sexual abuse of, women through movies, television, advertising, and 'girlie' magazines" is common, and accepted (Burt, 1980, p. 219). Under this logic, since women are often portrayed as sexual objects in mass media and society, sexual violence against them is normalized. In some ways, this explanation is aligned with social learning processes. In contrast to social learning theory, however, feminist scholars view this situation as stemming largely from long-standing patriarchy in American culture. Research examining how these images contribute to a "rape culture" is discussed below.

First, prior work has demonstrated that the sexual objectification of women appears prevalent in American society. To illustrate, in a review of media portrayals of women and violence, Belknap (2007, p. 280) pointed to one study of television music videos that indicated "aggressive sex [occurs] in about one-third of the implicit or explicit sex scenes ... [and that] females were typically viewed as recipients (not initiators) of sex and as enjoying aggressive sex more than the males did." A different study conducted by Bufkin and Eschholz (1996) examined the top-earning films of 1996. In their study (n=50) they found that the movies typically presented patriarchal views of rape. For example, approximately 20 percent of the sex scenes in the top-grossing films involved rapes and nearly all of these films showed a female victim being assaulted by a male perpetrator. Moreover, the rapists fit "stereotypical" notions of sex offenders. That is, they were depicted as deranged, sadistic, and poor.

A larger content analysis conducted by Stankiewicz and Rosselli (2008) examined the depiction of women in 1,988 advertisements from 58 popular U.S. magazines. In particular, the study examined the extent to which women were portrayed as "sex objects," "victims," or "aggressors." Findings indicate strong support for the notion that women are routinely sexualized in advertisements. That is, 50 percent of the advertisements portrayed women as sexual objects. In contrast, less support was found for the notion that women are often depicted as vulnerable, as only 10 percent of the advertisements featured women as victims. In stark contrast, only 3 percent of advertisements featured women as "aggressors." Notably, the "type" of publication where the advertisement appeared mattered. Men's, women's, fashion, and female adolescent magazines were significantly more likely to portray women as sex objects and as victims than news and business, special interest, or women's non-fashion magazines.

Some feminist scholars also view the widespread availability of pornographic media as evidence of the sexual objectification of women, and so as an important indicator of rape culture. Some for instance claim that any type—even "mainstream"—pornography degrades women—providing a "training manual" for how to sexually abuse women (for a review of these arguments see, Hald, et al., 2010). As we have already discussed, the social learning perspective—more precisely, differential association—posits that exposure to such media might teach viewers the techniques and values associated with sexual aggression, and in turn contribute to sexual violence against women. While some feminist theorists see social learning as helpful in understanding these impacts, their larger concern about pornography is that the content routinely degrades women, and so sustains a rape culture. Notably, not all feminists share this view (see e.g., Strossen, 1993; see generally, Kesler, 2002). More broadly however, the feminist perspective—these exceptions notwithstanding—has historically perceived the availability of pornography as problematic.

How might these images in popular media contribute to sexual violence against women? Per scholars, they perpetuate rape myths (e.g., women are only raped by delusional and sick men who are distinct from "normal" people), and may lead to sexual aggression and the acceptance of sexual violence among *both* men and women. This perspective has led scholars to further investigate the consequences of living in a "rape culture."

In one study conducted by Bleecker and Murnen (2005), a researcher took digital pictures of all of the images of women displayed in the rooms of 30 fraternity men and 30 non-fraternity men on a residential college campus. A rape myth acceptance scale was also administered to the samples. In total, close to 100 images were found in the form of posters, "pin-ups," advertisements, or computer screen savers. Results indicate that fraternity men had significantly more images of women displayed in their rooms; the images were rated as significantly more sexually degrading than those in the rooms of non-fraternity men (trained psychology students rated the images). Fraternity men were found to have significantly higher scores on a rape supportive attitude scale. In turn, these scores were positively related to the amount of degradation in the images found in men's rooms.

In a different study, Milburn, Mather, and Conrad (2000) investigated the effects of viewing scenes from R-rated popular films on perceptions of female responsibility for and enjoyment of either a date rape or a stranger rape, using an experimental design. College male participants viewed either scenes that sexually objectified and degraded women (the experimental group) or scenes from an animation festival (the control group). In a supposedly unrelated second experiment, participants then read a fictitious magazine account of a date rape or a stranger rape. Results suggest that males who viewed the sexually objectifying media felt that the victim in the date-rape condition experienced pleasure and "got what she wanted" (similar results have been reported in other earlier research, see e.g., Linz, Donnerstein, & Penrod, 1988).

Notably, the aforementioned studies focused on males. These images also affect women's tolerance for sexual violence. For example, Kalof (1999) reported in her study (n=44) that female participants exposed to "traditional" images of women in music videos (e.g., as sexualized, vulnerable), in comparison to females not shown these traditional images, had a significantly greater acceptance of interpersonal violence. In fact, women in the experimental group had higher scores of violence tolerance than men also shown the media. Johnson, Adams, Ashburn, and Reed (1995) report similar results in their study. In particular, African American teenage girls exposed to rap music videos had greater levels of acceptance of teen dating violence than young women who were not exposed to the media.

The feminist conception of "rape culture" and, more generally, feminist perspectives about rape has been criticized by some scholars. For example, one argument against the contention that sexual offending has reached epidemic proportions involves recent crime trends. Reports of forcible rape and other sexual offenses against women have been in consistent decline since the mid-1990s. Notably, both official (arrest) data and victimization data (thought to be a more reliable indicator of sex crime) support this general decline pattern (Finkelhor & Jones, 2004; Velázquez, 2008). Thus, this trend provides some evidence that sex crime may not be widely pervasive in society. Another claim made by opponents of rape culture is that feminist scholars are simply too "sensitive" in their measurement of sex crime, and so, their analysis of sexual offending substantially overestimates the extent of "true" sexual victimization.

Recall the criticism levied by Neil Gilbert concerning Mary Koss and colleagues' rape research. In particular, Gilbert has questioned Koss et al.'s findings that sexual victimization is highly prevalent, particularly the prevalence statistic that approximately 25 percent of women in the U.S. will be raped at some point during their lives. His particular criticism centered on one of Koss et al.'s main indicators of sexual victimization: "Have you had sexual intercourse when you didn't want to because a man gave you alcohol or drugs?" Gilbert (1992, p. 5) claimed the question was far too ambiguous, and that responses to it conflated "real victims" with those women who simply "regretted saying yes":

Table 4.3. Feminist Perspective Overview

Theoretical Focus	Argument and Summary
Patriarchy	*Argument*: Patriarchy, or the social, legal, and political climate that values male dominance and hierarchy, contributes to the endorsement of stereotypical views about women, rape victims, and sex crime. Patriarchal societies have higher rates of sexual victimization, particularly where perpetrators are male and victims are female. *Summary*: Feminist scholars have emphasized that sexual victimization—particularly against women—is highly prevalent in the U.S. They have also documented that the perpetrators of such crimes are overwhelmingly male. Not least, feminist research finds rape myths to be widespread in society. Other scholars, however, have critiqued some of this work. For example, one claim is that feminist scholars are much too sensitive in their measurement of sexual offending.
Rape Culture	*Argument*: Patriarchy has led to a rape culture—a society where the sexual objectification of, and violent abuse of, women is typical, accepted, and encouraged. *Summary*: In measuring indicators of a rape culture, researchers have examined the prevalence of sexual objectification of women. A large body of studies indicates that women, compared to men, are more likely to be sexually depicted in society. A smaller strand of research has examined how these images impact views about sexual offending. Generally, findings comport with feminist scholars' assertions that such images shape attitudes accepting of sexual violence—among men and women. A criticism of these findings however focuses on whether they are valid. That is, some scholars have emphasized that many of these studies have inflated the actual extent of sexual offending.

What does having sex "because" a man gives you drugs or alcohol signify? A positive response does not indicate whether duress, intoxication, force, or the threat of force were present; whether the woman's judgment or control were substantially impaired; or whether the man purposely got the woman drunk to prevent her from resisting his sexual advances. It could mean that a woman was trading sex for drugs or that a few drinks lowered the respondent's inhibitions and she consented to an act she later regretted ... While the item could have been clearly worded to denote "intentional incapacitation of the victim," as the question stands it would require a mind reader to detect whether an affirmative response corresponds to a legal definition of rape.

To summarize, some scholars have questioned the feminist perspective of rape by arguing that sexual offending is not nearly as prevalent as some (in their eyes, flawed) studies indicate, and also that feminists have overemphasized the extent of a "rape culture" in American society. Table 4.3 summarizes the feminist perspective in explaining sexual offending.

Chapter Summary

Criminologists have directed considerable scholarly attention toward understanding crime. As a result, numerous theories centered on offending currently exist. We could easily fill a rather lengthy monograph examining how these theories might explain sex crime; however, such an endeavor would leave little room to discuss other intriguing aspects of sex crime—such as patterns and trends in sexual offending, the public's response to sex offenders, sex crime reforms, and other important, but not nearly as researched issues. Thus, the goal of this chapter was to highlight three prominent perspectives regularly used to explain sexual offending. This chapter examined three broad perspectives that apply directly toward understanding the etiology of sex crime: the biological perspective, social learning theories, and the feminist perspective. Each framework emphasizes different factors in explaining sexual offending. The biological perspective highlights the role of hormone regulation and neurological processes in understanding sex crime. In contrast, social learning theories stress the theoretical concepts of differential association and neutralization or "drift" in better comprehending the propensity to sexually offend. Not least, the feminist perspective underscores how patriarchy has contributed to a rape culture which tolerates and encourages sexual victimization.

A supplementary reading list is presented below that directs interested readers to additional theory readings. The following section, "Societal Responses to Sexual Offending," begins by highlighting and evaluating prominent myths about sexual offending (Chapter 5).

Additional Suggested Readings

Baron, L., & Straus, M. A. (1989). *Four theories of rape in American society.* New Haven, CT: Yale University Press.

Crowell, N. A., & Burgess, A. W. (Eds.). (1996). *Understanding violence against women.* Washington, D.C.: National Academy Press.

Dworkin, A. (1997). *Life and death: Unapologetic writings on the continuing war against women.* New York: Free Press.

Ellis, L. (1988). *Theories of rape.* New York: Spectrum.

Estrich, S. (1987). *Real rape.* Cambridge, MA: Harvard University Press.

George, W., & Martinez, L. (2002). Victim blaming in rape: Effects of victim and perpetrator race, type of rape, and participant racism. *Psychology of Women Quarterly, 26,* 110–119.

Marshall, W. L. (1996). Assessment, treatment, and theorizing about sex offenders: Developments during the past twenty years and future direction. *Criminal Justice and Behavior, 23,*162–199.

Thornhill, R., & Palmer, C. T. (2000). *A natural history of rape: Biological bases of sexual coercion.* Cambridge, MA: MIT Press.

Ward, T., & Siegert, R. J. (2002). Toward a comprehensive theory of child sexual abuse: A theory knitting perspective. *Psychology, Crime, & Law, 8,* 319–351.

Part II

Societal Responses to Sexual Offending

Chapter 5

Societal Myths (and Facts) about Sex Offenders

Chapter Introduction

Along with the rapid proliferation of sex crime laws in the 1990s, scholars contend that many misperceptions about sexual offending have surfaced in the U.S. (see e.g., Fuselier, Durham, & Wurtele, 2002). For instance, one might logically conclude, given the intense policymaking in this area, that sex offender reform followed a substantial increase in reports of sexual victimization, particularly for violent offenses and crimes involving children. Strikingly however, prior to the unprecedented emergence of sex offender laws nationally, reports of sex offenses began to decline. Indeed, throughout an especially active period of sex crime policymaking (mid-1990s to 2010), national statistics indicate that sex offenses had declined by more than 64 percent (Planty, Langton, Krebs, Berzofsky, & Smiley-McDonald, 2013). Thus, the perception that sex offending has increased in the last twenty years constitutes a sex crime "myth." Notably, other misperceptions regarding sexual offending have been identified by scholars. The goal of this chapter is to examine ten prominent myths related to trends and characteristics of sexual offenses, sex offenders, and sex crime policy with a particular emphasis on explaining why these myths constitute misperceptions.

Trends and Characteristics of Sexual Offenses

Myth 1: Sex crime has increased in recent decades.

A prominent perception held by policymakers (see e.g., Sample & Kadleck, 2008) and the public (Mancini & Mears, 2010) alike is that sexual offenses have increased nationally over the last twenty years. For example, Sample and Kadleck (2008, p. 47) in their study of legislators' beliefs (n=35) regarding sex crime found that nearly all commented on the "growing sex-offender problem." In a similar direction, Mancini and Mears (2010) in their national study discovered that over three-quarters of Americans endorsed the view that the sex crime rate has increased.

As emphasized in Chapter 3, objective indicators of crime however provide no support for this widespread perception. That is, official and unofficial data sources indicate that sexual offending has been declining in the U.S. for quite some time. To illustrate, UCR data, or "official" data indicate a substantial decrease in reports of sexual offending, particularly for serious sex offenses. For example, Lonsway and Archambault (2012) analyzed arrest (UCR) trend data from the 1960s until 2008. Their results suggest that the number of reported forcible rapes per 100,000 residents increased dramatically from the 1960s to the late 1980s. But, by the early 1990s—notably, prior to the emergence of federal sex crime legislation—rape rates began declining to levels that are comparable with the late 1970s. Specifically, the researchers contend that the figure justifies "the conclusion on the UCR website that the rate of forcible rapes in 2008 was 'the lowest figure in the last 20 years'" (Lonsway & Archambault, 2012, p. 148).

Recall though that several limitations are associated with official data. Most relevant here is the tendency for sexual offenses not to be reported to law enforcement, resulting in statistics that do not account for the "dark figure of (sex) crime." At the same time, UCR data do not typically provide information about victim age. Given these shortcomings, victimization surveys are an important supplement to understanding contemporary crime trends. These surveys, as discussed earlier, aim to measure a greater array of victimization experiences among respondents—including those crimes that have not been reported to law enforcement. The largest victimization survey—the NCVS—conducted regularly by the U.S. Census Bureau—relies on a large and randomly derived sample of Americans (age 12 and older). Thus, using these data we can generalize about sex crime trends nationally. What do these data indicate regarding sex offense reports? Here again, as Chapter 3 described, the most recent NCVS statistics paint a similar portrait as the UCR data, pointing to a significant decrease in sexual offenses. From 1995 to 2005, the total rate of sexual violence (includes completed, attempted, or threatened rape or sexual assault) committed against females diminished by 64 percent from a high of 5 sexual victimizations per 1,000 females in 1995 to a low of 1.8 victimizations per 1,000 females in 2005. The sexual violence rate, as measured by NCVS statistics, remained unchanged from 2005 to 2010 (Planty et al., 2013). As previously mentioned, although unofficial data have clear advantages over official data, the NCVS is limited in that it only measures offenses committed against persons age 12 and older. Thus, it does not provide trend data for sexual offenses involving young children, specifically those 11 and younger.

As a result, some scholars advocate the use of other data sources to estimate crime trends for sexual offenses involving children. Finkelhor and his colleagues have pioneered several innovative methods to document sexual abuse trends among minors in the U.S. To be clear, Finkelhor and Jones (2012) do not discount the use of UCR and NCVS data to provide a general description of sex crime trends in the U.S. At the same time, though they emphasize reliance on other distinct data sources such as child protection system substantiations (NCANDS, discussed in Chapter 3, which aggregates data from state child protective agencies), cases known to professionals (such as the National Incidence Study), specialized victimization surveys (e.g., the Minnesota Student Survey, the National Survey of Family Growth, NatSCEV), and associated outcome indicators. With respect to this last data source, Finkelhor and Jones (2012, p. 3) explain that sexual abuse is typically associated with several other welfare problems among minors, such as teen pregnancy, suicidal tendencies, and running away. And so, "if [such indicators] were trending in the same way as sexual abuse, it could be seen as indirect support for a true decline [in sex crimes against children]." In analyzing these data, Finkelhor and Jones (2012, p. 3) conclude that "the decline in sexual abuse is about as well established as crime trends can be in contemporary social science."

The belief that sex crime is rising in the U.S. may be the result of many factors. Scholars for example have emphasized how the media contributes to a "moral panic" regarding the extent of sexual victimization, particularly for offenses involving children and recidivist offenders (see generally, Sample, 2011). In turn, such coverage, per Galeste, Fradella, and Vogel (2012, p. 4) "perpetuate[s] the acceptance of myths that run contrary to empirical knowledge about sex crimes and sex offenders." Concomitantly, over the last two decades states and the federal government have amplified efforts to incarcerate and punish sex offenders. To illustrate, the incarcerated population of sex offenders increased at a faster pace than for any other offender population in the 1990s (Greenfeld, 1997). At the same time, the registered sex offender population has dramatically increased since federal legislation requiring states to develop registries and notification policies was implemented in the mid-1990s. That is, as of 2012, nearly 740,000 sex offenders are now registered across the U.S. (National Center for Missing and Exploited Children, 2012). These legal changes, however, are not necessarily indicative of actual trends in sexual offending, as previously mentioned, both official and unofficial data indicate a significant decline in reports of sexual offending against both adults and minors. In contrast, the policy change represents a pronounced and more intense response by the criminal justice system than in years prior. Thus the origins of this misperception regarding sex crime trends may stem from media coverage of sexual offending and the prominent punitive shift in criminal justice policy toward addressing sexual victimization. We turn now to a second prominent myth related to trends and characteristics of sexual offending.

Myth 2: Sexual offenses are most often committed by stranger perpetrators.

The impression that sex offenses are most typically perpetrated by stranger offenders constitutes another myth concerning the characteristics of sex offending. To illustrate, some research has examined perceptions of risk of victimization among Americans. Overwhelmingly, this body of work suggests that the public perceives a greater risk of personal sexual victimization by strangers than acquaintances (Jacobs, Hashima, & Kenning, 1995). At the same time, survey research indicates that parents report more frequently cautioning their children about "stranger danger" than potential assaults by someone known to them (Collins, 1996). Not least, this same body of literature indicates that women take greater precautions to avoid sexual assault by strangers than by a known perpetrator (Gidycz, McNamara, & Edwards, 2006 in a review).

Thus, as evidenced by these behaviors the public most fears sexual assaults committed by strangers than by individuals known to them. By extension then, Americans perceive that a greater share of sexual offending is committed by stranger offenders. To what degree, though, does research support this belief? The answer is that on average known offenders—typically family members, friends, or acquaintances—commit the majority of all sex offenses. This pattern is evident among offenses involving children, and also, adults. Greenfeld (1997) in one of the largest and only national studies to systematically examine the incidence and prevalence of sexual victimization, the response of the justice system to sex crimes, and the characteristics of sex offenders using both official and unofficial data, found that nearly three-quarters of all sex offenses are committed by individuals known to the victim. Specifically, Greenfeld (1997) disaggregated sex offenses by number of perpetrators. His analysis indicates that strangers accounted for 20 percent of the victimizations involving a single offender. Single offender crimes constitute the most common offense—nearly 90 percent of sex crimes involve just one offender. However, about 10 percent of all rape/sexual assault victimizations involve multiple offenders. For these rarer offenses, a reverse pattern is evident—as approximately 76 percent of the victimizations involving multiple offenders are committed by stranger perpetrators. This exception notwithstanding, the vast majority of sex offenses involve a single perpetrator with whom the victim had a prior relationship (such as a family member, intimate, or acquaintance).

Moreover, this trend has persisted over time. That is, earlier sex crime statistics regarding the extent of stranger versus acquaintance sex offenses have remained virtually constant. For example, Planty and his colleagues (2013) report in their national study analyzing NCVS data from 1994 to 2010 that 78 percent of sex offenses involved a perpetrator familiar to the victim. Similar to Greenfeld's (1997) study, most sex offenses (90 percent) during this time period involved just one offender. In particular, Planty and his associates (2013) were able to disaggregate offenses by the offender-victim relationship. Here, about 34 percent of all rape or sexual assault victimizations were committed by an intimate partner (i.e., a former or current spouse, girlfriend, or boyfriend), 6 percent by a relative or family member, and 38 percent by a friend or acquaintance. Comparatively, strangers were infrequently identified as offenders during this time period (on average, constituting 22 percent of all offenders).

As discussed earlier, the NCVS is limited in that it examines the victimization experiences of those persons age 12 or older and the general population. To assess whether this pattern exists among other populations we can turn to specialized victimization data. For example, recent studies have begun to examine the prevalence of sexual victimization involving young children and teenagers. With few exceptions, results again indicate that sexual abuse against minors is most typically perpetrated by persons known to victims. In particular, the recent work of Finkelhor, Turner et al. (2009) in conducting the NatSCEV (discussed in Chapter 2) indicates that minors are significantly more likely to be sexually abused by a known adult or peer than by a stranger.

Other efforts to understand victimization experiences among a range of populations exist. To illustrate, as discussed earlier Bonnie Fisher and her colleagues (2000) were among the first researchers to conduct a large-scale survey (NCWSV) using a nationally representative sample of college women to better understand sexual victimization experiences on the nation's college and university campuses. Here again, stranger offenses constitute a very small proportion of all sex crimes involving college students. Indeed, Fisher et al.'s (2000) figures suggest that 90 percent of sex crimes against college women are committed by offenders familiar, in most cases, closely familiar to victims. In particular, "classmates" were identified most often as perpetrators (35.5 percent of offenders for completed rapes, 43.5 percent for attempted rapes); "friends" were the next most common group of offenders (34.2 percent for completed rapes, 24.2 percent for attempted rapes); "boyfriends/ex-boyfriends" were the third most typical offender category (23.7 for completed rapes, 14.5 for attempted rapes). Acquaintances were identified in 2.6 percent of completed rapes and 9.7 percent of attempted rapes. The remaining category comprised stranger perpetrators (4 percent for completed rapes, 8.1 for attempted rapes; Fisher et al., 2000, p. 19).

Collectively, findings across multiple data sources pertaining to sexual victimization patterns clearly indicate that with few exceptions most sexual offenses are committed by perpetrators known, and in some cases, intimately known by victims. The empirical evidence thus challenges the view that most sex crimes are committed by stranger offenders. This contradiction notwithstanding, the American public directs significantly more fear and crime prevention behavior toward potential stranger victimization. The reality, again, indicates that attention toward "acquaintance danger" is also warranted. Indeed, extrapolating current statistics regarding victimization risk, one's overall odds of experiencing sexual victimization by known offenders are significantly higher than for offenses involving strangers. Similar to the myth regarding sex crime trends, the "stranger danger" misperception likely stems from disproportionate media coverage toward atypical cases involving stranger (and often recidivist) offenders and child victims (Maguire & Singer, 2011). At the same time, there is evidence that the public is becoming more aware that stranger offenses account for only a small percentage of total sex crimes. For example, in Craun and Theriot's (2009) study of misperceptions held among the public and subsequent awareness of sex offenders, only 30 percent of the public endorsed the "stranger danger" myth. Craun and Theriot's (2009) investigation is limited to one county in the southeastern U.S., however. Thus, future research is needed to examine the extent to which the "stranger danger" myth still constitutes a widespread misperception held by the American public. Next, a third myth concerning sex crime characteristics is discussed.

Myth 3: Most sex crimes are reported to law enforcement.

The third myth involves beliefs about reporting of sex offenses. There is often an implicit view in sex crime legislation that sex offenses will be reported to police immediately after they occur. For example, sex crime laws require that victims come forth with allegations within a specific period of time for prosecution of offenders to ensue. By definition then, allegations of criminal misconduct must be reported to authorities. One empirical investigation conducted by Levenson, Brannon, Fortney, and Baker (2007) examined public opinion toward a range of issues related to sexual offending, including perceptions of victim reporting practices. In their study, respondents believed on average that nearly half of all sex crimes were reported to law enforcement. Going against this view, however, is research examining reporting patterns among sex crime victims. By all accounts this work indicates that sex crime is among one of the most underreported offenses in the U.S. A significant body of scholarship has been devoted toward understanding the extent of underreporting, and also, factors related to the likelihood of reporting. In what follows, this research is briefly summarized below.

According to victimization surveys, reporting of sex offenses constitutes the exception rather than the rule. For example, NCVS data indicate that on any given year only 30–35 percent of all rapes and sexual assaults committed against persons age 12 and older are reported to law enforcement (Hart & Rennison, 2003; Langton et al., 2012). The NCVS also reveals that sexual assault/rape offenses have consistently remained among the least reported violent offenses in the U.S. In comparison, robbery and aggravated assaults—also defined as serious violent crimes per the NCVS—are substantially more likely to be reported than rape offenses. Indeed, the reporting percentage of the former is nearly double that of the sexual assault/rape reporting percentage average (i.e., 60 percent of victims report violent property/assault crimes to law enforcement). Other studies indicate even smaller estimates of reporting. In a national study examining childhood sexual abuse experiences of adult women (NWS; Kilpatrick et al., 1992), it was revealed that only 12 percent reported the crime to authorities (Smith et al., 2000).

In a separate investigation, Finkelhor, Ormrod, and colleagues (2011) examined child and adolescent reporting patterns of sexual victimization using NatSCEV. Study results indicate that the likelihood of reporting varies by offense for minors. That is, reporting was most typical when perpetrators where identified as adults and the charge included "sexual abuse" (69 percent for offenses involving a known adult and 76.1 percent for a non-specified adult). In contrast, when offenses involved peers or "rape" offenses, reporting was much less frequent among minors. Here, only 10 and 13 percent of such offenses were reported, respectively. Finkelhor, Ormrod et al. (2011, p. 14) explain that the contrasting trend in reporting based on offense type, "may have to do with differences in perpetrator characteristics; for example, attempted and completed rape and dating assault often involve peer perpetrators. Incidents with adult perpetrators are more likely to be known, perhaps because the adult offenses are seen as more criminal or because peer allegiances may inhibit reporting of younger perpetrators."

Even so, such underreported offenses (i.e., peer perpetrated and rape offenses; n=66) were significantly more common than sexual abuse perpetrated by adults (n=15). Thus, when the focus is on the vast majority of sex offenses committed against minors, reporting is relatively low.

As discussed earlier, research has also sought to understand victimization experiences, and by extension, reporting patterns among college students. Within this focus, Fisher et al.'s (2000) NCWSV study is illuminating. In particular, study results indicate that approximately 5 percent of completed and attempted rapes against college students were reported to law enforcement. Thus, among students attending universities and colleges in the U.S., reporting is even lower than the national average as captured by the NCVS.

Other studies that have elicited information from offenders and other "unofficial" sources provide further support for the notion that a substantial number of sex offenses go undetected. For example, Marshall and Barbaree (1990) compared official police records of a sample of sex offenders with "unofficial" sources of crime data (i.e., self-reports, allegations of sexual abuse known to child protective agencies but were not substantiated). They found that the number of actual sex offenses revealed through the unofficial sources was nearly 2.4 to 2.8 times higher (for child molesters and exhibitionists, respectively) than the number that was recorded in official law enforcement reports.

In addition, research using information generated through polygraph examinations may provide some insight into the extent of underreporting. Ahlmeyer, Heil, McKee, and English (2000) used such methods to examine a sample of incarcerated sex offenders and sex offenders on parole living in Colorado with fewer than two known victims (on average). The researchers found that these offenders actually had an average of 110 victims and 318 offenses. A similar polygraph study (Ahlmeyer, English, & Simons, 1999) found that a sample of imprisoned sex offenders known to have extensive criminal histories, committed sex crimes for an average of 16 years before being apprehended. It should be noted, however, that other evaluations have questioned the reliability of polygraph methods for assessing the extent of sexual offending (see for a review, Meijer, Verschuere, Merckelbach, & Crombez, 2008).

Even so, a later study (Lussier and Mathesius, 2012) which focused on official records and victimization accounts rather than polygraph methods provides some replication of Ahlmeyer et al. (1999) in a Canadian sample. Specifically, Lussier and Mathesius (2012) estimate that "successful" sex offenders can evade detection for nearly seven years. Generally, the most successful sex offenders in their study—those who offended for significant periods of time without being detected—were those who were well known to victims and in positions of trust or authority.

In a different direction, some research has inquired about factors related to reporting patterns. For example, NCVS data (Langton et al., 2012) indicate that the number one reason for underreporting (when one was specified) given by victims was "fear of reprisal or fear of getting offender in trouble" (28 percent). Approximately 20 percent of victims reported that they "dealt with [crime] in another way" or "felt it was a personal matter." In contrast, 13 percent of victims believed "police would not or could not help." A small

Table 5.1. Myths (and Facts) about Trends and Characteristics of Sexual Offenses

Myth	Fact
Sex crime has increased in recent decades.	Official (UCR, NIBRS) and unofficial data (NCVS and other victimization surveys) indicate substantial declines for sex crimes involving adult and child victims over the last two decades.
Sexual offenses are most often committed by stranger perpetrators.	An overwhelming majority of sex crimes are committed by known perpetrators such as family members, acquaintances, and intimate partners. This pattern is consistent across sex offenses involving adult and child victims.
Most sex crimes are reported to law enforcement.	A minority of sex offenses are actually reported to law enforcement. On average, per NCVS data about one-third of rapes and sexual assaults committed against those 12 and older are reported to police. Reporting for child sexual abuse also appears to be underreported.

minority of respondents (6 percent) felt the offense was too trivial to report. Not least, a sizable minority (33 percent) relayed that some other reason or no single reason precluded them from reporting the offense.

In contrast, Finkelhor, Ormrod and his colleagues (2011) estimated logistic regression analyses to determine what factors predicted police being aware of sexual victimization involving child victims. The predictive factors were "the child feeling afraid" and offenses involving an adult perpetrator. Victim race and ethnicity also predicted the likelihood of law enforcement awareness of the crime. In particular, victimizations involving African Americans, mixed race/ethnicity children, and those identifying as "other" race were significantly more likely than victimizations involving other racial groups to be known to police.

Fisher and colleagues (2000, p. 24) in their study of sexual victimization experiences on college campuses also examined factors related to reporting. Specifically, college women relayed the following reasons for not reporting sexual victimizations (completed rape) to law enforcement (respondents were permitted to give more than one response): "did not want family to know" (44.4 percent), "did not want other people to know" (46.9 percent), "lack of proof that incident happened" (42 percent), and "fear of being treated hostilely by police" (24.7 percent).

If public opinion is any indication, the fact that most victims do not report sex offenses committed against them is striking. Put differently, although the public optimistically reports that close to half of all sex offenses are reported to law enforcement (Levenson et al., 2007), empirical research paints a different picture. The vast majority of sex crimes, with few exceptions, go undetected. Victims report a number of obstacles toward their reporting likelihood—such as fear of retaliation, social stigma, and concern about legal considerations. It should be emphasized that although several efforts now exist to increase reporting among sex crime victims (e.g., improved law enforcement training, criminal justice campaigns) future and systematic research is needed to fully assess the extent to which these efforts have translated into greater reporting among victims (see generally, Cohn, Zinzow, Resnick, & Kilpatrick, 2013). Table 5.1 highlights the myths concerning trends and characteristics of sex crime reviewed in this chapter. The discussion that follows centers on unpacking myths related to characteristics of sex offenders, beginning with the belief that most sex offenders reoffend.

Sex Offenders

Myth 4: Most sex offenders will reoffend.

We move now toward focusing on distorted perceptions of sex offenders. One of the more prominent claims—endorsed by legislators and the general public—is that most sex offenders will reoffend. Sample and Kadleck (2008, p. 50) in their study of policymakers' views toward sex offenders paint a portrait of public officials' views toward the "typical" sex offender, namely one "who is targeted by sex offender legislation … a 'sick' male who is afflicted with some biological or psychological irregularity that causes him to be unusually persistent in his offending." This assessment is not unique to public policy authorities. To illustrate, one large national study found that 93 percent of the American public believed that sex offenders would continue to reoffend no matter the punishment or intervention (Mancini & Mears, 2010; see also Fortney, Levenson, Brannon, and Baker, 2007).

Despite being widely accepted, this perception remains, however, empirically unsupported. It is certainly correct that similar to all criminal offenders, certain sub-types of sex offenders have higher rates of recidivism than others; but, at the same time, nearly all scholarly accounts indicate that the vast majority of sex offenders will not go on to reoffend. For example, a landmark study of offender recidivism in Illinois (n=146,918) provides little support for the perception that sex offenders have unusually high rates of reoffending (Sample & Bray, 2003). In the study, Sample and Bray (2003) analyzed the reoffending percentages for several offender "types" including those offenders with prior homicide, sex offense, robbery, non-sexual assault, kidnap, stalking, burglary, larceny, property damage, and public order charges. Their results indicate that only 6.5 percent of sex offenders were rearrested for a new sex crime in a five-year period. Other types of offenders also were rearrested for sex crimes, but the percentages were lower. For example, within a five year period, the robbery, kidnapping, and stalking categories all had between 2 percent and 3 percent of re-arrests for sexual offenses. Put differently, when relative rates of sex crime recidivism are compared (e.g., 6.5 percent versus 2.5 percent), it thus can appear that convicted sex offenders are two or three more times likely than other offenders to recidivate for a sex crime. Even so, these are relatively small differences given the low baseline rates of sexual reoffending generally as evidenced by Sample and Bray's (2003, p. 76) concluding observations, "based on rates of reoffending, sex offenders do not appear to be more dangerous than other criminal categories." An earlier study (n=106,216) using the same methodology and conducted by the federal government also reveals that most sex offenders (92.5 percent) will not be re-arrested for another sex offense over a three year period (Beck & Shipley, 1989).

Some work has examined whether this pattern persists over longer follow-up periods. For instance, Piquero, Farrington, Jennings, Diamond, and Craig (2012) relied on longitudinal data of South London males (the Cambridge Study in Delinquent Development) to determine the extent of sex offending. Findings from their study indicate that sex offending is relatively rare in comparison to other offenses, with less than 3 percent of the Cambridge males being convicted for 13 sex offenses through age 50. Additionally, there was no indication of continuity in sex offending from the adolescence to early adulthood periods. Overall, very few sex offenders were identified as persistent recidivist offenders, leading Piquero and his colleagues (2012, p. 421) to posit that "[such] results call into question the view that sex offenders are a highly chronic, specialist, recidivistic group of offenders."

To be clear, much of the research already reviewed has demonstrated that sex offenders, as a group, have lower than assumed levels of reoffending. Substantial heterogeneity exists within this broad offending category, however. As a result, some scholars have turned to examining the reoffending patterns of specific sex offender sub-types. To illustrate, A. J. R. Harris and Hanson (2004) conducted one of the largest studies of recidivism among a range of sex offenders (n=4,724) using long follow-up periods. Similar to other studies, their findings indicate that sex offenders as a group have fairly low odds of reoffending. In particular, the overall recidivism rates (14 percent after 5 years, 20 percent after 10 years, and 24 percent after 15 years) were similar for rapists (14 percent, 21 percent, and 24 percent, after 5, 10, and 15 years, respectively) and the combined group of child molesters (13 percent, 18 percent, and 23 percent after 5, 10, and 15 years, respectively). The lowest observed rates were evident for incest offenders (6 percent, 9 percent, and 13 percent after, 5, 10, and 15 years, respectively). There were, however, significant differences between the child molester sub-type, with the highest rates observed among the extrafamilial boy-victim child molesters (i.e., adult male offenders with a male child victim preference; 23 percent, 28 percent, and 35 percent after, 5, 10, and 15 years, respectively). In comparison, extrafamilial girl-victim child molesters have markedly lower rates (9 percent, 13 percent, and 16 percent after, 5, 10, and 15 years, respectively).

Notably, nearly all of these studies centered on sex offender recidivism preclude females, mainly due to their low representation as sex offenders. However, one review conducted by Cortoni, Hanson, and Coache (2010) synthesized results from ten studies (n=2,490 sex offenders) to determine the extent of reoffending among female sex offenders. The results from this meta-analysis suggest that only 3 percent of women will sexually reoffend over a six to seven year period.

To summarize, what has generally been gleaned from extant scholarship is that sex offenders, as a group, have low rates of reoffending across the life course. There is, of course, substantial heterogeneity across sex offender sub-types. Male offenders with a same-sex child victim preference evince the highest likelihood of reoffending. In contrast, incest offenders (those who abuse family members) have the lowest risk of reoffending. Moreover, females appear particularly less likely to reoffend based on the available evidence. Yet against that empirical backdrop, the view that all sex offenders inevitably reoffend remains pervasive in society. Many factors are likely associated with the origin of this view. Per some scholars (see e.g., Soothill, 2010, p. 167), intense media coverage has created and continues to perpetuate the myth as it ignores the "intricacies and complexities" in sex offending scholarship, and instead, provides "a distorted perception of recidivism based on a few sensational cases." To be clear, other myths about sex offenders exist. We turn now to another prominent view concerning the mental health of sex offenders.

Myth 5: Most sex offenders are mentally ill.

The belief that a majority of sex offenders suffer from mental illness is a pervasive myth in contemporary society. Once again, Sample and Kadleck's (2008) work is instructive. In their investigation, two-thirds of policymakers in the study made mention of sex offenders having a psychological abnormality. In another study, conducted by Levenson and her colleagues (2007, p. 149), the public estimated that 50 percent of sex offenders are "severely mentally ill" (see also Olver & Barlow, 2010). Compare this statistic with other studies that have posed a similar question, but have not specified sex offenders—on average, less than 30 percent of the public attributes mental illness as a cause of crime for violent offenders (see e.g., Doble, 2002). The view that sex offenders are mentally ill is also endorsed by authorities who have daily contact with incarcerated offenders. For instance, Weekes, Pelletier, and Beaudette (1995) report that sex offenders who had victimized children were perceived by prison officers as significantly more mentally ill than sex offenders who had assaulted women. In turn, both sub-groups were perceived to be more mentally ill than non-sex offenders.

However, the assumption of widespread mental illness among sex offenders, although widely endorsed across a range of populations, is not supported by extant scholarship. To be clear, it is certainly true that a small proportion of sex offenders have been deemed to have a mental abnormality that may contribute to their offending by states and the federal government. Having said that, mental illness does not appear to be widely distributed among the sex offender population. For example, in a seminal study conducted by Abel, Mittleman, and Becker (1985), 60 percent of convicted child molesters showed no evidence of psychopathology or psychosis. An earlier study conducted by Abel, Becker, and Skinner (1980), focusing on a sample of rapists, found that only 5 percent demonstrated signs of being psychotic during the commission of their crime. Some studies, as Levenson et al. (2007) emphasize indicate a higher prevalence of mood disorders among sex offenders, but more common were disorders such as ADHD, substance abuse disorders, and anxiety disorders—illnesses more prevalent in the general population and not necessarily linked to violence (see e.g., Kafka & Hennen, 2002). One national study of incarcerated offenders also provides little evidence that most sex offenders are mentally ill. For example, Ditton (1999) reported that 12 percent of the mentally ill offenders incarcerated in state prisons had committed a sex offense. Notably, this estimate is comparable to rates of mental illness for other violent crimes (the percentage of mentally ill offenders presented parenthetically): homicide offenses (13 percent), robbery (13 percent), and assault (11 percent). More precisely, major mental illness has not been detected as a predictor of sexually re-offending (see for a review, Hanson & Morton-Bourgon, 2004).

Civil commitment data provide the most compelling evidence against the belief that sexual offending is driven by mental illness. Specifically, these data indicate that an extremely small number of sex offenders are assessed by states or the federal government as having a mental illness prior to their release from prison. Approximately 4,249 rapists, pedophiles, and other sex offenders nationwide are currently detained in civil commitment centers (Jackson, Schneider, & Travia, 2010). Comparatively, using the registered sex offender population as a proxy for all known sex offenders (n=740,000; National Center for Missing and Exploited Children, 2012), this statistic indicates that less than one percent of sex offenders nationally have been determined to present a risk of reoffending due to an underlying mental illness.

The origins of this myth may lie, once again, in the sensationalism of unusual sex crimes (see e.g., Lancaster, 2011b). That is, per Douard (2008, p. 39), sex offenders are constructed by the media as "mentally disordered and addicted to harmful deviant sexual conduct ... in a way that is different from most violent criminals groups." To illustrate, there exists disproportionate attention to particularly gruesome sex crimes, such as those involving sexualized homicide, sadistic offenders, and children. As a result, the myth that sex offenders constitute a group of mentally ill offenders may be part of a larger mythology regarding the etiology of sexual offending perpetuated by the media. We move now toward reviewing a prominent myth concerning other factors that may contribute to sexual offending.

Myth 6: Most sex offenders were sexually abused as children.

The perception that prior sexual victimization is linked with offending constitutes a longstanding belief regarding sex crime. Some policymakers attribute past sexual abuse as a catalyst for subsequent sex offending later in life (Sample & Kadleck, 2008). Most Americans attribute this factor to increase the likelihood of sexual offending. Per one study, on average, Americans estimated that nearly two-thirds of sex offenders had been sexually abused as children (Levenson et al., 2007). Another investigation found an overwhelming majority of Americans (84 percent) agreed with the statement that "juvenile sex offenders typically are victims of child sexual abuse and grow up to be adult sex offenders" (Katz-Schiavone, Levenson, & Ackerman, 2008, p. 300; see also Fortney et al., 2007).

It is important to emphasize, as Jespersen, Lalumière, and Seto (2009, p. 190) conclude in a review, that "not all sex offenders have a history of sexual abuse, so sexual abuse history is neither a sufficient nor a necessary condition for adult sexual offending." Having said that, the sexual abuse-abuser relationship is complex and not fully understood. That is, although scholarship does not support the broad view that most sex offenders were sexually abused as children, there is some evidence of an association between prior abuse and subsequent offending. However, other factors may moderate this relationship. Below, highlights from this body of research are outlined.

First, extant studies have examined the prevalence of prior sexual abuse victimization among adult sex offenders. One early review examined 25 studies (retrospective studies, prospective studies, and research reviews) and estimated a range of sexual victimization prevalence of 3 to 29 percent among sex offenders (U.S. General Accounting Office, 1996). The report noted the limitations in studies that have used a retrospective design. In short, such methods typically ask adult offenders to recall their prior abuse histories as children. Retrospective studies thus are subject to recall bias; additionally, reports of abuse from offenders typically are not verifiable. In contrast, prospective designs follow individuals from childhood to adulthood. These designs are methodologically sounder for establishing cause and effect than retrospective studies. However, the report found that collectively the studies in their review were equivocal in establishing a causal link between prior sexual abuse victimization and subsequent offending (U.S. General Accounting Office, 1996).

A later meta-analysis conducted by Jespersen and her colleagues (2009) that examined 24 studies of sex offenders (n=1,037) and non-sex offenders (n=1,762) provides stronger support for the sexual abuse-offender link. It found a sexual abuse history prevalence rate of approximately 41 percent among sex offenders. Comparatively, offenders convicted of non-sex crimes evinced substantially lower sexual victimization rates (18 percent). Within the sexual offender population, there was a significantly lower prevalence of sexual abuse history among sex offenders against adults compared to sex offenders against children. At the same time, the review highlights important caveats.

First, extant research indicates that sexual abuse history is not predictive of sexual recidivism, but it appears most likely to affect the onset of offending. Not least, as Jespersen and her colleagues (2009) conclude, "the large majority of sexually abused children do not go on to offend, so individual differences must play a role in the association between sexual abuse history and later sexual offending … [additionally] not all sex offenders have a history of sexual abuse" (p. 190, citations omitted). Put differently, while it does appear that prior sexual abuse history may be linked with offending, this relationship is moderated by individual characteristics of offenders. At the same time, most sexually abused children will not go on to sexually abuse others as adults.

The belief that most sexual offenders have been prior victims of child sexual abuse is a distorted perception, even though some evidence indicates a greater prevalence of sexual abuse among sex offenders compared to non-sex offenders. The distortion involves degree. That is, most sex offenders, as recent statistics demonstrate (Jespersen et al., 2009), do not have childhood sexual abuse histories. But, it is true that as a group, sex offenders are more likely to report being prior sex abuse victims than non-sex offenders. At the same time, differences exist within sex offenders. Those who have sexually abused children are significantly more likely to report sexual abuse victimization than those who offend against adults (Jespersen et al., 2009). However, a large segment of the public endorses the view most sex offenders were prior victims of childhood sexual abuse (Fortney et al., 2007; Katz-Schiavone et al., 2008). This perception may flow from societal attempts to explain sex crime. That is, the etiology of sex offending is not fully understood. And so, the belief that "violence begets violence" is a logical inference toward understanding factors that may contribute to sexual offending. Indeed, Salter (2003) argues further that it is "strangely comforting" to believe because "if offenders are just victims, then no one has to face the reality … that there are people out there who prey on others for reasons we simply don't understand" (p. 74). Even so, empirical evidence suggests that experiencing prior sexual abuse is not a direct risk factor for offending among most sex offenders. A final myth centered on sex offenders is discussed below.

Myth 7: Youth rarely commit sex offenses.

Before moving on to discuss myths related to sex crime policy, it is important to emphasize one last misperception about sex offenders, particularly regarding their age. To illustrate, the prototypical image of a sex offender — popularized by the media — often portrays an adult who is significantly older than his or her victims. Finkelhor, Ormrod, and Chaffin (2009, p. 1) caution however that although those who sexually offend against children are typically described as "'pedophiles' or 'predators' and thought of as adults, it is important to understand that a substantial portion of these offenses are committed by other minors who do not fit the image of such terms."

Indeed, NIBRS statistics indicate that adolescents and children commit nearly 36 percent of all sex crimes (Finkelhor, Ormrod et al., 2009). In disaggregating this percentage, approximately 16 percent of all arrests for forcible rape involved juvenile offenders. Ten percent of "other" sexual offenses (e.g., sexual assault, molestation) for any given year are committed by minors (Snyder & Sickmund, 2006). Although a majority of juvenile sex offenders are teen-agers, approximately 16 percent are younger than age 12 (Finkelhor, Ormrod et al., 2009). In addition, juvenile sex offenders are most often males. National data of juvenile crime patterns suggest, for instance, that on average males comprise 98 percent of arrests for rape offenses and 91 percent of arrests for "other" sex offenses (Snyder & Sickmund, 2006). Victims are typically other minors or younger peers. For instance, Finkelhor, Ormrod, and colleagues (2009) in their national study report that the proportion of victims younger than the age of 12 is nearly 60 percent for juvenile sex offenders, compared with only 39 percent for adult sex offenders. Similar to patterns of adult perpetrated sex crime, in most instances, victims know their offenders. National data suggest that only 3 percent of juvenile sex crime cases involve a stranger offender. Compared to adults, however, juvenile sex offenders were somewhat more likely to victimize acquaintances (63 percent versus 55 percent). At the same time, slightly fewer juvenile offenders victimized family members compared to adult offenders (25 percent versus 32 percent). Victims of sex crimes involving juvenile offenders are overwhelmingly female (79 percent). However, this percentage is slightly less than estimates for adult perpetrated sex crimes (88 percent). Thus, juvenile sex offenders target male victims at a higher frequency than adult sex offenders. Juveniles are also more likely to commit sodomy and molestation offenses compared to adults (61.9 percent versus 48.6 percent).

Table 5.2. Myths (and Facts) about Sex Offenders

Myth	Fact
Most sex offenders will reoffend.	Broadly, sex offenders have relatively low levels of general recidivism, and lower than assumed levels of sexual recidivism. The prevalence of recidivism, however, varies by offender type.
Most sex offenders are mentally ill.	Little evidence exists to support the view that a majority of sex offenders have mental illness. Moreover, a small number of sex offenders (less than one percent) are civilly committed in the U.S., indicating that few meet the legal definition of being mentally ill.
Most sex offenders were sexually abused as children.	Compared to non-sex offenders, a greater number of sex offenders report histories of prior sex abuse victimization. Having said that, a majority of sex offenders (nearly 60 percent) have no such history. At the same time, most sexually abused children do not progress to committing sex offenses as adults. Thus, experiencing prior sexual victimization is not a direct risk factor for offending.
Youth rarely commit sex offenses.	Close to 40 percent of all sex crimes are perpetrated by juvenile offenders. Juvenile sex offenders share some similarities with adults, but differences also exist between the two offender groups.

Other distinctions are evident between juvenile and adult sex crimes. Sex offenses involving multiple perpetrators are significantly more prevalent for the former. To illustrate, NIBRS data indicate that approximately one-quarter of all offenses committed by juvenile sex offenders involve more than one perpetrator. In contrast, only 14 percent of sex offenses committed by adults involve multiple offenders per Finkelhor, Ormrod et al. (2009). Differences also exist within location of the crime. Finkelhor, Ormrod et al. (2009) report that fewer juvenile-perpetrated sex offenses are committed in the residence or home (69 percent) compared to adult-perpetrated crimes (80 percent). In contrast, a substantially higher number of sex offenses committed by juveniles take place in a school or college (12 percent) compared to adult sex offenses (2 percent). Similar estimates are evident for both groups in the remaining locations (i.e., "store/building," "outside," and "other/unknown"). Finally, the timing of day of offenses varies across juvenile and adult sex crimes. Per Finkehor, Ormrod et al.'s (2009) estimates, juvenile sex offenses are more likely than adult perpetrated sex offenses to occur in the afternoon (43 percent versus 37 percent, respectively). In contrast, adult sex offenses more typically occur in the evening or at night compared to juvenile offenses (38 percent versus 30 percent, respectively).

To summarize, juvenile sex offenders comprise a substantial percentage of all sex offenders. At the same time, the juvenile sex offender population is distinct from the adult offender population across a range of characteristics, indicating again, the substantial heterogeneity across offender "types." Thus, the perception that nearly all sex offenses are committed by "dirty old men" (see e.g., Fuselier et al., 2002, p. 272) is a distorted view that neglects the substantial number of offenses committed by minors, particularly against other young people. In line with the previously discussed myths, it may have originated from the media portrayal of sex offenders as typically older and victims as very young children (Wilson, McWhinnie, Picheca, Prinzo, & Cortoni, 2007). Table 5.2 reviews myths related to sex offenders. Next, we discuss prominent myths regarding sex crime policy and offender management.

Sex Crime Policy

Myth 8: Sex offender registries are effective.

We will discuss registry laws in greater depth in Chapters 7 and 8. For now, the policies can be easily summarized. Broadly, the federal government has required all states to develop and implement procedures to notify the public regarding released sex offenders. Nearly all registries are available online and include information about registrants' addresses, pictures, and other identifying information (Mancini et al., 2013). Judging by the substantial levels of policy support for these laws it appears that most Americans believe they effectively prevent sexual recidivism. To illustrate, on average, nearly 90 percent of the public endorses support for registry laws (see e.g., Kernsmith, Craun, & Foster, 2009; Levenson et al., 2007). At the same time, policymakers purport that registry and notification laws are needed because they promote public safety via increased surveillance of released sex offenders; indeed, the U.S. Supreme Court has upheld such measures, namely agreeing with lawmakers that such laws serve to protect the public from an especially dangerous population (see e.g., *Connecticut Department of Public Safety vs. Doe*, 2003).

Few studies, however, have reported significant crime-reducing effects of registry and community notification laws. For example, one study examined sex crime rates in the years before and after the implementation of Megan's Law (1985–2005) in New Jersey (Zgoba et al., 2008). Trend analysis of the data revealed that the registry law had no effect on reductions of sex offense rates in the state. That is, although reductions in sexual offending were observed during the study period, the implementation of Megan's Law occurred *after* sex offense rates began to decline. As a result, the researchers concluded that it could not be causally linked to the initial reduction of sex crimes in the state. Additionally, Zgoba and her colleagues (2008), in a separate analysis of the same study, found no evidence that Megan's Law reduced the recidivism odds of released sex offenders living in New Jersey.

In another, larger scale investigation, Vásquez and his colleagues (2008) examined sex crimes across ten states from 1990 to 2000, or before and after the enactment of Megan's Law in the U.S. Study results indicate that for most states, the registry law produced no statistically significant effect on rates of sex crime. Notably, the findings of Zgoba et al. (2008) and Vásquez et al. (2008) have been replicated across other studies (see e.g., Sandler, Freeman, & Socia, 2008; more recently see, Ackerman, Sacks, & Greenberg, 2012).

In contrast, some evidence indicates the crime-reducing potential of registry laws but with caveats. To illustrate, one study examined whether registry laws and community notification affected sex crime rates of adult offenders in South Carolina using time series data (Letourneau, Levenson et al., 2010). Specifically, Letourneau, Levenson, and colleagues (2010) assessed whether adult arrests for sexual offenses declined after the registry and notification policy was enacted in the state. Results indicate that the law was associated with an approximately 11 percent reduction in first-time sex crime arrests in the post-implementation period (1995–2005) relative to the pre-registry/notification period (1990–1994). Their findings however do not extend to non-sex offenses—suggesting that the deterrent effect is more likely the result of specific sex crime measures implemented in the state. Even so, their results do not show that the law affects recidivist, or repeat sex offenses. Furthermore, these significant findings were not demonstrated in a separate study examining sex offenses involving juvenile sex offenders in the same state (Letourneau, Bandyopadhyay, Armstrong, & Sinha, 2010). Put differently, the registry law had no statistically significant effect of sex offenses committed by minor offenders.

Notwithstanding the one positive effect of the registry law in deterring first-time (but not recidivist) offenses identified by Letourneau, Levenson et al. (2010), most studies have demonstrated virtually no deterrent effect of registry and community notification laws. Some scholars attribute these largely null findings to flaws in the implementation of the laws. For instance, the main presumption driving registry laws is that the general public will a) be aware of sex offenders living in the community, and b) implement protective behavior to reduce the risk of sexual victimization. Indeed, such laws take a "capable guardianship" theoretical rationale. Simply put, their efficacy depends on the public use of information and the extent to which individuals take precautions, upon learning about sex offenders living in their neighborhoods. Based on the available evidence, these presumptions are not well supported. To illustrate, most studies have shown that few Americans report accessing sex offender registries (see, most recently, Mancini, in press). Additionally, of the small sub-sample of individuals who access the registries, most Americans do not in turn, implement precautions that would theoretically reduce their likelihood of sexual victimization. For instance, Anderson and Sample (2008) demonstrate that in their study, that of a relatively small percentage of respondents who reported using the registry in the past (35 percent of all respondents), only 38 percent then incorporated preventive action (such as installing an alarm system, watching children more closely). As a result, the absence of widespread "consumer" use may explain the majority of studies showing null effects of registry and community notification laws.

Despite empirical evidence indicating little practical utility of registries, most Americans strongly support their use to track and monitor released sex offenders. Such views may have originated from the widespread implementation of such laws over a relatively short period of time; and the concomitant perception that if laws are enacted, they *must* be effective in reducing crime. Still, given the available evidence, the belief that such laws are effective constitutes a myth regarding registry procedures. This of course does not mean that such laws have little potential to be effective. Put differently, when properly implemented and with increased use by the public they very well may be. Even so, public views regarding registry effectiveness run counter to extant research showing few significant effects of such laws on sexual offending. In a similar direction, misperceptions exist about other prominent sex crime laws, such as the efficacy of residence restrictions. We turn now to a discussion about them.

Myth 9: Residence restrictions are effective in reducing sex crimes against children.

Along with registry laws, residence restriction policies are examined in greater detail later in the text. For now, to provide context for our discussion about sex crime myths, such laws are briefly described. Over the last twenty years, states have incorporated laws that prohibit convicted sex offenders from living near certain locations where children frequent, such as schools, bus stops, playgrounds, and day care centers. Indeed, as a direct indicator of their popularity, over thirty states have designed and implemented residence restrictions for sex offenders (Mancini et al., 2013). On average, restrictions range from 500 feet to 2,000 feet. Additionally, some states permit counties to enact additional prohibitions beyond the state's boundary. The public overwhelmingly endorses such legislation. Mancini, Shields, Mears, and Beaver (2010) in a study of Florida residents found nearly 82 percent of the public supported the use of residence restrictions. One other study conducted in Florida indicates strong support for such legislation (see e.g.,

Levenson et al., 2007). Not least, a study conducted by Comartin, Kernsmith, and Kernsmith (2009) reveals that on average, over 80 percent of Michigan residents support laws restricting sex offenders from living near schools and day care centers and other locations frequented by children.

Despite the overwhelming support for residence restrictions, the extent to which such legislation prevents sexual victimization, particularly among children, remains questionable. To be sure, research examining the effectiveness of residence restrictions is sorely lacking (see e.g., Socia, 2012). Thus, impact evaluations that investigate how such prohibitions affect sexual offending across a range of jurisdictions are needed. Having said that, the relatively small knowledge base that currently exists provides little indication that residence restrictions increase public safety. Thus, given the current state of evidence endorsing the belief that such laws are effective constitutes a myth regarding the efficacy of sex crime laws. Below, the highlights from extant research investigating residence restrictions are mentioned.

With few exceptions, residence restriction statutes aim to protect child victims of sex crime. For example, most residence restriction laws prohibit convicted sex offenders from residing in locations proximate to places children congregate. As a result, such laws are presumed to preclude opportunities to offend by reducing the potential for sex offenders to target and abuse child victims. Most studies, however, have demonstrated no statistically significant effect of residence restrictions on sexual offending. In particular, some research has determined the extent to which sex offenders "self-select" to live near places children frequent. Findings from two state studies examining sex offenders living in Colorado (Colorado Department of Public Safety, 2004) and Minnesota (Minnesota Department of Corrections, 2003) found no statistically significant relationship between recidivist sex crimes and residence of sex offenders. A separate study conducted in Iowa revealed that the statewide residence restriction law had no effect on sex crimes committed against minors in the state (Blood, Watson, & Stageberg, 2008).

Other studies have evaluated the actual impacts of the law in preventing sex crimes that occur near places outlined in residence prohibitions. For example, one study examining the effect of Florida's residence restriction boundaries used mapping analysis to determine if sex offenders who lived within 1,000 feet to 2,500 feet of schools or daycare centers (places outlined in Florida's residence prohibition) had higher odds of sexually reoffending than those who lived further away (Zandbergen, Levenson, & Hart, 2010). Their results showed no effect of the law. Sex offenders who lived further away from such locations were just as likely to reoffend against a minor victim as those who were required to abide by the prohibition. Thus, as underscored by Zandbergen et al.'s (2010) findings residence of sex offenders had little impact on their likelihood of recidivism against child victims.

Another study also focused on Florida's residence law. In particular, this investigation tested whether a larger municipal-level restriction implemented in Jacksonville, Florida (from 1,000 feet to 2,500 feet) reduced sexual offending (Nobles, Levenson, & Youstin, 2012). Simply, it aimed to address whether a larger boundary is more effective than a smaller one in reducing sex crime. The study addressed three research questions. First, does the larger residence boundary affect the extent of sexual recidivism in the city? Second, is the implementation of the boundary restriction associated with a decrease in reports of sex crime in Jacksonville? Third, does the law deter convicted sex offenders? Results from Nobles and colleagues' (2012) analysis reveal largely null effects of the ordinance. That is, in response to question one, no difference in sex offenses or recidivist (i.e., repeat) offenses was observed. At the same time in addressing question two, the city's sex crime trends before and after the implementation of the increased boundary were not markedly different. Finally, in line with question three, the timing of the law was not correlated with changes in arrests among individual offenders.

Another recent analysis investigated a residence restriction enacted in New York. Socia (2012) advanced scholarship by disaggregating offenses involving minor and adult victims. Specifically, he tested whether the restrictions were correlated with rates of recidivistic (or repeat) sex crime arrests that included child and adult victims. Additionally, his analysis also determined whether the boundary restrictions affect rates of non-recidivistic arrests for sex crimes involving children and adult victims. In contrast to the intent of the law, Socia's (2012) findings demonstrate that the prohibitions did not reduce recidivistic sex crimes involving child victims. However, when focusing on adult victimization, Socia's (2012) study uncovered a positive effect of the law. Put differently, only nonrecidivistic sex crimes (i.e., first-time offenses) involving adult victims declined when a residence restriction was adopted. Socia (2012, p. 628) contends that notwithstanding replication of his results, such laws may produce general deterrent effects, but cautions against making firm conclusions as "unfortunately, it still remains unclear as to exactly why residence restrictions were associated with significantly decreased arrest rates for sex crimes involving adult victims and not for those involving child victims." More precisely, given the intent of the law, specifically, the "child-centered" areas outlined in most residence restrictions, it is striking that such laws would reduce first-time sex crimes against adults but not at all affect offenses committed against child victims.

Across most states, residence restriction laws are clearly a preferred policy response toward sex offender management. At the same time, the public strongly favors such prohibitions. Their support likely stems from the assumption that such laws are effective in protecting potential victims, particularly child victims against offenders who may target them at certain locations. Notwithstanding their popularity, extant research casts doubt on the presumption that such laws effectively reduce the sexual victimization of minors. Indeed, most studies reveal no effect of the law (see, e.g., Nobles et al., 2012; Zandbergen et al., 2010). Findings from one study (Socia, 2012) indicate a positive effect of residence restriction laws, but only for first-time offenses involving adult victims. Accordingly, the potential exists for residence restriction laws to produce general deterrent effects. Research does not, however, support the view that they work as intended. Put differently, no extant research has revealed that recidivist sex crimes against minors decline as a result of the implementation of residence restrictions. We now turn to our final myth which centers on the belief that treatment is ineffective for sex offenders.

Myth 10: Treatment is ineffective in reducing sexual recidivism.

Although policymakers and the public overwhelmingly support "get tough" reforms to address sex offending, significantly less optimism is directed toward treatment efforts. For instance, in their study of state lawmakers, Sample and Kadleck (2008, p. 49) observed that "a large majority" perceived sex offenders as "compulsive in their behavior" and that "none believed that a cure [to end sex offending] was possible." The public appears equally pessimistic in their views toward sex offender rehabilitation. In a recent national study, Mancini (in press) determined that nearly three-quarters of the public believe sex offenders cannot be sufficiently rehabilitated to the extent that they no longer threatened children. Concomitantly, most Americans (85 percent) perceive sex offenders as significantly less amenable to treatment efforts compared to other serious non-sex offenders.

Does this assessment, however, accord with scholarship on treatment effects? The short answer is "no." Broadly, most studies indicate that treated sex offenders are significantly less likely to sexually reoffend compared to those who receive no treatment (for reviews, see e.g., Hanson & Bussière, 1998; Lösel & Schmucker, 2005). Certainly, there are caveats to this research. That is, not all treatment is equally effective in reducing sex offending. And, given the wide heterogeneity within the sex offender population, not all offenders experience similar benefits of treatment. Even so, the presumption that treatment is simply ineffective for most sex offenders constitutes a distorted perception. In what follows, extant research centered on sex offender treatment interventions is highlighted.

In a large-scale study, Lösel and Schmucker (2005) used meta-analysis to examine results from extant sex offender treatment studies (n=69) published in five languages and containing 80 independent comparisons between treated and untreated offenders. The researchers identified seven separate categories of treatment across these studies (i.e., "cognitive-behavioral," "classic behavioral," "insight-oriented," "therapeutic community," "other psychological, unclear," "hormonal medication," and "surgical castration"). On average, treated offenders showed six percentage points, or 37 percent less sexual recidivism than those offenders who did not receive treatment. Specifically, organic treatments such as surgical castration and hormonal medication were most effective in reducing sexual recidivism. Per the psychosocial treatment category, cognitive behavioral therapy was the most promising intervention. The other treatment methods were significantly less effective methods to treat sex offenders (see also, Schmucker & Lösel, 2008). One later but smaller analysis (n=23 studies) conducted by Hanson, Bourgon, Helmus, and Hodgson (2009) reported a similar estimate of treatment effects. In their study, Hanson et al. (2009) found that treated offenders on average were significantly less likely to sexually reoffend than controls (10.9 percent versus 19.2 percent, respectively).

Notably, Lösel and Schmucker's (2005) and Hanson et al.'s (2009) results replicated those found in an earlier study conducted by Gallagher, Wilson, Hirschfield, Coggeshall, and MacKenzie (1999). In that investigation, Gallagher and her colleagues (1999) synthesized the results of 25 studies to determine whether treatment intervention affects sexual offending. Results from their review indicate that treated offenders, on average, were less likely to reoffend compared to non-treated controls. Additionally, cognitive-behavioral therapy emerged as the most effective intervention.

One other meta-analysis conducted Hanson and Bussière (1998) bears emphasizing. In one of the most frequently cited studies examining sex offending and correlates of re-cidivism, Hanson and Bussière (1998) analyzed the results of 61 studies that included data on 23,393 offenders. Treatment effects emerged as statistically significant factors in predicting sexual recidivism. Specifically, offenders who failed to complete treatment (not disaggregated by type of intervention) were at "moderate" risk for sexually reoffending compared to those who completed treatment.

Additionally, some studies have assessed whether treatment interventions received in prison versus in the community affect the likelihood of reoffending. For example, Polizzi, MacKenzie, and Hickman (1999) analyzed the results of 21 sex offender prison and non-prison based treatment programs. Eight studies were excluded because they were not deemed to be scientifically rigorous (e.g., they did not control for other potential confounding factors, did not include a control group). Of the remaining studies, results indicate that non-prison-based sex offender treatment programs incorporating cognitive-behavioral treatment methods are most effective in reducing the likelihood of a new sex offense. In contrast, prison-based programs were less effective in reducing sexual reoffending.

Finally, some studies have investigated treatment effects by offender type. Hanson and his colleagues (2009) in their meta-analysis found that treatment served to reduce sexual

Table 5.3. Myths (and Facts) about Sex Crime Policy

Myth	Fact
Sex offender registries are effective.	Little evidence exists that indicates registries decrease recidivist sexual offenses. At the same time, some evidence indicates a reduction in sex offenses involving first-time offenders.
Residence restrictions are effective in reducing sex crimes against children.	Overall, most evaluations suggest null effects of residence boundaries in reducing sexual offenses, particularly for child sexual abuse. Having said that, some extant research indicates a significant impact of residence restrictions in reducing sex offenses involving adult victims and first-time offenders.
Treatment is ineffective in reducing sexual recidivism.	Overall, most studies demonstrate a significant reduction in sexual recidivism among treated sex offenders. To be sure, variation exists in the efficacy of treatment interventions. Concomitantly, variation exists in the success of treatment efforts for specific sex offender sub-types.

offending in both adult and juvenile sex offenders. That is, no statistically significant differences emerged between adult and juvenile sex offenders in their exposure to treatment. One other large study (n=7,275) followed offenders who participated in a cognitive-behavioral treatment program to assess reoffending rates and also whether differences existed between offender types (Maletzky & Steinhauser, 2002). In determining a new sex offense, the study utilized official records (arrest reports) and also self-reports. Analysis revealed the following about treatment effects for specific sub-types of offenders: "child molesters, with female victims" (i.e., men who molested at most two female children in a situational context), "child molesters, with male victims" (i.e., men who molested at most one male child), "heterosexual pedophiles" (i.e., men who molested more than one female child and showed a preference for female children or a predatory style of offending), and "exhibitionists" (i.e., men who exposed themselves and did not molest children or rape) had the lowest odds of sexually reoffending after treatment (6.3 percent, 9.4 percent, 9.7 percent, and 13.5 percent, respectively). "Rapists" (i.e., men who raped and did not molest children or expose themselves) and "homosexual pedophiles" (i.e., men who molested more than one male child and showed a preference for male children or a predatory style of offending) had comparatively higher recidivism rates after treatment than the other sub-types (21.2 percent versus 16.3 percent, respectively).

To summarize, prior research indicates that policymakers and a majority of Americans are pessimistic concerning treatment efforts for sex offenders. Yet, the belief that treatment is ineffective for sex offenders reflects a view that runs counter to a substantial body of scholarship on sexual offending. On average, as shown by several studies, treated sex offenders are less likely to recidivate than offenders who receive no treatment. To be clear, variation exists in treatment effects. That is to say not all treatment interventions are equally effective, and not all sex offenders will benefit from treatment. Table 5.3 summarizes myths about sex crime policy discussed in this chapter.

Chapter Summary

This chapter reviewed a range of distorted perceptions about sexual offending that run counter to a larger body of scholarship centered on understanding the etiology of sexual offending and sex crime. In particular, ten myths, across three broad domains — trends and characteristics of sexual offenses, sex offenders, and sex crime policy — were examined. To be sure, that is not to say that some myths are absolutely incorrect. More precisely, there are important nuances to discussions and debates about sexual offending that the identified myths overlook. In turn, to the extent that myths guide the development of sex crime laws, the greater the concern that such efforts will be ineffective in preventing sexual violence.

Additional citations to other work that has explored sex crime myths are recommended below. Chapter 6 continues with the focus on societal reactions to sex crime by examining public opinion toward sex offenders and sex crime policy.

Additional Suggested Readings

Chaffin, M. (2008). Our minds are made up — Don't confuse us with the facts: Commentary on policies concerning children with sexual behavior problems and juvenile sex offenders. *Child Maltreatment, 13*, 110–121.

Dowler, K. (2006). Sex, lies, and videotape: The presentation of sex crime in local television news. *Journal of Criminal Justice, 34*, 383–392.

Moscowitz, L., & Duvall, S. S. (2011). "Every parent's worst nightmare": Myths of child abductions in U.S. news. *Journal of Children and Media, 5*, 147–163.

Robinson, L. O. (2003). Sex offender management. *Annals of the New York Academy of Sciences, 989*, 1–7.

Wright, R. G. (Ed.). (2009). *Sex offender laws: Failed policies, new directions.* New York: Springer.

Chapter 6

Public Attitudes toward Sex Offenders

Chapter Introduction

This chapter examines public opinion about sex crime. This focus has become critically important in understanding the nation's policy response to sexual offending. As discussed earlier in the text, there was not a significant increase in reports of sexual violence during the 1990s — the period of the most intense policy attention toward sex offenders. Thus, contrary to what might be expected, an actual increase in sex offending did not precede an unprecedented shift in sex offender management. Accordingly, scholars have posited that other factors — distinct from objective indicators of sex crime — may have sparked the "tough on sex crime" movement. One of these factors has been increased public attention toward sexual offenses. For example, research has found that Americans rank responding to sexual violence as a top priority for the criminal justice system (Mears et al., 2008). In turn, policymakers appear to have responded to the public's concern. As but one example, a 2008 study published by the federally funded Center for Sex Offender Management (CSOM, 2008, p. 1) reported that when asked to list their top ten public policy concerns, state legislators rated "sex offenders and sexual predators" as "number 5." Notably, concern about sex offenders ranked higher than such social and health issues as "energy and environment," "the minimum wage," "higher education reform," "privacy," and "obesity." What this indicates is that the public prioritizes sex offender management as an important crime policy concern. As a result, policymakers have responded by enacting an array of diverse laws aimed at preventing sexual violence.

Beginning largely in the 1990s, scholars began to track and monitor public views about sex crime and offending. In particular, increasing empirical attention has been directed toward determining policy support for sex crime initiatives, public awareness and use of registry and community notification, perceptions of offenders and sex crime, and divides in public opinion. Despite this emphasis in criminal justice, scholars have yet to produce a systematic body of research that examines public opinion about sex crime. Consequently, what is known about public attitudes toward sexual offending remains an underdeveloped literature. Thus, the objective of this chapter is to assist with understanding the prominent role of public opinion in discussions and debates about sexual offending. What follows below is a review of extant research, and also an assessment of work that needs to be conducted to better understand public views toward sex crime, offenders, and sex offender management.

Policy Support for Sex Offender Laws

Several studies have determined the public's level of support for various sex crime initiatives. For instance, studies have examined public support for sex offender registries and notification laws (Kernsmith, Craun et al., 2009; Phillips, 1998), residence restrictions (Schiavone & Jeglic, 2009), "get tough" child pornography laws (Mears, Mancini, Gertz, & Bratton, 2008), supervised monitoring (Button, Tewksbury, Mustaine, & Payne, 2013), civil commitment (Pickett, Mears, Stewart, & Gertz, in press), sanctions aligned with reform such as chemical castration and treatment efforts (Levenson et al., 2007), and the death penalty (Mancini & Mears, 2010). This research has demonstrated that the public overwhelmingly supports laws designed to address sexual offending. Studies examining public support for these specific initiatives are discussed below.

Registry/Notification Policies

Registry laws garner significant policy support. To illustrate, in a study examining Melbourne, Florida residents' perceptions about a range of sex offender sanctions (n=193), Levenson et al. (2007) reported that the greatest support was found for registry laws that list the names and provide photos of sex offenders (95 percent) and community notification laws (83 percent). Similar findings have been reported in different studies examining policy support among other populations, with some exceptions.

To illustrate, Kernsmith, Craun et al. (2009) in a sample of Michigan residents (n=733) were among the first researchers to examine public support for registering specific types of sex offenders. Similar to Levenson et al.'s (2007) study, overwhelming majorities of the public supported efforts to register sex offenders (see also, Phillips, 1998; Proctor, Badzinski, & Johnson, 2002). However, levels of support were contingent on the type of offender. The greatest support (97 percent) was found for registering "pedophiles" and "incest offenders." The public was least willing to extend registry laws to "spousal rapists" (71 percent) and "statutory rapists" (65 percent). This finding reflects that the public views sex offenders who target children as a more dangerous population in need of greater restrictions.

In a different study, Beck and Boys (in press) explored public attitudes toward registry requirements for statutory rapists. Using a sample of California and Wisconsin residents (n=338), they determined that little public support exists for extending registry requirements to statutory rape offenders. Specifically, overwhelming majorities from both states (approximately 95 percent of residents) felt that if teen-agers, under the age of consent, engage in consenting sexual acts, then the charge should only be a misdemeanor offense, regardless of whether the two teens were the same age. Respondents were also unanimous in their views about sex offender registration. An overwhelming majority in both states (Wisconsin=96.8 percent and California=94 percent) would not support sex offender registration in such instances.

Residence Restriction Laws

Significantly less attention has been directed toward documenting policy support beyond registries and notification laws. However, at least one study examined Floridians' support for residence restriction laws. In that study, Mancini et al. (2010) reported that most Florida residents saw merit in the law. That is, four out of five Floridians endorsed support for policies that restrict where convicted sex offenders can live upon release (see also, Schiavone & Jeglic, 2009). In another study, that also examined Florida residents, Levenson et al. (2007) found somewhat less, but still majority support for residence restriction laws (58 percent). One last study examined Michigan respondents' support for residence boundaries. Comartin and colleagues (2009) reported high levels of support for laws prohibiting sex offenders from living near schools and day cares (88 percent) and other places children frequent (83 percent).

Penalties for Child Pornography Crimes

Given the increasingly prominent emphasis on prosecuting child pornography offenders in the U.S., scholars have begun investigating public approval for pornography related sanctions. Once again, the public views these reforms favorably. For instance, Mears and colleagues (2008), relying on national data, established that the public overwhelmingly supports incarcerating non-contact sex offenders convicted of distributing (89 percent) and accessing (68 percent) child pornography (for similar results using a Canadian university college sample, see Lam, Mitchell, & Seto, 2010). As these results indicate, the public considers the severity of the offense before ascribing punishment. Thus, most Americans perceive accessing pornographic images of children to be less criminal than distributing the media.

Increasing Supervision of Sex Offenders

Some scholars have also assessed public support for efforts to increase supervised monitoring of sex offenders. Button and colleagues (2013) determined levels of public support for GPS monitoring using survey data of Virginia residents. Drawing on a composite measure of support (with items such as "Sex offenders should be placed on GPS or other electronic monitoring as long as they are not in prison"), Button et al. (2013) demonstrated that most respondents held a positive view of GPS procedures. In all, the mean level of public support for GPS monitoring was estimated to be 9.4 (range in values of 3 to 12). In a different study of Florida residents, Levenson et al. (2007) found that 62 percent of the public supported electronic monitoring for convicted sex offenders. Thus, most Americans support efforts to increase monitoring of convicted sex offenders.

Civil Commitment Laws

Relatedly, recent research has also focused on assessing Americans' support for civil commitment laws. In particular, Pickett and his colleagues (in press) asked Florida residents whether they supported efforts to detain sex offenders past their original prison sentence. Their results indicate that most of the public saw merit in the law. To illustrate, respondents were asked the extent to which they endorsed support for a law that would "hold dangerous sex offenders past their sentence" (response options were: 1=strongly oppose to 5=strongly favor). Overall, the average response value, 3.60, indicates that most respondents endorse some to moderate support for civil commitment policies.

Chemical Castration and Sex Offender Treatment

A small handful of studies assessed policy support for other recently implemented laws aligned with reform, such as chemical castration and treatment efforts. Here again, Levenson et al.'s (2007) work is illustrative. Overall, a slight majority of the public (51 percent) endorses support for chemical castration. In a more recent study of Michigan residents Comartin et al. (2009) found less, but a still substantial level of support for castration—approximately 40 percent of the sample expressed approval for it. These differences may derive from measurement. For instance, Levenson et al. (2007) specified the reversible "chemical castration" policy whereas Comartin et al. (2009) relied on a more general indicator of "castration" (which conceivably includes irreversible, physical castration). Even so, a nontrivial percent of Americans, overall, endorses support for castration policies.

At the same time, work also indicates that the public is supportive of treatment efforts. In Levenson et al.'s study, an overwhelming number of respondents also supported treatment efforts in prison (71 percent) and in the community (65 percent). Mears et al. (2008) investigated the extent to which the public was willing to pay for treatment efforts for sex offenders. For instance, a majority of Americans—51 percent—supported a tax increase of at least $25 a year to fund rehabilitation programs for sex offenders. In a study examining UK residents' views, Brown (1999) reported that the public was largely in favor of the development of treatment facilities for sex offenders. For instance, 51 percent of the sample believed sex offender treatment was "a good idea," and nearly all respondents (95 percent) recommended that incarcerated sex offenders receive treatment in prison. At the same time, the public strongly endorsed punishment. That is, 81 percent felt a treatment only approach would be too "soft" of an option. Brown's (1999) findings, along with the scholarship cited above, indicate that public opinion toward crime and justice is nuanced. It simultaneously reflects both punitive and progressive ideals, or as Cullen, Fisher, and Applegate (2000, p. 60) characterize, "the hybrid mission that most Americans believe the correctional system should work vigorously to realize."

Capital Punishment

Majorities of the public are also willing to extend the death penalty—typically a sanction reserved only for homicide offenders—to sex offenders, with some caveats. Using national public opinion data, Mancini and Mears (2010) demonstrated that a majority (albeit slim) of the public (51 percent) favored applying capital punishment to convicted sex offenders who had victimized children. Support, however, was contingent on offender type. To illustrate, only 27 percent of Americans endorsed support for executing offenders convicted of sex crimes against adults. Once again, support is found for the contention that the public perceives child victims as being especially vulnerable and in need of additional protections, and so are particularly supportive of punitive efforts to deal with sex offenders.

Contributors Driving Widespread Support for Sex Crime Policies

Some research has investigated reasons why the public—with few exceptions—overwhelmingly supports sex crime laws. It appears that most Americans believe that the laws are effective in reducing sex crime. To illustrate, Schiavone and Jeglic (2009) using an online message board elicited responses from the public about the efficacy of sex offender laws. Nearly two-thirds of the public believed that residence restriction laws would enhance community safety. Slightly less, but still a majority (54 percent), felt that registry and notification laws resulted in reduced offending. Similarly, in Levenson et al.'s (2007) study, an average of 71 percent of the public endorsed the view that current sex crime reforms are effective in reducing sexual offending. Additionally, as a last example, Brannon, Levenson, Fortney, and Baker (2007) assessed public perceptions of the effectiveness of community notification laws using a Florida sample (n=193). A striking majority—90 percent of the sample—reported that notification laws were effective in preventing sex crime (see also Redlich, 2001). Put differently, evidence exists for the notion that public support for sex crime laws is driven largely by the belief that they can effectively reduce sex crime and future reoffending. Even so, evidence exists for the view that these also represent "symbolic" policies among the public—or, per Anderson, Sample, and Evans (2011, p. 27) those laws passed to "appease public concern without necessarily influencing... behaviors for which they are meant to address." Indeed, Levenson et al. (2007, p. 150) posed to respondents the question of whether they would support sex crime reforms even if "there is no scientific evidence showing that they reduce sexual abuse." Their analysis revealed that nearly half of the public would continue to favor ineffective sex crime laws. At the same time, the public is willing to substantially invest in crime control programs to reduce sexual assault/rape. In a national study, Cohen, Rust, Steen, and Tidd (2004) calculated that public "willingness to pay" (WTP) for sex crime initiatives (on average, $237,000 per sex offense) was higher than willingness to fund programs to prevent other offenses such as burglary ($25,000), serious assault ($70,000), and armed robbery ($232,000).

Accordingly, while there is the impression among the public that sex crime laws are fairly effective in reducing sexual victimization and support for funding such reforms, there is the concomitant and unwavering endorsement of the laws—at least among half of the American population—even if they are shown to be ineffective in preventing sex crime. Table 6.1 summarizes prior research centered on determining public support for sex crime laws.

Public Awareness, Use of Sex Offender Registries and Community Notification, and Protective Action

A smaller strand of literature has examined public awareness and utilization of the federally implemented sex offender registries and community notification procedures. Survey research has also focused on the subsequent protective behavior of citizens after registry use/notification. Recall that these policies emphasize increased capable guardianship in preventing sexual victimization. To a large extent then, as recognized by Anderson and Sample (2008, p. 372), "citizens' actions are expected to augment the public safety afforded by sex offender legislation and law enforcement activities." Thus, determining the extent to which the public is aware of and utilizes them is an important first step in assessing the likely efficacy of the laws.

Table 6.1. Policy Support for Sex Crime Laws

Policy	Prior Research	Sample(s)
Registry/ Notification	• Support ranges from 83 percent (notification) to 95 percent (registries with pictures of offenders; Levenson et al., 2007). • Support varies by offender type; the greatest support has been found for registering "pedophiles" (97 percent) and "incest offenders" (95 percent) and the least for "statutory rapists" (Kernsmith, Craun et al., 2009; see also Beck & Boys, in press).	• Melbourne, FL residents (n=193; Levenson et al., 2007) • MI residents (n=733; Kernsmith, Craun et al., 2009) • WI and CA residents (n=338; Beck & Boys, in press)
Residence Restrictions	• Estimates for approval of residence restrictions range from 58 percent (Levenson et al., 2007) to 82 percent (Mancini et al., 2010); greater support found when specific locations were specified—83 percent ("places children congregate") to 88 percent ("day cares"; Comartin et al., 2009).	• Melbourne, FL residents (n=193; Levenson et al., 2007) • FL residents (n=1,067; Mancini et al., 2010) • MI residents (n=703; Comartin et al., 2009)
Child Pornography Laws	• Overwhelming support found for incarcerating offenders convicted of distribution (89 percent); less, but still majority approval found for accessing child pornography (68 percent; Mears et al., 2008).	• U.S. residents (n=425; Mears et al., 2008)
Supervision Laws	• Broad policy support evident for increased monitoring procedures—nearly 62 percent of the public in favor of GPS (Levenson et al., 2007; see also, Button et al., 2013).	• Melbourne, FL residents (n=193; Levenson et al., 2007) • Norfolk/Virginia Beach, VA residents (n=746; Button et al., 2013)
Civil Commitment	• Most of the public is supportive of civil commitment statutes (average response on a 1 to 5 point scale=3.60; Pickett et al., in press).	• Leon county, FL residents (n=1,693; Pickett et al., in press)
Chemical Castration/ Treatment	• Policy support for chemical castration ranges from 40 percent (Comartin et al., 2009) to 51 percent (Levenson et al., 2007). • More generally, widespread approval of sex offender treatment in prison (71 percent) and the community (65 percent; Levenson et al., 2007; see also Brown, 1999).	• MI residents (n=703; Comartin et al., 2009) • Melbourne, FL residents (n=193; Levenson et al., 2007) • UK residents (n=312; Brown, 1999)
Capital Punishment	• Levels of support for the death penalty are dependent on sex offender "type." Less approval for executing offenders convicted of crimes against adults (27 percent) compared to sex offenders who have abused children (51 percent; Mancini & Mears, 2010).	• U.S. residents (n=1,101; Mancini & Mears, 2010)

Public Awareness of Registries and Use

To illustrate, Craun (2010) used hierarchical linear modeling (HLM) and examined community awareness of convicted sex offenders' residences in a southeastern county in the United States (n=631). Her results indicate that the majority of the public is not knowledgeable about convicted sex offenders' whereabouts. Approximately 70 percent of the residents who lived within a close distance (one-tenth of a mile) of a registered sex offender were unaware of a sex offender's presence.

In a separate study of residents living in Nebraska (n=1,821) Anderson and Sample (2008) examined public awareness of the state's registry and subsequent protective action. They found nearly all Nebraskans (90 percent) reported being aware of the state's sex offender registry. A much smaller proportion—however—approximately 35 percent of the sample—had accessed the state's sex offender registry in the past. Of those respondents who admitted accessing the registry, most endorsed positive views about its potential efficacy. For example, overwhelming majorities reported "feel[ing] family is safer" (87.6 percent) and "personally feel[ing] safer" (88 percent) after using the registries. A smaller proportion of users (38 percent) reported taking some type of preventive action after accessing the registry (e.g., installing an alarm system, monitoring children more closely; p. 383). In another study extending the focus on Nebraskans, Sample, Evans, and Anderson (2011) examined the motivations for accessing the state's sex offender registry. Since registries are premised on an instrumental logic—that is, such policies have been designed and implemented to control what has been seen by policymakers as an especially dangerous and threatening population of offenders—large segments of the public should be motivated primarily by safety concerns to access the registry. Sample et al. (2011) find some support for this notion. Nearly 57 percent of the public reported accessing the registry out of safety concerns. However, the remainder of the public endorsed other reasons for accessing the registry: because of "curiosity or personal interest" (29 percent) or "job obligations" (10 percent). The remaining 4 percent indicated using the registry for "some other reason."

A study conducted by Kernsmith, Comartin, Craun, and Kernsmith (2009) also provides some evidence that social and demographic variation in registry awareness and use is evident. Their results indicate that while most Michigan residents (n=733) report awareness of publicly available sex offender registries (89 percent), only a small proportion (35 percent) had accessed the state's sex offender registry in the past. Predictors of use included younger age, having children, and having been the victim of a sex crime. Notably, those who had accessed the registry in the past were significantly more likely to be aware of sex offenders living in their neighborhoods. Thus, this last finding indicates some support for the notion that particularly vulnerable populations are utilizing the registries and are therefore becoming more knowledgeable about sex offenders' residences. At the same time, Kernsmith, Comartin et al.'s (2009) findings also indicate that only half of the population is taking advantage of a tool designed to prevent sexual victimization. Additionally, given the primary focus on registry awareness and predictors of registry use, their study left open the question of whether registry utilization translates into protective action. We now turn to that literature.

Protective Action

A related focus of sex crime policy research is whether citizens take protective action after registry utilization. Note that this is a critical premise behind sex offender registry and notification laws. Put differently, sexual victimization should decrease as citizens become more knowledgeable about potential offenders and institute protective measures. Extant findings indicate mixed support for this premise. For instance, a recent investigation conducted by Bandy (2011) finds no evidence of citizen protection. In her study of Minneapolis residents (n=407), no statistically significant effect of registry use was observed on protective behaviors. These findings echo results of Anderson and Sample's (2008) study of Nebraskans. To illustrate, in their study, Anderson and Sample (2008) reported that of a relatively small sub-sample of respondents who reported accessing the registry (35 percent of the total sample), only 38 percent reported taking some type of preventive action (e.g., installing an alarm system, monitoring children more closely; p. 383). Two earlier studies also reveal null effects of registry use on the adoption of protective behaviors (Caputo & Brodsky, 2004; Phillips, 1998).

However, some studies have uncovered positive effects of registry utilization and community notification on subsequent protective behaviors. For example, Beck and Travis (2004) examined Hamilton county, Ohio respondents exposed to community notification (n=87) and a control group of uninformed citizens (n=149). Their results indicate that the former (i.e., notified) group was significantly more likely to report adding outside lighting to their homes and becoming familiar with self-defense.

Using the same sample, Beck, Clingermayer, and Travis (2004) further investigated whether perceived risk of victimization might affect the relationship between community notification and self-protective or altruistic behaviors. Results indicate that community notification directly affects altruistic-protective behavior, regardless of one's level of perceived risk of behavior. Community notification, however, only affects self-protective behavior if one perceives a high risk of victimization. Put differently, individuals exposed to community notification are significantly more likely to exhibit protective behaviors toward others. However, the extent to which community notification impacts self-protective measures is contingent on one's level of perceived self-risk of victimization.

In a different study, Anderson, Evans, and Sample (2009) found that registry effects exerted a significant effect on increasing protective behaviors only among certain groups. Women, lower income respondents, those with greater Internet access, and parents were significantly more likely to take preventive action as a result of checking the state's sex offender registry.

Collectively, these findings are notable for underscoring several important points. First, while most Americans are aware of registry and notification policies, only a minority of the public report having accessed them in the past. Second, most registry users convey feeling safer after using them. Third, registry use appears to be motivated by safety concerns, although large swaths of the public also report accessing them for other, non-safety related reasons. Fourth, research has not consistently supported the contention that registry and notification laws spur protective actions. Relatedly and finally, the relationship between prior registry use and protective actions is not direct, but rather is contingent on individual social and demographic characteristics. Table 6.2 reviews the major findings of research examining awareness of registries/notification, utilization, and subsequent protective action among the public.

Perceptions of Offenders and Sex Crime

Public opinion literature centered on sex crime has also investigated views about sex offenders and contributors to sex crime. This area is critical for understanding how the public perceives sex offenders, and also, their assessment of potential contributors to sex

**Table 6.2. Sex Offender Registries/Community
Notification and Protective Action**

Outcome	Prior Research	Sample(s)
Awareness	• Substantially few Americans (30 percent) are aware of convicted sex offenders living in their neighborhood (Craun, 2010). • A majority of the public (nearly 90 percent) is aware of registry laws (Anderson & Sample, 2008; Kernsmith, Comartin et al., 2009).	• Residents from an unnamed city in the Southeast (n=631; Craun, 2010) • NE residents (n=1,821; Anderson & Sample, 2008) • MI residents (n=733; Kernsmith, Comartin et al., 2009)
Use	• Most Americans do not access sex offender registries; utilization estimates range from 35 percent (Anderson & Sample, 2008) to 37 percent (Kernsmith, Comartin et al., 2009).	• NE residents (n=1,821; Anderson & Sample, 2008) • MI residents (n=733; Kernsmith, Comartin et al., 2009)
Protective Action	• Inconsistent support exists for the notion that registry and notification laws spur protective action; Bandy (2011) discovered null effects of the laws on increasing protective action, whereas Beck and Travis (2004) and Beck et al. (2004) report that notified respondents are more likely than non-notified residents to take protective action.	• Minneapolis, MN residents (n=407; Bandy, 2011) • Hamilton County, OH residents (n=236; Beck & Travis, 2004; Beck et al., 2004)

crime. In turn, such examination provides insight into the current public policy landscape. That is, a determination of the specific perceptions about sex crime and beliefs about sexual offending held among the public has the potential to explain the current "tough on sex crime" movement in criminal justice.

This literature has examined the following: a) whether perceptions toward sex offenders differ from those of non-sex offenders, b) attitudes toward specific "types" of sex offenders, and c) beliefs about offender reform. Each of these strands of research is discussed below.

Attitudes toward Sex Offenders Compared to Non-Sex Offenders

The argument that the public views sex crime differently from other offenses has been supported by a handful of studies centered on systematically examining public views about sex offenders compared to violent criminals who have not sexually offended. To illustrate, Rogers and Ferguson (2011) relying on data from a vignette survey (n=355) of college students assessed whether differences existed in public views toward sex offenders compared to non-sex offenders. In particular, they tested whether the public differentially responded to a crime that involved "fondling" versus a non-sex crime, "hitting." As hypothesized, the public was the most punitive toward offenders who had "fondled" a victim versus physically assaulting them. In a separate national analysis, Manza, Brooks, and

Uggen (2004) examined public opinion toward felon disenfranchisement (n=1,000). Their results revealed that Americans were least willing to restore voting rights to convicted sex offenders, compared to other offender types (white collar and violent, non-sex offenders). A more recent analysis of public opinion conducted by Chiricos, Padgett, Bratton, Pickett, and Gertz (2012) replicated Manza et al.'s (2004) general findings using a Florida sample (n=1,575). Once again in the Chiricos et al. (2012) study, the public was least in favor of restoring voting rights to convicted sex offenders compared to other offender types (e.g., felony non-sex offenders).

In a different study, Levenson, Shields, and Singleton (in press) using data from a survey administered to Ohio and Kentucky residents (n=255) investigated whether the public varied in their views about driving under the influence (DUI) offenders compared to convicted sex offenders. In particular, the researchers theorized that the public would judge residence restrictions to be a more punitive policy for DUI offenders compared to sex offenders. Results were supportive of this hypothesis. Residence restrictions were viewed as a more punitive sanction for DUI offenders than for sex offenders. These divergent assessments likely stem from societal differences in how DUI offenses and sex offenses have been addressed. Under this logic, Levenson et al.'s (in press) observation is illustrative:

> DUI is seen as a public health problem requiring prevention, treatment, and education initiatives in addition to a criminal justice response ... as a result, emphasis has been placed not only on increased penalties but also on generating a societal commitment to responsible drinking behavior and recognizing the need for treatment for those with substance addiction problems. Conversely, approaches to sexual violence have been oriented almost exclusively toward criminal justice despite attempts to conceptualize sexual assault as a public health problem (pp. 15–16).

Collectively, these findings indicate that the public distinguishes between sex crime and other non-sexually motivated crimes. In turn, these distinctions amplify negative views toward sex offenders.

Public Opinion toward Sex Offender Types

While most studies of sex crime perceptions have inquired about public views of sex offenders "generally" (i.e., "sex offenders" with no description of offender types, see as an example Mancini et al., 2010; for an exception see Comartin et al., 2009), there have been calls to understand nuances in public views about specific sex offender "types" (e.g., offenders who commit crimes against children versus adults, non-contact offenders versus violent predators). Such examination is warranted for two reasons. First, as discussed earlier in the text wide heterogeneity in offending patterns and motives exist across sex offender classifications (e.g., rapist of adults, incest offender, child molester). However, most sex crime laws have adopted the opposite logic—that is, most reforms make little distinction concerning individual recidivism risk, victim preference, and offender amenability to treatment. This perception seems to be widely accepted among the general public and policymakers (see e.g., Sample & Kadleck, 2008). Accordingly, public misconceptions about sex offenders may have triggered policy responses that are ineffective in reducing sex crime. Second, Americans might express substantially different views when asked specifically about offender types. That is, they may hold especially negative attitudes toward offenders who commit crimes against children, a group historically seen as vulnerable and in need of special protection from predators (Mears et al., 2007).

Indeed, extant work reveals that the public expresses the most concern about sex offenders who commit crimes against children. Rogers, Hirst, and Davies (2011) using a hypothetical vignette survey design examined whether victim age (as 10, 15, or 20 years old) and offenders' completion of a sex offender treatment program affected public attitudes toward sex offenders (n=235). Lending support to the point concerning child victims, in their study, public views became decidedly more negative as victim age decreased. The public expressed the most negative attitudes toward perpetrators who had victimized a 10 year-old female and who did not receive treatment. In another study, Mancini and Mears (2010) assessed whether "type" of offender affected levels of death penalty support for executing sex offenders. The public was most willing to execute sex offenders convicted of crimes against children (51 percent) versus those offenders convicted of crimes against adult women (27 percent). Mears and his colleagues (2008) in an earlier investigation found substantially greater endorsement of punitive sanctions for offenders convicted of crimes against children rather than adults. For example, 80 percent of Americans believed that offenders who commit indecent exposure offenses against children should receive a prison or jail sentence. Conversely, support for incarcerating indecent exposers drops by nearly half when the victims were specified as adults (46 percent). Similar results — in particular, more negative views toward offenders who have victimized children — have been reported in studies that have disaggregated offender types (see e.g., Comartin et al., 2009).

Other studies have explored public views toward juvenile sex offenders. For example, Sahlstrom and Jeglic (2008) developed a vignette survey designed to tap into whether public assessments of juvenile sex offenders vary by offender age (8, 9, 11, or 13 years old), offender gender, or offender race/ethnicity (White, African American, Hispanic/Latino, East Indian). In particular, respondents (n=208) were given three scenarios of a hypothetical case of sexual assault while the victim was being babysat or socially interacting with another youth-perpetrator. After reading all scenarios respondents were first asked to judge how the case should be handled. They could choose "formally" (by involving law enforcement or child protective services) or "informally" (involving parents of the victim and perpetrator only). Next, the survey asked respondents to rate the seriousness of each offense. Results indicate that perpetrator age did not significantly alter views about the crime. However, offender race/ethnicity did. Specifically, results suggest that greater support for parental versus police involvement for Hispanic perpetrators was evident among the public. Sahlstorm and Jeglic (2008, p. 189) attribute this result to the sample which overrepresented Hispanic Americans, as evident by their observation, "this [finding] may have resulted in respondents identifying more with Hispanic perpetrators and therefore advocating for more lenient intervention." Overall though respondents felt that the sex crimes described were serious enough to warrant criminal justice intervention. Crime seriousness rating varied by offender and victim sex. Mixed-gender (e.g., male perpetrator, female victim) scenarios were judged more harshly by the public than scenarios depicting same-sex cases. Additionally, respondents were significantly more likely to believe that mixed-gender scenarios required formal involvement compared to same-sex scenarios. Specifically, cases involving female perpetrators and male victims were judged more harshly than all other gender scenarios. For these crimes, respondents were significantly more inclined to feel formal intervention was required and that the event was more serious. In explaining this finding, particularly for how it goes against the idea that female sex offenders are not judged as harshly as male offenders, Sahlstorm and Jeglic (2008, p. 189) explained, "it appears that once a female is identified as a sex offender, attributions toward the female perpetrator are more negative perhaps because she is violating traditional norms of the passive and nurturing caregiver."

Along a similar line, drawing on a sample of White college students (n=220) Stevenson and colleagues (2009) determined the extent to which juvenile offender race impacted public views about punishment. Their study revealed that women, compared to men, were significantly more supportive of registering a juvenile offender as a sex offender, but only when the victim was White. In addition, women (but not men) expressed stronger retributive attitudes toward sanctioning the defendant when the victim was White rather than Black by indicating that they would register the defendant "even if registration does not reduce abuse." Per the researchers, their results indicate:

> gender-related social categorization caused women to attend to characteristics of the female victim more than men ... women's positive in-group associations toward women [and] their sympathetic attitudes toward victims of child sexual abuse might have driven them to pay attention to the female victim in this case more than men. In turn, women's heightened awareness of the female victim may have caused them to be more susceptible to her characteristics, namely race. Men, in contrast, likely categorized the female victim as an out-group member and paid less attention to her than did women, and in turn were less influenced by her racial characteristics (p. 973, citations omitted).

A separate study that also focused on perceptions of juvenile sex offenders reveals the public holds juvenile offenders as accountable for their actions as adult offenders. To illustrate, Salerno et al. (2010) using a convenience sample of Chicago residents found that laypersons supported juvenile and adult sex offender registration equally, despite also believing that juvenile sex offenders were generally less threatening than adult sex offenders. Notwithstanding these generally comparable levels of support, when age of the juvenile offender was disaggregated, greater variation in public views was evident. That is, the public was more likely to support registry requirements for a 16-year-old than for a 12-year-old juvenile sex offender.

Similarly, Comartin, Kernsmith, and Kernsmith (2013) investigated whether public judgments to require registration for "sexting" offenses depend on age, gender, and sexual orientation of the offender. Findings indicate that the option to require registration differed for sex and sexual orientation, depending on the sexting behavior. Among those offenders who received a nude photo, the public felt that males and juveniles involved in a same-sex relationship should be placed on the registry. For youth or young adults who sent a nude photo to others, a same-sex relationship was more predictive of a respondent's likelihood of supporting registration. No gender differences emerged for this latter outcome.

Overall, these findings indicate that variation in public views concerning offender types is evident. Americans feel most negatively toward offenders who have abused children. At the same time, the age, gender, and to some extent ethnicity of offenders appear to impact public judgments about appropriate responses to sex crime and the seriousness of offenses. Additionally, some evidence indicates that the public holds juvenile offenders as accountable as adults. However, variation in public views is evident when considering specific characteristics of juvenile offenders.

Beliefs about Sex Offender Rehabilitation

Some extant research has also considered public views about sex offender rehabilitation. Understanding public assessments of sex offender reform is important as some scholars charge that sex crime laws incorrectly assume that most sex offenders are driven to reoffend. Thus, to the extent that the public influences the emergence of sex offender legislation, determining their perceptions of offender rehabilitation is critical toward comprehending the recent proliferation of sex crime laws.

Payne and his colleagues (2010) in a study of Virginia Beach residents (n=746) examined public attitudes toward sex offender rehabilitation. In general, their findings indicate that the public holds largely pessimistic views about sex offender reform. A majority of residents (52 percent) believed that successful sex offender rehabilitation was not likely. However, a non-trivial percent (36 percent) of the public appeared convinced that sex offender reform was indeed possible. The remaining percentage of respondents (12 percent) was unsure. Thus, while a slight majority of Americans judge sex offender reform as unlikely, nearly half of Americans believe it may be possible.

In a related study of views among college students, Rogers and Ferguson (2011) assessed rehabilitation views toward sex offenders and violent, non-sexual offenders. The public held significantly less positive perceptions toward sex offender amenability compared to the treatment potential of other types of violent offenders. Mancini (in press) relying on national poll data (n=1,006) assessed two indicators of public attitudes toward sex offender reform. She first examined the extent to which the public perceived rehabilitation to be possible to "the extent that the offender no longer represents a threat to children." In line with prior research (Payne et al., 2010) most Americans (73 percent) were unconvinced that such reform could occur. Mancini (in press) also inquired about whether respondents felt differently about reform prospects for sex offenders versus other violent criminals. Here again, results indicate that the public views sex offenders as having unusually high odds' of reoffending. Specifically, 85 percent of the sample reported that sex offenders could not be rehabilitated as effectively as violent non-sex offenders.

Thus, these findings indicate the public remains skeptical about the potential for sex offenders to desist from offending. At the same time, public views are more negative toward sex offenders' amenability to be reformed than for other offenders. Table 6.3 summarizes public opinion of sex offenders and sex crime.

Divides in American Public Opinion

Beyond establishing general public views about sex crime policy and offending, extant literature has also identified determinants of public attitudes.[1] Accordingly, there exist certain factors—social and demographic characteristics and perceptions about sex crime—that may in turn shape attitudes about sexual offending and appropriate policy responses. Below, multivariate research examining these divides is discussed.

Social and Demographic Factors

A wider public opinion literature has identified certain social and demographic characteristics (e.g., sex, race, educational attainment) that shape public attitudes toward crime and justice. For example, sex is often associated with less punitive attitudes toward offenders. Females on average are less supportive of retributive sanctions such as the death penalty, and more inclined to endorse rehabilitative reforms for offenders (Applegate,

---

1. Given the focus on explaining American public opinion, the following discussion focuses on multivariate studies examining public opinion data from residents of the U.S. The "Additional Suggested Readings" section provides citations for a sampling of studies conducted in other countries.

Table 6.3. Perceptions of Offenders and Sex Crime

Focus	Prior Research	Sample(s)
Sex Offenders versus Non-Sex Offenders	• The public is most punitive toward sex offenders compared to other serious non-sex offenders; Rogers and Ferguson (2011) reported greater punitive attitudes toward offenders convicted of "fondling" compared to offenders convicted of "hitting." • Americans are least approving of restoring voting rights to sex offenders compared to non-sex felony offenders (Chiricos et al., 2012; Manza et al., 2004). • The public is more likely to judge residence restrictions as punitive for DUI offenders but not for sex offenders (Levenson et al., in press).	• Students from a large Midwestern U.S. public university (n=355; Rogers & Ferguson, 2011) • FL residents (n=1,575; Chiricos et al., 2012) • U.S. residents (n=1,000; Manza et al., 2004) • OH and KY residents (n=255; Levenson et al., in press)
Sex Offender Types	• Americans are most punitive toward sex offenders convicted of crimes against children; Rogers et al. (2011) found the public expressed strong punitive attitudes as victim age decreased. • The public is most supportive of "get tough" sanctions when victims are children (Kernsmith, Craun et al., 2009; Mears et al., 2008). • Some evidence that offender age, race, gender, and crime impact public views about juvenile sex offenders (Comartin et al., 2013; Sahlstrom & Jeglic, 2008; Salerno et al., 2010; Stevenson et al., 2009).	• UK residents (n=235; Rogers et al., 2011) • MI residents (n=733; Kernsmith, Craun et al., 2009) • U.S. residents (n=425; Mears et al., 2008) • MI residents (n=770; Comartin et al., 2013) • Students from a large urban university (n=208; Sahlstrom & Jeglic, 2008) • Students from the University of Illinois at Chicago (n=472; Salerno et al., 2010) • Midwestern residents (n=220; Stevenson et al., 2009)
Beliefs about Sex Offender Reform	• A majority of the public holds largely negative views about the possibility of sex offender rehabilitation (Mancini, in press; Payne et al., 2010). • Public opinion is more positive toward the possibility of reform for non-sex offenders than for sex offenders (Mancini, in press; Rogers & Ferguson, 2011).	• U.S. residents (n=1,006; Mancini, in press) • Norfolk/Virginia Beach, VA residents (n=746; Payne et al., 2010) • Students from a large Midwestern U.S. public university (n=355; Rogers & Ferguson, 2011)

Cullen, & Fisher, 2002). Similarly, race is also thought to shape public views. Findings from extant studies indicate that Whites, compared to minorities, tend to more strongly endorse support for "get tough" laws (Messner, Baumer, & Rosenfeld, 2006). Additionally, Whites, in contrast to minorities appear significantly less willing to accept offender reintegration (Hirschfield & Piquero, 2010). Along a similar line, conservatives express greater support for increased sanctions for adult and juvenile offenders (Moon, Wright, Cullen, & Pealer, 2000; Vogel & Vogel, 2003). In contrast, higher educational attainment is associated with reduced support for retributive crime legislation, such as capital punishment and three-strikes laws (Soss, Langbein, & Metelko, 2003; Stack, 2003). Public opinion research has examined these correlates in addition to others such as age, parental status, prior victimization, income, and residence.

Although most of this investigation has focused on public attitudes toward capital punishment, "get tough" sentencing, and juvenile justice initiatives, within the last two decades, criminologists have begun to conduct studies specifically focused on understanding public attitudes toward sex offenders and sex crime policy. In particular, there has been a focus on the following social and demographic variables: age, sex, race/ethnicity, education, political ideology, parental status, victimization, income, and residence.

Extant work indicates that age exerts effects on public views, with some exceptions. Some studies have revealed significant effects of age on public opinion and others have reported null effects. Among the significant findings, older age reduces punitiveness and support for sex crime laws. To illustrate, McCorkle (1993), in a study of Las Vegas, Nevada residents (n=397) demonstrated that older age decreased punitveness toward rapists and child molesters. In a separate study, Cohen and colleagues (2004) determined that older respondents were significantly less willing than younger respondents to support increased taxes to fund new sex crime programs. Even so, many studies report non-significant effects of age (see e.g., Button et al., 2013; Chiricos et al., 2012; Levenson et al., in press; Mancini & Mears, 2010; Mancini et al., 2010; Payne et al., 2010; Pickett et al., in press).

The relationship between sex and public attitudes toward sex offenders is not entirely clear. In contrast to what has been observed in the larger public opinion literature examining punitive attitudes toward offenders, some extant research suggests that women are generally more supportive of "get tough" sex crime efforts. To illustrate, compared to men, women are more supportive of electronic monitoring (Button et al., 2013) and civil commitment for sex offenders (Pickett et al., in press). One study found that women held stronger punitive views toward offenders who have victimized children (McCorkle, 1993). However, despite these results, mixed findings are evident in other studies. For example, at least one study (examining college students' views about sex offenders; n=316) found that gender served to temper negative views about sex offenders. Church, Sun, and Li (2011) reported that compared to men, women were significantly more likely to hold positive assessments about sex offenders (e.g., believing they could be reformed, are not necessarily driven to reoffend). At the same time, null effects of sex have been observed. No sex effects emerged in a study assessing support for capital punishment of sex offenders (Mancini & Mears, 2010). Some other studies have demonstrated similar null effects of sex on views about sex crime and offenders (e.g., Chiricos et al., 2012; Cohen et al., 2004; Levenson et al., in press; Mancini et al., 2010).

Empirical attention has also focused on determining the effects of race and ethnicity on shaping public views about sex offenders. Some evidence exists for the notion that race and ethnicity impacts views about sex crime laws and sex offenders. To illustrate, Whites, compared to other racial and ethnic groups, are more likely to support tougher sanctions for child pornography offenses (Mears et al., 2008), residence restrictions (Mancini et al., 2010), and civil commitment (Pickett et al., in press). They also express less optimism about sex offender reform (McCorkle, 1993; Payne et al., 2010). One study found Latinos to be more supportive of residence restrictions compared to non-Latinos (Mancini et al., 2010). Some evidence suggests that African Americans are more willing to accept sex offenders back into the community, however this effect has been observed in only one study (Chiricos et al., 2012). In contrast, Payne et al. (2010) reported that minorities were significantly less likely to believe sex offenders could be rehabilitated. Notably, such results go against what has been uncovered in a larger public opinion literature—namely, that minorities are more accepting of ex-offenders (see generally, Hirschfield & Piquero, 2010). In explaining this discrepancy, the authors (p. 581) reasoned that: "Different factors potentially influence attitudes about criminal justice issues for Whites and Blacks. In other words, Blacks [are] believed to be punitive for one set of reasons, while Whites are believed to be punitive for another set of reasons."

Education has been shown to influence support for "get tough" policies and punitive attitudes toward sex offenders. Specifically, greater educational attainment has been associated with reduced support for increased punishment for offenders who access child pornography (Mears et al., 2008), residence restrictions (Mancini et al., 2010), capital punishment for sex offenders (Mancini & Mears, 2010), and civil commitment (Pickett et al., in press). At the same time, education has been linked to greater acceptance of sex offender reintegration (Chiricos et al., 2012), increased concern about offender harm (Mancini, in press), and reduced punitiveness toward sex offenders (McCorkle, 1993).

As mentioned earlier, political conservatives are more punitive toward individuals who offend. While this is generally the case for sex offenders, the effect is not as consistent. Some studies indicate that conservatives, compared to liberals and moderates, are more opposed to the re-enfranchisement of sex offenders (Chiricos et al., 2012). However, other studies find no effect of political ideology on public opinion about sex crime (see e.g., McCorkle, 1993; Mears et al., 2008; Pickett et al., in press).

Parental status has only recently been examined in studying views about crime. Research has produced mixed findings. Mancini et al. (2010) found that parents were significantly more likely to support residence boundaries for sex offenders. In their study, having more than one child was associated with additional increases in support for the law. In contrast, Levenson et al. (in press) found no effect of parental status on views about sex offender policy.

Research has not clearly discovered a victim effect on views about sex offenders. Although it could be argued that prior victimization should drive negative views toward sex offenders, some studies indicate the opposite outcome. For instance, Levenson et al. (in press) reported that prior victimization increased the view that residence restrictions amount to additional punishment; put differently, respondents who had been previously victimized rated residence restrictions as punitive. The authors reasoned that "[while] this seems somewhat counterintuitive ... many crime victims know their perpetrator, so they might have a more humanistic approach to criminal offenders" (p. 16). Along a similar dimension, Mancini and Mears (2010) found that vicarious victimization (i.e., knowing a sex crime victim) reduced support for a particularly punitive sanction—capital punishment of sex offenders. They relied on a similar logic as Levenson and colleagues (in press) to explain their unexpected findings. Namely, since sexual crimes most typically involve a known offender it is likely that respondents who have experienced vicarious victimization may also be familiar with both the victim and perpetrator, and so, may be opposed to extreme punishment. However, McCorkle (1993) reported that perceived risk of victimization increased punitiveness toward sex offenders. At the same time, a number of studies have found no effect on being a victim of a violent or sexual crime on views about sex offenders (Button et al., 2013; Mancini & Mears, 2010; Payne et al., 2010).

In a similar direction, extant research indicates mixed effects of income on public views about sex crime. One study found that higher annual income was associated with reduced support for tougher child pornography crimes (Mears et al., 2008). Mancini (in press) reported that higher income Americans expressed less concern about the unintended effects of sex offender laws. Other studies have revealed null effects of income. To illustrate, Comartin et al. (2009) found no significant effect of income on support for "punitive" (e.g., residence restrictions, imposing nighttime curfew) and "severely punitive" (e.g., castration, life imprisonment) sex crime policies (see also Cohen et al., 2004; Payne et al., 2010).

Some research has examined whether residence or perceptions of residence affects views about sex offenders. Overall results have yielded ambiguous findings. One national study found that urban residence increased "softer" views toward offenders. Specifically, Mancini (in press) found that urban residents were significantly more likely to express concern about registered sex offender harassment. Another study found that residents living in "vulnerable" communities (e.g., percentage of households in the zip code with residents below age 18, percentage of the population that are female, percentage of females who live alone) were more supportive of electronic monitoring (Button et al., 2013). Still others have reported null effects of residence on public opinion (Payne et al., 2010) or have not included residence as a control (e.g., Mancini & Mears, 2010; Mears et al. 2008).

Findings from this body of research indicate social and demographic divides in public views. At the same time, this literature is incomplete. Thus, greater empirical attention toward unpacking these social and demographic cleavages is needed. Generally, age has been shown to decrease punitive views, although null effects are also evident. Sex is less understood — with some studies finding that women are more punitive toward sex offenders than men, and others finding that women are more willing to believe that sex offenders can be reformed. Still other work has revealed null effects of sex. Race appears to shape views about sex offenders. Overall, extant research indicates that compared to minorities, Whites are more punitive toward sex offenders, tending to support a range of "get tough" sanctions. Having said that, at least one study found that minorities, compared to Whites, were more pessimistic concerning sex offender rehabilitation efforts. Research examining the effects of education offers a clearer interpretation. On average, more highly educated Americans are less punitive toward sex offenders and express greater acceptance of convicted sex offenders. Although it can be argued that political ideology shapes views about crime and offenders, it is to a lesser degree for sex offenders. For instance, politically conservative Americans are less accepting of sex offenders. At the same time, evidence suggests that political ideology may play less of a role in influencing crime views than has been previously theorized. The impact of parental status is also not clearly understood. Some work suggests a negative effect of parental status — where parents express greater support for "get tough" sex crime laws than individuals without children. However, other studies indicate null effects of parental status on views about sex crime and policy. Along a similar direction, victim effects on public views are not clearly understood. That is, some studies find that prior and vicarious victimization tempers views about offenders. Still others suggest that perceived risk of victimization amplifies punitive attitudes toward sex offenders. Not least, some investigations report null effects of victimization. Income effects have also not been consistent across studies. At least one study demonstrated that greater income reduced support for punitive sex crime laws. At the same time, higher income has been shown to reduce concern about offender harm. Not least, null effects of income have also been reported in extant studies. Finally, the effect of residence and perceptions of residence have exerted unclear findings. Results from one study indicate that residence reduces punitive attitudes toward convicted sex offenders. In contrast, other work suggests that living in vulnerable neighborhoods increases approval for increased monitoring of sex offenders. However, non-significant effects of income have also been reported in prior studies.

Sex Crime Perceptions

Beyond examining the effects of social and demographic factors, research has also explored the effect of specific sex crime-related perceptions (e.g., perceptions of sex offender reform) on views about offenders and policy. Put differently, it may be that certain views about crime and sex offenders impact public opinion about sexual offending. In particular, research has explored the impact of the following on public opinion about sex crime and policy: perceptions of crime and offending, assessments of sex offender amenability to be rehabilitated, and views of the criminal justice system and law.

One source of punitive attitudes toward sex offenders may stem from broader crime perceptions held among the public. For example, endorsing punitive sanctions for offenders generally (e.g., supporting efforts to make prison life "tougher," approving of more severe sentences for all offenders) may extend to attitudes about sex offenders. Indeed, at least one study supports this logic. Chiricos and his colleagues (2012) in their study of Floridians' perceptions of offender re-enfranchisement (n=1,575) demonstrated that general punitive attitudes (e.g., "making sentences more severe," "limiting death sentence appeals," "using chain gangs") served to increase opposition toward restoring sex offender rights. At the same time, general crime concerns may shape views about sex offenders and sex crime policy. For example, using national poll data Mears et al. (2008) tested whether concern about crime (measured on a ten-point scale where "0=unconcerned" to "10=very concerned") influenced support for increasing punishment for offenders who access child pornography. Results indicate that each additional increase in crime concern amplified support for punitive sanctions for child pornography offenders. Not least, fear of crime might arguably affect public views of sex crime and policy. Comartin et al. (2009) in a study examining Michigan residents' perceptions of sexual offending and support for "get tough" sex crime laws reported that fear of crime significantly increased approval for punitive and severely punitive sex crime laws. A separate investigation found that fear of crime significantly amplified support for sex offender registration among Michigan citizens (Kernsmith, Craun et al., 2009). Furthermore, a recent study of college students attending Texas and Wisconsin universities found that concern about becoming a crime victim resulted in higher approval of more punitive treatment for criminal offenders convicted of sexual assault and molestation (Tajalli, De Soto, & Dozier, in press).

Not least, Craun and Theriot (2009) demonstrate the relationship between sex offender notification and sex crime misperceptions using a sample of citizens in a southeastern U. S. county (n=631). In particular, their study tested the relationship between awareness of sex offenders in the community and holding the misperception that most offenses are committed by strangers. Their results illustrated that awareness of a local sex offender has a strong positive relationship to an increased likelihood of holding a misperception about sex offending (i.e., that most sex offenders are stranger perpetrators).

Another potential driver of attitudes about sex offenders involves public perceptions of sex offender amenability to be reformed. That is, those who feel sex offenders are unlikely to desist from offending will likely hold strong views about appropriate responses toward sex crime. In a national study, Mancini (in press) determined that having the belief that sex offenders are driven to recidivate reduced concern about registered sex offender harassment among the public. In a separate investigation, Mancini and Mears (2010) demonstrated that holding the view that "most sex offenders continue to repeat their crimes no matter what the punishment" increased approval for capital punishment for sex offenders who victimized children and rapists of adults. A separate study conducted by Levenson and her colleagues (in press) provides additional support that pessimism about sex offender reform amplifies punitive attitudes. In their study, respondents who judged sex offenders as having a high likelihood of recidivating were less likely to view residence restriction laws as punitive. Not least, in a public opinion study of Virginia residents Payne et al. (2010) identified predictors of negative views about sex offender rehabilitation. Although the study did not focus on determining how rehabilitation views affect policy support for sex crime initiatives, their study is instructive for highlighting divides in how the public perceives sex offender reform. Specifically, race, corporal punishment experience, and prior use of force against a partner emerged as statistically significant predictors of rehabilitation views. Minorities and those who experienced corporal punishment as children expressed less positive views about the possibility of sex offender rehabilitation. In contrast, residents who had used force against their partners "to get their way" (p. 584) were significantly more optimistic about sex offender rehabilitation.

Views about the criminal justice system might also impact public views. Some research indicates that holding negative perceptions of criminal justice system effectiveness increases support for sex crime laws and punitive attitudes. Once again, Mancini and Mears' (2010) investigation is noteworthy. Respondents who believed that "the state court system does not do enough to prevent sexual assault" were substantially more supportive of capital punishment for convicted sex offenders compared to individuals without such views. Additionally, it may be that positive assessments of the efficacy of sex crime reform influence punitive attitudes toward offenders. Levenson and her colleagues (in press), however found no support for that notion. In particular, public perceptions about the efficacy of residence restriction laws did not influence attitudes regarding whether the law was too punitive. Indeed, this result may reflect a general willingness to support "get tough" sex crime measures regardless of their efficacy (see e.g., Levenson et al., 2007).

How do perceptions of crime, offending, and the criminal justice system impact views about sex crime and offenders? The answer is that broader perceptions of crime—such as concern about crime and fear of victimization—substantially increase punitive attitudes toward sex offenders and approval of "get tough" reforms. At the same time, awareness of sex offenders living in the community increased stereotypical views about sex offenders. Perceptions of sex offender amenability to be reformed also significantly affects public attitudes about sex offenders and policy. In particular, negative assessments of sex offender rehabilitation efforts are associated with increased punitive attitudes. Additionally, rehabilitation views appear contingent on social and demographic characteristics of the public. In contrast, perceptions of the justice system affect views to a smaller extent. That is, some work finds that negative views of the court system increase approval for punitive sex crime laws. However, other research has found no effect of perceptions of the efficacy of laws on support for punitive sex offender sanctions. Table 6.4 highlights research findings concerning divides in public opinion about sex crime, offenders, and policy.

Future Directions for Public Opinion Research

We turn now to a discussion about next steps for public opinion research. As mentioned earlier, a much larger public opinion literature has examined public perceptions about crime, offending, the criminal justice system, and punishment. It is only recently that criminologists and public policy researchers have begun to investigate public attitudes about sexual offending and sex crime policy. Thus, a large knowledge base focusing on public views about sex crime has yet to be developed. Moreover, extant studies—while

Table 6.4. Variation in Public Views

Predictor	Prior Research	Sample(s)
Age	• Some evidence that older age decreases punitiveness toward sex offenders (McCorkle, 1993) and reduces policy support for "get tough" sex offender laws (Cohen et al., 2004). • At the same time, null effects have also been observed (e.g., Button et al., 2013; Mancini & Mears, 2010; Pickett et al., in press).	• Las Vegas, NV residents (n=397; McCorkle, 1993) • U.S. residents (n=1,300; Cohen et al., 2004) • Norfolk/Virginia Beach, VA residents (n=746; Button et al., 2013) • U.S. residents (n=1,101; Mancini & Mears, 2010) • Leon county, FL residents (n=1,693; Pickett et al., in press)
Sex	• Sex has been shown to have some impact on public opinion. • Females compared to males are significantly more supportive of "get tough" sanctions such as electronic monitoring (Button et al., 2013) and civil commitment (Pickett et al., in press). • In comparison to men, women are also more likely to hold punitive views toward offenders who have prior convictions for abusing children (McCorkle, 1993). • However, some evidence exists for the notion that women relative to men are more willing to believe sex offenders can be reformed (Church et al., 2011). • Other studies have reported null effects of sex on public opinion (e.g., Chiricos et al., 2012; Levenson et al., in press).	• Norfolk/Virginia Beach, VA residents (n=746; Button et al., 2013) • Leon county, FL residents (n=1,693; Pickett et al., in press) • Las Vegas, NV residents (n=397; McCorkle, 1993) • Students from a Southern public university (n= 316; Church et al., 2011) • FL residents (n=1,575; Chiricos et al., 2012) • OH and KY residents (n=255; Levenson et al., in press)
Race	• Prior studies indicate that race shapes views about sex crime and offenders. • Generally, research indicates that Whites relative to non-Whites are more supportive of punitive laws (Mancini et al., 2010; Mears et al., 2008; Pickett et al., in press). • Racial effects on attitudes about offender rehabilitation are less clear; some research finds Whites are less optimistic about offender reform (McCorkle, 1993), whereas other work indicates that minorities, not Whites, express greater pessimism about the possibility of sex offender rehabilitation (Payne et al., 2010).	• FL residents (n=1,067; Mancini et al., 2010) • U.S. residents (n=425; Mears et al., 2008) • Leon county, FL residents (n=1,693; Pickett et al., in press) • Las Vegas, NV residents (n=397; McCorkle, 1993) • Norfolk/Virginia Beach, VA residents (n=746; Payne et al., 2010)
Education	• Higher educational attainment has been associated with reduced support for increased punishment for sex offenders (Mancini & Mears, 2010; Mancini et al., 2010; Mears et al., 2008; Pickett et al., in press).	• U.S. residents (n=1,101; Mancini & Mears, 2010) • FL residents (n=1,067; Mancini et al., 2010)

Table 6.4. Variation in Public Views, *continued*

Predictor	Prior Research	Sample(s)
Education, *continued*	• Education is also associated with reduced punitiveness toward sex offenders (McCorkle, 1993). • Additionally, more highly educated individuals, compared to individuals with less education, report greater acceptance of sex offender reintegration (Chiricos et al., 2012; Mancini, in press).	• U.S. residents (n=425; Mears et al., 2008) • Leon county, FL residents (n=1,693; Pickett et al., in press) • Las Vegas, NV residents (n=397; McCorkle, 1993) • FL residents (n=1,575; Chiricos et al., 2012) • U.S. residents (n=1,006; Mancini, in press)
Political Ideology	• Some evidence that political conservatives are opposed to the re-enfranchisement of sex offenders (Chiricos et al., 2012). • The effect to which political ideology shapes public perceptions about sex crime is not consistent across studies, however (e.g., McCorkle, 1993; Mears et al., 2008).	• FL residents (n=1,575; Chiricos et al., 2012) • Las Vegas, NV residents (n=397; McCorkle, 1993) • U.S. residents (n=425; Mears et al., 2008)
Parental Status	• Prior research findings indicate mixed effects of having children on views about sex crime and policy; Mancini et al. (2010) found that parents, compared to non-parents, were more willing to support residence boundaries; however, Levenson et al. (in press) reported null effects of parental status on views about sex crime.	• FL residents (n=1,067; Mancini et al., 2010) • OH and KY residents (n=255; Levenson et al., in press)
Victimization	• Findings concerning the impact of prior victimization on public opinion are mixed. • Levenson et al. (in press) reported that crime victims were significantly more likely to rate residence restrictions as punitive. • Moreover, Mancini and Mears (2010) found that vicarious victimization reduced approval for executing sex offenders. • However, perceived risk of victimization increases punitive attitudes toward sex offenders (McCorkle, 1993). • At the same time, some studies have reported null effects of prior victimization (see e.g., Button et al., 2013).	• OH and KY residents (n=255; Levenson et al., in press) • U.S. residents (n=1,101; Mancini & Mears, 2010) • Las Vegas, NV residents (n=397; McCorkle, 1993) • Norfolk/Virginia Beach, VA residents (n=746; Button et al., 2013)
Income	• Income effects are not fully understood. • Some evidence that higher income is associated with reduced support for punitive sex crime laws (Mears et al., 2008). • However, greater annual income has also been shown to reduce concern about the unintended effects of sex crime laws (Mancini, in press).	• U.S. residents (n=425; Mears et al., 2008) • U.S. residents (n=1,006; Mancini, in press)

Table 6.4. Variation in Public Views, *continued*

Predictor	Prior Research	Sample(s)
Residence	• The impact of residence is not fully understood. • One study found that Americans living in urban areas expressed greater concern about sex offender harassment (Mancini, in press). • A separate investigation revealed that living in vulnerable areas amplifies support for "get tough" sex crime laws (Button et al., 2013). • Other studies have revealed null effects of residence (Payne et al., 2010) or have not included it as a control (e.g., Mancini & Mears, 2010).	• U.S. residents (n=1,006; Mancini, in press) • Norfolk/Virginia Beach, VA residents (n=746; Button et al., 2013) • Norfolk/Virginia Beach, VA residents (n=746; Payne et al., 2010) • U.S. residents (n=1,101; Mancini & Mears, 2010)
Crime Perceptions	• Holding punitive attitudes toward offenders generally may shape specific views about sex offenders. • One study demonstrated a link between general punitiveness and reduced approval for sex offender re-enfranchisement (Chiricos et al., 2012). • Other research has shown that general crime concerns positively affect support for punitive sex crime laws (Mears et al., 2008). • Fear of crime has also been associated with increased support for "get tough" sex offender sanctions (Comartin et al., 2009). • Sex crime perceptions are also shaped by community notification of sex offenders; Craun and Theriot (2009) demonstrated the relationship between being aware of sex offenders living in the community and the endorsement of sex crime myths.	• FL residents (n=1,575; Chiricos et al., 2012) • U.S. residents (n=425; Mears et al., 2008) • MI residents (n=703; Comartin et al., 2009) • Residents from an unnamed city in the Southeast (n=631; Craun & Theriot, 2009)
Perceptions of Sex Offender Rehabilitation	• Generally, research has uncovered that pessimistic views about sex offender rehabilitation shape perceptions about sex offenders and increase support for punitive sex crime policy. • Mancini (in press) found that respondents who believed sex offender rehabilitation was not possible were less concerned about registered sex offender harassment. • Mancini and Mears (2010) demonstrated that negative views about sex offender rehabilitation increased approval for laws designed to execute sex offenders.	• U.S. residents (n=1,006; Mancini, in press) • U.S. residents (n=1,101; Mancini & Mears, 2010) • OH and KY residents (n=255; Levenson et al., in press) • Norfolk/Virginia Beach, VA residents (n=746; Payne et al., 2010)

Table 6.4. Variation in Public Views, *continued*

Predictor	Prior Research	Sample(s)
Perceptions of Sex Offender Rehabilitation, *continued*	• The belief that sex offenders cannot be reformed has also been associated with perceptions that residence restrictions do not constitute punitive sanctions (Levenson et al., in press). • Predictors of rehabilitation views include race, corporal punishment experience as children, and prior use of force against a partner (Payne et al., 2010).	
Views about the Criminal Justice System	• Perceptions of the criminal justice system to prevent sex crime significantly influences views about sex crime and sex offender laws; however the relationship is not consistent across studies. • Holding the belief that the court system does not sufficiently respond to sex crime shapes increased approval for capital punishment (Mancini & Mears, 2010). • Other research indicates that perceptions of the efficacy of sex crime laws are not associated with public support for them (Levenson et al., in press).	• U.S. residents (n=1,101; Mancini & Mears, 2010) • OH and KY residents (n=255; Levenson et al., in press)

providing great insight in complex attitudes about sex offenders — are limited. Below, implications for future studies are discussed.

Longitudinal Data

Virtually all studies centered on public opinion about sex crime have relied on cross-sectional data. Recall from our previous discussion about sex crime measurement that cross-sectional data represent a "snap-shot" in time. Accordingly, cross-sectional data are limited for several reasons. First, they are unable to track trends over time. Thus, if data from only one year are examined, it is not possible to determine whether it is representative of other years. Second, the use of cross-sectional data can potentially introduce historical bias. That is, if data are collected during a time period in which a celebrated event occurs (e.g., a high profile sex crime case), responses may be unduly biased by that particular event and not reflective of actual trends in public opinion over time. In contrast, longitudinal data allow researchers to test whether public opinion fluctuates over time. Public opinion data that are collected on a regular basis allow criminologists to consistently monitor trends in public views. Another strength of longitudinal data involves its ability to determine if responses are typical of prior years. Put differently, the use of longitudinal data permits researchers to assess whether historical events have impacted public opinion (i.e., whether certain "outlier" or atypical years exist).

At the same time, adopting a "life course" approach toward tracking and monitoring public views about crime has been proposed by some scholars (Cullen et al., 2000). No national database following individuals over time currently exists. As a result, little is known about whether public views remain stable over time or whether certain life events (e.g., marriage, having children) affect views about crime and punishment. The life course method would require creating a panel study by following young individuals over time — say, during adolescence, early adulthood, later adulthood, and so on, and tracking their perceptions about crime, offending, and punishment. Such a method, per Cullen and his colleagues (2000, pp. 63–64) has the advantage of "offer[ing] rich research possibilities by focusing attention on how developmental continuities and changes — factors that affect so much else in people's lives — may also play a role in shaping their views on punishment and corrections."

National Focus

There is also a need to conduct national studies of public opinion. Indeed, this is a critique of the larger public opinion literature centered on understanding public perceptions of crime and justice (Cullen et al., 2000). And, it is equally applicable to studies examining public opinion about sex offending. For instance, several extant studies have relied on convenience or college samples (Kleban & Jeglic, 2011; Olver & Barlow, 2010; Rogers & Ferguson, 2011; Schiavone & Jeglic, 2009). Of the more rigorous investigations available nearly all have relied on data collected from a single city (Levenson et al., 2007) or state (Mancini et al., 2010; Payne et al., 2010). This void represents a potentially significant research gap as it is not known how generalizable these findings are to the larger national population since states vary considerably in how they manage sex offenders (Mancini et al., 2013), and so views might be contingent on the types of efforts states have experimented with in recent years.

Additional Measures

Outside of these methodological shortcomings, conceptual gaps are also evident in this body of research. Beyond determining policy support for sex crime initiatives much less attention has been given to examining other facets of opinion, such as beliefs about the causes and correlates of sex crime (for an exception, see Levenson et al., 2007 who reported primarily descriptive statistics about respondent beliefs of factors that influence sex offending). For instance, what factors do Americans attribute as the cause of sex crime? Biological influences (e.g., hormonal imbalance, brain injury), social inequality, low self-control, social learning, or some other factor? This area is a critical one to explore as misperceptions about sex offenders appear to be endorsed by the public and policymakers (Sample & Kadleck, 2008). Moreover, there has also been an almost universal focus on determining punitive views about sex offenders. Greater attention is needed toward understanding public views toward reform and rehabilitation. Indeed, some preliminary evidence indicates that the public holds relatively pessimistic views about the possibility of sex offender rehabilitation, despite evidence indicating that sex offenders have low rates of general recidivism and lower than assumed rates of sexual recidivism (Payne et al., 2010). Exploring beliefs about the causes of sex crime and views about offender reform among the public may go far in understanding the widespread myths and misperceptions about sex offenders that currently exist.

Concomitantly, most extant studies have focused on perceptions about the generic and catch-all "sex offender" (see e.g., Mancini & Mears, 2010; Payne et al. 2010; for an exception see Kernsmith, Craun et al. 2009). This oversight stands out given the variability in offending patterns among sex offender classifications (e.g., rapist of adults, incest offender, child molester). This heterogeneity suggests that future public opinion studies should inquire about a range of sex offenders and crimes to more fully understand how public views diverge when the focus is on specific offender types.

Theoretical Context

Ideally, research will couch future investigations of public opinion within a theoretical framework. Theories centered on explaining punitive attitudes have been developed in the general public opinion literature. For example, threat theory has been used to argue that majority populations are more supportive of "get tough" sanctions because they perceive an increasing threat to their economic and social hegemony in the presence (or assumed presence) of large numbers of minorities (Blalock, 1967). However, the extent to which sex crimes have been racialized is unknown. Thus, it is unclear if this perspective could explain public views about sex crime and offenders. Certainly, other theories exist that may apply toward understanding public opinion about sexual offending. What is needed requires a greater theoretical focus on determining why support exists for sex crime policies, how perceptions of sex offenders differ from beliefs held about other, non-sex offenders, what factors account for divides in public opinion, and factors that shape punitive attitudes toward sex offenders.

Chapter Summary

Public opinion has been critical to the implementation of sex offender reforms. This chapter reviewed extant research centered on understanding public views toward sex offenders and sex crime. In particular, it discussed policy support for sex offender laws, awareness and use of registry and community notification policies, perceptions of offenders and sex crime, and divides in public opinion. Clearly, the public feels addressing sexual offending should be a top priority for the criminal justice system. With few exceptions, Americans are aware of and supportive of sex crime reforms. Moreover, public opinion concerning sex crime and offenders is dependent on many factors, such as characteristics of the offenders and victims. At the same time, divides in opinion are evident—indicating that public views about sexual offending are nuanced and complex. Recommendations for developing this body of work include relying on longitudinal data, focusing on national samples of the public, including additional measures, and framing analyses within a theoretical context.

The additional suggested reading list below provides a sampling of citations to prominent public opinion studies of crime and justice. Chapter 7 concludes the focus on societal reactions to sex offenders by reviewing efforts to curtail sexual offending in the U.S. across time.

Additional Suggested Readings

Burstein, P. (2003). The impact of public opinion on public policy: A review and an agenda. *Political Research Quarterly, 56,* 29–40.

Frost, N. A. (2010). Beyond public opinion polls: Punitive public sentiment and criminal justice policy. *Sociology Compass, 4,* 156–168.

Green, D. A. (2006). Public opinion versus public judgment about crime correcting the "comedy of errors." *British Journal of Criminology, 46,* 131–154.

Indermaur, D., Roberts, L., Spiranovic, C., Mackenzie, G., & Gelb, K. (2012). A matter of judgment: The effect of information and deliberation on public attitudes to punishment. *Punishment & Society, 14,* 147–165.

Roberts, J. V., Stalans, L. J., Indermaur, D., & Hough, M. (2002). *Penal populism and public opinion: Lessons from five countries.* New York: Oxford University Press.

Unnever, J. D., & Cullen, F. T. (2010). The social sources of Americans' punitiveness: A test of three competing models. *Criminology, 48,* 99–129.

Chapter 7

Historical Emergence of Sex Offender Laws in the U.S.

Chapter Introduction

Many experts have highlighted the sharp increase in the types of sex crime policies adopted nationally in recent decades (Sample & Bray, 2003; Zevitz, 2006). Indeed, Duwe and Donnay (2008, p. 412) observed that in the last twenty years "lawmakers across the country have enacted a variety of policies designed to increase public safety by decreasing the incidence of sexual recidivism." The goal of this chapter is to put this change into historical perspective by reviewing how sex crimes have been characterized and addressed in the past. Seven time periods are examined—the "Colonial Period" (1600s–early 1800s), "Progressive Era" (late 1800s–1920s), "Medical Model Era and Sexual Psychopath Laws" (1930s–1950s), "Deinstitutionalization Decades" (1960s–1970s), "Get Tough Justice Era" (1980s), "Decade of the Predatory Sex Offender" (1990s), and the modern era (2000s)—"A Potpourri of Laws."

The 1600s–Early 1800s: Colonial Period

Historical accounts suggest that efforts to curtail sexual deviance began as early as the American colonial days in the 1600s. In the Massachusetts Bay Colony, acts such as homosexuality, bestiality, sodomy, adultery, statutory rape, and other "immoral offenses," were, in some cases, considered capital crimes. Scientifically derived explanations for understanding sexual offenses were virtually non-existent. Instead, religious doctrine was often consulted to explain crime. That is, a prevailing belief was that supernatural forces such as demonic possession and witchcraft led to criminal offending and deviance (Block, 2006; Erikson, 1966). As a result, punishment was extreme. In most instances of sex crime—which included offenses not likely to be sanctioned today (e.g., adultery)—banishment and physical punishments such as public flogging and execution were typical sentences (Godbeer, 1995).

The colonial system of identifying sexual offending and apprehending the accused differed markedly from contemporary criminal justice. That is, there was a gendered "division of labor" in investigating claims of sexual violence. To illustrate, female relatives were charged with inspecting the victim for signs of sexual assault. This method was seen as particularly important for cases involving young victims who had not had sexual intercourse yet, and so, were thought to have difficulty comprehending whether in fact they were sexually assaulted. As reflected by Block's (2006, p. 162) observation—"Women's examinations of young women and girls who had been raped could reassure the victim of her story's veracity, introduce her to the community's definitions of rape, and eventually bolster or destroy her claims of her body's experiences"—this approach served a vital purpose in the community. Male relatives in contrast were responsible for apprehending the offender and working with law enforcement to ensure the accused was tried in a criminal court.

At the same time, the onus was on the victim to "prove" she had indeed been sexually assaulted. Block's (2006, p. 37) analysis is illustrative: "An early modern belief in women as temptresses could make women's claims of rape look like consensual sex postcoitally regretted." Relatedly, in a historical examination of responses to sex crime over the years, Gavey (2005, p. 17) concluded that although rape was a serious and "detestable" crime in early colonial days, there was a hesitancy by the community to condemn men accused of sex crime, as there appeared to be "an overriding concern for the wrongs of falsely accusing a man of rape, over and above the wrongs of the rape itself." Indeed, some accounts indicate that female accusers could even be charged with other offenses in the course of making claims of sexual assault. For example, in 1710, Maine courts convicted Mary Jinkins, a woman who claimed she was the victim of an attempted rape, of "lewdness" based on witness testimony and other evidence. She and her accuser received a corporal punishment (as reported in Block, 2006, p. 38).

Because sex offenses at this time were viewed as "un-Christian" or "unspeakable crimes," it is difficult to assess the full range of policy responses used by early Americans, as historical records of these offenses are scarce (Godbeer, 1995). However, what can be gleaned from extant historical analysis is that the process of uncovering sexual offending, judging which allegations were credible, and punishing sex offenders took a "community" approach— whereby relatives, other community members, and societal norms were integral in the process.

A departure in understanding sexual offending occurred after America gained independence from England in 1776. Although official records are difficult to come by, it appears that sex crime policymaking, like general crime policy, followed a "rational choice" logic stemming from classical criminology. The classical school of crime was heavily influenced by the Age of Enlightenment in Europe during the 18th century. Jeremy Bentham and Cesare Beccaria were among the notable classical criminologists who emphasized that God instilled in humans free will and the ability to exercise judgment about the consequences of their actions (Pratt, Cullen, Blevins, Daigle, & Madensen, 2006). Following this logic, the perspective outlined six principles for developing a fair and effective criminal justice system. First, punishment should not be revenge-oriented. Instead, it should be proportionate to the crime. Moreover, it should ideally have a practical purpose. That is, criminal sanctions should deter individual offenders and the general public from engaging in crime. Third, laws should be enacted in advance of crimes (i.e., to avoid "ex post facto" lawmaking). Fourth, the perspective emphasizes the importance of transparent criminal justice practices. Thus, criminal proceedings should be made public and laws should be openly publicized. Fifth, the use of torture should be avoided; rather, offenders should be treated humanely. Sixth, and finally, the accused should be granted several rights—the right to a speedy trial, the right to confront witnesses, and the right to bring forth evidence of innocence (Pratt et al., 2006).

Indeed such views influenced the U.S. Constitution and the nation's legal system, and have continued to do so in modern decades. Although such notions are today taken for granted, such a shift in understanding represents a radical departure from earlier colonial days. Illustrative of this influence on sex crime policymaking, is the following 1779 passage regarding rape statutes. The bill, "Bill for Proportioning Crimes and Punishment in Cases Heretofore Capital (Bill 64)" was one of 126 bills submitted to the Virginia Assembly in the late 1700s by the "Committee of Revisors." The committee, led by Thomas Jefferson, worked for several years revising colonial law, as Virginia began making the legal transition from colony to commonwealth. The goal of the bill was to outline proportionate punishment for various offenses:

Whosoever shall be guilty of Rape, Polygamy, or Sodomy with man or woman shall be punished, if a man, by castration, if a woman, by cutting thro' the cartilage of her nose a hole of one half diameter at the least (as cited by Crompton, 1976, pp. 286–287).

This bill reflects the prominent belief at the time that punishment should be balanced to the crimes committed; at the same time, it should serve as a general and specific deterrent. Notably, the prior punishment for such offenses was much more extreme. Indeed, as mentioned earlier several rape offenses were considered capital crimes in the earlier colonial period. The bill, however, was never adopted in Virginia (Crompton, 1976).

Yet, Jefferson's logic influenced several other state legislatures. For example, in 1796, New Jersey enacted a law that reduced the crime of sodomy to a fine and a term of hard labor. In the same year, New York implemented "An Act Making Alterations in the Criminal Law" that retained capital punishment for treason and murder but mandated that any person convicted of any other offense (e.g., a sex offense) should instead be punished by life imprisonment. In contrast, Rhode Island's "Public Laws of 1798" distinguished between first-time and repeat offenses and afforded more serious punishment to the latter, reflecting a proportionate logic. Specifically, it stated "that every person who shall be convicted of sodomy ... shall, for the first offence, be carried to the gallows in a cart, and set upon the said gallows, for a space of time not exceeding four hours, and thence to the common gaol, there to be confined for a term not exceeding three years, and shall be grievously fined at the discretion of the Court; and for the second offence shall suffer death" (as reported in Crompton, 1976, p. 287).

Despite classical criminology's influence on the American legal code, toward the latter part of the 1800s criminologists began to challenge the notion that offending could be simply explained as choice. Relatedly, the belief that crime could be easily prevented via purely legal measures was also critiqued. We turn now to exploring this paradigm shift in the study of crime.

The Late 1800s–1920s: The Progressive Era, Moral Hygiene, and Sex Offenders

Positivism, with strong roots in the eugenics movement and social Darwinism, appeared to dictate approaches toward sex offenders throughout the Progressive era. Notably this scientific paradigm warrants brief discussion. This perspective is distinct from others in that it makes three assumptions about deviance. First it assumes that individual pathology (i.e., abnormal physical or mental conditions of criminals) leads to crime. Additionally, it maintains that such pathology is often inherited from parents to offspring. Finally, it presumes that offenders can be identified by their unique physical or mental characteristics (for a review, see Gould, 1996).

Under positivist thought, scientific innovations were curative. Thus, scientifically derived approaches were thought to reflect the best "antidote" to address undesirable criminal tendencies. As a result, these efforts focused heavily on individualized treatment and rehabilitation programs tailored to address an offender's unique shortcomings. Cullen and Gendreau's (2000, pp. 116–117) historical analysis of this emphasis is illustrative:

First, [positivism] embraced the belief that crime was caused by an array of psychological and social factors that, in a fashion unique to each individual, intersected to push a person to the other side of the law. Second and relatedly, the way to prevent future crime was to change the unique set of factors that drove each individual into crime. Third, the process of corrections should be organized to identify these crime-causing factors and to eliminate them ... Sanctions would be directed to the individual needs and circumstances of offenders. Much like physicians do with those who are physically ill, correctional decisionmakers would use their expertise, rooted in the emerging social sciences, to diagnose and cure offenders. To do so effectively, they had to be trusted to exercise their discretionary decisions wisely and not coercively ... this line of thinking helped to refashion the criminal justice system. The roster of changes was remarkable: the invention of a nonadversarial juvenile justice system, whose purpose was to "save" wayward children; the development of substantial indeterminacy in sentencing; the spread of probation, with its focus on presentence reports and offender supervision; and the rise of parole boards, parole release, and parole officers. Together, this package of reforms was intended to make possible the individualized treatment of offenders.

Reflected in this observation is the medical analogy between treating crime in the same fashion as treating disease. In short, positivist thinking reflects a sharp retreat from earlier schools of thought stressing crime as a function of the "devil's work," or choice.

This radical change in responding to crime was also illustrated in scholarly efforts and campaigns to "better society." For instance, influenced heavily by this intellectual thought and a larger "child-saving" movement, scholars began to devote significantly more empirical attention toward examining sex crime and its effects, particularly the sexual exploitation of children and young adults. This focus in part reflects larger societal changes. Beginning in the late 1800s and early 1990s, there was a mass migration of rural and foreign people to the larger and more industrialized cities. For these new urbanities, finding legitimate work was not always feasible, and some, not yet in their teens, turned to prostitution to generate income (Sacco, 2002). Prominent scholarly accounts like W.L. Gibb's "Indecent Assault of Children" (1894) revealed the extent of the sex crime problem, including accounts of child prostitution and inspired an outpouring of public concern about these conditions. Thus, while such empirical focus contributed to a nascent sex crime literature, it also motivated public action to address sexual violence and exploitation.

At the same time, there was a larger medical concern that sex offending led to the spread of sexually transmitted diseases (STDs). Venereal disease and syphilis were two highly prevalent STDs that afflicted a substantial proportion of children in the Progressive era. According to experts, the Progressives' movement to reduce sex offending highlighted both a societal shift in how to best address crime and also an emphasis on improving public health (Sacco, 2002).

As mentioned earlier, the positivist approach emphasized applying scientifically derived punishment to offenders. For instance, toward the end of the nineteenth century, medical-professional and legal realms mandated that repeat or habitual sex offenders, deemed to be "incurable," be institutionalized for life, or executed (Jenkins, 1998, p. 40). Once again, such efforts highlight the medical model that so prominently influenced Progressives. Thus, permanently incapacitating extreme offenders assisted with "containing" pathology to a sterile environment. For first-time or "nuisance" sex offenders (e.g., those convicted of non-contact sex offenses such as indecent exposure or lower level offenses), treatment options varied. To illustrate, typical sanctions included indeterminate sentences often fused with required psychiatric counseling and physical castration (Leon, 2011a).

According to Lynch (2002, p. 533) this latter intervention — castration — was particularly attractive to Positivists because "sexual perversion was considered to be in the same category as defectiveness and degeneracy; therefore, those deemed perverts could be subject to sterilization to prevent their deficient genes from being reproduced." Thus, physical castration was an influential policy response that served dual purposes. First, castration served to decrease sexual urges and fantasies. Thus, it was believed that reduced sexual arousal would lead to fewer sexual offenses. Second it also served to permanently sterilize the offender, so that his "condition" could not be passed to offspring (Scott & Holmberg, 2003, p. 502). The use of sterilization, with its emphasis on the containment of pathology became an increasingly popular sanction during the Progressive era.

The legal environment at this time was also shaped by positivistic thinking. In describing this impact, Jenkins (1998, p. 43) noted, "these laws often mixed criminal and civil functions together in a confusing and perilous manner." Regardless of the possible unintended effects of these hybrid policies, "sweeping new laws were implemented with minimal criticism" (Jenkins, 1998, p. 43). Indeed, positivist reforms appeared to be embraced by many influential groups, including psychiatrists and women's and child-saving organizations, which were actively involved in shaping sex crime policy efforts (Gibb, 1894). Stereotypes about sex offenders were endorsed by the public and the research community, and so, punishments for them were rarely challenged. Some of the beliefs were that sex offenders suffered from mental abnormalities (e.g., "feeble-mindedness") and that certain ethnic and racial groups, and those living in poverty were more prone to commit sex crimes than Whites and the more affluent (Sacco, 2002). These perceptions pervaded public opinion and influenced policy into later decades. We turn now to discussing a later time period, the Medical Model and Sexual Psychopath Laws (1930s–1950s).

The 1930s–1950s: The Medical Model and Sexual Psychopath Laws

A series of sexually motivated homicides involving youths in 1937 alerted the public and policymakers to the risk sex offenders posed to children and women (Freedman, 1987). Perhaps partially influenced by these media accounts and the prevailing view that science could "fix" criminal pathology, beginning in the 1930s and continuing well into the 1950s sexual psychopath laws emerged in the U.S. These laws were designed to force sex offenders into medical treatment (Fitch, 1998). Although few sex offenders were actually considered legally insane, psychiatrists often referred to sex offenders as "sexual psychopaths" and were instrumental in the passage of these laws (Cole, 2000). States varied in their implementation of these reforms, but the general criteria of the legislation required that either the offender committed more than one sex crime or that the offender suffered from mental abnormalities such as emotional instability or sexual impulsivity. Sexual psychopath laws are one of the first documented civil commitment attempts of sex offenders in America (Freedman, 1987).

According to scholarly accounts, words such as "fiend," "degenerate," and "pervert" were used to describe sex offenders in the sex crime literature and popular media throughout this era (Leon, 2011a). The prevailing view was that sex offenders were "neither sane nor insane," but lacked the ability to control sexual impulses and were likely to recidivate, and therefore, should be segregated until "cured" (Lieb, Quinsey, & Berliner, 1998, p. 56). In some instances, treatment for sex offenders included doses of testosterone-lowering hormones, given in the belief that these drugs could help control the sexual urges of repeat offenders (Scott & Holmberg, 2003).

Sutherland (1950, p. 547) was one of the first scholars to critique sex offender legislation. Specifically, he claimed that sex offenders as a group had low rates of recidivism and that such laws, "although dangerous in principle," were rarely invoked, and thus, had little appreciable effect on subsequent sex offending. Many scholars blamed "mass hysteria" as a driving catalyst responsible for these new laws, brought on, in part, because of grisly media coverage of atrocious, but exceedingly rare, sex crimes, such as the case of Albert Fish. Fish, a self-proclaimed pedophile, had confessed to the murder, cannibalism, and sexual assault of numerous children. Fish's crimes represented an extreme offender; however, many in favor of sexual psychopath laws contended that if policymakers could identify such dangerous offenders and treat them before their crimes escalated numerous lives would be saved (as discussed in La Fond, 1998).

Although such cases outraged the public, sexual psychopath laws were not intended as punitive sanctions. The laws were created in an attempt to force offenders into treatment and to incapacitate them, as a popular misconception among policymakers and the public at the time was that sex offenders had high rates of recidivism compared to other offenders (Lieb et al., 1998). Accordingly, Freedman's observation (1987, p. 98) is illustrative:

> The sexual psychopath laws did not necessarily name specific criminal acts, nor did they differentiate between violent and nonviolent, or consensual and non-consensual, behaviors. Rather, they targeted a kind of personality, or an identity, that could be discovered only by trained psychiatrists. Whether convicted of exhibitionism, sodomy, child molestation, or rape, sexual psychopaths could be transferred to state mental hospitals or psychiatric wards of prisons for an indefinite period, until the institutional psychiatrists declared them cured. The laws rested on the premise that even minor offenders (such as exhibitionists), if psychopaths, posed the threat of potential sexual violence. Indefinite institutionalization of sex offenders would protect society from the threat of violent sexual crimes, and psychiatric care would be more humane than castration, life imprisonment, or execution.

Put differently, as discussed earlier this response represents an early form of civil commitment in the U.S. For example in 1939, California became one of five states to enact a sexual psychopath law (Leon, 2011a). Its particular statute mandated that "sexual offenders apprehended by the law are examined by court-appointed psychiatrists to determine whether they are 'sexual psychopaths' as defined by California law and need treatment in a mental hospital" (Rapaport & Lieberman, 1956, p. 232). Notably this penalty was sometimes blended with biological "treatment" designed to be "therapeutic" in nature. To illustrate, in her analysis of sex crime legislation in California, Leon (2011a, p. 49) observed of sexual psychopath legislation enacted in the state in 1923, "Sterilization is included [as a sanction] 'in addition to such other punishment' for child molesters with young girl victims."

The social and legal focus on the most extreme sex offender — homicidal and mentally deranged — ignored other prevalent types of abuse. For example, in a historical analysis, Devlin (2005, p. 609) observed, "consensus on father-daughter incest during the postwar years in the United States is that it was fully and effectively denied — by social workers, courts, of law, criminologists, psychoanalysts, social scientists, and ultimately the public at large" — despite emerging research at that time that such forms of abuse were becoming increasingly more common. What this emphasis indicates is that the strong focus on extreme cases in this era resulted in sex crime policy that did not address more typical forms of sexual victimization. We turn now to exploring sex offender policies nationally in the 1960s and 1970s.

The 1960s–1970s:
Deinstitutionalization Decades

The 1960s and 1970s were marred by social and political turmoil. To illustrate, prominent movements emphasizing equal treatment of women and minorities, and the resultant backlash of these movements, as well as highly publicized scandals involving government corruption indicated that conflict existed in society. As a result, public support in the government to effectively control and reduce crime had significantly waned during this time period than in prior decades. Finckenauer's (1988, p. 84) description of this era is pertinent:

> Crime rates (however imperfectly measured) surged between the mid-1960s and the early 1970s; this period also was characterized by assassinations, urban riots, campus disorders, antiwar protests, the hippie movement, and a widespread increase in drug use. At the same time, there was a massive national effort to fight poverty, unemployment, and urban decay, as well as to control crime and ensure safe streets. In addition, Watergate and the war in Vietnam shook public confidence both in the government's integrity and in its ability to govern.

In turn, the criminal justice system experienced a radical shift in how it responded to crime during this decade. In stark contrast to prior decades, strategies to divert individuals from the "system" were implemented. Policies and laws implemented during this time tended to reflect the view that prisons were criminogenic environments, and that contact with the justice system increased recidivism, rather than prevented it, particularly among juveniles and lower level offenders. Diversion strategies were implemented throughout the nation (Cullen & Gendreau, 2000).

Although concern continued to be expressed about sexual violence, much of the extant research on sex crime was thought to be antiquated and based on misconceptions about crime and offenders (Petrunik, 2002). In reaction, research began to focus on debunking prevalent sex crime myths and pointing to unintended effects of sex crime policies, such as racial disparities in sentencing.

Thus, this change in empirical direction reflected the larger intellectual movement that stressed decriminalization and deinstitutionalization (Lilly, Cullen, & Ball, 2007). Sex crimes began to be disaggregated and studied separately. A distinction was made between "mere molestation" and "serious" sex offending. Scholars began to view molestation and certain types of pedophilia as less damaging to victims than previously assumed. For instance, a number of scholarly accounts such as Abrahamsen (1960) and Kempe and Kempe (1978) were published at this time suggesting that child victims often suffered no serious damage as a result of molestation, and may, in fact, have enjoyed the victimization experience. Rather than focusing on the harmful consequences of sexual victimization, many scholars emphasized the racial disparities of sex crime policies, particularly in the South. In this region, lynching and executions of African American men accused of sexually assaulting White women continued until this practice was eventually outlawed by the Supreme Court in the 1960s (Petrunik, 2002).

In the legal arena, encompassing sex offender laws like civil commitment were routinely struck down. Throughout this era, the U.S. Supreme Court appeared to adopt a liberal orientation toward the legality of policies — one that emphasized offenders' rights, as evidenced by a series of "offender friendly" cases like *Miranda v. Arizona* (1966), which involved a convicted rapist. In particular, Ernesto Miranda was convicted of sexual battery offenses and kidnapping in 1963. He was sentenced to 20 to 30 years in prison. In 1966, the U.S. Supreme Court overturned his conviction because law enforcement had not informed him of his Constitutional rights before he confessed to the crime.

In *Specht v. Patterson* (1967), the U.S. Supreme Court ruled against a state sex offender statute that allowed for a man who originally faced a possible 10 year sentence for "indecent liberties" with a child to face an indeterminate penalty of possibly life in prison contingent on a psychological evaluation. The Court ruled that such legislation did not afford an offender basic due process rights, such as the right to counsel and to confront witnesses. In a similar case four years later, the Supreme Court in its ruling of *Lessard v. Schmidt* (1974) made it more difficult for states to civilly commit sex offenders that "posed no risk to society." The Court ruled in *Lessard v. Schmidt* (1974) that states had to afford those in jeopardy of civil commitment due process rights such as the right to confront witnesses testifying against them, counsel, and the right to a jury trial. Thus, these U.S. Supreme Court decisions represent a radical shift away from imposing strict regulations to offenders, including sex offenders, and toward protecting defendants' rights in the criminal justice system.

Towards the end of the 1970s, the emphasis on rehabilitation and treatment, which previously shaped theory and empirical research and guided sex offender policies, appeared to wane. Jenkins (1998, p. 113) put it a bit more forcefully when he concluded that "these attacks all but killed the rehabilitative ideal as a respectable component of American social policy." We now move toward examining sex offender laws in the 1980s.

The 1980s: "Get Tough" Justice Era

Whereas previous decades stressed treatment and decriminalization, beginning in the 1980s, criminal justice policy was guided by the "just deserts" philosophy (Akers & Sellers, 2004; Lilly et al., 2007). Per scholars, the publication of the "nothing works" Martinson (1974) report had a profound impact on the criminal justice system's response to sex offenses (Lucken & Latina, 2002, p. 22). In a 1974 essay published in *The Public Interest*, Robert Martinson summed up results from a forthcoming meta-analysis conducted with his colleagues (Martinson, Lipton, & Wilks, 1975). The study analyzed the effects of over 200 rehabilitation programs implemented in correctional facilities between 1945 and 1967. The results indicated that few rehabilitation efforts successfully reduced recidivism; that is, as Martinson (1974, p. 49) concluded, "[programming] at its best, cannot overcome, or even appreciably reduce, the powerful tendency for offenders to continue in criminal behavior." Interestingly, Martinson believed his research would result in the decriminalization of offenses, and ultimately, the "emptying" of prisons. In stark contrast however, his work paved the way for a new penology — one that emphasized "get tough" punishment and "just deserts."

The political atmosphere at this time seemed to embrace this new paradigm shift in criminology. Lucken and Latina (2002, p. 23) noted that "the Reagan/Bush era provided a ripe environment for the return of criminology theories based on individual responsibility." Put differently, sexual criminality was thought to be due to a lack of moral aptitude. Jenkins (1998, p. 121) observed, "for moral traditionalists, a campaign against sex crime provided an effective weapon for combating what they saw as a slide toward decadence, which had been unchecked since about 1965 and which was symbolized by the tolerance of divorce, abortion, homosexuality, drugs, and sexual promiscuity."

Throughout this decade, several "get tough" initiatives aimed at incapacitating and punishing offenders emerged in the U.S. Sentencing guidelines and determinate sentences were key policies used in the criminal justice system, "with the intent of bringing certainty, fairness, and uniformity to sentencing and punishment" (Lucken & Latina, 2002, p. 24). Most sexual psychopath laws reminiscent of the 1930s and 1940s were repealed in the latter part of the 1980s, seen as discriminatory by liberals and too lenient by conservatives (Lieb et al., 1998). Perhaps fueled by celebrated cases described in the media, instead of focusing on the habitual "pervert" or sexual psychopath, policies began to target child pornographers and child sex abusers (Terry, 2005). Such laws imposed stricter penalties for child sexual abuse and the manufacture, sale, or possession of child pornography. For instance in describing child pornography laws at the time, as Jenkins (1998, p. 150; see also Jenkins, 2001) explained, "a crime was committed by anyone who 'knowingly receives or distributes' or 'knowingly possesses' images, in addition to anyone who made or sold them."

Constitutional challenges to these increasing child pornography laws were often unsuccessful. For example, in 1982 the U.S. Supreme Court heard a challenge to one of these laws. In *New York v. Ferber*, the Court ruled that the First Amendment did not prohibit states from banning the manufacturing of material depicting minors engaged in sexual activity. The decision was a landmark case that eroded earlier "constitutional assumptions"—such as the right to privacy in the home.

Throughout the 1980s, Americans began to recognize incest and "acquaintance rape" as widespread forms of sexual abuse. Popular talk-shows often featured sex crime victims who recalled vivid accounts of child sex abuse during this era (Gavey, 2005; Terry, 2005). Another change occurred in the legal arena. Courtroom procedures were relaxed so that convictions were easier to obtain against offenders known to the victim. For example, several states suspended statutes of limitations for certain sex crimes, allowing victims of sex abuse several years to report victimization (Terry, 2005). The acknowledgement that the bulk of sex crime was committed by perpetrators familiar to the victim was a radical departure from previous accounts suggesting that sex crime overwhelmingly involved strangers (Gavey, 2005).

More broadly, during this "get tough" era, a greater emphasis on crime victims was evident. Empirical work examined the long-term effects of sexual abuse including illnesses such as post-traumatic stress disorder (PTSD). The National Crime Victimization Survey (NCVS) which was first conducted in 1973 suggested that a substantial proportion of sex crimes go unreported to law enforcement (Rand & Catalano, 2006; Terry, 2005). Memory recall therapy, developed by psychiatrists at this time, allowed alleged victims of sex abuse to recall their repressed victimization through psychiatric counseling. A number of alleged incidents of sexual abuse were recalled at this time period, suggesting an epidemic of sexual victimization among children. However, the validity of this method was questioned, and as Jenkins (1998, p. 180) commented, "If a person was convicted of a crime on the basis of recollection, whether of an adult or a child, was this any more just or reliable than that of the spectral evidence used with deadly effect in seventeenth-century Salem?"

Juxtaposed against such observations, we turn now to describing the unprecedented emergence of sex crime laws in the 1990s, an era depicted by experts as the "decade of the predatory sex offender" (Nash, 1999, p. 45).

The 1990s: The Decade of the Sex Offender

Clearly, as several scholars have demonstrated, the nation witnessed an unparalleled growth in sex crime laws throughout the mid-1990s. In questioning the emergence of these laws during this decade, experts have linked a series of highly publicized child abduction and murder cases to them. In particular, scholars have identified three specific cases that appeared to act as catalysts for the emergence of subsequent sex crime legislation. We begin first with Jacob Wetterling's abduction. In 1989, eleven year-old Jacob Wetterling was kidnapped at gunpoint while riding his bicycle with friends in St. Joseph, Minnesota. The search for Jacob continued for several months and made national headlines. Jacob has never been found and is presumed to be dead. Less than four years after Jacob's abduction, twelve year-old Polly Klass was kidnapped from her home during a sleepover party in Petaluma, California and murdered by a violent offender with a long history of sexual offenses against women. Her body was found weeks later in a deserted field. Less than a year later, in Hamilton Township, New Jersey, seven year-old Megan Kanka was lured into her neighbor's home, a convicted sex offender, and sexually assaulted and murdered (Sample & Bray, 2006).

These widely publicized tragedies of child abduction, sexual assault, murder, and repeat offenders sparked national outrage. In response to these crimes, policymakers around the country began to enact stricter legislation aimed at tougher sentences for sex offenders, identifying and monitoring sex offenders living in communities, and equipping communities with information about registered sex offenders living in nearby neighborhoods (Sample & Kadleck, 2008). For instance, after his daughter's death, Marc Klass was instrumental in working with California lawmakers to enact "three strikes and you're out" sentencing policies designed to incarcerate violent offenders for long periods of time (Tier & Coy, 1997).

Jacob's and Megan's parents were also active in the development of legislation designed to increase penalties for sex offenders. Convinced that a sex offender abducted and murdered their son, Jacob's parents, Jerry and Patty Wetterling helped pen the Jacob Wetterling Crimes against Children and Sexually Violent Offender Registration Act in 1994. This was one of the first legislative attempts to institute a state sex offender registry in the country (Sample & Bray, 2006).

After the death of their daughter, Megan's parents sought to increase community awareness about the prior histories of released sex offenders. Partially due to their efforts, Megan's Law was adopted by the federal government in 1996. The law requires states to notify community members when sex offenders move into their neighborhoods. States must develop and implement sex offender registries or risk losing federal funding for other criminal justice programs (Center for Sex Offender Management, 1999). The Jacob Wetterling Act (1994) and Megan's Law (1996) marked the beginning of an emergence of a broad range of expanded sex crime policies across the country. With the advent of the Internet in the mid-to-late 1990s, states began to create sex offender registry websites with the intent of providing concerned citizens with information about released sex offenders (Sample & Bray, 2006).

Notably, the Pam Lychner Sex Offender Tracking and Identification Act (1996) mandated additional provisions of registries and community notification laws. It required the development of a National Sex Offender Registry to ensure the FBI could track certain sex offenders. The Pam Lychner Act also sets forth provisions to allow the FBI to better monitor convicted sex offenders.

Other prominent sex crime polices enacted at this time hit on a number of other dimensions. The laws included controversial practices such as the enactment of civil commitment statutes, castration of sex offenders, the implementation of sex offender residence restrictions, capital punishment, the enactment of laws designed to protect children on the Internet, and mandatory HIV testing for sex offenders and related intentional transmission statutes.

In the mid-1990s, states considered enacting civil commitment statutes to indefinitely detain sex offenders judged to be at high-risk of reoffending. Recall that a prior generation of civil commitment laws emerged in the early part of the 20th century, as part of the sexual psychopath statutes. However, with its reemergence in the 1990s, the law was challenged in the federal courts. In 1997, the U.S. Supreme Court heard the case of *Kansas v. Hendricks* and ruled that civil commitment was not unconstitutional because its primary objective is to treat, not punish, the offender. In that decision, the Court concluded that states have the right to enact statutes that are designed to protect citizens from dangerous offenders. Florida for instance has enacted the Jimmy Ryce Involuntary Civil Commitment for Sexually Violent Predators Treatment and Care Act (1998). The law requires that high-risk sex offenders be indefinitely detained and committed to a mental health facility for treatment. Release occurs only after health professionals have deemed the offender to no longer represent a threat to society.

One other debated effort was the enactment of castration policies across the nation. As noted earlier, the U.S. practiced castration of offenders at the turn of the 20th century and during the sexual psychopath decade (1930s to 1950s). However, the practice lost its appeal in later decades due to concerns about its legality and effectiveness (Scott & Holmberg, 2003; Spalding, 1998). In describing the castration policies of the mid-1990s, Meyer and Cole (1997, p. 2) observed that the reemergence of such punishments was likely "in response to increased public awareness and outcry" about sexual offending. The authors further noted that "attention is being focused on castration because it is believed that decreasing testosterone will decrease sexual interest and activity and thus lead to a decrease in sexual offenses and violence" (p. 4). With the development of reversible chemical castration treatments (such as Medroxyprogesterone acetate or MPA) in earlier decades, more states began to consider chemical castration as treatment for certain types of sex offenders (Spalding, 1998). In the late 1990s, California and Florida passed castration statutes for sex offenders. Typically, this approach requires that certain male offenders (e.g., repeat offenders) receive injections of synthetic hormones to reduce sexual arousal (Scott & del Busto, 2009). By and large, federal courts have upheld the use of chemical castration as a constitutional practice, as it appears such sanctions are considered treatment rather than criminal punishments (Scott & Holmberg, 2003).

Concerned that convicted sex offenders reoffend soon after release, during the latter part of the 1990s states began to implement residence restriction laws that prohibit sex offenders from living within a certain distance of places children congregate, such as schools, school bus stops, playgrounds, or daycare centers. Boundary restrictions ranged widely from state to state to a minimum of 500 feet to a maximum of over 2,000 feet. Premised on the belief that sex offenders prey on victims that live in close vicinity to them, the legislation soon spread as states across the country began to enact such laws (Meloy, Miller, & Curtis, 2008).

Beginning in the mid-1990s, a small handful of states enacted legislation that extends the death penalty to sex offenders. Proponents of the law argue that such legislation produces deterrent effects and has retributive value. It bears emphasizing that prior to this legislation some states (e.g., Georgia) had extended the death penalty to rapists of adults. However, the U.S. Supreme Court struck down those provisions in *Coker v. Georgia* (1977). In contrast, this new wave of death penalty laws specifically targeted sex offenders who had committed crimes against children. For example, Louisiana became the first state to enact a law that allowed for the execution of first-time sex offenders convicted of rape of a child. Not long after other states—including Georgia and Texas—adopted statutes that permitted the execution of child rapists (D'Avella, 2006).

With the advent of the Internet in the 1990s, other efforts focused on controlling the online distribution, manufacturing, and downloading of child pornography. For example, in 1996 the U.S. Congress passed the Child Pornography Prevention Act (CPPA). The CPPA expanded the federal ban on child pornography from pornographic images created using actual children engaging in sex acts to include computer-generated, or "virtual" depictions of children participating in sexually explicit conduct. Thus, the law would prohibit any individual in any state from creating, distributing, or accessing virtual child pornography.

Not least, states also began to implement mandatory HIV testing and related procedures for convicted sex offenders in the 1990s. Two pieces of federal legislation allowed states to enact these policies: the Ryan White Comprehensive AIDS Resources Emergency (CARE) Act (1990) and the amended Omnibus Crime and Control Act of 1968 (as reported by Radeloff & Carnes, 2008). For example, the CARE Act amended in 1996 includes a provision that permits states to mandate HIV testing for charged or convicted sex offenders (Webber, 1997). Additionally, some states have incorporated additional punishment in "intentional transmission" cases, or instances where sex offenders were aware of their HIV status prior to committing sex crimes. Alaska for example allows known HIV status to be considered an aggravating factor in a felony sex conviction (Radeloff & Carnes, 2008).

These policies represent some of the prominent efforts to respond to sex crime in the 1990s. This policymaking activity continued well beyond this decade. With that in mind, we now turn toward discussing prominent sex crime policies in the 2000s.

2000s: A Potpourri of Laws

One notable observation about the historical emergence of sex crime laws is that such policymaking flourished well into the 2000s, particularly on a federal level. In this decade, the federal government became increasingly active in developing sex offender legislation. It also created an agency designed to specifically manage the sex offender population.

We begin with a discussion of these federal initiatives. For example, in 2000 the Campus Sex Crimes Prevention Act (CSCPA) was implemented nationally. The federal Act is an extension of the prior registry and notification laws. In particular, it requires universities and colleges to publicize information to students, faculty, and staff about convicted sex offenders to whom they may come in contact with on campus. Thus, higher educational institutions are required per the CSCPA to disclose information about students or members of the campus community who may also be convicted sex offenders.

In contrast, the Prosecutorial Remedies and Other Tools to end the Exploitation of Children Today (PROTECT) Act enacted in 2003 targets offenders convicted of child sexual abuse. The federal law has three main provisions. It first mandates stricter punishments for child sex offenders. For example, it includes a "double strike" provision, or life imprisonment clause for sex offenders convicted of crimes against minors in cases where the offender had a prior conviction for crimes against children. It also prohibits jurisdictions from allowing pretrial release of persons charged with specific sex offenses against children. A second emphasis of the law involves responses to kidnapping offenses. For example, PROTECT establishes a national AMBER (America's Missing: Broadcast Emergency Response) alert system that provides states with resources for issuing public alerts in suspected kidnapping cases. The law also eliminates waiting periods before police can investigate incidents of missing persons ages 18–21. A third provision of the law focuses on controlling the distribution and sale of child pornography. For instance, the PROTECT Act mandates that child pornography convictions for possession and distribution be set at five and ten years of incarceration, respectively.

Two years later in 2005, the U.S. Congress introduced a bill modeled after a Florida law, the Jessica Lunsford Act, which aimed to implement new sex offender regulations. Jessica Lunsford was kidnapped from her home in Homosassa, Florida in 2005. Her abductor, John Couey, a twice convicted sex offender, failed to register with law enforcement in his community. Couey kept Jessica alive for days and raped her repeatedly, before finally burying her alive in his backyard. The tragic case brought national attention to the failure of states to effectively monitor sex offenders living in the community. Florida legislators, along with assistance from Jessica's father, Mark Lunsford, developed and enacted the Jessica Lunsford Act in 2005. The law requires thorough background checks of school employees who may come into contact with children (Couey was a mason at Jessica's school), more stringent monitoring of sex offenders, greater reliance on global positioning system (GPS) for sex offenders, increased penalties for sex offenders who fail to register in their state, and other requirements. The federal version of Jessica's Law has not yet been enacted by Congress; however, since 2005, 33 other states have adopted some form of the legislation (Terry & Ackerman, 2008).

The Adam Walsh Child Protection and Safety Act (2006; AWA), which was passed in memory of Adam Walsh, who was kidnapped from a Florida mall and murdered in 1981 is illustrative of federal efforts to tighten sex crime laws. This new piece of legislation expands the scope of crimes covered by the prior registry law outlined in the Wetterling Act. Notably, the U.S. Supreme Court upheld challenges to national registry and notification laws in a series of decisions heard in the early 2000s (*Connecticut Department of Public Safety v. Doe*, 2003; *Smith v. Doe*, 2003). This is notable because it highlights that few legal obstacles have stood in the way of the development of the AWA which aims to strengthen existing registry and notification laws. For example, in contrast to prior legislation, the AWA includes offenses of child pornography and conspiracy as registerable offenses and extends registration beyond adults to include certain juveniles convicted of serious sex offenses. Moreover, the AWA strengthens reporting requirements by requiring that sex offenders submit substantially more information to law enforcement compared to the requirements of the Wetterling Act. This provision mandates that offenders disclose their social security number, employer and school information, fingerprints, physical description, photograph, and a DNA sample. Related to this requirement, under the AWA sex offenders are now required to personally appear at law enforcement agencies to allow for a current photograph to be taken and to update and verify the accuracy of current registration information (Rogers, 2007).

Additionally, the AWA makes failure to register with a state agency a federal crime (Rogers, 2007). Prior to this federal law, failure to register in most states was considered a misdemeanor offense. Thus, this provision directly addresses concerns that sex offenders may purposely avoid registering in their respective states, and thus evade detection from law enforcement.

Moreover, the Act includes provisions to create a national sex offender database. To illustrate, in 2005 the federal government created a national registry, the Dru Sjodin National Sex Offender Public Website (NSOPW), which provides the public with access to a federal database of sex offenders as well as additional links to individual state registry websites (U.S. Department of Justice, 2012). According to the NSOPW, this innovation represents "an unprecedented public safety resource" designed to assist parents, employers, and other concerned citizens with finding "location information on sex offenders residing, working, and attending school ... in their own neighborhoods ... [and in] nearby states and communities as well" (U.S. Department of Justice, 2012).

A separate provision of the AWA—the Sex Offender Registration and Notification Act (SORNA)—mandates that states revise their registry and notification procedures according to federal guidelines. SORNA is designed to standardize states' registration and community notification practices by dividing sex offenders into three tiers based solely on the conviction of offense. Tier 3 offenders, the highest risk group, are required to be registered on a national database for life. Tier 2 offenders, those with a moderate risk, under SORNA, will remain on the registry for a 25 year period. Finally, Tier 1 offenders, the lowest risk group, per the federal law would be required to be on the registry for 15 years. The Act also increases penalties for failure to register. Under SORNA, not registering within a specified period of time or failure to update residential information could result in felony charges, punishable by ten years in prison (Terry & Ackerman, 2008). In addition, SORNA sets minimum standards for in-person verification. Under the new law, Tier 3 offenders must verify their information every three months, Tier 2 offenders, every 6 months, and Tier 1 offenders, every year. SORNA also removes states' discretion in determining what types of offenders will appear on their states' registry. That is, under SORNA, all convicted sex offenders (not just those who have been deemed "high-risk") must appear on states' registries. Per the federal provision, states will also be required to collect DNA samples of all registrants. Not least, SORNA mandates that juveniles be listed on state registry websites. Notably, some states have not required that juvenile sex offenders register with the state. Additionally, some states have prohibited jurisdictions from revealing identifying information about juvenile sex offenders via community notification procedures. This is notable because under SORNA states' discretion would be removed; thus, all juvenile sex offenders who were at least 14 years of age at the time of the crime would be required to register. Additionally, juveniles who have been convicted of aggravated sexual abuse would be subjected to community notification procedures (Terry & Ackerman, 2008).

It is unclear the extent to which SORNA has been fully enacted by states. A 2010 review has shown that the costs associated with SORNA implementation (e.g., reclassification, expanded enforcement personnel) "far outweigh" the costs of losing federal funding for not implementing the changes (Freeman & Sandler, 2010, p. 44). Because of the substantial costs associated with the law, states thus far, according to A. J. Harris and Lobanov-Rostovsky (2010, p. 219), have adopted a "wait and see" approach to compliance. The absence of uniformity in the implementation of the law presents a situation which could potentially generate state-level variability in the enactment of laws—precisely the situation SORNA sought to redress—whereby some states with greater fiscal resources may come into substantial compliance with the law and others, perhaps because the costs of implementing the law exceed the costs of sanctions for non-compliance, may not.

In 2007, the federal government created the Office of Sex Offender Sentencing, Monitoring, Apprehending, Registering, and Tracking (SMART). SMART represents one of the only federal agencies designed specifically to respond to sex crime, and thus highlights the new federal focus on preventing sexual violence. Per its mission statement, "the agency is responsible for all matters related to the implementation of the AWA including, administering the Sex Offender Registration and Notification Act ('SORNA'), administering grant programs relating to sex offender registration and notification as well as other grant programs authorized by the AWA, cooperating with and providing technical assistance to states and other public and private entities in relation to sex offender registration and notification and other measures for the protection of the public from sexual abuse or exploitation, and performing such other functions as the Attorney General may delegate" (Rogers, 2007, p. 1).

Beyond these federal reforms, another striking feature about the sex crime policy landscape in this modern era is the diversity of laws and initiatives that exist. As discussed earlier, per federal law, all states currently have in place sex offender registration and community notification policies. In addition, well into the 2000s, states have continued to strengthen current sex offender reforms or enact new ones. Illustrative of efforts to strengthen extant laws include a focus on the following: civil commitment, chemical castration, residence restrictions, capital punishment for sex offenders, and Internet-related restrictions. In the 2000s, states also began to enact new reforms: electronic monitoring, Halloween restrictions, driver's license and related identifying requirements, sex offender lifetime supervision laws, and gateway legislation (Wright, 2008).

Although states began to enact civil commitment statutes in the 1990s, this containment strategy continued well into the 2000s. As of 2008, 19 states had implemented some form of civil commitment for sexually violent or repeat offenders (Mancini et al., 2013). Additionally, in 2010 the U.S. Supreme Court upheld a federal statute as part of the AWA that allowed for detainment of sex offenders past their federal sentence (*U.S. v. Comstock*). Notably the U.S. Supreme Court in prior cases challenging civil commitment sanctions has upheld the use of the regulation.

A recurring theme of policies enacted in the 2000s has also been on greater use of chemical castration. Since the late 1990s when Florida and California first implemented chemical castration laws for convicted sex offenders, a number of states followed their lead. Put differently, in a relatively short period of time, at least eight states have enacted chemical castration laws (Mancini et al., 2013).

As mentioned previously, in the 1990s, states also began to design and implement residence restrictions or laws that prohibited convicted sex offenders from living near certain "hot spots." It bears emphasis that this push continued well into the 2000s. For example, one recent analysis of sex offender laws found that a vast majority of states (n=33) had implemented a state-level restriction as of 2008 (Mancini et al., 2013). Not least, states have allowed additional or supplemental residence boundaries, beyond the state-level restriction, to be implemented at the county or municipal level (Zgoba, 2011). Thus, in some instances boundaries can reach as high as 2,500 feet, as is the case for some Florida counties (Nobles et al., 2012).

States also continued to emphasize capital punishment for sex offenders well into the 2000s. Proponents have argued that the application of the death penalty for sex offenders is warranted given the serious nature and consequences of sexual victimization. At least five states have enacted death penalty statutes since Louisiana did so in 1995 (Mancini & Mears, 2010). However, in 2008 the U.S. Supreme Court in *Kennedy v. Louisiana* invalidated the state's child rapist law. The extent to which this ruling impacts other states' death penalty laws is questionable. It bears emphasizing that the Louisiana statute applied to first-time sex offenders (unlike other states' capital punishment laws). As a result, it constituted an extreme penalty in the eyes of the U.S. Supreme Court. Thus, it is unclear whether states that have enacted similar laws that target repeat offenders are in violation of the *Kennedy v. Louisiana* (2008) decision. Even so, some states have retained their death penalty laws for sex offenders or have vowed to revise the statutes to comport with Constitutional standards (Mancini & Mears, 2010). This approach however appears to be relatively symbolic as virtually no offenders have been tried under any states' child rapist law since the *Kennedy v. Louisiana* (2008) ruling.

As discussed earlier the federal government enacted the CPPA which prohibited the online distribution and downloading of virtual, computer-generated child pornography. Notably in 2002, in *Ashcroft v. Free Speech Coalition*, that law was struck down by the U.S. Supreme Court for being "overly broad and restrictive." Additionally, the Court questioned the logic of the law. For example, the premise behind the prohibition of child pornography is that merely its creation constitutes sexual abuse of the children shown in the image. Yet, if an image is created by use of computer technology or by photographing adults pretending to be children, there is no legal basis to ban the image. Despite the *Ashcroft v. Free Speech Coalition* (2002) ruling, the federal government has continued to legislate in this area. For example, as discussed earlier in 2003 the PROTECT Act was created. In particular, the federal law included provisions to criminalize a separate act of "pandering" or acts where one:

> advertises, promotes, presents, distributes, or solicits through the mails, or in interstate or foreign commerce by any means, including by computer, any material or purported material in a manner that reflects the belief, or that is intended to cause another to believe, that the material or purported material is, or contains (i) an obscene visual depiction of a minor engaging in sexually explicit conduct; or (ii) a visual depiction of an actual minor engaging in sexually explicit conduct.

Accordingly, under PROTECT, any instance where an individual *advertises* virtual images that depict child pornography is criminalized. For example, the PROTECT Act would criminalize an instance where an adult sends a minor virtually created child pornography via the Internet. As an extension to the earlier *Ashcroft v. Free Speech Coalition* decision, in 2002, the U.S. Supreme Court has upheld the "pandering" provision of PROTECT (in *U.S. v. Williams*, 2008). Even so, merely possessing virtually created child pornography—where there is no intent to promote or advertise it—is still legally permissible per the Court's earlier provision in *Ashcroft v. Free Speech Coalition* (2002).

Relatedly, a concomitant argument is that sex offenders may use the Internet to identify victims who are unaware of their prior crimes. Under this logic, states have enacted laws that restrict Internet access. Some of these initiatives require convicted sex offenders to publicize their offender status on social networking accounts. For example, Louisiana recently implemented a law that requires convicted sex offenders to list their status on "Facebook" or "MySpace" accounts (Onishi, 2012). Indiana bars sex offenders from using social networking websites, instant messaging services, and chat rooms. The extent to which these efforts to control offender Internet use and access are generalizable to other states' current laws is unknown as no systematic analysis of them exists. At the same time, the laws have been recently challenged in federal courts—as discussed in Chapter 11. Even so, as these accounts suggest, it may be that more states consider them as debates continue about how best to respond to Internet facilitated sex offending.

In addition to these efforts, other modern reforms have emphasized increasing supervision and tracking of sex offenders using recent technological advances. As a result, starting in the early 2000s some states began requiring that sex offenders be monitored with GPS or electronic monitoring technology (Payne & DeMichele, 2010). Perhaps speaking to their popularity these initiatives have proliferated nationally over a relatively brief time frame. For example, Armstrong and Freeman (2011) reported that at least thirty-nine states have enacted electronic monitoring or GPS statutes specific to sex offenders as of 2008. In short, the national emergence of these reforms suggests that states perceive electronic monitoring to be an effective strategy to manage what is perceived to be an especially dangerous class of offenders. At the same time, scholars have attributed the proliferation of such initiatives to "an increasingly get-tough, punitive response to sex offenders ..." (Payne & DeMichele, 2010, p. 276).

In line with efforts to reduce sex offenders' opportunities to recidivate, a handful of states beginning in the mid-2000s began experimenting with "Halloween" and more generally holiday restrictions. These laws prohibit convicted sex offenders from participating in holiday related festivities (e.g., greeting trick-or-treaters on Halloween, dressing up as "Santa Claus"). In some states, such as New Jersey, New York, Virginia, Wisconsin, California, South Carolina, and North Carolina, convicted sex offenders must abide by a curfew for particular holidays. In other states (e.g., Ohio, Illinois, and Virginia) offenders are required to be in contact with their probation or parole officer during Halloween evening (Chaffin, Levenson, Letourneau, & Stern, 2009). The premise driving such legislation centers on reducing opportunities to sexually reoffend by legislating steep punishments for non-compliance. For example, as reported by Durling (2006), offenders who violate this provision in South Carolina can face up to three years in prison (p. 322).

At the same time, efforts to better identify convicted sex offenders living in the community have been developed by states. For example, some commentators have voiced concern that sex offenders all too often easily evade registration requirements by moving to other jurisdictions. Although the extent to which registered sex offenders are "missing" from registry databases has been debated (see generally, Levenson & A. J. Harris, 2012), states have responded to the concern by enacting laws—such as driver's license restrictions—designed to better monitor convicted sex offenders (U.S. Government Accountability Office, 2008). As of 2008, the most current year for which national data are available, at least eleven states have enacted laws that require sex offenders to display a special driver's license notation identifying their registration status (Mancini et al., 2013).

Other states during this decade have expanded supervision requirements for sex offenders. Such laws are premised on the logic that sex offenders have an unusually high risk of committing repeat offenses over the life course, compared to other offenders, and so, must be monitored by law enforcement until death. Recent accounts indicate that lifetime supervision for sex offenders exists in 14 states as of 2008 (Mancini et al., 2013).

States have also experimented with efforts to expand registries and DNA databases to include non-sex offenders. Under this "gateway" legislation, offenders who have committed "predicate" crimes believed to lead to sexual offending in the future (e.g., burglary) would be required to preemptively register as sex offenders or to submit DNA to a sex offender database. To illustrate, Illinois enacted a measure that mandated that burglars submit DNA to a sex offender registry (Sample & Bray, 2003). Louisiana recently passed a law that requires offenders convicted of prostitution-related offenses (offering oral or anal sex for money) to register as convicted sex offenders (Lancaster, 2011a). On November 6, 2012, California residents voted nearly unanimously (81 percent) to incorporate "Proposition 35" a law that aims to tighten restrictions on human traffickers. One provision of the law mandates that such offenders register with the state's sex offender registry (Minugh, 2012). Notably, 17 other states have considered or are considering gateway-related legislation (Sample & Bray, 2003). Despite their popularity, such laws may be subject to legal challenges. For example, Louisiana's law has recently been struck down by a federal court (Lancaster, 2011a).

As this review indicates, a varied array of policy responses to sex crime currently exists in the U.S., many of which have been enacted over the last two decades. Figure 7.1 outlines the major sex offender reforms in contemporary criminal justice.

Figure 7.1. Timeline of Major Sex Offender Legislative Reforms, 1990s–2000s

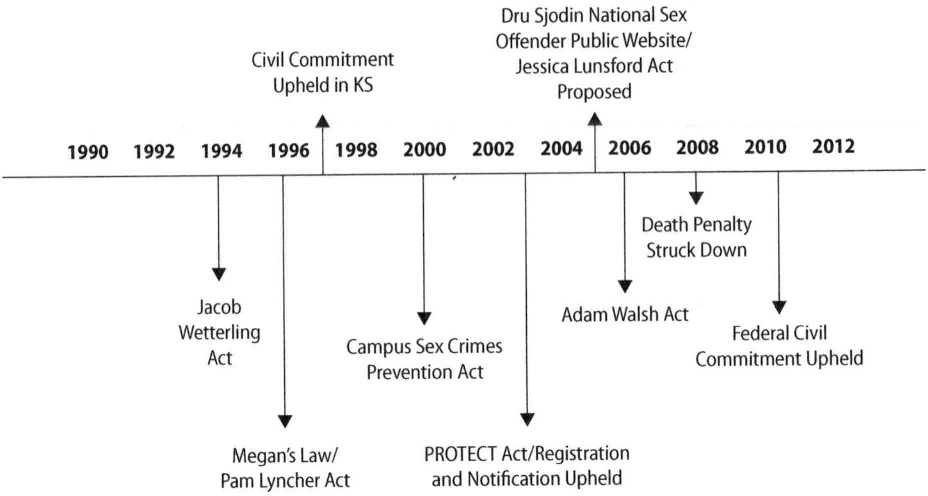

Chapter Summary

Although addressing sexual offending has at times been highly prioritized on the crime agenda in the U.S., sex crime policymaking has become a "growth industry" in the last two decades. In short, the federal government and states have recently developed and implemented an array of laws *exclusively* targeting sex offenders. Overall, these laws make three presumptions about sex offenders. First, they are premised on the belief that sex offenders—compared to other violent offenders—are significantly more likely to recidivate upon release. Second, sex crime legislation—to a large extent—assumes that stranger sex offenders, as opposed to known offenders, extend significant risk to victims. Third, and finally, current policies, with few exceptions, focus on containment strategies to manage sex offenders—registries, notification, residence laws—over approaches aligned with reform. The extent to which these premises are supported by empirical research will be discussed later in the text. For now, it is important to emphasize that a diverse set of sex crime laws exist, and that they derive from certain assumptions about sexual offending.

Below, a reading list is suggested—which includes some accounts already discussed—that traces the historical development of sex crime policy in the U.S. Chapter 8 begins the focus on the text's final theme, "Sex Crime Policy and Reform." In particular, it examines the logic and efficacy of prominent sex crime laws.

Additional Suggested Readings

Bancroft, J. (Ed.) (2003). *Sexual development in childhood* (Vol. 7). Bloomington, IN: Indiana University Press.

Block, S. (2006). *Rape and sexual power in early America*. Chapel Hill, NC: University of North Carolina Press.

Jenkins, P. (1998). *Moral panic: Changing concepts of the child molester in modern America.* New Haven, CT: Yale University Press.

Lancaster, R. N. (2011b). *Sex panic and the punitive state.* Berkeley: University of California Press.

Leon, C. S. (2011a). *Sex fiends, perverts, and pedophiles: Understanding sex crime policy in America.* New York: NYU Press.

Laws, D. R., & Marshall, W. L. (2003). A brief history of behavioral and cognitive behavioral approaches to sexual offenders: Part 1. Early developments. *Sexual Abuse: A Journal of Research and Treatment, 15,* 75–92.

Marshall, W. L., & Laws, D. R. (2003). A brief history of behavioral and cognitive behavioral approaches to sexual offender treatment: Part 2. The modern era. *Sexual Abuse: A Journal of Research and Treatment, 15,* 93–120.

Petrunik, M., & Deutschmann, L. (2008). The exclusion-inclusion spectrum in state and community response to sex offenders in Anglo-American and European jurisdictions. *International Journal of Offender Therapy and Comparative Criminology, 52,* 499–519.

Part III

Sex Crime Policy and Reform

Chapter 8

Logic and Efficacy of Sex Offender Laws

Chapter Introduction

As mentioned in prior chapters, over the last two decades the American public has expressed increased concern about sex crime (Velázquez, 2008). In response, the federal government and states have adopted a variety of laws aimed at reducing sexual offending and victimization. Since many of these reforms have been enacted relatively recently, research that has examined the efficacy of these laws is noticeably absent. This void is potentially problematic because emerging studies suggest that many members of the public and policymakers subscribe to myths about sex offending (Sample & Kadleck, 2008). Given these observations, it is unclear if extant sex crime reforms rest on these misconceptions or on sound theoretical and empirical foundations. The goal of this chapter is to contribute to a greater understanding of the efficacy of sex offender legislation by exploring the theoretical logic underlying prominent laws. In particular, sex offender registration and community notification laws, residence restrictions, civil commitment, and castration laws are reviewed. This focus is, of course, not exhaustive. As discussed earlier several other reforms currently exist. However, the policies this chapter focuses on represent a sampling of the more prevalent and controversial laws that have been identified by scholars (see e.g., Mancini et al., 2013).

Causal Logic Framework

Evaluating the theoretical or causal logic behind a program or reform is an important first step in policy development and implementation. The underlying logic as to why a policy should achieve stated goals is "just as subject to critical scrutiny within an evaluation as any other important aspect of the program" (Rossi, Freeman, & Lipsey, 2004, p. 135). Sex offender policies—particularly ones that have focused on implementing post-incarceration sanctions—have proliferated in recent years. At the same time, there is the concern that such policies may rest on inaccurate premises about sexual offending. Under this logic, Kruttschnitt, Uggen, and Shelton's (2000, p. 66) observation is illustrative: "Decisions about what to do with sex offenders are often made without the benefit of theoretical insights or sound empirical evaluations." The emergence of these recently implemented laws provides a unique opportunity to examine their causal and theoretical logic and to assess whether the assumptions behind them accord with theoretical accounts of sex offending, general logic, and prior research.

For a policy to achieve its intended goals and objectives, it is often necessary to understand why the program should work, from a theoretical or causal standpoint. Understanding the causal logic behind a law can also assist in modification or improvement of the initiative, likely increasing the effectiveness of the policy. Causal logic evaluations are used in the public policy field to assess various social programs (Rossi et al., 2004). Typically, these evaluations focus on causal pathways and immediate and distal goals of the program, policy, or law.

Consider, for example, a dietary awareness program instituted at school that targets overweight children and includes nutritional classes and exercise. The causal logic behind this program is that exposing children to dietary knowledge and encouraging exercise in school should lead to immediate weight loss. A more distal goal is that children will adopt healthy eating habits as adults, resulting in a reduced risk for specific illnesses such as diabetes and heart disease.

Note, however, that some of the assumptions about nutrition and weight loss underlying this program may be faulty. For instance, studies suggest that changing the dietary habits of children while at school may have little impact on overall weight loss and nutrition, as most meals are consumed at home (Golan & Crow, 2004; McLean, Griffin, Toney, & Hardeman, 2003). Thus, for such a program to effectively achieve weight loss among students it also would have to target parents and educate them about proper nutrition and the importance of exercise. In addition, research has found that poor eating habits may be linked to unmet emotional and psychological needs, suggesting that for a weight loss program to achieve its long-term goals, it should also include psychological counseling (Braet, Tanghe, Decaluwé, Moens, & Rosseel, 2004). This example is illustrative of the importance of outlining a policy's causal pathway or theoretical logic, which can assist in evaluating and improving the program (Rossi et al., 2004).

Broadly—as observed by scholars—there have been "increased calls from policymakers for 'evidence-based practice' in health and human services that have extended to criminal justice" (Lipsey, Petrie, Weisburd, & Gottfredson, 2006, p. 272). The recent proliferation of sex offender policies, for instance, has affected a large number of offenders and communities, without the benefit of systematic theoretical evaluations. Indeed, this view is reflected in an observation made by Fortney and colleagues (2007, p. 1) in their study of sex crime legislation: "sex offender policies are often hastily passed and are not based on scientific evidence, but on emotional reactions to high profile, violent, disturbing cases." Evaluating whether these relatively new laws accord with theory, logic, and prior research can provide policymakers with a better understanding of their rationales and may offer guidance about how to examine their impact and about how to modify or improve them to increase their potential effectiveness. Despite these arguments, little systematic analysis that unpacks the logic behind popular sex crime initiatives currently exists.

Causal Logic Evaluations of Sex Crime Laws

Below the causal logic behind four prominent sex crime laws—sex offender registration and community notification laws, residence restrictions, civil commitment, and castration laws is discussed. Thus, the analysis also considers the extent to which these reforms accord with theory, logic, and prior research. In particular, a summary of the policy is first presented. Next, the theoretical perspective driving the law is described. The third section reviews the general logic of the policy. Finally, an assessment is made concerning the extent to which the underpinnings of the policy are supported by prior research.

Sex Offender Registration and Community Notification Laws

Description of Policy

As reviewed earlier in the text, in compliance with federal laws (the Jacob Wetterling Act and Megan's Law) all states have enacted some form of sex offender registration and community notification (SORN) legislation. SORN laws require that state agencies maintain, verify, and update sex offender databases. At the same time, SORN laws mandate that law enforcement institute policies to notify community members about convicted sex offenders living in their neighborhoods.

Typically, sex offenders living in the community are required to register with the state police, departments of public safety, offices of the attorney general, or departments of corrections. The public is then notified about sex offenders living in the community via a state website that lists sex offenders by name, posts their pictures, and in some cases, displays their addresses and work locations (Tewksbury, 2005). In reviewing notification methods across the nation, Matson and Lieb (1996) reported that community notification methods may also include press releases, flyers, phone calls, door-to-door contact, and neighborhood meetings coordinated by law enforcement. In some instances, registration is only required for offenders deemed to be at "high-risk" for reoffending. Almost fifty percent of states assign offenders to one of three risk levels and notify the public according to the recidivism risk of the offender. In contrast, other states rely on a more liberal community notification approach, publicizing the location of all sex offenders without regard to recidivism risk (Mancini et al., 2013). As discussed in Chapter 7, some attempts have been made to standardize state registry and notification procedures. However, the extent to which these efforts have been implemented nationally is currently in question. The discussion that follows examines the general theory, logic, and research behind SORN laws.

Theory

At least two theoretical logics exist to describe this policy. The first is that these laws assume a capable guardianship effect. Registries alert community members to potentially dangerous offenders living in close proximity to neighborhoods. As community members become more aware it follows that offenders may encounter significantly less opportunities to offend, which should then deter them from committing future sex crimes.

As Tewksbury and Lees (2006, p. 310) have observed, sex offender registries and notification policies were "also created with the intent of promoting public shaming and societal ostracism." Thus, a second theoretical underpinning is that registered sex offenders will be perceived as social outcasts, which in turn reinforces both the moral code and serves as retributive action. It follows that a decrease in sex crime—via deterrence— among these offenders, and more generally, among potential offenders should occur. Lending support to this assertion is Quinn, Forsyth, & Mullen-Quinn's (2004, p. 219) contention that "the belief that sex offenders are unredeemable predators is so widely accepted in modern society that it provides a rallying point for victims' groups, conservative politicians, and others with the desire to build consensus on the need to make penal sanctions harsher." Thus, under this logic, sex offender registries and notification laws serve to both establish social solidarity and retribution. In turn, registered sex offenders are deterred from committing future offenses. Furthermore, a general deterrent effect may be achieved by deterring potential, or "would-be" sex offenders.

Logic

There are two goals of registration and notification policies. Collectively, an immediate goal of both policies is to ensure increased monitoring of sex offenders. This goal is presumed to be achieved soon after registration occurs. Proponents of registration and notification laws claim that due to this increased surveillance in the long term, registry and notification laws have the potential to reduce overall sex crime rates among registered offenders (see generally, Tewksbury, 2005). Figure 8.1 depicts a visual presentation of how this policy is expected to achieve its stated outcomes.

As inspection of Figure 8.1 suggests, there are several intervening mechanisms by which this process should follow. First, sex offender registration and community notification should lead to more effective monitoring of sex offenders from community members. In this instance, citizens are acting as capable guardians and upon learning about sex offenders' locations take precautionary steps to reduce sexual victimization (e.g., install additional locks, monitor children more closely). A second pathway is that closer monitoring of sex offenders should result in reduced opportunities to sexually offend. A third and final mechanism by which these policies should achieve success, is through specific deterrence. In turn, a decrease in the sexual recidivism among registered sex offenders should be observed.

Conversely, a second logic by which registries and notification may affect sex crime rates is depicted in Figure 8.2. Here, registries and notification result in sex offenders labeled as "social outcasts." In turn, proponents of these laws assert that such labeling serves two functions—it reinforces the moral code that sex offending will not be tolerated in the community and, also it serves as a retributive sanction. The end result? These mechanisms should lead to deterrence and eventually a decrease in sex crime among registered sex offenders and potential offenders.

The pathways by which these policies should work depend on several assumptions about the criminal justice system, citizen behavior, and sex offenders. First, these policies assume law enforcement can effectively track sex offenders living in the community. Second, both laws require that efforts to notify the public about sex offenders' whereabouts are actually successful. Put differently, these laws assume the public uses information about sex offenders and subsequently takes precautions based on that knowledge. Third, registries and community notification laws are assumed to have potential deterrent effects. Fourth, SORN laws hinge on the assumption that the bulk of sex offending is committed by sex offenders already formally convicted, but unknown to community members. Thus, these policies reflect a "stranger-danger" rationale, as opposed to "acquaintance-danger" logic.

Prior Research

To recap, the theoretical or causal logic underpinning these policies is buttressed by four broad assumptions about sex offenders and sex crime. The following claims are presented here and further discussed below:

Figure 8.1. Causal Pathway Model of Sex Offender Registration and Community Notification Laws: Capable Guardianship

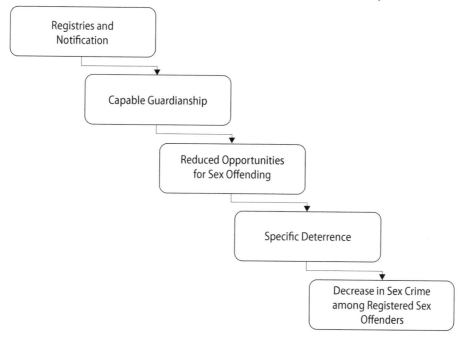

Figure 8.2. Causal Pathway Model of Sex Offender Registration and Community Notification Laws: Shaming/Retribution/Deterrence

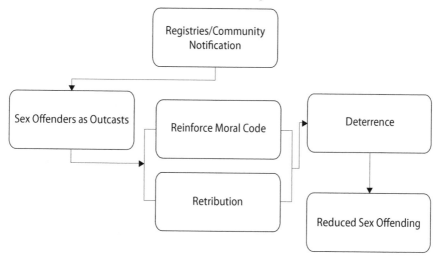

1) law enforcement can effectively track sex offenders living in the community
2) the public will use information obtained from sex offender registries/notification and take proactive measures to avoid victimization
3) sex offender registries/notification produce deterrent effects
4) most sex crimes are committed by stranger perpetrators with a known history of offending

1) Law enforcement can effectively track sex offenders living in the community. The number of registered sex offenders has increased exponentially over the last two decades. Current estimates indicate that approximately 740,000 offenders nationwide are required to register per federal and state laws (National Center for Missing and Exploited Children, 2012). Broadly speaking, the registry process is fairly standardized across states. Typically, law enforcement or other state agencies monitor and update online sex offender registries and also inform citizens about sex offenders living in close proximity. Few studies have examined whether these agencies can effectively supervise and monitor sex offenders, and sufficiently notify communities about dangerous sex offenders. However, among those that have, results suggest law enforcement faces significant challenges in maintaining these registries and notifying the public.

Avrahamian (1998) and Tewksbury (2002) both found that a significant number of sex offenders either do not register as required or, upon registration, provide a false address to law enforcement. For example, in a study of a state sex offender database (n=537), Tewksbury (2002, p. 23) found that a significant percentage of registered and listed sex offenders (around 25 percent) did not have sufficient information provided about them to allow identification by the public or furnished inaccurate information about their actual whereabouts, questioning law enforcement's ability to adequately maintain sex offender records. Levenson and Cotter (2005a) found similar results in a study examining whether sex offender databases list accurate information about registrants. In particular, the study revealed that more than half of the sample of convicted sex offenders (n=183) reported that information posted about them (e.g., address, offense history) on Florida's online registry was incorrect. More recently, Levenson and A. J. Harris (2012) reported that at least four percent of registered sex offenders fail to register with law enforcement. While this estimate is nowhere near the oft-cited, but empirically invalidated, claim that 100,000 sex offenders are currently "missing," it does indicate that at least 30,000 have absconded and thus are not being monitored.

Having said that, Tewksbury (2002, p. 25) as early as a decade ago has cautioned against making definitive assumptions about law enforcement's ability to manage the sex offender population as "the need for additional research is clear," but also acknowledged that "doubts voiced by some observers appear credible." Tewksbury's (2002) observation is particularly apt given the ever-growing registered sex offender population.

2) The public will use information obtained from sex offender databases and take proactive measures to avoid victimization. Proponents of online sex offender registries claim that such tools enable citizens to become better capable guardians, and thus, subsequent changes in potential victims' behaviors should reduce sex offenses. However, there is little empirical evidence to support this assumption. For example, in a 2006 review of the literature centered on examining public utilization of sex offender registries, Zevitz pointed to only two published studies. Both investigations that Zevitz (2006) identified, Matson and Lieb (1996) and Zevitz and Farkas (2000), focused on community members' reactions to the knowledge that sex offenders were living in their neighborhoods. Results from both studies cast doubt on the notion that registry use/notification triggers better capable guardianship in crime prevention. One other early study bears mention. In examining a sample of Washington residents (n=400), Phillips (1998) found that although eighty percent of the public endorsed support for a community notification law, more than half reported that they took no precautions (such as monitoring their children more closely) based on the knowledge that sex offenders were living in their communities.

More recently, Anderson and Sample (2008), in one of the only studies to systematically examine public awareness, use of sex offender registries, and subsequent protective action (n=1,821), found that approximately 35 percent of Nebraskans reported accessing the state's sex offender registry. In addition to registry use, the study also inquired about reasons for accessing the registry. Overall, most respondents endorsed positive views about its potential efficacy. For example, overwhelming majorities reported "feel[ing] family is safer" (87.6 percent) and "personally feel[ing] safer" (88 percent) after using the registries. A smaller percentage of users (38 percent)—reported taking some type of preventive action after accessing the registry (e.g., installing an alarm system, monitoring children more closely; p. 383). Here, the authors concluded that although most respondents knew the registry existed, "the majority of citizens had not accessed registry information and few respondents took any preventative measures as a result of learning [about] sex offender information" (p. 371).

More generally, other studies examining registries and awareness of sex offenders exist. To illustrate, Craun (2010) examined awareness of registered sex offenders' presence in a county in the southeastern United States using hierarchical linear modeling (HLM). She found that approximately three out of ten residents who lived within one-tenth of a mile of an RSO were aware of a sex offender's presence. Alternatively, this finding indicates that most citizens—nearly 70 percent—are unaware that registered sex offenders live in close proximity to them.

There are exceptions. To illustrate, Beck and Travis (2004) examined Ohio respondents exposed to community notification (n=87) and a control group of unaware citizens (n=149). Their results indicate that the notified group was significantly more likely to have taken some type of precautionary effort (e.g., installing outside lighting to their homes and becoming familiar with self-defense) than those who were uninformed. These findings however were not replicated in recent research. For instance, Bandy (2011) found no evidence that registry use resulted in increased citizen protection in her study of Minneapolis residents (n=407).

Collectively, these findings are notable for underscoring three general points that call into question the assumption that registry/notification laws result in better informed citizenry. First, the public is generally aware of the existence of registries/notification procedures and of registered sex offenders. Even so, most citizens have not accessed the registries in the past. And finally, while most Americans convey feeling safer after viewing the registries, with few exceptions, there is little evidence that they go on to take protective measures that would theoretically prevent sexual victimization. Accordingly, a main assumption of the registry/notification law is not clearly supported by extant research.

Overall, prior research has not systematically addressed a) the national prevalence and consistency of public use of sex offender databases, and b) the intervening mechanisms by which self-protective measures translate into reduced sex crime rates. For example, registries are dynamic and subject to change. Under this logic, citizens would need to regularly check the registries and keep abreast of community notification alerts about sex offenders. Concomitantly, research has not yet determined if the specific self-protective behaviors produced by registry use/community notification result in reduced sexual victimization.

This void potentially represents a significant research gap given that a key assumption behind sex offender registries and community notification is that they lower sex crime rates precisely because the public regularly makes use of them and also takes proactive measures to protect themselves. In short, based on published findings, it is clear that sex offender registries are not regularly accessed by citizens, and even among those members of the public who report accessing these sites, few take the necessary precautions to prevent sexual victimization.

3) Sex offender registries produce deterrent effects. According to scholars, sex offender registries and notification policies were "also created with the intent of promoting public shaming and societal ostracism" (Tewksbury & Lees, 2006, p. 310). Thus, registries may potentially produce a deterrent effect by increasing offenders' (or potential offenders') fear of being apprehended or labeled as a sex offender. Put differently, to the extent that SORN laws invoke fear of punishment in convicted sex offenders or potential offenders, reductions in sex crime should follow the enactment of such legislation.

Some evidence exists to suggest registries may produce a deterrent effect perhaps through fear of being formally labeled a sex offender. For example, Letourneau, Levenson, and colleagues (2010) used time series data to examine whether South Carolina's SORN policy exerted a general deterrent effect on adult sex crimes. In particular, the study tested whether adult arrests for sexual offenses decreased after the implementation of South Carolina's registry and notification policy. Study findings suggest that the law produced a general deterrent effect with an approximately 11 percent reduction in first-time sex crime arrests in the post-registry/notification period (1995–2005) relative to the pre-registry/notification period (1990–1994). Notably, comparison analyses with violent non-sex offenses against persons (assault and robbery) failed to produce similar effects. This is a noteworthy finding because it highlights that the deterrent effect is attributable solely to sex crime-specific legislation. Such deterrent results, however, were not evident in a separate analysis examining juvenile-perpetrated sex offenses (Letourneau, Bandyopadhyay et al., 2010).

However, other studies have revealed no significant deterrent effects of sex offender registry and community notification laws. These findings provide null support for the notion that registries may deter offenders (and would-be offenders) through the fear of sanctions or stigma. For example, in a study examining the effectiveness of a state sex offender registry in New Jersey, Zgoba and her colleagues (2008, p. 37) noted that "sex offense rates began to decline well before the passage of Megan's Law, [and so] the legislation itself cannot be the cause of the drop in general. It may, in fact, be the case that continuing reductions in sex offending in New Jersey, as well as across the nation, are a reflection of greater societal changes." In a separate study, Vásquez and colleagues (2008) investigated the impact of sex offender laws on reports of forcible rape across ten states from 1990 to 2000. Overall, they concluded that "sex offender legislation seems to have had no uniform and observable influence on the number of rapes reported in the states analyzed" (p. 188). Having said that, in three of the ten states examined by Vásquez et al. (2008), forcible rape rates significantly declined after the passage of Megan's Law. It is however equally true that in the seven other states no deterrent effect was observed. Other research has produced similar null effects of the deterrent impact of SORN laws (e.g., Ackerman et al., 2012; Sandler et al., 2008).

So, what can be concluded about the potential deterrent effects of registries and community notification laws? More precisely, how can the positive findings from Letourneau, Levenson et al. (2010) be reconciled with studies finding null effects of the registry/ notification laws? The disparity potentially derives from a number of factors. One that bears emphasis and is a theme of Chapter 10 involves state-level variability in the implementation of registry and notification systems. In short, states differ in their registry and notification laws. It may be that in some states (e.g., South Carolina) the law targets a greater number of offenders, or is better publicized to ensure potential offenders are aware of the consequences of offending. As a result, greater deterrence is achieved (see e.g., Letourneau, Levenson et al. 2010, p. 549). Indeed, while the Vásquez et al. (2008) study indicates little consistent effect of the registry/notification systems across most states, the fact that three states experienced significant declines in reports of sex crime after the enactment of Megan's Law suggests the potential for state-level factors to influence the efficacy of registry/notification policies. Even so, research to date does not clearly demonstrate that registry and notification laws significantly reduce sex crime nationally.

4) Most sex crimes are committed by stranger perpetrators with a known history of offending. Some accounts argue that registry/notification laws are premised on "stranger danger" logic. To illustrate, SORN laws assume that most sexual offenses involve perpetrators who have no prior relationship with victims. Under this logic, publicizing the names, addresses, pictures, and other identifying information of convicted sex offenders has the potential to encourage greater capable guardianship, or deterrence.

Moreover, SORN laws apply exclusively to offenders who have been convicted of sexual offenses. Thus, offenders who have been accused of a sex crime, but not convicted, or those who are never apprehended for their crimes will not appear on the registry. The extent to which prior research supports these assumptions is discussed below.

We will begin with the "stranger danger" logic. Notably, several scholars have pointed to widespread misconceptions about sex offenders and the nature of sexual offenses. Among these beliefs is the widely endorsed view that sex offenders typically target stranger victims. Per experts, such a characterization "distracts attention from more common types of offenders in a manner that unnecessarily inflates public fear and antagonism. It creates unnecessary fear among parents while diverting attention ... from the fact that most child molesters are known and trusted by the families they victimize" (Quinn et al., 2004, p. 222). Supporting this assertion is a growing body of research that has found that sex offenders typically have some type of prior relationship with their victims (Levenson et al., 2007; Terry, 2005). Indeed, several reports indicate that the vast majority of sex crimes (nearly 85 percent) are committed by offenders known to victims—such as a family member, close friend, spouse, neighbor, and other such individuals (Greenfeld, 1997; Logan, 2011; Sample & Bray, 2003; Terry, 2005). Put differently, this consistent finding appears at odds with the overall assumption that underpins sex offender registries and community notification laws—namely that sex crimes are often committed by offenders unknown to victims.

At the same time, a premise of SORN laws is that convicted or "known" sex offenders represent the greatest risk to society, and so, should appear on the registry sites and be subjected to community notification procedures. Questions arise however, about a) those offenders who are arrested but never convicted of a sex offense, and b) "successful" offenders who will never come in contact with the criminal justice system. Stated differently, to what extent are registries exhaustive? Prior research indicates that approximately 35 percent of sexual assault arrests result in offender convictions (Belknap, 2007, p. 303). Alternatively, this means the overwhelming majority of offenders accused of sex crime are never officially sanctioned, and so, would not be mandated to appear on a state or federal registry. Relatedly, emerging research has identified characteristics of "successful" sex offenders, or those offenders who have committed several offenses but are able to evade legal detection for significant periods of time (Lussier, Bouchard, & Beauregard, 2011). By definition, such offenders would not be required to register with law enforcement because they would be proficient in avoiding the legal system. Certainly, the competing assertion can be made. That is, one argument is that registrants include offenders who committed offenses serious enough to be convicted of a registerable offense. Having said that, because sexual offending is notoriously underreported, registered sex offenders likely comprise only a portion of the actual sexual offending population. Concomitantly, of those reported offenses, many—as Belknap's (2007) observation indicates—result in no legal sanction for offenders. Collectively, the available evidence indicates that registries may not include an exhaustive nor representative list of sex offenders.

Table 8.1 summarizes the logic and assumptions driving registry and notification laws.

Table 8.1. Logic and Assumptions of Sex Offender Registration and Community Notification Laws, Summarized

Logic	Assumptions
1) If capable guardianship is increased crime reduction will occur 2) Public shaming will deter convicted and potential sex offenders	1) Law enforcement can effectively track sex offenders living in the community 2) The public will use information obtained from sex offender databases and take proactive measures to avoid victimization 3) Sex offender registries produce deterrent effects 4) Most sex crimes are committed by stranger perpetrators with a known history of offending

Sex Offender Residence Restriction Laws

Description of Policy

Current research indicates that most states have enacted residence restrictions (n=33; Mancini et al., 2013). These laws prohibit sex offenders from residing in close proximity to places where potential victims frequent, such as a school, park, day care center, or school bus stop. Law enforcement typically is responsible for confirming that certain offenders do not live within a specified number of feet near areas that are outlined in the law (Tewksbury & Levenson, 2007). States differ in the length of boundary restriction. Nationally, residence restrictions range from 500 feet to 2,000 feet (Levenson & D'Amora, 2007). Furthermore, many states allow for counties or municipalities to enact additional boundaries beyond the state-level restriction (Zgoba, 2011).

Theory

The theoretical logic behind residence laws is that by restricting sex offenders from living near certain locations, the supply of potential sex crime victims will be greatly reduced. First, residence restrictions should present reduced opportunities for sex offenders to reoffend in places where children frequent, such as a school or playground. Offenders should then experience reduced exposure and proximity to children. A decrease in sex offender recidivism among affected offenders should then follow.

Logic

Figure 8.3 depicts how residence boundaries are expected to achieve stated outcomes. Specifically, an immediate goal of this policy is that residence restrictions will keep offenders away from areas in which children congregate. In turn, the opportunities to offend should be significantly reduced. Ultimately, this separation should result in a decrease in the number of reported sex crimes among convicted sex offenders.

There are several intervening mechanisms by which residence restrictions should effectively reduce sex crime. Figure 8.3 depicts this process. Since offenders cannot live

Figure 8.3. Causal Pathway Model of Sex Offender Residence Restriction Laws

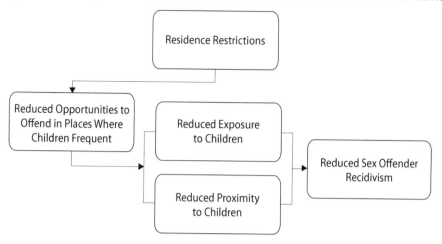

within close proximity to areas in which large groups of children frequent, such as schools and playgrounds, opportunities to sexually offend are presumed to be significantly limited. This reduction in exposure to potential victims and reduced proximity to them thus should lead to reduced recidivism among offenders affected by the law.

In particular, the theoretical or causal logic behind restricting where sex offenders can live rests on three beliefs about the nature of sex crime. First, this policy assumes that sex offenders have high rates of recidivism and must, therefore, be isolated from certain segments of the population. Second, residence restrictions assume that sex crimes are committed close to places children frequent. Third, this policy assumes that the vast majority of sex crime victims are children. To illustrate, recall that restrictions typically prohibit an offender from living near certain areas such as a school, park, day care center, or school bus stop. Note that these locations are places where children usually frequent, not necessarily adults.

Prior Research

The theoretical or causal logic underpinning sex offender residence restriction policies hinge on three assertions about sex offenders and sex crime. These claims are further reviewed below:

1) sex offenders have high rates of recidivism
2) a significant proportion of sex crimes are committed near places children congregate
3) the majority of sex crime victims are children

1) Sex offenders have high rates of recidivism. The majority of studies suggest that sex offenders as a group have relatively low levels of general and sexual recidivism (Craig, Browne, & Beech, 2008). In a comprehensive analysis of Canadian sex offenders (n=4,274), A. J. R. Harris and Hanson (2004) found that after 15 years, 73 percent of sex offenders had not been charged with, or convicted of another sex offense. Their study findings echo results found in Hanson and Bussière's (1998) quantitative review of recidivism studies which demonstrated an average recidivism rate of 13.4 percent for offenders after a follow-up period of four to five years (n=23,393). A similar large-scale study conducted by Langan, Schmitt, and Durose (2003) of U.S. sex offenders (n=9,691) found a recidivism rate (measured by criminal conviction) of 5.3 percent after three years.

In their study of Illinois offenders (n=146,918), Sample and Bray (2003, p. 76) found that only 6.5 percent of convicted sex offenders were re-arrested for a sex crime five years later. Among the burglar, stalker, and kidnap offenders, approximately two to three percent were re-arrested for a new sex crime. The difference suggests "that the overwhelming majority of offenders in all listed crime categories were not rearrested for a sex crime, including those persons classified as sex offenders" (Sample & Bray, 2003, p. 74). Even more, the authors concluded that "empirical research suggests that sex offenders are not as dangerous as sex offender policies would lead us to believe" (p. 76). Based on prior findings, extant literature does not support the assumption that sex offenders have unusually high rates of recidivism.

2) A significant proportion of sex crimes are committed near places children congregate. There is little empirical evidence that suggests that sex crimes are committed near schools, school bus stops, day care centers, playgrounds, and other locations where children frequent (Barnes, Dukes, Tewksbury, & De Troye, 2009; Levenson & Cotter, 2005b). For example, some indirect evidence indicates that sex offenders do not "self-select" to live near places children congregate. To illustrate, a study of sex offenders living in Colorado found that pedophiles who recidivated while under parole supervision were randomly scattered throughout the area and did not live closer to areas children frequent, compared to pedophiles who did not recidivate (Colorado Department of Public Safety, 2004). In another state study, researchers found no statistically significant relationship between proximity to schools or parks and sex offender recidivism (Minnesota Department of Corrections, 2003). Similar null effects of the law have been reported using an Iowa sample of sex offenders (Blood et al., 2008).

At least three other recent studies have directly tested whether convicted sex offenders go on to reoffend within certain distances of "hot spots." For example, in 2010 Zandbergen, Levenson, and Hart drawing on data of a matched sample of recidivists and nonrecidivist sex offenders from Florida (n=330) used mapping analysis to test whether male sex offenders who lived within 1,000 feet to 2,500 feet of schools or daycares were more likely to reoffend sexually in a two year period against children than those who lived farther away. Study results indicated that no statistically significant association existed between where a sex offender lived and whether he sexually reoffended against a minor victim. Put differently, sex offenders who lived in closer proximity to schools and daycares were no more likely to recidivate than those offenders who lived farther away.

In a separate study, Nobles and his colleagues (2012) examined whether a law designed to increase the boundary restriction in Jacksonville, Florida (from 1,000 feet to 2,500 feet) affected reports of sex crime. This municipal-level ordinance represents one of the largest boundary restrictions to be enacted nationally. Thus, the study tests the effect of the most stringent version of the law. Using a quasi-experimental design, measures of recidivism before and after the implementation of the ordinance were compared. Analysis revealed no statistically significant change in the number of sex crimes or recidivist sex crimes in the city after the law was implemented. Additionally, analyses do not support the notion that residence restrictions deter offenders. For instance, after controlling for several demographic factors (e.g., age, sex, race), individual-level multivariate results indicate that the timing of the residence restriction policy was not associated with a significant decline in sex crime arrests or sex offender recidivism after the law's implementation date.

In contrast, Socia (2012) examined the impact of county-level residence restrictions adopted in New York. Drawing on county-level data from all New York counties (n=62) over a ten-year period, the study assessed the extent to which residence restrictions were associated with rates of recidivistic sex crime arrests that involve children and adult victims. In addition, the study investigated whether the boundary zones impacted rates of non-recidivistic sex crime arrests that involve children and adult victims. Results indicate that residence boundaries did not significantly affect recidivistic sex crime rates involving children. This finding accords with the extant research mentioned earlier (Nobles et al., 2012; Zandbergen et al., 2010). In contrast to these prior studies, however, Socia's (2012) study uncovered a significant effect of residence restrictions on adult victimization. That is, only nonrecidivistic sex crimes involving adult victims significantly decreased when a residence restriction was present. This finding indicates that residence laws may impose a general deterrent effect, albeit, only for adult sex crimes. Thus, the laws may have prevented sex crimes being committed by first-time offenders involving adult victims. Having said that, in the absence of other studies replicating such results, Socia (2012) cautions against making strong conclusions about the potential for residence laws to reduce sex crime. Under this logic, his explanation is instructive (p. 628):

> It is still unclear whether residence restrictions themselves are associated with this decrease in nonrecidivistic sex crimes committed against adult victims. Rather, this decrease may be the result of two separate processes: First, it may be that the increased awareness of sex crimes by residents, which stems either directly from the passage of a residence restriction policy or occurs in concurrence with efforts to pass such legislation, leads to increased protective measures taken by adults and thus fewer overall sex crimes. However, it is not clear why this would have led only to a significant decrease in one of the four types of sex crimes. Second, it may be that the passage of residence restrictions results in, or occurs in conjunction with, an increased awareness by potential offenders of the entire package of consequences of sex crimes (not just residence restrictions), thus deterring potential first-time sex offenders.

Put differently, as Socia's (2012) observation indicates, it may be that general awareness and greater education about sex offenders have resulted in increased protective measures taken by potential victims, and thus, reduced opportunities for sex crime to occur. Concomitantly, potential offenders may be more aware of the punishments associated with sex offending, and so, are deterred from committing first-time offenses. Moreover, it is unclear why residence restriction laws—which were designed with the intent to protect child victims—would affect sex crimes involving adult victims, but not children in Socia's (2012) study. Still undetermined is why no deterrent effects in reducing sex crimes involving child victims have been detected by prior studies. In an evaluation of the goals of residence restrictions, Tewksbury and Levenson (2007) offered a potential explanation for the absence of significant findings. They concluded that "residence restrictions control where sex offenders sleep, but do little to prevent a motivated predator from visiting places where he or she can cultivate relationships with children and groom them for sexual abuse" (p. 56). Thus, residence restriction laws do little to restrict the day-to-day mobility of sex offenders.

3) The majority of sex crime victims are children. Because residence restrictions prohibit offenders from living near places children usually frequent, a central belief underlying sex offender residence restrictions is that most sex crime victims are children (Levenson et al., 2007). Indeed, empirical studies indicate that a substantial proportion of sex crime victims are minors. For example, Greenfeld (1997, p. 1) reported that "in self-reported victimization surveys of the public age 12 and older, teenagers report the highest per capita rates of exposure to rape and sexual assault" (p. 1). He further noted that almost half (44 percent) of rape victims were under the age of 18. More recent estimates consistently indicate that minors represent nearly half of all sex crime victims (Holmes & Holmes, 2009).

Thus, extant research appears to suggest that around half of sex crime victims are children. Bearing this finding in mind, recall that residence restrictions assume that almost all victims of sex crime are children, as evidenced by the types of locations that are listed in the law, such as playgrounds and school bus stops. For instance, bars, nightclubs, colleges and universities, and other places adults tend to frequent are typically not included as restricted locations in these statutes. At the same time, many states require that all convicted sex offenders abide by some type of residence restriction. These broad restrictions indicate that the typical residence law would do little to prevent sexual victimization of adults.

Table 8.2 provides a brief overview of the logic and assumptions of residence restriction laws.

Table 8.2. Logic and Assumptions of Sex Offender Residence Restriction Laws, Summarized

Logic	Assumptions
Restricting sex offenders' residences away from "hot spots" will reduce opportunities to reoffend	1) Sex offenders have high rates of recidivism 2) A significant proportion of sex crimes are committed near places children congregate 3) The majority of sex crime victims are children

Civil Commitment

Description of Policy

Civil commitment laws are designed to incapacitate sex offenders beyond the length of their original sentence. Although some states (e.g., California) had enacted such legislation well before the 1990s, most states have only recently implemented such laws. Current accounts suggest that at least 16 percent of states have enacted some form of civil commitment reserved for sex offenders (Mancini et al., 2013). Essentially, the civil commitment process involves a blending of the legal and mental health systems. Although state level variability exists in individual statutes, the general process can be easily summarized. That is, "sexually dangerous" or "sexually violent" offenders with a presumed mental disorder or defect are identified by the state in the months prior to their release. Mental health professionals—typically forensic psychologists—examine this group of offenders to determine the extent of recidivism risk. At this point, the state considers these clinical evaluations in its decision to impose civil commitment. If the clinical observations indicate that the offender poses little risk of reoffending, the state may release the offender. In contrast, if the evaluations indicate a high likelihood of future reoffending, the process continues. For instance, under this scenario, legal proceedings ensue to determine if sufficient evidence exists to indicate that the offender's mental illness may contribute to future offending. Offenders are typically allowed to retain counsel and present evidence showing that they are not at risk of reoffending during the hearings. Judges or juries decide if evidence exists to warrant civil commitment (Doren, 2002). In cases where such determinations are made, offenders are detained in a mental health facility indefinitely. Clinicians regularly assess offenders and ultimately determine when, if ever, offenders may be released. Some states (e.g., Washington) allow for an annual progress review by the court or a jury (Washington Department of Corrections, 2012).

Theory

There are two theoretical frameworks behind civil commitment laws. First, the law emphasizes offender incapacitation. Under civil commitment, offenders can be easily controlled by the state if they are not permitted to re-enter society. At the same time, civil commitment can be viewed as a rehabilitation-based effort. Typically, detained offenders are offered programming and rehabilitative interventions during their indefinite detainment. Thus, civil commitment may result in desistance from crime as offenders acquire social skills and learn techniques to manage their sexual urges. The end result in each instance is reduced reoffending.

Logic

Since there are two causal logics expressed by civil commitment laws, two causal logic models are presented in Figures 8.4 ("Incapacitation" model) and 8.5 ("Rehabilitation" model). Figure 8.4 outlines how incapacitation should impact sex offending. From the model, indefinite incapacitation permits the state to separate the offender from society, and thus, potential victims. In turn, offending is prevented.

A second pathway model (Figure 8.5) shows the rehabilitative potential of civil commitment. Notably, the U.S. Supreme Court in three decisions has upheld the use of civil commitment. Rather than judging the law as ex post facto or punitive punishment, the Court instead has viewed the penalty as having a rehabilitative value (see, *Kansas v. Hendricks*, 1997; *Kansas v. Crane*, 2002; *U.S. v. Comstock*, 2010). Thus, a clear logic stemming from civil commitment is that it provides additional opportunities—above and beyond what may be offered in correctional facilities during offender sentences—to reform offenders. As inspection of Figure 8.5 indicates civil commitment laws may lead to offender rehabilitation via programming and treatment opportunities. Thus, while detained, offenders have access to treatment programs designed to reduce their motivation to sexually offend. At the same time, such programming may assist with the development of interpersonal skills, anger management strategies, and other life skills that may be deficient in offenders.

Prior Research

The theoretical or causal logic behind civil commitment laws derive from two assertions about sex offenders and sex crime:

1) states can identify "high-risk" offenders
2) exposure to treatment during detainment will result in desistance from offending among offenders eventually released

1) **States can identify "high-risk" offenders.** Implicit in civil commitment statutes is the premise that sex offenders most at risk of reoffending can be identified. Under this

**Figure 8.4. Causal Pathway Model of Civil Commitment Laws:
Incapacitation Model**

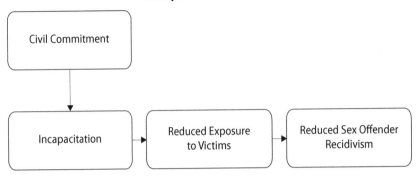

**Figure 8.5. Causal Pathway Model of Civil Commitment Laws:
Rehabilitation Model**

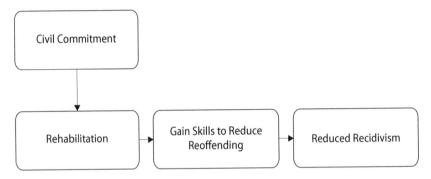

logic, psychologists, psychiatrists, and criminologists rely on their clinical judgments or risk-assessment[1] tools to determine offenders' risk of recidivism. Thus, a key question about this assumption is, does research in fact support the view that states can effectively identify "at-risk" offenders? From most accounts, the answer is "yes." For example, Levenson (2004) examined two groups of sex offenders who were considered for civil commitment under Florida's Jimmy Ryce Act. The first group consisted of offenders who were recommended by forensic evaluators to be civilly committed by the state (n=229). The second group included 221 sex offenders who were recommended for release. Study results indicate that the first group scored significantly higher on actuarial (statistically-derived) risk assessment instruments. Given these findings, Levenson (2004) endorsed a positive review of Florida's selection criteria, "Florida evaluators are selecting for commitment those sex offenders who are more sexually deviant and are at higher risk for reoffense as measured by factors known to be associated with sex offense recidivism" (p. 645). Other studies indicate that civilly committed offenders share traits that suggest a greater propensity to commit crime than offenders who are not civilly committed (see generally, Boccaccini, Murrie, Caperton, & Hawes, 2009; Doren, 2002; Levenson & Morin, 2008).

---

1. Generally, these instruments consider a number of factors (e.g., prior history of offending, victim preference, relationship history) in determining offenders' risk of recidivism. Risk assessment tools also identify treatment needs. A more detailed discussion about them, including their strengths and limitations, will be discussed in the following chapter.

Collectively, these findings indicate that current strategies to identify high-risk sex offenders are believed to be generally valid. Having said that, to date data from only a small handful of states' civilly committed sex offender populations have been made available through published research (see e.g., McLawsen, Scalora, & Darrow, 2012). At the same time, states rely on different methods to assess sex offender risk. Thus, the extent to which published findings accord with other states' civil commitment procedures is unknown.

Not least, researchers have pointed to methodological issues in accurately determining offender risk of reoffending. One glaring issue is that sexual recidivism occurs relatively infrequently (i.e., low baseline rates of sexual offending exist). For example, Abracen and Looman (2006) in their study of civil commitment reported that only 13.3 percent of their sample of high-risk sex offenders (n=188) recidivated after a five-year follow-up period (they note similar results have been reported in other studies). Accordingly, these low baseline estimates of reoffending indicate that current risk assessment tools have the potential to produce biased results when identifying "high-risk" offenders. Abracen and Looman's (2006, p. 136) observation is illustrative of this possibility:

> The phenomenon of relatively low rates of sexual offense recidivism is commonly referred to as the base rate problem. The base rate problem is critical ... with a base rate of under 30 percent given the current state of the art in risk assessment, prediction will be wrong most of the time ... the fact that there is a relatively low base rate of long term sexual recidivism suggests that evaluators may have a difficult time differentiating those offenders who are going to offend sexually in the future from those who are not.

2) Exposure to treatment during detainment will result in desistance from offending among offenders eventually released. A second premise of civil commitment statutes centers on the assumption that detainment affords additional opportunities to treat high-risk sex offenders. Complicating matters in assessing the rehabilitative value of civil commitment is that few systematic studies exist that a) demonstrate the types of treatment programs currently in use by states, and b) directly test the impact of a civil commitment sanction on subsequent sexual offending. Thus, the review of research that follows discusses extant work that may be only indirectly related to whether civil commitment can effectively reduce future offending through treatment.

For example, one study conducted by D. Harris, Knight, Smallbone, and Dennison (2011) examined specialization and persistence among two groups of offenders—those civilly committed to a mental health facility in Massachusetts between 1959 and 1984 (n=247) and a sample of similarly situated non-committed sex offenders (n=189). Two findings from the study are notable. First, civilly committed sex offenders were significantly more likely to recommit sex offenses compared to non-committed offenders. In addition, committed offenders were nearly three times as likely as non-detained offenders to specialize in their offending—that is, they tended to recommit similar types of offenses for which they were originally detained. Per D. Harris and her colleagues (2011, p. 254), "this might suggest that the period of commitment was patently unsuccessful in reducing one's tendency to recidivate." At the same time, the researchers point to other reasonable interpretations. For example, civilly committed offenders may have been exposed to ineffective treatment during their detainment. Not least, it must be cautioned that civilly committed offenders, by definition, represent the "worst of the worst" offenders, and so, are assumed to be significantly more likely to reoffend despite treatment interventions.

Fundamentally, civil commitment assumes treatment can be effective in reducing sex offending. While most research indicates that treated sex offenders, on average, are less likely to recidivate than those who receive no intervention, there are caveats. To illustrate, it is equally true that many sex offender treatment programs have been found to be ineffective; strikingly, some may actually increase recidivism (see, e.g., Quinsey, Khanna, & Malcolm, 1998). Not least, the potential efficacy of any given intervention can vary greatly depending on the type of treatment and the type of sex offenders (Terry, 2005, p. 163). For example, Lösel and Schmucker (2005) used meta-analysis to examine results from extant sex offender treatment studies (n=69). They identified seven separate categories of treatment (e.g., "hormonal," "cognitive-behavioral," "insight-oriented," "therapeutic community"). Organic treatments (such as surgical castration and hormonal medication) showed the most promise in reducing sexual recidivism. Under the psychosocial treatment category, cognitive behavioral therapy was the most effective intervention. In contrast, the four other treatment methods were significantly less effective. Other research has reported a similar pattern of disparate treatment effects. Gallagher, Wilson, Hirschfield, Coggeshall, and MacKenzie (1999, p. 19) in a meta-analysis of 25 studies, revealed that "Cognitive behavioral approaches appeared particularly promising [in reducing sexual recidivism], whereas the data produced less support for behavioral, chemical, and generalized psychosocial treatment." Thus, civil commitment centers that rely on proven interventions would likely be most effective in reducing future recidivism. At issue, however, and as discussed earlier, is that virtually no systematic analysis of state-level civil commitment programming efforts currently exists. Accordingly, it is unknown if states who practice civil commitment include evidence-based treatment strategies as opposed to the less effective interventions.

Table 8.3 summarizes the general logic and premises behind civil commitment legislation.

Table 8.3. Causal Logic of Civil Commitment Laws, Summarized

Logic	Assumptions
1) Indefinite confinement precludes high-risk offenders from committing further offenses 2) Detainment allows for additional rehabilitation	1) States can accurately identify "high-risk" offenders 2) Exposure to treatment and programming during detainment will result in desistance from offending among offenders eventually released

Castration Laws

Description of Policy

Castration policies are perhaps the most unique and controversial response to sex crime in the U.S. (Lösel & Schmucker, 2005). As mentioned earlier, these policies require that sex offenders are administered MPA, a synthetic hormone, to induce reversible chemical castration (Mancini et al., 2013). Wright (2008) reported that an increasing number of states have enacted or are considering implementing castration laws. Castration can be a court-ordered sanction (normally applied only to offenders living in the community), a condition of parole or probation, or a voluntary procedure (i.e., an offender can elect to undergo the procedure in exchange for a possible reduced sentence).

Although states vary in their implementation of castration policies, it appears that overall, castration is a sanction reserved for repeat or predatory sex offenders (Mancini et al., 2013). Typically, it involves a multi-step process. To assess risk, an offender is first

Figure 8.6. Causal Pathway Model of Castration Laws

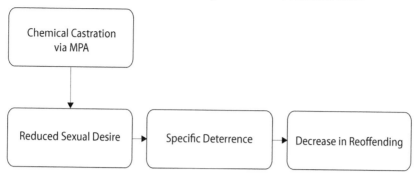

psychologically evaluated. Then, if deemed eligible for castration, the offender may go through a lengthy legal proceeding. If the sanction is eventually handed down, the offender is then required to take medication that reduces sexual urges (Scott & Holmberg, 2003).

Theory

A theoretical assumption behind castration laws is that if males[2] are physically restrained from maintaining an erection, they will be unlikely to commit sexual offenses involving penile penetration. By extension, such policies assume that sexual battery is the most prevalent type of sex crime, and also a crime primarily committed to fulfill sexual urges.

Logic

Figure 8.6 illustrates the causal pathway by which castration is expected to reduce sexual offending. The underlying rationale underpinning the sanction is that biological interventions can be used to reduce sex offending among males. Specifically, as Figure 8.6 shows, chemically castrated males should experience a reduction in sexual urges which should specifically deter them and result in reduced sexual offending involving penile penetration.

Prior Research

Three main rationales are typically offered to support castration policies. Below, these claims are presented and their logic further explored:

1) only males commit sex crimes
2) sexual battery is the most prevalent type of sex crime
3) sex crime is motivated by sexual desire

1) Only males commit sex crime. Since castration applies exclusively to male offenders, a central belief about this sanction is that only males commit sex crime. Overall, empirical

2. Although chemical castration statutes have been typically written to be gender neutral, the drugs that induce chemical castration have no effect on the female sex drive (Spalding, 1998).

evidence supports this assertion, but it also points to instances in which females commit sex acts. Greenfeld (1997, p. 2) reported that nearly all arrestees for forcible rape in 1995 were male (99 percent) and that almost one in ten arrestees for other sex offenses were female. In a later study, the Center for Sex Offender Management (2007) relayed that approximately one percent of women were arrested for forcible rape and less than six percent were arrested for other types of sex crimes.

Although the assertion that males commit the majority of sex crimes appears soundly supported by empirical research, female offenders still account for almost ten percent of sex crimes reported to law enforcement. Castration policies only target male offenders and do not address female sex offending. Extant research focusing on "this unique segment of the sex offender population" remains quite limited and there appears to be little "evidence-based guidance or other consensus" about the most effective approaches toward working with female offenders (Center for Sex Offender Management, 2007, p. 1). Experts appear to agree, however, that understanding female sex offenders "remains a significant area of need within the criminal and juvenile justice fields" (Center for Sex Offender Management, 2007, p. 1). Having said that, castration policies would not appreciably affect sex offenses committed by female offenders.

2) **Sexual battery is the most prevalent type of sex crime**. Another belief surrounding castration policies is that sexual battery or forcible rape offenses (defined, typically, as sexual contact involving the penis, another body part, or foreign object) occur more frequently than other types of sex crime (Terry, 2005). Empirical literature suggests that although sexual battery/rape offenses account for a substantial number of sex crimes, the vast majority of offenses reported to law enforcement involve other types of victimization, including sexual assault (e.g., fondling, touching, or threatening sexual violence), lewd and lascivious acts (e.g., allowing children to view pornography, exposing children to inappropriate sexual conduct), and other sex acts (see generally, Terry, 2005). To illustrate, in a national study of sex offenses, Langan and colleagues (2003, p. 7) reported that of the released 9,691 sex offenders in 1994, 3,115—approximately 30 percent—were considered "rapists." Alternatively, nearly 70 percent of offenders (n=6,576) according to Langan et al.'s (2003) estimates were "sexual assaulters" who had committed non-sexual battery crimes. These numbers accord with earlier research. For example, in a similar study of national sex crime reports, Greenfeld (1997, p. 8) relayed that in 1995, state law enforcement agencies recorded approximately 34,650 arrests for forcible rape and 94,500 arrests for other types of sex offenses.

Thus, the clear majority of sexual offenses committed in the U.S. can be described as acts that do not involve sexual battery or forcible rape offenses. By extension, the bulk of sex crimes can be described as conduct other than sexual contact involving penetration of the penis, body part, or other object (Greenfeld, 1997; Langan et al., 2003), suggesting that castration policies would not necessarily affect non-penetrative sex crimes (e.g., molestation offenses).

3) **Sexual crime is motivated by sexual desire**. A widespread belief held about sex crime and one that appears to drive the proliferation of castration laws, is that such offenses are motivated primarily by the sexual urges of offenders. As mentioned previously, various typologies of sex offenders currently exist. Most of these typologies presume that sex crime is motivated by non-sexual needs. For example, in Knight and Prentky's (1990) MTC: R3 rapist typology, only one classification—the "sexual gratification rapist"—of four sub-types identified (i.e., "opportunistic," "pervasively angry," and the "vindictive rapist") was characterized as being driven to offend for purely sexual reasons. More generally, in a review of the literature, Terry (2005, p. 72) explained that certain types of sex offenders, in particular, the "power-control rapist" and the "mass rapist" are more

likely to offend out of a need to express power or domination over victims. At the same time, Terry (2005, p. 72) acknowledged that other types of sex offenders, such as the "exclusively sexual" or "sadistic" rapist, appear to commit sexual battery for purely sexual needs. In another investigation, Groth, Burgess, and Holmstrom (1977) examined the motivation behind sexual battery. In their study, 133 offenders and 92 victims were interviewed to assess whether the sex crime was motivated by power, anger, or to fulfill sexual needs. Notably, the authors found that there were "no rapes in which sex was the dominant issue; sexuality was always in the service of other, nonsexual needs," such as a need to control or impose power over a victim (Groth et al., 1977, p. 1239).

Other scholars have pointed to the difficulties in ascertaining the motivations behind rape. Baker (1997, p. 566) noted that extant research suggests that "all rapes are not alike ... some are predominately about sex, some rapes are predominately about masculinity." This point is important to highlight because it indicates wide heterogeneity in the motivation to sexually offend. At the same time, an empirical limitation of this research is that assumptions about the motivation behind an offense are often made based on responses of offenders or victims. Offenders may be unwilling or unable to accurately recall the primary motivation behind the sex crime. Moreover, victims may be traumatized from the offense and may not be able to report the reason behind the sexual offense. The assumption that sex crime is motivated by sexual desire appears only partially supported by the literature, calling into question the efficacy of castration policies applied to a wide range of offenders.

Table 8.4 reviews the general logic and assumptions behind castration legislation.

Table 8.4. Causal Logic of Castration Laws, Summarized

Logic	Assumptions
Reducing sexual urges will result in reduced reoffending among convicted sex offenders	1) Only males commit sex crimes 2) Sexual battery is the most prevalent type of sex crime 3) Sex crime is motivated by sexual desire

Implications

Reflecting in part the increased attention to sexual victimization, the "1990s ushered in an unprecedented amount of sex offender legislation" (Sample & Kadleck, 2008, p. 40). Scholars have argued that these laws have been developed and implemented without the benefit of prior empirical investigation. Thus, an examination of this sort can be particularly helpful in identifying how these laws should achieve intended goals. In particular, analyses suggest that some of the widely held assumptions driving sex crime laws are in direct contrast to what empirical research has uncovered. Concomitantly, the extent to which some assumptions are empirically supported by research is difficult to ascertain as several gaps remain in the sex offending literature. Below, the implications of this chapter are highlighted.

Although sex offender registries and community notification laws have been enacted nationwide some of the assumptions surrounding these laws do not appear to accord with theoretical accounts of sex offending or extant research. For instance, one main premise behind these laws is that better capable guardianship will reduce sexual offending. Within that assumption is the belief that the public frequently visits state sex offender registry websites and upon learning about sex offenders' whereabouts adopt behaviors to reduce victimization. Although research is limited, extant studies suggest a majority of citizens do not visit these sites and that if they do, many neglect to take any precautionary measures to reduce sexual victimization (Anderson & Sample, 2008; Phillips, 1998; Zevitz & Farkas, 2000). A separate premise underlying registry and notification laws is that state agencies can effectively manage and update sex offender websites. At least two studies suggest law enforcement often faces difficulties in accurately maintaining sex offender databases (Levenson & Cotter, 2005a; Tewksbury, 2002). Notwithstanding these critiques, some research suggests that registries may produce general deterrent effects, particularly among first-time adult sex offenders (Letourneau, Levenson et al., 2010). However, the precise mechanism by which SORN laws may produce deterrent effects is not fully understood. At the same time, observed deterrent effects of the registry/notification laws could be solely attributable to larger societal changes, and not the actual law (see e.g., Zgoba et al., 2008).

Sex offender residence restrictions have also been implemented across the nation. A central assumption underlying these laws is that sex offenders often commit crimes near places children regularly congregate. However, there is virtually no empirical evidence that suggests that sex crimes are committed near schools, school bus stops, day care centers, playgrounds, and other locations where children typically frequent (Barnes et al., 2008; Minnesota Department of Corrections, 2003; Zandbergen et al., 2010). Moreover, research indicates that residence restrictions have not been successful in reducing recidivistic sex offenses. Having said that, some emerging work indicates the law may produce general deterrent effects, particularly for offenses involving adult victims (Socia, 2012). To be clear, however, these findings may be the result of other factors— such as greater knowledge in preventing sexual victimization—rather than actual impact effects of residence restrictions.

Civil commitment procedures are in use by states concerned about high-risk sex offenders. Thus, these laws presume that states can effectively identify offenders at greatest risk of reoffending. Overall, extant studies provide support for this assumption. That is, states—at least those for which empirical evaluations exist—are accurately identifying through the use of actuarial/risk assessment tools those offenders who appear most at risk of reoffending (see e.g., Levenson, 2004). Having said that, relatively few evaluations have been conducted for only a small handful of states. At the same time, the second assumption driving civil commitment laws—specifically that treatment can effectively reduce reoffending—is substantially less supported by extant research. That is, virtually no systematic analysis examining the types of treatment/programming options offered in civil commitment centers currently exists. By extension, it is unknown whether civil commitment centers provide effective treatment for committed offenders. Moreover, the extent to which civilly committed offenders go on to recommit offenses once released from detainment has not been sufficiently investigated by prior research.

States have also experimented with castration laws, which are designed to reduce sexual urges of sex offenders. These laws rest on some accurate and some faulty assumptions about sex crime and offenders. For example, castration laws target serious offenders most likely to commit sex offenses. Thus, such legislation derives from a correct presumption about sex crime (i.e., that most sex offenses are perpetrated by male offenders). It is notable, however, that such policies would not apply to female sex offenders who commit upwards of ten percent of all sex offenses (Center for Sex Offender Management, 2007). At the same time, there are some faulty assumptions expressed in the law. To illustrate, one major premise driving the enactment of castration laws is that sex crimes typically involve sexual battery. Yet, the clear majority of sex offenses include sexual acts other than sexual battery or forcible rape. Put differently, the majority of sex crimes can be described as conduct other than sexual contact involving penetration of the penis, a body part, or other object (Greenfeld, 1997; Langan et al., 2003). In turn, castration policies would only reduce acts of sexual battery which occur relatively less frequently than other types of offenses (e.g., molestation, sexual assault crimes).

Several implications emerge from this study. First, the study examined the causal or theoretical logic of prominent types of sex offender laws—sex offender registries and community notification, residence restrictions, civil commitment, and castration, and found along some dimensions, that these laws lack clear theoretical foundations. As discussed earlier, states across the nation have not just implemented the four laws studied here. In recent years, a plethora of other laws have been enacted across the U.S. These laws include Halloween restrictions, laws requiring sex offenders to carry special identification cards, lifetime supervision of sex offenders, and an assortment of other sanctions. If study findings are any indication, it might also be the case that these other policies lack a clear theoretical foundation. Should such problems be enduring to these laws, it suggests these newer types of laws should be modified in some way to increase their likely effectiveness.

Such efforts may also inform subsequent impact studies of these reforms. A natural next step then is to examine the impacts of these laws currently implemented nationally. Leading with the premise that America's sex offender laws have been developed with little empirical guidance, this study examined the theoretical basis for prominent sex crime laws. It did not, however, assess the actual impacts of these laws. Notably, in the past twenty years, states have enacted a broad array of other reforms not examined in this study. Many scholars have questioned not only the theoretical and empirical basis behind sex offender legislation, but have also doubted the likely effectiveness of these reforms. Indeed, scholars have observed that impact studies about these numerous laws are virtually "non-existent" (Vásquez et al., 2008, p. 175). Heeding calls for additional research in this area, future studies, informed by prior causal logic evaluations, should conduct evaluations of these laws. Ideally, such research will account for the significant variation in the content of these laws across states. That is, to ensure impact evaluations produce generalizable results, studies should be conducted across a wide variety of sites across the U.S.

Study findings presented here also hold implications for policy. Similar to findings from other studies, this study found that some sex crime policies lack an obvious coherent theoretical based or empirical based foundation. For example, a central assumption behind sex offender registries and community notification laws is that citizens will view these sites and upon learning about the whereabouts of sex offenders, will better protect themselves and their children. Given that prior research has found that citizens do not typically access online registries and make behavioral changes after viewing them, policymakers may want to consider developing and implementing public relations campaigns in which they disseminate information about these registries and community notification procedures and encourage members of the public to visit these sites.

Chapter Summary

An overriding lesson that emerged from review of prominent sex crime legislation is that sexual offending constitutes a significant social problem in America. Policymakers, often in response to mounting public concern about sex offenders, may feel compelled to act, to 'do something' about sexual offending and sexual victimization (Sample & Kadleck, 2008, p. 43). However, the extent to which sex crime reforms reflect "best practices" to reduce sexual offending is questionable. To illustrate, some of the assumptions upon which sex crime laws rest upon are directly contradicted by a larger body of research. At the same time, a more comprehensive knowledge base — one that systematically examines the impact of these laws across a range of jurisdictions, their implementation, and unintended effects — is needed to fairly assess the efficacy of sex crime legislation. In particular, this chapter examined the causal logic behind sex offender registration and community notification laws, residence restrictions, civil commitment, and castration laws. While these initiatives are popular and widespread, numerous other laws have recently been enacted nationally. Studies assessing the causal logic behind these reforms are virtually non-existent. What this situation reflects is that greater empirical attention to this ever-growing range of policy responses and the assumptions of these laws are needed to assess the extent to which current reforms constitute "evidence-based" policy.

Below, a suggested reading list centered on sex crime policy and evidence-based practice is recommended. In line with understanding sex crime policy and reform in the U.S., Chapter 9 reviews prominent methods to determine sex offender recidivism and potential treatment issues.

Additional Suggested Readings

Council of State Governments. (2010). *Sex offender management policy in the states: Strengthening policy and practice.* Lexington, KY: Author.

Tabachnick, J., & Klein, A. (2011). *A reasoned approach: Reshaping sex offender policy to prevent child sexual abuse.* Beaverton, OR: Association for the Treatment of Sexual Abusers.

Terry, K. J. (2011). What is smart sex offender policy? *Criminology & Public Policy, 10,* 275–282.

Wright, R. G. (Ed.). (2009). *Sex offender laws: Failed policies, new directions.* New York: Springer.

Chapter 9

Methods to Assess Sex Offender Recidivism and Treatment Needs

Chapter Introduction

The preceding chapter reviewed prominent sex crime laws and policies. In contrast, the goal of this chapter is to understand risk analysis in determining sex offender recidivism risk and treatment needs. Notably, researchers have developed several assessment tools to predict the extent of reoffending and to identify potential treatment issues. This chapter focuses on the following five risk assessment tools: the Static-99/ Static-2002, Stable-2007/Acute-2007, the Minnesota Sex Offender Screening Tool-Revised (MnSOST-R)/Minnesota Sex Offender Screening Tool-3 (MnSOST-3), the Juvenile Sex Offender Assessment Protocol-II (J-SOAP-II), and the Estimate of Risk of Adolescent Sexual Offense Recidivism (ERASOR). Although other methods to assess offender risk and treatment needs exist, these represent common types used across the nation. The suggested reading list provides citations to research centered on validating other risk assessment tools. The chapter first discusses the value of risk assessment methods. It then moves toward understanding the different types of risk assessment tools that are used to determine the probability of reoffending and treatment needs. Finally, it concludes by summarizing controversies regarding the current state of risk assessment.

Risk Assessment Tools for Predicting Recidivism Odds and Treatment Needs

With advancements in psychology and criminology, several risk assessment tools have been developed over the last two decades. Given the critical importance of identifying potential recidivists, risk analysis is now frequently utilized in the criminal justice system. At the heart of the process is the determination of whether released offenders will pose a threat of reoffending in the future. For example, many states depend on risk assessments in part to judge whether convicted sex offenders should be detained past their sentences through the process of civil commitment. At the same time, risk assessment procedures can also be used to identify offenders' treatment needs. For instance, if certain risk factors are identified, interventions can be tailored to address specific treatment needs of offenders. Two broad types of risk assessment procedures exist (Martinez, Flores, & Rosenfeld, 2007). The first, purely clinical assessment refers to instances where clinicians form an opinion about offender risk relying on his/her expertise and clinical training. In contrast, actuarial assessments and structured clinical/empirically guided assessments, the second method, involve empirically derived instruments to identify potential risk factors; depending on the specific tool, clinicians may be permitted to weight the importance of individual factors in determining risk. Generally, states and the federal government have come to rely on the latter method (i.e., actuarial/empirically guided assessments) rather than unstructured judgments to determine offender risk, and in some cases treatment needs in part because unstructured clinical assessments are based on individual practitioners' anecdotal experiences. Accordingly, as Worling and Curwen (2001, p. 2) observe, it is thus difficult, if not impossible, to determine how precisely clinical risk ratings were generated and, "as such, these predictions are difficult to question, challenge, or support." More specifically, some research shows that purely clinical assessments are not valid indicators of potential sex offender recidivism risk. Doren (1998) for instance demonstrated that clinical judgments have the potential to underestimate sex offender recidivism risk particularly for rapists and child molesters (Doren, 1998). Concomitantly, there is the related concern that unstructured clinical judgments are unreliable measures of risk prediction. Put differently, there is likely to be reduced consensus among clinicians when relying on this non-empirical approach. Thus, the discussion that follows centers exclusively on five prominent actuarial/empirically guided tools widely used in the U.S.

Static-99/Static-2002

Description. The Static-99 (Hanson & Thornton, 2000) is an actuarial (i.e., empirically derived) risk prediction instrument used to estimate the odds of sex offender recidivism. It is one of the most widely used tools in the U.S. and other countries (Helmus & Hanson, 2007). It measures only "static" (i.e., unchangeable) factors such as official criminal history, offender age, and victim characteristics that have been identified by prior research as predictors of sexual recidivism. Information regarding these characteristics is typically readily available and easy to obtain. That is, official records, sentencing reports, and case file data routinely provide static or historical information about offenders. In 2003, Static-99 was revised to better reflect current knowledge about sex offender prediction (Hanson & Thornton, 2003). The redesign—Static-2002—however, retained the key features of the original tool as it identifies stable risk factors to assess the long-term potential for sexual and violent reoffending.

Target Population. Both the Static-99 and Static-2002 are designed for use with adult males who have already been charged with or convicted of at least one sex crime against a child or adult. Both versions are suitable for first-time offenders. In contrast, neither version is recommended for female offenders, juvenile offenders (i.e., those less than 18 years old at time of release), offenders convicted of prostitution-related offenses (e.g., "pimping"), and statutory rape offenders.

Instrument. The original version, Static-99, consists of 10 measures that cover a range of items empirically related to sexual deviance (A. J. R. Harris, Phenix, Hanson, & Thornton, 2003).

The first item, "age," refers to the offender's age at the time of risk assessment, or at exposure to risk (depending on the goal of assessment). The logic for including this measure stems from prior research indicating that younger adults are at increased risk for committing sex offenses. Thus, if the offender is between 18 and 25 at the time of assessment, he scores a "1" on Static-99. Older offenders receive no points for the age item.

A second item determines whether the offender "ever lived with an intimate partner." Developmental research indicates that offenders who have a close intimate relationship with a romantic partner are significantly less likely to reoffend in the future. This trend is also evident for sexual recidivism (Hanson & Bussière, 1998). Hence, scoring for this item is instructed as follows. If the offender has had an intimate relationship with another person for at least two years in the past, he scores a "0" for this item. In contrast, offenders who have not had such a relationship receive a score of "1" for this measure.

Static-99 also includes five measures of criminality. These items are included because prior offending characteristics (the frequency, extent, and nature of offending) are associated with increased offender persistence in offending. First, it documents item 3, "index non-sexual violence" (i.e., count of simultaneously occurring non-sexual offenses committed during the index, or most recent sex crime). For example, if an offender is convicted of a sex offense and also a kidnapping offense on the same sentencing occasion, he would receive a "1" for this item. Offenders not fitting this criterion would receive a "0."

A second criminality measure and the fourth item in the assessment tool, "any prior non-sexual violence," refers to any prior non-sexual violent crime convictions (i.e., non-sexual offenses committed before the index sex offense). Here, offenders who have been convicted of violent, non-sexual offenses in the past (e.g., aggravated assault, robbery), specifically prior to the index offense would receive a score of "1." Offenders without such convictions are scored as "0."

In contrast, "prior sex offenses," the third criminality indicator (and fifth overall item), measures the number of prior sex offense charges/convictions prior to the index offense. Thus, an offender receives "0" points if he has no prior sex offense charges or convictions. Offenders with one or two prior charges or one conviction receive a final score of "1" for this item. In contrast, offenders with three to five prior charges or two to three convictions receive a score of "2." Finally, offenders with six or more sex crime charges or four or more convictions receive the highest score of "3." Coders are reminded that whichever column either "charges" or "convictions" results in the "higher" total score is the column that determines the offender's final score for this item (A. J. R. Harris et al., 2003).

The fourth criminality item and sixth overall measure, "prior sentencing dates," serves as a proxy for measuring the extent of an offender's criminal career. Accordingly, offenders who have records that document four or more separate sentencing dates (for any offense) prior to the index sex offenses score a "1" on this measure. Thus, offenders with three or fewer separate sentencing dates receive a "0" score.

The fifth and final criminality item and seventh item in the Static-99 instrument gauges "any convictions for non-contact sex offenses." Here, coders are requested to record any prior convictions for sex offenses that do not involve direct contact with victims. For example, non-contact sex crimes would include exhibitionism, possessing child pornography, voyeurism, and Internet related offenses (e.g., solicitation of a child). Offenders convicted of at least one of these offenses receive a score of "1" for this item. Offenders without non-contact sex crime convictions receive zero points. As a result, this measure serves as a proxy for determining whether the offender may have a paraphilic disorder, and thus may indicate if the offender is at increased risk to reoffend (A. J. R. Harris et al., 2003).

The last three items of the Static-99 instrument record information about the offender's victims. First, coders are asked to record whether the offender has committed offenses against "any unrelated victims" (item 8). This item is included because prior studies indicate that having victims outside of the immediate family is significantly associated with an increased risk of sexual recidivism. As a result, offenders with at least one unrelated victim are scored as "1" for this measure. Offenders who have committed offenses exclusively against family members receive zero points.

The second victim-related measure and ninth item in the instrument, "any stranger victims" refers to offenses where the perpetrator has victimized an unknown person. Prior studies suggest that offenders who commit sex crimes against strangers are significantly more likely to reoffend than offenders with known victims. For this item, a victim is defined as a stranger if he or she did not know the offender 24 hours before the crime. Hence, offenders with stranger victims are scored as "1" for this item. In contrast, offenders with known victims are coded as "0."

The final victim-related item and last measure (item 10) of the Static-99 determines whether the offender committed crimes against "any male victims." Having male victims is empirically related to increased sexual deviance. Accordingly, in cases where the offender has male victims, he receives a "1" score. In instances where an offender's victims are female, the offender is scored as "0." The developers of the instrument caution that the offender must know the victim is a male to receive a "1" score.

Thus, total scores on the Static-99 can range from "0" to "12." Offenders who receive a score of "6" or greater are all considered high risk and treated similarly. The Static-99 provides recidivism risk estimates based on these scores. For example, an offender with a total score of "4" is estimated as having a 26 percent chance of sexual reconviction in the first five years after release, a 31 percent chance of sexual recidivism over ten years of release, and a 36 percent likelihood of sexual recidivism over a 15 year time period (A. J. R. Harris et al., 2003).

In contrast to the earlier Static-99 instrument, the Static-2002 sought to increase coherence and conceptual clarity. Specifically, it includes five additional items designed to measure the following theoretical domains: age, persistence of sex offending, deviant sexual interests, relationship to victims, and general criminality (Phenix, Doren, Helmus, Hanson, & Thornton, 2008). Additionally, the Static-2002 also excludes two prior items from the earlier version ("ever lived with an intimate partner," "index non-sexual violence") from the original Static-99 given missing data and theoretical concerns, respectively. Thus, the total number of items in the Static-2002 equals 13. The first new item is "juvenile arrest for sex offense." Put differently, it serves as a proxy for age of onset of offending. Generally, offenders who begin offending early in life persist in deviant behavior for longer durations than offenders with a later age of onset (Hanson & Bussière, 1998). Offenders score a "1" if they have at least one arrest as minors (under the age of 18) for a sex offense; all others are scored as "0."

The second addition, "high rate of sex offending," indicates the extent to which sex offenders have specialized in sexual offenses. Offenders with no prior sentencing dates for sexual offenses score "0" if they have had less than one sentencing occasion every 15 years and a "1" if they have had one or more sentencing occasions every 15 years.

A third measure documents whether offenders had "two or more victims, at least one unrelated." This item serves as a proxy for measuring sexual interest in minors, which is a robust predictor of sexual recidivism, particularly against child victims. The coding here is as follows: offenders score a "1," if he has two or more victims less than age 12 (one of them must be unrelated). If the offender does not have victims under the age of 12, or has only one victim under the age of 12, he receives a score of "0." If the offender has victimized two or more victims under the age of 12 in the past but they are all related to the offender, he would receive a score of "0."

The fourth new item, "breach of conditional release," refers to instances where offenders violate the conditions of their probation or parole. The literature has identified failure to conform to the demands of community supervision as a consistent predictor of sexual and violent recidivism (Hanson & Morton-Bourgon, 2004). If the offender's record indicates any violation of conditional release the offender is scored a "1" on this item. In all other cases, the offender receives a zero.

The final new item "years free prior to index sex offense" taps into persistence of offending. Thus, offenders with shorter time spans in-between their offending would be considered more persistent offenders. Coders are advised to score "1" if the offender has less than 36 months free (in the community) prior to committing the index sexual offense, or less than 48 months free prior to the conviction date for the index sex offense. For all other cases, the offender receives a "0."

Additionally, the latest instrument provides greater theoretical context for the inclusion of certain items. Not least, the new version introduces coding changes for some measures. Although the Static-2002 is a revision of its earlier version, its developers caution that both versions are not necessarily comparable and should be considered separate instruments. Specifically, they caution "future research will determine whether the two instruments provide sufficient incremental information to justify scoring both, or whether one of the instruments can 'replace' the other" (Phenix et al., 2008, p. 3).[1]

Strengths. Both the Static-99 and Static-2002 have several strengths. Three of these are discussed below. First, both instruments require information that can be easily obtained by coders. Generally, three sources of information are needed to evaluate offenders: demographic information, the offender's official criminal record, and victim information. An interview or evaluation with the offender is not necessary although it can be helpful for coders (A. J. R. Harris et al., 2003). Second, the scoring process is straightforward. Coders need only sum the individual items together to generate an overall total score. The coding instructions for both versions instruct that coders simply consult a table that provides estimates of reoffending over certain periods of time. As a result, coders need not possess an advanced degree in psychology or criminal justice-related fields. However, training is strongly recommended for individuals administering the assessment (Phenix et al., 2008). Third, and finally, both the Static-99 and Static-2002 have shown "moderate" predictive accuracy in estimating the likelihood of sexual recidivism for a range of sex offenders (Helmus & Hanson, 2007), with the latter performing slightly better than the former for predicting sexual recidivism across studies (see e.g., Helmus, Thornton, Hanson, & Babchishin, 2012). Specifically, the area under the receiver operating characteristic curve (AUC) value for the Static-99 has been calculated across studies to be 0.68, whereas the Static-2002 has performed slightly better (AUC= 0.72; Hanson & Thornton, 2003). AUC values range from .5, meaning the tool is not much better than chance in predicting reoffense, to 1, meaning that there is a 100 percent chance that a randomly selected recidivist will have a higher score on the instrument relative to a randomly selected nonrecidivist. Simply put, instruments with AUC scores closer to "1" indicate greater predictive validity than tools with lower AUC values.

Limitations. Notwithstanding these attractive features, researchers have critiqued both the Static-99 and Static-2002. Three main criticisms have been levied against the assessment tool. One concern is that both instruments rely on measuring unchangeable offender characteristics. Put differently, they do not account for factors that are dynamic and subject to change over time. Potentially then static risk assessment tools may tell only part of the story. For instance, while static risk factors may reveal *which* offenders are most likely to reoffend overall, dynamic risk factors may signal *timing* to reoffending. Accordingly, scholars have identified two types of dynamic risk factors (see e.g., Hanson & A. J. R. Harris, 2000; Ward & Beech, 2004): stable dynamic factors, which may change but remain relatively constant over significant periods of time (e.g., cognitive distortions, intimacy

---

1. Indeed, revisions of the Static-99 and Static-2002 (i.e., Static-99R and Static-2002R) have focused on changing the age categories to better reflect current knowledge about age and its impact on future reoffending. Beyond this change, the Static-99R and Static-2002R are comparable to their earlier versions.

Table 9.1. Static-99/Static-2002 Overview

Target Population	Risk Factors	Scoring
• Adult males who have been charged with or convicted of at least one sex crime against a child or adult • Not recommended for certain offenders (e.g., females, statutory rape offenders)	• Static factors (e.g., prior crime characteristics, victim preference)	• Total score equals the sum of all items

deficits), and acute dynamic factors, which can rapidly change over a short period of weeks, days, or even hours (e.g., feelings of anger, stress).

Second, some researchers have cautioned that both assessment tools were developed using relatively homogenous samples of offenders (i.e., white males) and may produce variable predictive accuracy when used for different samples of offenders. Långström (2004) investigated whether ethnicity of offender affected the accuracy of Static-99 in predicting reoffense rates among Swedish sex offenders. His results demonstrated that the Static-99 risk assessment was able to distinguish between recidivists and non-recidivists in those of Nordic ancestry. However, it did not have success differentiating recidivists and non-recidivists in the African and Asian samples. More recently, Babchishin, Blais, and Helmus (2012) determined the extent to which the Static-99 and Static-2002 predicted reoffending odds among Aboriginal offenders in Canada. Study results indicate that the Static-99 instrument similarly predicted recidivism risk among Aboriginal and non-Aboriginal populations. At the same time, Static-2002 showed significantly less promise in accurately predicting reoffending in minority populations. Collectively, findings from these two studies may be indicative of different risk factors associated with offending across diverse populations.

Third, both instruments rely on official data sources to determine the extent of offender criminality. Accordingly, it may be that only offenses for which offenders have been officially processed are actually "counted." Sex crimes are notoriously underreported nationally, particularly for offenses involving known perpetrators (Lussier & Mathesius, 2012). As a result, given that both tools use official arrest/conviction data, the recidivism estimates they generate may not reflect the extent of unreported sex offenses. Table 9.1 outlines the broad features of the Static-99 and Static-2002.

Stable-2007/Acute-2007

Description. In response to the observation that dynamic risk factors serve as robust predictors of future offending, researchers have developed tools designed to tap into the changeable characteristics of offenders. To illustrate, Hanson, A. J. R. Harris, Scott, and Helmus (2007) introduced instruments designed to measure the presence of dynamic risk factors: the Stable-2007 and the Acute-2007. The former is designed to measure "stable" risk factors. Recall that these include personal skill deficits, learning behaviors, and other characteristics that are associated with sexual recidivism but that can change over long periods of time potentially through treatment interventions. In contrast, the Acute-2007 instrument purports to measure the impact of quickly changeable traits on reoffending. For example, the emotional state of an offender (e.g., angry, depressed) would be illustrative of an acute characteristic. At a minimum, archival records (e.g., prior criminal conviction data) and structured interview data are needed to appropriately administer both instruments (Hanson et al., 2007).

Target Population. The instrument has been used primarily for adult males who are currently under community supervision (i.e., probation or parole). Generally, the instruments may not apply to juvenile offenders, female offenders, or to those offenders whose only sex crime involved consenting adults (e.g., prostitution offenses).

Instrument. Hanson and his colleagues (2007) developed two separate instruments designed to account for the effects of dynamic risk factors on offending. The first, Stable-2007, measures factors which are potentially changeable but more typically endure for significant periods of time (i.e., months or years). In particular, it uses a guided interview process administered by correctional practitioners approximately every six months. The instrument covers six major areas of stable risk in the offender. The first indicator, "significant social influences" documents the people in the offender's life "who were not paid to be with him." Final scores for this item are computed based on the number of positive and negative influences in the offender's life.

The second set of items tap into "intimacy deficits" that the offender may exhibit. These include five measures: stability of the offender's current relationship with a significant other, emotional identification with minors, hostility held toward women, general social rejection/loneliness, and lack of concern for others.

The instrument also measures the extent of the offender's sexual self-regulation (which constitutes the third domain of the instrument). Here, Hanson et al. (2007) recommend documenting whether the offender exhibits a "high sex drive/sexual pre-occupations," whether he "uses sex as a coping mechanism," and, last, "deviant sexual interests" held by the offender (p. 7).

The fourth area was designed to tap into offenders' attitudes held toward sex. Specifically, the following items are included in this sub-scale: sexual entitlement, pro-rape attitudes, and attitudes accepting of adult-child sexual relationships.

A fifth domain centers on officers' perceptions of the extent to which the offender is co-operating with his supervision requirements. In particular, officers are asked in their evaluation whether the offender was "working with" or "working against" him or her.

The final section measures "general self-regulation." Here, three items are relevant: the extent to which offenders commit impulsive acts, whether they exhibit poor cognitive problem-solving skills, and whether they display negative emotional states or hostility.

Final scores are generated by the following scoring scheme. For each of the sixteen factors, coders use a three-point rating: "0=no problem," "1=some concern/slight problem," and "2=present/definite concern." Additionally, coders are instructed to also assess the offender's Static-99 score. This approach ensures that relevant static factors are also accounted for in evaluating the offender's overall risk of sexual recidivism. After scoring the relevant items, the highest score in each sub-section counts as the section score resulting in overall scores with a range from 0 to 12. Hanson et al. (2007) suggest the following ranking: "0 to 4=low need," "5 to 8=moderate," and "9 to 12=high."

By comparison, Hanson et al.'s (2007) second instrument, Acute-2007, taps into rapidly variable "acute" factors and is designed to be administered on a regular basis (i.e., during every supervision meeting). Specifically, it includes seven items: "access to victims," "emotional collapse," "collapse of social supports," "hostility," "substance abuse," "sexual preoccupations," and "rejection of supervision." Additionally, officers are permitted to document any other unique characteristics of offenders that may contribute to future offending. For example, evaluators may note that the offender does not have stable housing or is not complying with psychiatric treatment. For each item, the following responses exist: "0=no problem," "1=maybe/some problem," "2=yes, definite problem," and "3=intervene now." This last category refers to extreme instances in which "the officer felt that the risk of new offending was sufficiently high that preventative actions were immediately necessary" (Hanson et al., 2007, p. 8). For each factor, evaluators are requested to note whether the offender's behavior "became worse," "stayed the same," or "improved since last meeting."

Before calculating final scores, evaluators were asked to consider the most recent assessment in determining the offender's level of risk. Specifically, the acute score is tallied based on each individual item and includes a recommended level of supervision: "normal supervision" (no risk factors), "extra attention" (one risk factor for low to moderate priority offenders), "elevated supervision" (one risk factor for high priority offenders or two risk factors for low or moderate priority offenders), and "intervene now" (any intervene now scores). Hanson and colleagues (2007) provide technical rules in their manual for overall scoring that also accounts for Static-99 (i.e., static factors) scores.

Strengths. The development of the Stable-2007 and Acute-2007 was motivated in part by the concern that earlier risk assessment tools neglected to account for changeable factors. Thus, given the strong effect of dynamic characteristics on criminal propensity, the Stable-2007 and Acute-2007 are believed to be superior in predicting the likelihood of recidivism compared to tools that account only for static risk factors (AUC=0.67 and 0.74, respectively; Hanson et al., 2007). Concomitantly, both the Stable-2007 and Acute-2007 are theorized to better predict the timing of reoffense, compared to tools that only measure unchangeable factors (Hanson et al., 2007; see also, Eher, Matthes, Schilling, Haubner-MacLean, & Rettenberger, 2012).

Limitations. The tools may also have potential shortcomings. One limitation involves the information and time needed to score the Stable-2007 and Acute-2007. In contrast to the Static-99 both the Stable-2007 and Acute-2007 require that practitioners meet with offenders and administer the instrument on a consistent basis. This means Hanson et al.'s (2007) approach requires substantially greater resources to administer over time compared to the Static-99. A related but separate concern involves the reliance on correctional officers to provide specific information about offenders. Some studies have found that the more complex Stable-2007 and Acute-2007 instruments, compared to the Static-99, pose challenges to implementation (i.e., not all officers appear equally competent in making specific judgments about the offender). It follows, as A. J. R. Harris and Hanson (2010, p. 305) explained that "risk assessments involving sensitive judgments (does this offender use sex to cope with negative emotions?) require more attention to staff selection, training, supervision, support, and middle-management 'buy in' than do risk assessments based on simple, static variables (any male victims?)." Below, Table 9.2. summarizes the Stable-2007 and Acute-2007.

Table 9.2. Stable-2007/Acute-2007 Overview

Target Population	Risk Factors	Scoring
• Males over the age of 18 who are under community supervision (i.e., probation or parole) • May not apply to specialized populations such as juvenile offenders, female offenders, and/or offenders whose only sex crime involved consenting adults (such as prostitution offenses)	• Stable-2007 measures stable dynamic risk factors (i.e., factors that slowly change over time such as learning difficulties) • Acute-2007 taps into quickly changing factors (e.g., mood)	• The total calculation includes two separate scores for each scale • Cut-offs regarding risk level are based on these scores

Minnesota Sex Offender Screening Tool-Revised (MnSOST-R)/Minnesota Sex Offender Screening Tool-3 (MnSOST-3)

Description. The Minnesota Sex Offender Screening Tool-3 (MnSOST-3; Duwe & Freske, 2012) is a revision of the MnSOST-R (Epperson et al., 2005), which is among one of the most widely used actuarial tools in the nation (McGarth, Cumming, Burchard, Zeoli, & Ellerby, 2009). Both instruments measure static and dynamic risk factors. The earlier version (Epperson et al., 2005) developed in 2003 relied on a sample of 256 sex offenders released from Minnesota prisons in the 1980s and 1990s. Its most recent version was developed using a contemporary sample that included 2,315 sex offenders released from prisons in Minnesota between 2003 and 2006 (Duwe & Freske, 2012). In creating the revised instrument, advanced statistical modeling techniques were used to refine the selection of predictors and to also internally validate the items used in the instrument. The MnSOST-3 also includes revised coding schemes for certain items.

Target Population. Both the MnSOST-R and the MnSOST-3 are designed for assessing recidivism risks of adult males who have previous convictions for sex offenses. Caution is warranted however for use with the following offenders: incest offenders, offenders whose only offense was committed as a minor, and those who have prior convictions exclusively for child pornography crimes. Neither instrument is recommended for women who have committed sexual offenses.

Instrument. In total the MnSOST-R (Epperson et al., 2005) includes 16 items (12 measure static risk factors and 4 tap into dynamic/institutional factors). The historical factors focus on measuring aspects of the offense, victim characteristics, personality traits of offenders, and their prior employment history. First, the instrument records the number of sex/sex-rated convictions, including current conviction (coding: "1=zero," "2=two or more"); second, the length of the offender's sexual offending history ("-1=less than one year," "0=more than six years," "3=one to six years"); third, whether the offender was under any form of supervision when he committed any sex offense that resulted in a charge or conviction ("0=no," "2=yes"); fourth, whether any sex crime (charged or convicted) was committed in a public place ("0=no," "2=yes"); fifth, whether force (or threat of force) was used to complete sex crime (charged or convicted) ("-3=no force in any crime," "0=force used in at least one crime"); and six, whether any sex offense (charge or conviction) involved multiple acts on a single victim within any single contact event ("-1=no," "1=yes"). The seventh question measures the versatility of offending against different minor age groups. Here, evaluators are advised to record the number of different age groups victimized across sex crimes (includes charges or convictions): a) "age 6 or younger," b) "age 7 to 12 years," c) "age 13 to 15 years and the offender is more than five years older than the victim," and d) "age 16 or older." Coders are then instructed to note "0=no age group or only one age group checked," or "3=two or more age groups checked." The eighth item asks whether the offender "offended against a 13 to 15 year old victim and the offender was more than five years older than the victim at the time of the crime (charged or convicted" ("0=no," "2=yes"); the ninth indicator measures the extent of stranger victims ("-1=no victims were strangers," "0=uncertain due to missing information," "3=at least one victim was a stranger"). The last three measures tap into antisocial personality traits, prior substance abuse, and employment history of the offender: specifically, the tenth item asks whether the offender exhibits adolescent antisocial behavior ("-1=no indication," "0=some relatively isolated antisocial acts," "2=persistent, repetitive pattern"); the eleventh factor measures the offender's prior problems with alcohol and drugs one year prior to arrest for the index offense ("-1=no," "1=yes"); and, the final static item taps into the offender's employment history one year prior to arrest for their index crime (where "-2=stable employment for one year or longer/homemaker, retired, full-time student in good standing, or officially disabled," "0=part-time, seasonal, unstable employment, or file contains no information," "1=unemployed or significant history of unemployment").

In contrast, the four dynamic risk factors include the following: discipline history while incarcerated, excluding refusal to complete treatment programs ("0=no major discipline reports or infractions," "1=one or more major discipline reports"); whether the offender participated in drug/alcohol treatment while incarcerated ("-2=treatment recommended and successfully completed or in program at time of release," "0=no treatment recommended, not enough time to participate in treatment program, or no opportunity," "1=treatment recommended but offender refused, quit, or did not pursue," "4=treatment recommended but terminated by staff"); sex offender treatment history while incarcerated ("-1=treatment recommended and successfully completed or in program at time of release," "0=treatment recommended but offender refused, quit, or did not pursue/no treatment recommended, not enough time to participate in treatment program, or no opportunity," "3=treatment recommended but terminated"); and, offender age at time of release ("-1=age 31 or older," "1=age 30 or younger").

The final score involves adding the values to each item together (although the developers caution that specific scoring directions must be followed and administrators must be trained prior to scoring offenders, see Epperson et al., 2005). Based on this scoring, offenders can fall into three categories: "low risk" (score of 3 or below), "moderate risk" (score of 4 to 7), and "high risk" (score of 8 and above).

The MnSOST-3 retains some of the features of the MnSOST-R. That is, the revised instrument still includes both static and dynamic risk factors. There are differences, however. In comparison to the MnSOST-R, the MnSOST-3 relies on a relatively recent sample of offenders (most were released from Minnesota prisons in 2003–2006). Additionally, it uses a multiple logistic regression model when scoring responses. Thus, final scores indicate an offender's predicted probability for sexual recidivism and an offender's percentile rank. This approach allows for modeling interaction effects (e.g., "committing prior offenses in public" x "length of sex offending career") and also a straightforward interpretation of risk (Duwe & Freske, 2012). Not least, the MnSOST-3 reduces the number of items on the instrument, includes new ones, and revises some of the original measures. The revised instrument (which contains a total of nine items) is briefly summarized below (additional details can be found in Freske, 2012).

For the first item, "predatory offenses for which an offender has been sentenced," coders are asked to document any offenses that involve criminal sexual conduct crimes, kidnapping offenses, solicitation offenses, and any other felony crimes committed during a criminal conduct offense. They may report up to 25 offenses. The second measure accounts for the offender's total number of felony convictions. These offenses include juvenile and adult convictions and both sexual and non-sexual felonies. Administrators are advised to record up to a maximum of 20 offenses. The instrument also taps into the offender's prior history of harassment and related offense. This third item counts the number of sentences (adult or juvenile; misdemeanor or felony) for stalking, harassment, and violations of orders for protection offenses on the offender's prior record. The maximum count an offender can receive for this item is five offenses. For the fourth item, coders are advised to record the number of disorderly contact sentences (adult or juvenile; misdemeanor or felony) in the three years prior to the offender's most recent commitment to prison (maximum count of two). The fifth measure notes the offender's age at the time of his anticipated release date. Sixth, the instrument documents whether the offender will be supervised after his discharge from prison. The scoring for this item is dichotomous: "0" if the offender will have some type of supervision after release and "1" if the offender will have no further correctional supervision. Item seven determines whether the offender received sex offender and drug/alcohol treatment during incarceration. Offenders receive a score of "0" if they have not completed both types of treatment (they are however given credit for treatment completion if they completed one treatment program and are actively participating in the second treatment program). Conversely, a score of "1" is given to offenders who have completed both types of treatment or if they are actively participating. The eighth item calculates the extent of predatory offenses that involve male victims. Here, offenders can receive a maximum score of "4" which corresponds to having four or more sentences for predatory sex offenses with male victims. The ninth and last item on the MnSOST-3 taps into whether the offender has a prior criminal history (charges and/or convictions) of committing sex/sex-related offenses in a public place. Offenders can receive a score of "0" if none of their sex offenses occurred in a public place or "1" if at least one crime was committed in public.

Final scores for risk are computed using a copy of the MnSOST-3 Excel spreadsheet. These values reflect the offender's predicted probability for sexual recidivism (with 95 percent confidence intervals), and an offender's percentile rank of reoffending risk (Freske, 2012).

Strengths. Both the MnSOST-R and MnSOST-3 risk assessment tools offer clear advantages for determination of offender risk of sexual recidivism. One observation is that both instruments indicate moderate to strong predictive accuracy. That is, the MnSOST-R shows an average AUC of 0.73 (when applied to older samples; Epperson, Kaul, Huot, Goldman, & Alexander, 2003). The revised version indicates a higher level of predictive discrimination (AUC=0.82; Duwe & Freske, 2012). A second strength of both instruments involves their use of both static and institutional/dynamic factors in determining risk of recidivism. As mentioned previously, such an approach accounts for several types of factors that may affect reoffending.

Limitations. The MnSOST-R and MnSOST-3 also have shortcomings. The most frequent critique involves the limited generalizability of both instruments. To illustrate, in a study that detailed the development of the MnSOST-3, Duwe and Freske (2012) observed that the MnSOST-R performed poorly when predicting recidivism among a contemporary sample of offenders (AUC=0.55). This result indicates that although the MnSOST-R performed fairly well in predicting the recidivism likelihood of offenders released from prison two decades ago, its predictive ability for contemporary samples is less than ideal. At the same time, both instruments have been developed using samples of Minnesota offenders. Thus, the fairly high predictive accuracy of the MnSOST-3 found in preliminary studies may not generalize to sex offender populations in other states. Specifically, Duwe and Freske (2012, p. 370) have observed that "Minnesota is, in several potentially important ways, different from the rest of the United States ... it has the second lowest incarceration rate in the nation ... [and] relies more heavily on local sanctions (e.g., jail and community supervision) ... prison beds are generally reserved for offenders who have committed very serious offenses and/or have lengthy criminal histories." More generally, the MnSOST-3 is a recently developed instrument. As a result, few studies have cross-validated the instrument (i.e., evaluated its predictive ability using other populations). Thus, there is a clear need for future research to determine the extent to which it is appropriate for use on diverse samples of sex offenders. Table 9.3 highlights the major features of the MnSOST-R/MnSOST-3.

Table 9.3. MnSOST-R/MnSOST-3 Overview

Target Population	Risk Factors	Scoring
• Both versions apply only to adult males who have previous convictions for sex crimes • Should not be used for specific groups of offenders: incest offenders, offenders whose only offense was committed as a minor, those who have prior convictions exclusively for child pornography offenses, and female sex offenders	• The earlier and later versions measure both static and dynamic factors	• Final scores for overall risk are calculated using a MnSOST-3 Excel spreadsheet which permits complex regression analysis for determining overall risk

Juvenile Sex Offender Assessment Protocol-II (J-SOAP-II)

Description. Recall from our earlier discussion about typologies (Chapter 1) that the J-SOAP-II is also helpful for classifying sex offender "types." For this discussion however we focus on the J-SOAP-II's utility for assessing risk levels of sex offenders. Its original version was developed in 1994. The instrument—which measures both static and dynamic factors—was empirically based and sought to predict the extent of both sexual and non-sexual recidivism among juvenile males with a prior history of committing sex crimes. Additionally, it may also assist with identifying treatment needs of juvenile sex offenders.

Target Population. The J-SOAP-II is one of the first risk assessment tools to be designed specifically for juvenile sex offenders. In particular, it is intended to assess risk in male youth ages 12 to 18 who have committed sex offenses in the past.

Instrument. The instrument has 28 items divided into four subscales. The first two scales center on historical (i.e., static) factors. Scale 1 measures "sexual drive/sexual pre-occupation." Specifically, the scale is comprised of eight indicators (briefly described below; detailed information regarding all of the items in the instrument is provided by Prentky & Righthand, 2003). These items include: prior legally charged sex offenses (coding: "0=none," "1=one offense," "2=more than one offense"); number of sexual abuse victims—from any reliable source (i.e., a legal charge/conviction is not required) ("0=only one known victim," "1=two known victims," "2=three or more known victims"); male child victim—ten or younger and at least four years younger than the offender ("0=no known male child victims," "1=one known male victim," "2=two or more known male victims"); duration of sex offense history—includes information from official and unofficial sources ("0=only 1 known sexual offense and no other history of sexual aggression," "1=multiple sex offenses within a brief time period—six months or less," "2=multiple sex offenses that extend over a period greater than six months and involve one or more victims"); degree of planning in sexual offense ("0=no planning," "1=mild degree of planning," "2=moderate-detailed planning"); sexualized aggression ("0=no gratuitous or expressive aggression," "1=mild amount of expressive aggression," "2=moderate-high amount of expressive aggression"); sexual drive and preoccupation ("0=normative/minimal," "1=moderate," "2=high"); and finally, sexual victimization history ("0=no prior sexual victimization of offender," "1=juvenile was a victim of non-penetrative sexual abuse that included no excessive force or physical injury," "2=juvenile was a victim of penetrative sexual abuse that included excessive force or physical injury").

In a different direction, Scale 2 measures "impulsive/antisocial behavior." Here again, eight measures exist: caregiver consistency (coding: "0=lived with biological parents until current age or age 10," "1=one or two changes in caregivers," "2=three or more changes in caregivers before age 10"); pervasive anger ("0=no evidence," "1=mild," "2=three or more changes in caregivers before age 10"); school behavior problems ("0=none," "1=mild," "2=moderate-severe"); history of conduct disorder before age 10 ("0=no evidence," "1=mild-moderate evidence," "2=strong evidence"); juvenile antisocial behavior—ages 10–17 ("0=none/minimal—no more than a single incident," "1=moderate—2 or 3 different criteria present," "2=strong—four or more different criteria present"); charges or arrests before age 16 ("0=none," "1=one," "2=more than one"); multiple types of offenses—limited to legally charged offenses (coders are instructed to select as many types of charges that apply to offenders; "0=one type," "1=two types," "2=three or more types"); and the final item, history of physical assault/and or exposure to family violence ("0=no/unknown," "1=yes," "2=moderate/severe").

The third and fourth scales incorporate dynamic risk factors. To illustrate, Scale 3, "intervention items," consists of seven factors related to offenders' attitudes toward their criminality and reform: accept responsibility for offenses ("0=accepts full responsibility for sexual and nonsexual offenses without any evidence of minimizing," "1=accepts some, but not total, responsibility—occasional minimizing present, but offender does not deny crime," "2=accepts no responsibility, or there is full denial"); internal motivation for change—offender has a genuine motivation to desist from crime ("0=appears distressed by offenses and exhibits a genuine desire to change," "1=there is some degree of internal conflict and distress, mixed with a desire to avoid consequences of recidivism," "2=no internal motivation for change"); understands risk factors and applies risk management strategies ("0=good understanding and demonstration of knowledge of risk factors and risk management strategies," "1=incomplete or partial understanding of risk factors and risk management strategies," "2=poor or inadequate understanding of risk factors and risk management strategies"); empathy ("0=offender appears to have genuine capacity for feeling empathy for his sexual abuse victims," "1=offender expresses some degree of empathy, but these may be socially desirable responses," "2=offender expresses little to no empathy toward others"); remorse and guilt ("0=offender appears to have genuine remorse for his actions," "1=offender expresses some level of remorse or guilt, but potentially does so for self-serving reasons, such as to avoid further punishment," "2=little evidence exists to indicate the offender has remorse for victims"); cognitive distortions ("0=expresses no distorted thoughts, attitudes, or statements about behavior," "1=occasional comments, attitudes, or statements reflecting cognitive distortions," "2=frequent comments, attitudes, or statements reflecting cognitive distortions"); and the last item determines the quality of peer relationships ("0=offender is socially active, peer-oriented, and rarely alone—friends are not delinquent," "1=offender has a few casual non-delinquent friends and some involvement in structured activities," "2=offender is withdrawn from peer contact and socially isolated").

By comparison, Scale 4 is composed of five items designed to indicate the extent of community stability/adjustment (i.e., how the offender has adjusted to reentry after release from a juvenile or correctional facility). Prentky and Righthand (2003) advise that this section does not apply to currently detained or incarcerated offenders or those offenders living in a secure residential treatment program. The specific indicators include: management of sexual urges and desire ("0=well managed expression of sexual urges and desires," "1=sexual urges and desires are managed appropriately most of the time," "2=sexual urges and desires are poorly managed"); management of anger ("0=no evidence of inappropriate anger," "1=anger managed appropriately most of the time," "2=anger poorly and inappropriately managed"); stability of current living situation ("0=stable," "1=moderate instability," "2=severe instability"); stability in school ("0=stable," "1=unstable," "2=highly unstable"); and the final indicator, evidence of positive support systems ("0=considerable support systems," "1=some support systems," "2=no known positive support systems or only negative supports").

Scoring the J-SOAP-II yields a "Static" and "Dynamic" scale score (each based on the corresponding subscales), and an overall score (the total items summed together). The J-SOAP-II does not provide cut-off ratings (e.g., "high" versus "low" risk); however, higher scores relative to lower ones indicate greater presence of risk factors for reoffending.

Strengths. Several strengths of the J-SOAP-II are evident. One involves its focus on juvenile sex offenders. At the time of its initial development, this approach represented a significant advancement in risk assessment tools. Indeed, Martinez and colleagues (2007) observe that it is one of the most well-known assessment procedures and among a fairly limited number of assessment tools designed exclusively for juvenile sex offenders. Second, some studies indicate that the J-SOAP-II significantly predicts reoffending (Martinez et al., 2007; Rajlic & Gretton, 2010). For example, findings from a recent meta-analysis examining prior studies of J-SOAP-II and other risk assessment methods indicate an average AUC value of 0.66 for general recidivism and 0.67 for sexual recidivism (Viljoen, Mordell, & Beneteau, 2012). Notably, results from this same study also indicate that the J-SOAP-II performed as well as other risk assessment tools in predicting reoffending among juveniles. Even higher AUC values for general (AUC=0.76) and sexual recidivism (AUC=0.78) were reported by Martinez and his colleagues (2007) in a sample of Latino and African American youth. At the same time, prior investigations reveal that the J-SOAP-II demonstrates acceptable inter-rater reliability (intraclass correlation; ICC=0.70) indicating that the instrument results in relatively consistent scores across coders (Martinez et al., 2007).

Limitations. Three broad limitations of the J-SOAP-II have also been identified by prior research. For instance, some preliminary work highlights that J-SOAP-II may not be appropriate for use outside of Western countries. To illustrate, Chu, Ng, Fong, and Teoh (2012) investigated the predictive ability of the J-SOAP-II in a sample of Singapore youth. Their results indicate that the J-SOAP-II was no better than chance in identifying which youth would reoffend in the future; although other tools appeared more effective in accurately predicting risk. More generally, these findings indicate that future research is needed to determine the extent to which the J-SOAP-II predicts recidivism in diverse populations. Second, other studies have found that J-SOAP-II scores are not significantly predictive of timing to re-offense. That is, survival analyses have revealed no statistically significant association between J-SOAP-II scores and time to sexual recidivism (Viljoen, Scalora et al., 2008). Third, and finally, prior research has found that the J-SOAP-II may differentially predict recidivism based on offender age. For instance, Viljoen, Scalora et al. (2008) in a sample of adolescents living in a Midwestern city in the U.S. found that the J-SOAP-II was less predictive of reoffending among younger juveniles (12 to 15 years of age) than for older juveniles (16 years and older). Thus, it might not be appropriate to administer to younger children. The J-SOAP-II is summarized in Table 9.4

Table 9.4. J-SOAP-II Overview

Target Population	Risk Factors	Scoring
• Exclusively applies to male juvenile sex offenders (12 to 18 years old) who have committed a sex offense in the past	• Taps into static and dynamic risk factors associated with reoffending among youth	• Scores include static and dynamic scale scores and an overall score (the total items summed together) • No cut-off ratings (e.g., "high" versus "low" risk) are provided • Higher scores relative to lower ones indicate greater presence of risk factors for reoffending

Estimate of Risk of Adolescent Sexual Offense Recidivism (ERASOR)

Description. The Estimate of Risk of Adolescent Sexual Offense Recidivism (ERASOR; Worling & Curwen, 2000), developed in 2000, is an empirically-guided approach toward determining the short-term risk of a sexual reoffense for male and female juveniles ages 12 to 18 years, who have committed a sex crime in the past. The instrument is comprised of 25 theoretically relevant risk factors that measure both static and dynamic factors. Its developers advise evaluators to administer the instrument fairly regularly—every two years, or when at least one risk factor changes significantly. Although it is an empirically guided tool, clinicians use their professional judgment in determining overall risk level. Generally, the greater the number of indicators (see below), the higher presumed risk an offender has for reoffending.

Target Population. The ERASOR is designed to assess the risk of sexual recidivism in youth (ages 12–18) who have committed at least one prior offense.

Instrument. The 25 risk factors included in the ERASOR—16 dynamic and 9 static items—are divided into five categories (complete information regarding the specific operationalization of each item is available in Worling & Curwen, 2000). The first area, "sexual interests, attitudes, and behaviors," contains four items that tap into sexual deviancy and preferences among offenders: "deviant sexual interests" (refers to sexual preferences for children and/or sexualized violence); "obsessive sexual interests/preoccupation with sexual thoughts" (e.g., unusually frequent masturbation, excessive use of sexual behaviors/fantasy to cope with negative emotional states, like boredom); "attitudes supportive of sexual offending" (offender exhibits willingness to believe in "rape myths"/beliefs endorsing sexual offending against victims); and, the final item, "unwillingness to alter deviant sexual interests/attitudes" (extent of offender willingness to change deviant behavior).

The second domain, "historical sexual assaults," incorporates nine items related to the offender's prior sexual offending history. Evaluators are asked to determine the following: "ever sexually assaulted two or more victims" (the extent to which offender has victimized multiple victims); "ever sexually assaulted same victim two or more times" (whether offender has a history of sexually offending multiple times against one victim); "prior adult sanctions for sexual assault(s)" (the extent to which the offender has been officially sanctioned for a sex offense/sexual deviance); "threats of, use of, violence/weapons during sexual offense" (whether the offender used physical force or threats of force during assault);

"ever sexually assaulted a child" (whether offender sexually assaulted a prepubescent child); "ever sexually assaulted a stranger" (measures if offender has committed at least one sex offense against a stranger); "indiscriminate choice of victims" (the extent to which the offender shows no preference for victims); "ever sexually assaulted a male victim" (for male offenders only); and, the final item, "diverse sexual-assault behaviors" (variation in the extent of offender's sexual offending).

The third area of the instrument determines the offender's "psychosocial functioning" using six items: "antisocial interpersonal orientation" (whether the offender exhibits at least four antisocial behaviors, such as the endorsement of antisocial or pro-criminal attitudes, defiance of authority figures); "lack of intimate peer relationships/social isolation" (the extent to which the offender has close peer relationships); "negative peer associations and influences" (whether offender has contact/formed relationships with deviant peers); "interpersonal aggression" (evident by a number of verbally or physically abusive behaviors against others); "recent escalation in anger or negative affect" (the extent to which the offender has tantrums, exhibits verbal or physical aggression, makes threats or experiences depression, anxiety, etc.); and last, "poor self-regulation of affect and behavior" (whether offender exhibits impulsive behavior).

The fourth domain, "family/environmental functioning," includes four measures: "high-stress family environment" (the extent of family dysfunction experienced by the offender); "problematic parent-offender relationships/parental rejection" (offender's experience with parental rejection/discord); "parent(s) not supporting sexual-offense-specific assessment/treatment" (i.e., parents' level of support for offenders' treatment needs); and, "environment supporting opportunities to reoffend sexually" (e.g., poor monitoring/supervision of offender, increased access to potential victims).

The fifth and final domain centers on an offender's treatment-related risk factors. Two items are included here: "no development or practice of realistic prevention plans/strategies" and "incomplete sexual-offense-specific treatment." In particular, the first factor measures whether the offender has established acceptable methods to avoid sexual offending in the future. In contrast, the second item taps into whether the juvenile has completed a majority (at least 75 percent) of the specific treatment goals that were recommended following initial assessment.

Not least, the ERASOR includes a provision for an "Other Factor" category. The logic here is to permit the evaluator to qualitatively note other items that might be related to reoffending risk. For example, if it is known that the juvenile experiences the greatest urge to offend when abusing alcohol, the offender's current use of alcohol would be relevant to document.

Scoring is fairly straightforward. Because ERASOR permits evaluators to assess overall risk, no determinate coding scheme exists. For all items, evaluators record (after reading a short description for each) whether the risk factor is "present," "partially/possibly present," "not present," and "unknown." Then a total numeric score is calculated by simply tallying the number of factors that exist (minimum of 0 to maximum of 25). Finally, the evaluators determine an offender's overall risk rating as "low," "moderate," or "high."

Strengths. The ERASOR demonstrates several strengths. First, some studies indicate that it outperforms other instruments in predicting sexual recidivism. For example, Chu and colleagues (2012) drawing on a sample of youths living in Singapore reported that the ERASOR's overall rating (i.e., as low, moderate, or high) and total numeric score significantly predicted sexual reoffending (AUC values=0.83, 0.74, respectively). The other instruments included in the study did not (e.g., J-SOAP-II's AUC value=0.51). Similar findings have been replicated in some other research (see also, Rajlic & Gretton, 2010).

A meta-analysis conducted by Hanson and Morton-Bourgon (2009) revealed moderate predictive ability of the ERASOR in determining sexual recidivism risk (AUC=0.66), specifically for the total numeric score. Separately, the ERASOR has demonstrated acceptable inter-rater reliability for total numeric scores and overall clinical assessments (Viljoen, Elkovitch, Scalora, & Ullman, 2009). Thus, overall evaluators come to similar conclusions in assessing sexual recidivism risk using the ERASOR.

Furthermore, some scholars see additional benefits of the ERASOR given its inclusion of mostly dynamic factors (n=16). That is, reliance on such indicators means evaluators can assess change in recidivism risk and treatment needs over time (Miccio-Fonseca & Rasmussen, 2011; Worling & Curwen, 2000).

Limitations. Although some scholarship has uncovered moderate to strong predictive validity of the ERASOR, results from other studies are less positive. For example, Viljoen and colleagues (2009) reported no statistically significant findings regarding the ERASOR's ability to predict sexual recidivism in a sample of juvenile offenders in a residential facility. Along a similar direction, Worling, Bookalam, and Litteljohn (2012) discovered that the ERASOR's clinical rating was unrelated to offenders' odds of sexually recidivating (although the ERASOR's total numeric score significantly predicted new sex offenses, AUC=0.72).

Relatedly, some scholars have critiqued the ERASOR on the grounds that it differentially predicts recidivism among offenders. For example, Miccio-Fonseca and Rasmussen (2011) observed that prior scholarship shows the ERASOR is less accurate in predicting sexual recidivism among adolescents who have committed more serious sex offenses and have a violent criminal history. This gap is potentially limiting per the authors given that adolescent sex offenders with histories of violent and other nonsexual offenses are among those most likely to persist in their sexual offending. Given that the ERASOR is one of the more recent assessment tools to be developed, future efforts are needed to explain these divergent findings and the extent of ERASOR's predictive ability across populations.

Not least, given ERASOR's measurement of several dynamic indicators, the instrument must be administered any time a risk factor changes. It follows that ERASOR scores have a short shelf life. Put differently, ERASOR scores at one point in time may not necessarily reflect risk of reoffense over time (see generally Chu et al., 2012). This consideration is potentially limiting as it suggests that additional resources from the criminal justice system are needed to appropriately administer the ERASOR. Table 9.5 provides a summary of the ERASOR.

Table 9.5. ERASOR Overview

Target Population	Risk Factors	Scoring
• Designed for use with juvenile sex offenders aged 12 to 18 years old with a prior history of committing sexual offenses	• Measures both static and dynamic risk factors to determine youth's overall recidivism risk	• Numeric scores involve the evaluators' tally of the total number of risk factors that offenders have exhibited • Overall risk assessment levels (i.e., low, moderate, and high) are determined by the evaluator

Sex Offender Risk Assessment Controversies

Risk assessment tools represent a significant advance in sex offender management. However, controversies regarding their use exist. Three prominent critiques are summarized below. The suggested reading list provides additional references about current discussions and debates surrounding sex offender risk assessment.

On one level, there is the concern that risk assessment tools represent an ecological, or more specifically, an actuarial fallacy. To illustrate, statisticians have observed that the behavior of aggregates does not necessarily generalize to the behavior of any one individual. However, this logic appears to underpin risk assessment (see e.g., Hart, Michie, & Cooke, 2007). Put differently, risk analysis assumes that the risk posed by an individual offender can be predicted based on knowledge about groups of offenders. Fitzgibbon (2007, p. 97) recognized the potential consequence of this problem: "The result is a tendency towards inflation taking the form of over-prediction of dangerousness of individuals, such dangerousness being conflated with the risk characteristics for the group to which the individual has been allocated."

To be clear, as Craig and Beech (2010, p. 287) have observed in a review of research, the view "that it is wrong to base individual decisions on 'group data' has been refuted" (citations omitted). They note, for example, that a significant body of scholarship has shown "that average predictive effects [of risk assessment tools] ... are large and are distributed as expected by psychometric principles and the laws of probability." Per this argument, applying knowledge regarding the behavior of aggregates to individuals in terms of a relative risk does not necessarily bias risk analysis (Doren, 2007). Even so, debates are on-going regarding the extent to which group estimates can be extrapolated to determine an individual's level of risk for reoffending.

Related to this concern is the view that actuarial tools may be biased in determining recidivism risk given low base rates of sexual offending. Recall that the "base rate problem" (Abracen & Looman, 2006) was highlighted earlier in our discussion of the efficacy of civil commitment procedures in Chapter 8. Simply put, contrary to public perceptions, sexual recidivism is relatively rare. To highlight, research indicates that over a five-year period, the vast majority (93 percent) of sex offenders will not go on to commit another sex offense (Sample & Bray, 2003). As a result, samples of recidivists are fairly small. This situation presents potential methodological difficulties in accurately determining the risk that any one individual offender presents to society. For example, assume that one in ten sex offenders will be convicted of another sex offense over a five-year period (an estimate on par with prior research). This example implies that always predicting reoffense would result in nine incorrect evaluations and only one correct one. If however, estimates are substantially higher, say that six in ten sex offenders will be convicted of another sex crime in the same period, we would be correct in predicting reoffense a majority of the time (60 percent) and incorrect only 40 percent of the time. This rather crude example thus illustrates that it is substantially more difficult to accurately predict a rare event than one that occurs with greater frequency.

Scholars have proposed remedies to address this problem. For instance, studies that extend follow-up periods will capture a greater number of recidivist events (Hanson, 2002). Separately, increasing sample sizes ensures that information is gathered on a wide range of sex offenders, increasing opportunities to observe reoffenses. Additionally, given that official conviction or charge data underestimate the extent of sexual offending, the use of self-report data should be considered to account for reoffending. Not least, the use of specialized statistics (e.g., AUC values) designed to deal with rare events may serve as more robust estimates of the predictive ability of risk assessment tools (Craig & Beech, 2010).

A final critique involves concern about the measurement of recidivism among evaluation studies examining the predictive ability of risk assessment tools. Miccio-Fonseca and Rasmussen (2011, p. 6) contend that "a limitation of risk assessment tools is lack of universal agreement on terms 'recidivism' or 'reoffense.'" Indeed, inconsistency exists across developmental/validation studies in their operational definitions of recidivism. To illustrate, some studies measure reoffense as convictions whereas others include arrests and charges, still others include self-reported offenses. The end result? This discrepancy potentially invites problems when attempting to synthesize large bodies of research to determine the relative utility of any one risk assessment tool compared to another (Reitzel & Carbonell, 2006).

Chapter Summary

Risk analysis—the science of determining offender recidivism odds and identifying treatment needs—has become a critical component of sex offender management in the U.S. Several risk assessment tools have been developed in the last decade. This chapter reviewed five prominent ones: the Static-99/Static-2002, Stable-2007/Acute-2007, the Minnesota Sex Offender Screening Tool-Revised (MnSOST-R)/Minnesota Sex Offender Screening Tool-3 (MnSOST-3), the Juvenile Sex Offender Assessment Protocol-II (J-SOAP-II), and the Estimate of Risk of Adolescent Sexual Offense Recidivism (ERASOR). These instruments vary in their target population, reliance on static and dynamic risk factors, and scoring. Controversies surrounding risk assessment tools exist, particularly concerning their ability to accurately identify offenders' recidivism risk odds. Although the limitations of risk assessment tools have been identified, some scholars question alternatives that do not rely on empirically derived assessments. Put differently, with few exceptions, purely clinical assessments have been shown to be poor indicators of sex offender recidivism risk particularly for rapists and child molesters. Even so, discussions and debates regarding offender risk assessment will likely continue in the future given the expanding registered sex offender population in the U.S.

The additional suggested reading list provides citations to other research in this area. The following chapter continues the emphasis on sex crime policy and reform by examining variation in sex crime laws across the U.S.

Additional Suggested Readings

Appelbaum, P., Saleh, F. M., Grudzinskas, A. J., Bradford, J. M., & Brodsky, D. J. (Eds.). (2009). *Sex offenders: Identification, risk assessment, treatment, and legal issues.* New York: Oxford University Press.

Craissati, J. (2004). *Managing high-risk sex offenders in the community: A psychological approach.* New York: Routledge.

Janus, E. S., & Prentky, R. A. (2003). Forensic use of actuarial risk assessment with sex offenders: Accuracy, admissibility, and accountability. *American Criminal Law Review,* *40,* 1443–1499.

Knight, R. A., & Thornton, D. (2007). *Evaluating and improving risk assessment schemes for sexual recidivism: A long-term follow-up of convicted sexual offenders.* Washington, D.C.: National Institute of Justice.

Thornton, D. (2002). Constructing and testing a framework for dynamic risk assessment. *Sexual Abuse: A Journal of Research and Treatment, 14,* 139–153.

Rich, P. (2009). *Juvenile sexual offenders: A comprehensive guide to risk evaluation.* New York: Wiley.

Chapter 10

National Variation in
Sex Crime Reforms

Chapter Introduction

In prior chapters, we discussed the difficulties of determining the efficacy of sex crime reforms. Part of the challenge stems from the significant variation across sex crime laws and also within the content of these laws. For example, some states have elected to enact a myriad of sex offender laws, beyond the federally required registries and notification policies. Others have enacted only those two reforms. Additionally, states differ in the implementation of prominent policies. Residence restriction laws, for example, can vary considerably across states. That is, some states have incorporated large boundaries (e.g., 1,500 feet to 2,000 feet), whereas others have implemented significantly shorter restrictions (e.g., 500 feet). Still others permit counties and municipalities to set wider restrictions beyond the state's mandated boundary. At the same time, and complicating matters further, seemingly all sex crime laws have appeared simultaneously in the U.S. Accordingly, in order to systematically assess the impact of any one given policy, evaluations must account for the effects of the other laws that may currently be in place. It follows then, that such variation affects research efforts to assess the impact of any one law. The goal of Chapter 10[1] is to highlight the variability within sex offender laws and, also the implications of this variation for policy evaluation.

An Examination of Sex Crime
Laws Nationally

In the past decade, every state has passed some type of sex crime legislation (Letourneau, Levenson et al., 2010; Sample, 2011). Many of these policies have been critiqued as being "built on weak theoretical and logical foundations" (Barnes, 2011, p. 406), or as being, per some scholars, "hastily passed [laws] not based on scientific evidence, but on emotional reactions to high profile, violent, disturbing cases" (Fortney et al., 2007, p. 1). Others have identified potential collateral consequences of such laws—offender stigma, unemployment, and residential displacement (see e.g., Burchfield, 2011; Levenson, 2011)—which may significantly reduce sex offenders' chances of successful reentry into communities.

---

1. The content for this chapter derives from a revised version of an earlier publication: Mancini, C., Barnes, J. C., & Mears, D. P. (2013). It varies from state to state: An examination of sex crime laws nationally. *Criminal Justice Policy Review, 24,* 166–198.

Even so, federal courts have upheld the laws and, in so doing, have given states wide latitude to develop and implement ever-new sex crime laws and policies or to expand the purview of existing ones (Bandy, 2011; Sample & Kadleck, 2008; Terry, 2011). The result is that efforts to address sex crime now include a wide range of initiatives, including offender registries, community notification laws, tougher sentences, civil commitment of sex offenders, and chemical castration (Beauregard & Lieb, 2011; Wright, 2009).

The range of sex crime laws and policies would seem to lend support to the notion that the United States has uniformly toughened its response to sex crime. According to some experts, states are engaged "in a race to the bottom to see who can most thoroughly ostracize and condemn ... the most despised members of our society [sex offenders]" (Geraghty, 2007, p. 514). Borrowing from the medical literature, Carpenter (2010) recently observed that the sweeping number of sex crime laws enacted by the federal government and states is tantamount to a "legislative epidemic," one triggered by "high-profile cases, emotion-laden rhetoric, and inaccurate assumptions about crime and criminals" (p. 66).

Collectively, these assessments appear to fit what is known about *general* trends in U.S. sex crime policymaking. As we argue, however, whether *all* states have embraced the "tough on sex crime" movement is a largely unaddressed empirical question. Given the significant range of laws, there is the potential for states to differ dramatically in sex crime policymaking. There also is considerable room for state-level variation in the design of sex crime laws and the intensity of sex crime legislation. Such variability has implications for depictions of the emergence of a putative era of "get tough" criminal justice policy (Gottschalk, 2008). If, for example, some states are highly aggressive in pursuing sex crime legislation while others are more tentative, it suggests that the country as a whole has not uniformly toughened its response to sex crimes. In addition, it raises the following question: *why* have some states adopted more aggressive, tougher responses to addressing sex crime?

The potential variability in sex crime legislation across states highlights a critical policy issue. Evaluations of sex crime laws and policies have burgeoned in recent years, especially in response to calls for evidence-based practice (Freeman, 2012). Given the apparent increase in such laws and policies, policymakers quite rightly may want to know which ones are effective and which are not. The challenge, however, that to date has gone largely unrecognized is that there are at least two types of variation, one recognized in the broader evaluation research literature (see, e.g., Mears, 2010), that may delimit our ability to generalize from one study to another. First, different types of policy responses exist (e.g., residence restrictions, chemical castration). It would be a mistake to generalize the results of a study focused on one type of response (e.g., residence restrictions) to another type (e.g., chemical castration). It also would be a mistake, given the nearly simultaneous implementation of many sex crime policies, to assume that any one policy, or even a set of policies, contributed to a change in reports of sex crime.

The second constraint on generalizing from one study to another is that the content and scope—more generally, the design—of any specific policy can vary considerably from state to state. To illustrate, a wide range of residence restrictions for sex offenders exists across states. In some states, sex offenders are prohibited from living within 500 feet of a school or school bus stop. In other states, offenders may not live within 2,000 feet of places children congregate (Levenson & D'Amora, 2007). An evaluation of one residence restriction law (in one state) may not necessarily generalize to another (in another state). For example, the 500-feet versus 2,000-feet distinction may be relevant to limiting or reducing sex offending (see, e.g., Levenson & Cotter, 2005b, p. 170). The former, for example, allows considerably more freedom for offenders to come into contact with potential victims.

These concerns are largely moot if states have uniformly adopted a similar number and type of sex crime laws and if there is little within-law variation among states. Should, however, there be substantial variation, it would point to the need to restrict the generalizability of analyses of "get tough" developments among states and of evaluations of particular laws and policies. In fact, despite an increasingly large body of research on sex crime policy, there remains little systematic analysis of the state of sex crime policies nationally. At the same time, sex crime policymaking continues to result in ever new sets of laws or variants of existing ones. Against this backdrop, the goal of this chapter is to answer two related questions and, in so doing, highlight the critical need for the development of a more systematic and comprehensive body of research on sex crime laws and policies. First, what variation exists in the types and number of sex crime laws and policies enacted across states? Second, to what extent do particular types of laws and policies vary in their design? We begin first by describing the major types of sex crime laws and policies that have emerged in recent decades. We then examine variability in these laws and policies and discuss the implications of the chapter's findings for research and policy.

Sex Crime Laws and Policies Nationally

In canvassing the literature on criminal justice policy that targets sex crime, seven broad types of laws and policies surface: sex offender registries, community notification, residence restrictions, civil commitment, lifetime supervision, sex offender driver license notation requirements, and castration laws. As previously discussed, these are not the only laws or policies; electronic monitoring is, for example, beginning to be used in a manner that targets sex offenders (see, e.g., Payne & DeMichele, 2010). However, these are laws and policies that, as the literature on sex crime laws attests, have dominated the policymaking landscape in recent decades (Velázquez, 2008). For example, Miethe, Olson, and Mitchell (2006, pp. 205, 224) observed that sex offenders have become "a major focus of current crime-control policies ... contemporary public policy involving sex offenders includes offender registries, community notification campaigns, civil commitment laws, chemical castration, and increased sentences [and monitoring] for sexual offenses." Thus focusing on this subset of crime laws ensures that our analysis represents the major types of initiatives states have pursued in recent decades. Below, we describe each of these types of approaches to addressing sex crime and then turn our attention to analysis of the implications of the variability within these types of laws and between them.

Sex Offender Registries

As reviewed in prior chapters, two pieces of federal legislation enacted in the 1990s are primarily responsible for the emergence of sex offender registries. The Jacob Wetterling Act (1994) and Megan's Law (1996) require all states to develop public registries that list information about released sex offenders (Levenson, Letourneau et al., 2010). States that do not comply risk losing ten percent of their Byrne Formula funding for criminal justice programs (Center for Sex Offender Management, 1999). Typically, sex offenders must register with local agencies, such as the state police, department of public safety, office of the attorney general, or the department of corrections (Terry & Furlong, 2006). Depending on the specific state statute, offenders may be required to register for a period of ten years or less to life (Tewksbury, 2005).

Community Notification

Community notification laws are closely related to registries. For instance, community notification laws were mandated under the same federal acts that spurred the creation of sex offender registries (Bandy, 2011). Under this approach, contact information about sex offenders living in local neighborhoods is published typically via a website (Tewksbury, 2005). Also, similar to registries, community notification laws appear to vary from state to state. For example, in one review of sex offender statutes, Velázquez (2008) reported that other community notification methods may include press releases, flyers, phone calls, door-to-door contact, and neighborhood meetings coordinated by law enforcement. In some instances, registration is only required for high-risk offenders. Some states reserve notification only for offenders who are deemed to be at increased risk of recidivism. Other states rely on a more liberal community notification approach, publicizing the location of all sex offenders without regard to recidivism risk (Beck & Travis, 2005).

Residence Restrictions

Unlike sex offender registries and notification laws, states do not lose federal funding if they decline to enact residence restrictions. These restrictions have been implemented to prohibit sex offenders from residing in close proximity to schools, school bus stops, parks, daycare centers, and other locations (Barnes et al., 2009; Mercado, Alvarez, & Levenson, 2008). Law enforcement and other state agencies (e.g., department of safety, community supervisory agencies) are typically responsible for ensuring that certain offenders do not live within close vicinity of prohibited areas that are outlined in the law (Tewksbury & Levenson, 2007). As discussed earlier, states differ in the range of boundary restrictions they establish (Zgoba, 2011).

Civil Commitment

Civil commitment is also a sanction that states have implemented in the past two decades to respond to concerns about sexual recidivism. Sex offender commitment typically requires that certain high-risk offenders undergo psychiatric evaluation (Birgden & Cucolo, 2011). If found to meet certain criteria, the sex offender is required to stand trial by a judge or jury. If the offender is committed, he or she is held in confinement until a clinician determines, based on clinical judgment, that the offender is no longer a threat to the community (Levenson, 2004).

Lifetime Supervision

Developed primarily to address repeat offending, lifetime supervision laws require that high-risk sex offenders be monitored for the duration of their lives (Armstrong & Freeman, 2011; Nieto, 2004). Colorado, for example, implemented the Lifetime Supervision Act in the early 2000s (Colorado Department of Corrections, 2002). The underlying logic of such efforts stems from the assumption that sex offenders cannot be "cured"; accordingly, they must be "managed" through, as in the case of Colorado, "treatment and carefully structured and monitored behavioral supervision conditions [to] assist many sex offenders to develop internal controls for their behaviors" (p. 21).

Driver's License Notation

Several states have recently enacted laws that require sex offenders to display a special driver's license notation identifying their registration status (Bonnar-Kidd, 2010). These laws were developed and implemented, in part, to address concerns that states failed to update their registry records once offenders moved to different jurisdictions. Driver's license-related screening "could, in concept, help improve the level of compliance with state sex offender registration requirements as well as enhance monitoring" (U.S. Government Accountability Office, 2008, p. 30). Sex offenders who move from one state to another, for example, can easily be identified as sex offenders.

Chemical Castration

Some states have experimented with chemical castration as a way to reduce sex crime. As prior chapters described, this approach requires that certain types of male offenders receive injections of synthetic hormones to reduce sexual arousal (Scott & del Busto, 2009). Some states allow eligible offenders to choose chemical castration in lieu of other types of sanctions. A handful of states permit offenders to elect surgical castration as a permanent solution instead of the reversible chemical castration treatment (Scott & Holmberg, 2003).

Evaluations of the Effectiveness of Sex Crime Laws

A large body of work has focused largely on issues other than the impacts of these laws. For example, they focus on the characteristics of sex offenders affected by sex crime reforms (Levenson, Letourneau et al., 2010; Wright, 2008), descriptive analyses of the "new generation" of sex crime laws (Harris & Lobanov-Rostovsky, 2010; Wright, 2009), policymakers' and public perceptions of various sex crime laws (Levenson et al., 2007; Mears et al., 2008; Sample & Kadleck), and not least, collateral consequences of the "tough on sex crime" movement (Levenson, 2011; Tewksbury, 2005).

Much less is known about the specific impacts of these policies (Harris & Lurigio, 2010; Mears, 2010). That said, as mentioned in prior chapters, a small handful of evaluation studies exist. Most of them, as Harris and Lurigio (2010) demonstrate, have focused on examining select reforms—registries and notification laws (Vásquez et al., 2008; Zgoba, Veysey, & Dalessandro, 2010) and residence restrictions (Zandbergen et al., 2010). Two themes emerge from review of this research. First, by and large these studies have not detected significant sex crime reducing effects of these policies—this situation possibly reflects that many of these laws appear to be poorly designed (Barnes 2011), and per scholars, have been developed primarily to address unusual and rare sex crime (Terry, 2011). The absence of systematic examination of the many other types of laws (lifetime supervision, state-level castration laws, and mandatory identification policies for sex offenders) indicates that knowledge about their effects remains a "black box"—that is, outside of descriptive endeavors, very little is known about whether and how these laws may affect sex crime.

The limited research on sex crime laws is important. There is, however, a related critical issue—the pronounced diversity of sex crime laws increasingly will make it difficult to arrive at credible estimates of impact. For example, virtually no empirical evaluation of sex crime laws (e.g., registry evaluations) has been able to control for the effects of other laws in place in particular areas (e.g., the effect of residence restrictions, castration law). The inability to disentangle the effects of these various policies means the potential effects of any one law are potentially obscured or, more precisely, cannot be identified. There is a related implication—the marked variability within and across types of sex crime laws limits the external validity of evaluations of any given law. For example, extant evaluations of sex crime laws have typically consisted of single state-level examinations (e.g., Zgoba et al., 2010) that investigate specific variants of sex crime laws. Generalizing from a single state and a single manifestation of one type of law limits substantially the ability of studies to generate findings that can be safely assumed to extend to other states, especially if those states use different types of sex crime laws or ones that vary considerably from those examined in particular studies.

The Present Analysis

Given the wide array of laws enacted to prevent sex crimes, this chapter seeks to provide a better foundation for assessing the state of sex crime laws in America. In particular, it examines seven sex crime laws and policies—sex offender registries, community notification, residence restrictions, civil commitment, lifetime supervision, sex offender driver's license notation requirements, and castration laws—and their implementation across each of the 50 states. The goal is to document (1) which laws and policies have been enacted in each state, and (2) the extent to which there is variation in the design (e.g., the types of restrictions) of each law and policy. In turn, the chapter argues that the marked variability of sex crime laws, and the likely increase in such variability in future years, increasingly will make it difficult to generate credible, generalizable estimates of the impact of any given type of sex crime law, especially those that aim to reduce macro-level sex crime trends. To this end, analysis draws on several sources of information. The first is an extensive and detailed compilation of state sex crime statutes in effect as of 2008 (Velázquez, 2008). The second is a review of state statutes in effect at the same time and specifically focused on chemical castration and driver's license notations; these were not examined in the Velázquez (2008) report. The chapter's appendix lists each state statute.

Findings

Variation in Sex Crime Laws and Policies across States

The first research question is addressed: what is the extent of the variation in the number of sex crime laws enacted across states? Several patterns emerge from Table 10.1, which was created by tallying the types of laws each of the 50 states had enacted as of 2008. Beginning with the first two laws—registries and community notification—inspection of Table 10.1 shows that every state enacted some type of registry or community notification statute. The explanation is straight-forward: as noted earlier, in the 1990s, the federal government required states to enact such laws or risk losing federal funding for criminal justice programs. From this perspective, then, the national "get tough" on sex crime movement was spurred on primarily by the federal government. That is, every state adopted two prominent efforts to address sex offending and did so because of a federal inducement.

What, though, about other types of sex crime laws and policies? When all seven are examined, it is clear that states vary greatly in the extent to which they have embraced a "get tough" stance against sex crime. Figure 10.1 depicts the percentages of states that have enacted only two of the seven laws and policies, three of them, four of them, or five or more. Notably, ten percent of states—that is, five of them—have adopted *only* the two federally required sex crime laws (i.e., registry and notification). One-third of states have adopted three of the sex crime laws and policies. Just over one-third have adopted four of the laws and policies, and roughly one-fifth have adopted five or more. No state enacted all seven of the laws and policies.

In short, when viewed from this perspective, it is evident that some states, such as Maine and Wyoming, have restricted their sex crime efforts to the minimum necessary to retain federal funding, while other states, such as Florida and Texas, have pursued a wide range of efforts to address sex crime. Put differently, states like Florida and Texas appear to be, on the face of it, substantially tougher on sex crime when compared to other states such as Maine and Wyoming.

Beyond sex offender registries and community notification laws, which types of approaches to addressing sex crime are most prevalent? As can be seen in Table 10.1, 33 states have enacted sex offender residence restrictions, 19 have enacted civil commitment provisions, 14 have enacted lifetime supervision laws, 11 have implemented driver's license restrictions, and 8 have allowed for chemical castration. Residence restrictions, thus, are the third-most common type of sex crime policy among states, followed by civil commitment provisions.

Are some regions of the country more aggressive, as might be expected based on prior studies (e.g., Borg, 1997), in addressing sex crime? As the last column in Table 10.1 reveals, the South, Midwest, and West are all relatively similar. For example, the average number of laws enacted in Southern states is 4.1, compared with 3.9 in Midwestern states, and 3.6 in Western states. Within each of these regions, there are states at the high end of the "intensity" spectrum—Florida and Texas in the South, Illinois and Wisconsin in the Midwest, and Arizona in the West. The average among Northeastern states (2.9), by contrast, is well below these averages. The highest "intensity" Northeastern state is Massachusetts, which enacted four of the seven types of sex crime laws and policies.

Variation in the Design of Sex Crime Laws and Policies

We move next to our second research question: to what extent is there variability in the design of sex crime laws and policies enacted nationally? That is, for a given type of sex crime law, is there marked consistency or variability in the focus or content?

Sex Offender Registries. As shown in Table 10.2, there is considerable variation concerning registration laws (the first policy examined). In all but one state (Colorado), the length

Table 10.1. Sex Crime Laws, by State and Region, as of 2008

	Registry	Notification	Residence Restriction	Commitment	Lifetime Supervision	Drivers' License	Castration	# of Laws (Average)
Northeast								26 (2.9)
Connecticut	X	X			X			3
Maine	X	X						2
Massachusetts	X	X		X	X			4
New Hampshire	X	X		X				3
New Jersey	X	X		X				3
New York	X	X		X				3
Pennsylvania	X	X						2
Rhode Island	X	X			X			3
Vermont	X	X			X			3
South								65 (4.1)
Alabama	X	X	X			X		4
Arkansas	X	X	X					3
Delaware	X	X	X			X		4
Florida	X	X	X	X		X	X	6
Georgia	X	X	X				X	4
Kentucky	X	X	X					3
Louisiana	X	X	X			X	X	5

Maryland	X	X	X					3
Mississippi	X	X	X			X		4
North Carolina	X	X	X					3
Oklahoma	X	X	X					3
South Carolina	X	X	X	X				4
Tennessee	X	X	X		X			4
Texas	X	X	X	X		X	X	6
Virginia	X	X	X	X				4
West Virginia	X	X	X		X	X		5
Midwest								**47 (3.9)**
Illinois	X	X	X	X	X			5
Indiana	X	X	X			X		4
Iowa	X	X	X	X				4
Kansas	X	X		X		X		4
Michigan	X	X	X			X		4
Minnesota	X	X	X	X				4
Missouri	X	X	X	X				4
Nebraska	X	X	X	X				4
North Dakota	X	X		X				3
Ohio	X	X	X					3

Table 10.1. Sex Crime Laws, by State and Region, as of 2008, *continued*

	Registry	Notification	Residence Restriction	Commitment	Lifetime Supervision	Drivers' License	Castration	# of Laws (Average)
South Dakota	X	X	X					3
Wisconsin	X	X		X	X		X	5
West								47 (3.6)
Alaska	X	X						2
Arizona	X	X	X	X	X	X		6
California	X	X	X	X			X	5
Colorado	X	X			X			3
Hawaii	X	X						2
Idaho	X	X	X					3
Montana	X	X	X		X		X	4
Nevada	X	X	X		X			4
New Mexico	X	X			X			3
Oregon	X	X	X		X		X	5
Utah	X	X	X		X			4
Washington	X	X	X	X				4
Wyoming	X	X						2
N (Percent)	50 (100%)	50 (100%)	33 (66%)	19 (38%)	14 (28%)	11 (22%)	8 (16%)	

Figure 10.1. Percentages of States with Multiple Sex Crime Laws, as of 2008

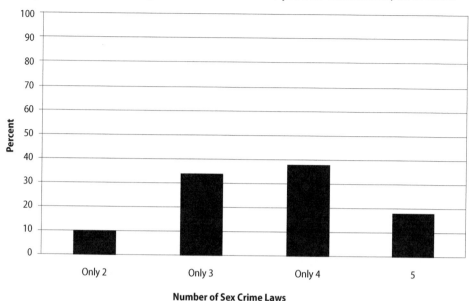

of sex offender registration ranges from 10 years to life. Specifically, 36 states have a 10- to 15-year length requirement for a range of sex offenders. Eleven states mandate that certain sex offenders must register for 16 to 25 years. Almost all states (n=48) require specific types of sex offenders (e.g., those convicted of crimes against children) to register for life. Eleven states require all convicted sex offenders to register for life (i.e., the state statutes make no clear distinction between offender types). Not shown in Table 10.2 is that three states—Arizona, Kansas, and New Hampshire—have special juvenile provisions in which youth sex offenders, as compared with adult sex offenders, are required to register for shorter durations (e.g., only until they reach age 25).

Community Notification. Federal law requires that states develop and implement sex offender registries and that they notify neighborhoods about sex offenders released into communities. Beyond that, states were afforded considerable leeway in the design of their laws. Analysis found, for example, that notification laws varied in (1) how they are carried-out (e.g., Internet registries, flyers, neighborhood meetings, e-mail, telephone calls), (2) who they serve (e.g., all members of the public versus only those living in close vicinity to registered sex offenders), and (3) who they affect (e.g., all registered sex offenders versus only high-risk offenders).

All states have developed Internet registries that list the names and addresses of convicted sex offenders. However, some states also disseminate information about offenders via flyers, community meetings, and e-mail. In addition, some states, such as Kentucky, notify citizens via telephone about sex offenders living in close vicinity to their residences. Other states, such as Louisiana, use e-mail to notify citizens living in close proximity to convicted offenders.

Inspection of Table 10.3 shows that most states (n=32) disseminate information about all types of registered sex offenders. For example, North Carolina's community notification statute requires public notification about virtually all sex offenders—those considered low, medium, and high-risk. However, 18 states only provide information to the public

Table 10.2. Length of Registration for Sex Offenders, by State, as of 2008

State	10 to 15 years	16 to 25 years	Life
Alabama	Juveniles		Adults
Alaska	1st offense		2nd offense or aggravated sex offense
Arizona	1st offense		2nd offense
Arkansas	1st offense		2nd offense, sexually violent predators, those convicted of aggravated sex offense
California			All registered sex offenders
Colorado	Class 1, 2, or 3 felony sex offense	Class 4, 5, or 6 felony sex offense	Felony sex assault involving children, sexual assault on a client by a psychotherapist, incest, or aggravated incest (State has a five year registration requirement for offenders convicted of misdemeanor sex crimes such as voyeurism)
Connecticut	All registered sex offenders		Those convicted of sexual assault of victim under age 13
Delaware	Tier 1 sex offenders	Tier 2 sex offenders	Tier 3 sex offenders
Florida			All registered sex offenders
Georgia			All registered sex offenders
Hawaii			All registered sex offenders
Idaho	All registered sex offenders		Violent and repeat sex offenders
Illinois	All registered sex offenders		Sexually violent predators
Indiana	1st offense		2nd offense
Iowa	1st offense		2nd offense and sexually violent predators

	First offense		
Kansas	First offense		Second offense, sexually violent predators, and those convicted of sex crimes against children
Louisiana	All registered sex offenders		Second offense, sexually violent predator
Maine	Determined by court	Determined by court	Determined by court
Maryland	All registered sex offenders		Aggravated sex crimes, sex crimes against children under age 12, sexually violent offender
Massachusetts	All registered sex offenders		Those convicted of two or more sex crimes or of a sexually violent crime
Michigan		All registered sex offenders	Those convicted of two or more crimes, sexually violent offense, sex crimes involving victim under age 13
Minnesota	All registered sex offenders		Those convicted of two or more crimes, committed murder during a sex assault, sexually dangerous person
Mississippi	Misdemeanor sex offenses	Felony sex offenses	Those convicted of crimes against children under age 14, repeat sex offenses, and sexually violent offenses
Missouri			All registered sex offenders
Montana			All registered sex offenders
Nebraska	All registered sex offenses		Offenders who were convicted of an aggravated offense or have prior convictions for sex-related offenses
Nevada	Tier 1 offenders	Tier 2 offenders	Tier 3 offenders
New Hampshire	All registered sex offenders		If convicted of aggravated felonious sexual assault, felonious sexual assault, habitual indecent exposure, offenses against children, and those with a second sex-related conviction
New Jersey			All registered sex offenders
New Mexico	1st sex offense		2nd sex offense

Table 10.2. Length of Registration for Sex Offenders, by State, as of 2008, *continued*

State	10 to 15 years	16 to 25 years	Life
New York		Level 1 sex offenders	Level 2 or 3 sex offenders, sexual predators, sexually violent offenders, those convicted of multiple sex crimes
North Carolina	All registered sex offenders		Violent sex offenders, offenders who commit multiple sex offenses, and if convicted of aggravated sex offense
North Dakota	Low-risk sex offenders	Moderate-risk sex offenders	High-risk sex offenders
Ohio	Tier 1 sex offenders	Tier 2 sex offenders	Tier 3 sex offenders
Oklahoma	Those required to register because of an out-of-state offense, level 1 sex offenders	Level 2 sex offenders	Level 3 sex offenders, habitual sex offenders, and those convicted of an aggravated sex offense
Oregon			All registered sex offenders
Pennsylvania	1st sex offense		2nd sex offense
Rhode Island			All registered sex offenders
South Carolina			All registered sex offenders
South Dakota			All registered sex offenders
Tennessee	All registered sex offenders		Violent sex offenders and those convicted of more than one sex offense
Texas	Offenders convicted of prohibited sexual conduct, indecent exposure, online solicitation of a minor and any attempt, conspiracy or solicitation to commit a sex offense		All other registered sex offenders

Utah	All registered sex offenders	Repeat sex offenders, sex crimes involving children, aggravated sex crimes
Vermont	All registered sex offenders	Sexually violent predators
Virginia	All registered sex offenders	Sexually violent offenders
Washington	Class "a" felony without "forcible compulsion"; class "c" felony	Class "b" felony	Sexually violent offenders, forcible crimes, and sex offenses involving minors
West Virginia	All registered sex offenders		The offender has one or more prior convictions, is a sexual predator, has committed sex crimes involving children, has a documented mental illness
Wisconsin	All registered sex offenders		
Wyoming	All registered sex offenders		

Table 10.3. Group to which Community Notification Law Applies, as of 2008

State	Notification Applies to ...
Alabama	All juvenile and adult registered sex offenders, where risk is high
Alaska	All registered sex offenders
Arizona	More serious (level 2 and level 3) registered sex offenders
Arkansas	All registered sex offenders
California	All registered sex offenders
Colorado	All registered sex offenders
Connecticut	All registered sex offenders
Delaware	More serious (tier 2 and tier 3) sex offenders
Florida	All registered sex offenders
Georgia	All registered sex offenders
Hawaii	More serious (felony) registered sex offenders
Idaho	All registered adult sex offenders
Illinois	All registered sex offenders
Indiana	All registered sex offenders
Iowa	All registered sex offenders
Kansas	All registered sex offenders
Kentucky	All registered sex offenders
Louisiana	All registered sex offenders
Maine	All registered sex offenders
Maryland	All registered sex offenders
Massachusetts	More serious (level 2 and level 3) registered sex offenders
Michigan	All registered sex offenders
Minnesota	More serious (level 2 and level 3) registered sex offenders
Mississippi	All registered sex offenders
Missouri	All registered sex offenders
Montana	All registered sex offenders
Nebraska	More serious (level 3) registered sex offenders
Nevada	More serious (tier 2 and tier 3) registered sex offenders
New Hampshire	Sex offenders convicted of aggravated sex crimes and sex crimes against children
New Jersey	More serious (tier 2 and tier 3) registered sex offenders

**Table 10.3. Group to which Community Notification
Law Applies, as of 2008,** *continued*

State	Notification Applies to …
New Mexico	Sex offenders convicted of aggravated sex crimes and sex crimes against children
New York	More serious (level 2 and level 3) registered sex offenders
North Carolina	All registered sex offenders
North Dakota	All registered sex offenders
Ohio	All registered sex offenders
Oklahoma	All registered sex offenders
Oregon	Predatory and sexually violent registered sex offenders
Pennsylvania	All registered sex offenders
Rhode Island	More serious (level 2 and level 3) registered sex offenders
South Carolina	All registered sex offenders
South Dakota	All registered sex offenders
Tennessee	All registered sex offenders
Texas	All registered sex offenders
Utah	All registered sex offenders
Vermont	Sex offenders convicted of aggravated sex crimes and sex crimes against children
Virginia	All registered sex offenders
Washington	More serious (risk 3) registered sex offenders
West Virginia	All registered sex offenders
Wisconsin	Sexually violent registered sex offenders
Wyoming	All registered sex offenders

about high-risk offenders. For example, Vermont's community notification law requires that information be released only for sex offenders convicted of aggravated sex crimes and sex crimes against children. One state (Idaho) publicizes identifying information only for adult registered sex offenders.

Residence Restrictions. Here, again, variability emerges as a prominent theme. Table 10.4 describes the boundaries states use in their residence restriction laws. One striking pattern is the degree of variation in the buffer zone sizes of residence restrictions. The interval cut-offs are used to highlight this variability. Of the 33 states that have a residence restriction policy, seven states have enacted residence restrictions that range from 500 feet to 999 feet. Thirteen states prohibit sex offenders from living within 1,000 feet to 1,499 feet of specific "hot spot" locations (e.g., schools). There is one state, Mississippi, that has enacted a 1,500-feet restriction, however, some states have gone well beyond this

Table 10.4. Residence Restrictions, by State, as of 2008

	500 to 999 ft.	1,000 to 1,499 ft.	1,500 to 1,999 ft.	2,000 ft.	General Law[1]	Other Law[2]	Child Victim[3]
Alabama				X		X (victim)	
Arizona		X					X
Arkansas				X			
California				X			
Delaware	X						X
Florida		X					X
Georgia		X					
Idaho	X						X
Illinois	X						X
Indiana		X		X			
Iowa							X
Kentucky		X					
Louisiana		X					X
Maryland					X (parole commission decides)		
Michigan		X					
Minnesota					X (end of confinement review committee decides)		

State								
Mississippi						X		
Missouri	X						X	
Montana				X (judge decides)				
Nebraska								X
Nevada	X						X	
North Carolina							X	
Ohio							X	
Oklahoma					X			
Oregon			X					
South Carolina		X (campus housing)						
South Dakota								X
Tennessee							X	
Texas				X (parole board)				
Utah		X (victim)						
Virginia								X
Washington	X							X
West Virginia							X	

1. These laws do not list an exact distance, thus allowing local municipalities to specify a boundary restriction.
2. Refers to laws that restrict offenders from living proximate to certain types of persons (e.g., students).
3. These laws only apply to offenders previously convicted of sex crimes against children.

range. In particular, five states—Alabama, Arkansas, California, Iowa, and Oklahoma—have adopted 2,000-feet restrictions.

A smaller number of states have residence laws that do not fit easily into a single category. For example, Minnesota and Oregon have general residence restrictions in which the exact boundary restriction is determined by local authorities (such as the county or city). Some states have special provisions in place that apply to other locations outside of schools and playgrounds. For instance, Alabama and Utah statutes require that convicted sex offenders not live within 1,000 feet of their victims' residences, making no reference to other potential hot spots with regards to this boundary. South Carolina law forbids sex offenders from residing in student housing at public institutions of higher learning.

Given that sex crime legislation appears to have been prompted by concerns about the victimization of children, to what extent have states designed their residence restriction laws to focus specifically on protecting children? Review of Table 10.4 shows that close to one-third of states have applied their law exclusively to offenders convicted of crimes against children (see also Meloy, Miller, & Curtis, 2008). By contrast, the other states have made no distinction between sex offenders who have victimized children or adults. This raises some theoretical complications when considering the rationale behind residence restriction laws.

Civil Commitment. The fourth policy examined here, civil commitment, can be more easily generalized (see Table 10.1). As Levenson (2004, p. 639) has emphasized, the process is "similar among states." With few exceptions, a judge or jury must find the offender "sexually violent" or "sexually dangerous" within the state's definition of the term. Approximately 38 percent of these state statutes (n=14) describe the length of confinement for sex offenders as "indeterminate." All statutes list eligible sex offenders as needing to suffer from a "mental abnormality," or "personality disorder," and/or listed as "sexual predators" to be eligible for civil confinement. For example, in Massachusetts, only sex offenders who "suffer from a mental abnormality or personality disorder that makes them more likely to engage in sex offenses" are eligible for civil commitment (see Massachusetts General Laws, Chapter 123A).

Lifetime Supervision. Variation in the content of the fifth law, sex offender lifetime supervision, is also easily summarized. By and large, states that have lifetime supervision statutes have used a similar approach. For example, almost all states target repeat or high-risk sex offenders. Among the states that have this law in place, roughly half require that sex offenders convicted of crimes against children receive lifetime supervision upon release. For example, Arizona law allows that in cases in which probation is an available sentence for certain felonies against children, the probation term ordered may be up to and including life. Some of the states' statutes (n=4) contain specific language that permits offenders to petition the court for release of lifetime supervision after a set period of time. Wisconsin, for example, "provides procedures for petition for termination of lifetime supervision" (National Conference of State Legislatures, 2003, p. 2).

Driver's License Identification. In recent years, there has been an emphasis on requiring sex offenders to obtain either special identification cards or to bear driver's licenses with special annotations (the sixth law examined). In Florida, for example, registered sex offenders are required to have either the marking "943.0435, F.S." (the specific state statute concerning registered sex offenders) or "775.21, F.S." (the state statute describing Florida's sexual predator law) imprinted on their driver's license or identification cards. Similarly, in Delaware, the identification cards of offenders are stamped with a "y" denoting their registered sex offender status (National Conference of State Legislatures, 2008a).

Chemical Castration. Most states that provide for this approach to reducing sex offender recidivism require chemical castration treatment via medroxyprogesterone acetate (MPA), a drug designed to control the production of testosterone in male offenders (see, e.g., Giltay & Gooren, 2009) as a prerequisite for release. Virtually all of these statutes apply to repeat sex offenders. About half of the states that use chemical castration (n=4) require that offenders with child victims undergo this sanction. Notably, two states (Louisiana and Texas) allow sex offenders to choose surgical castration in lieu of chemical castration. However, both statutes "prohibit a judge from requiring a defendant to undergo such a procedure as a condition of community supervision" (National Conference of State Legislatures, 2008b, p. 2).

Conclusion and Implications

Summary of Research

In the 1990s, the federal government and many states enacted new sex crime legislation in what was, according to some scholars, the equivalent of a "legislative panic" (Logan, 2003, p. 1288). Since that time, a broad range of efforts to address sex crime have emerged. Most of them have prioritized imposing tougher prison sentences and creating a wide range of post-incarceration penalties and restrictions for sex offenders (Sample, 2011; Wright, 2008). The reforms as well have illustrated the symbolic role of "get tough" lawmaking, as Leon's (2011b, p. 421) observation indicates— "Passing new laws that tighten surveillance and other restrictions on sex offenders lets policymakers signal their concern with crime and their solidarity with victims and their families." At first glance, the responses to sex crime seem to align well with the "tough on crime" philosophy that gained ascendance in American criminal justice policy during the past two decades. Upon closer inspection of state laws, however, that assessment appears to be incomplete. It overlooks the fact, for example, that significant variation exists in how aggressively states have responded to sex crime. The goal of the present chapter was to explore this possibility and, to this end, to investigate two interrelated questions: to what extent is there variability across states in the types and number of laws and policies in place, and to what extent is there variation in the design of these laws and policies?

After systematically compiling and examining information on state-level sex crime laws and policies, no variability was found in the enactment of sex offender registries and community notification. This finding reflects the fact that federal law requires such policies to be in place in order for the state to receive federal funding. However, we found considerable variation in the enactment of five other types of laws and policies: residence restrictions, civil commitment, lifetime supervision, driver's license restrictions, and castration laws. Some states have implemented none of these policies, while others have adopted most all of them. Notably, no state has enacted all of them. In short, viewed from the state level, it would appear to be incorrect to conclude that states have uniformly adopted a "get tough" approach to sex offenders. Some states, such as Texas, Florida, and Arizona have clearly done so—each state has implemented six of the seven laws. Other states, however, have enacted only the two policies required to receive federal funding (i.e., registry and notification laws).

To test arguments about the putatively tougher punishment philosophy of the South, we examined regional variation in sex crime law. We found that most regions have been similarly "tough" in their responses to sex crimes. The one exception was the Northeast; states in this region were, on average, less likely to adopt sex crime laws and policies.

Within each region, however, substantial variability existed. For example, in the West, Alaska had only enacted two sex crime policies, whereas Arizona had enacted six.

In investigating the chapter's second question, analysis indicates that considerable variability also exists in the design of these laws and policies. For example, across states, registries vary greatly in how long offenders must be registered, residence restriction zones vary in the distances used, and notification about the release of sex offenders occurs in a myriad of ways and targets varying groups of sex offenders. In these cases, the variation sometimes is sufficient as to raise questions about how generalizable the results of one policy would be for other states with similar polices. That said, for other laws and policies aimed at managing or sanctioning sex offenders—as with civil commitment, lifetime supervision, driver's license identification, and chemical castration laws—greater uniformity was found.

Research Implications

Several implications for future research flow from this chapter's findings. The first is that accounts of a new era in getting tough on sex crime do not correspond well with the variation in sex crime laws and policies that exists among states. Accordingly, an adequate explanation of the "get tough" movement must be able to show why some states have toughened their responses considerably while others have done so to a much lesser degree.

One assumption is that sexual offending has increased in recent years and that some states have differentially responded by prioritizing "get tough" approaches to sex crime. Yet, according to some sources, the rapid emergence of sex crime laws in the U.S. did not follow a sharp increase in national reports of sex crime (Veysey & Zgoba, 2010). Rising sex crime rates, then, do not appear to be an especially compelling factor explaining the *national* proliferation of sex crime laws. However, that assessment is based on an inspection of trends of sex crime across the U.S. It may well be the case that the very states that have responded most aggressively to sex crime are the same states that have experienced significant increases in reports of sexual offenses. That said, and although prior work has found tougher state sanctioning (e.g., increased reliance on incarceration, the development and implementation of "three-strike" laws) to be associated with violent crime rates (Beckett & Western, 2001), Greenberg and West (2001) have emphasized that "institutionalized punishment practices are not entirely determined by the functional necessity of preventing crimes" (p. 638). In short, the national proliferation of sex offender laws, and the greater intensity of sex crime-focused policymaking activity in some states, is not simply explained by trends in sex crime.

Against this backdrop, it is notable that scholars have identified several other types of factors that may be associated with the proliferation of "get tough" reforms among some states. For instance, under the "symbolic threat," view, states with a large minority population may respond to the perceived threat of certain social groups by enacting punitive crime control policy targeting certain offenders (see, e.g., Stemen & Rengifo, 2011). Scholars have also theorized that the extent of economic development in a state might explain differential emphases on punitive responses to crime. States with high levels of unemployment and poverty, as Sorensen and Stemen (2002, p. 460) have argued, tend to "rely more on formal mechanisms of social control, including imprisonment, to control its underclass." Not least, the level of cultural acceptance for punitive measures in particular jurisdictions has been argued to drive crime policy. For example, research indicates that southern states, on average, tend to have residents who are more likely to endorse punitive crime control (e.g., the death penalty) compared to individuals who reside in other areas.

This shared philosophical orientation among residents might explain the seemingly greater emphasis on punitive approaches adopted by certain states (see, e.g., Baumer, Messner, & Rosenfeld, 2003). However, the analyses here suggested that such an explanation does not apply to sex offender laws. Other regions of the country, excluding the northeast, are as tough on sex crime as are southern states.

The fact that the states and regions of the country vary greatly in the intensity of sex crime policymaking, and in the specific types of laws and policies enacted, and the fact that this variation does not neatly map onto arguments about more general tough-on-crime movements or increases in sex crime underscores that more careful investigation of sex crime policymaking is needed. Doing so holds the potential not only for creating a greater understanding of why states have responded to sex crime in varying ways, but also for understanding why broader societal trends in criminal justice policymaking have unfolded in a way that appears to differ from the trend in how sex crimes have been targeted by policymakers. Research on the emergence of sex crime laws and policies would provide an important step in developing a meaningful and accurate characterization of sex crime laws nationally, and in turn would contribute to debates and discussions about a putatively "get tough" era in criminal justice.

A second research implication involves the evaluation efforts of sex crime laws. A prominent finding of the current study was that the overwhelming majority of states (90 percent) have developed and implemented laws beyond the federally required registries and community notification laws. Studies examining the effect of any one law must, therefore, account for the effects of the other laws, or as scholars have described "the specific constellation of sanctions available in a particular [jurisdiction]" (Mears & Barnes, 2010, p. 706). For example, a researcher investigating the effect of a sex offender registry on sex crimes in a particular state must somehow address the fact that other sanctions may also be in place in that state. The considerable variability among states, and within states over time, in the types of sex crime laws and policies and the intensity with which they are implemented limits the ability of studies to develop credible estimates of the effects of these laws and policies.

This observation gives rise to a related implication for research. The substantial variability across states in the design of some sex crime laws and policies limits the external validity of studies of them — that is, it highlights the need for caution in generalizing about the effects of evaluations of any law or policy. For example, if an evaluation shows that requiring sex offenders to register for a period of 10 years with state agencies significantly reduces sexual recidivism, it does not necessarily follow that requiring offenders to register for 15 years would equally exhibit decreases in levels of sex crime that are equivalent to the increased punishment level (i.e., a 50 percent increase in the punishment level does not necessarily mean that sex crimes will be reduced by another 50 percent — it is more likely that the punishment-crime link follows a diminishing returns logic).

The same line of reasoning applies to evaluations of residence restrictions. Nationally, the boundary restrictions that have been adopted by a majority of states range from 500 feet to 2,000 feet. Some studies exist that have examined the effects of boundaries 1,000 feet or greater (Zandbergen et al., 2010). Findings indicate that the restrictions did not impact offender recidivism. It is not clear, however, if the findings from this state study apply to state laws with different boundaries. It seems illogical to anticipate that larger boundaries would be less effective than shorter boundaries. Even so, it may well be that shorter boundaries result in lower recidivism rates relative to what would occur with larger boundaries. The issue is complicated further by the fact that sex offender residence restrictions target different "types" of sex offenders. In one state, for example, all sex offenders may be targeted; in another, the law may apply only to sex offenders who have victimized children. Not least, additional or supplemental residence boundaries, beyond the state-level restriction, may exist at the county or municipal-level (Zgoba, 2011). In short, comparing the effect of one variant of a law in a particular state to another may result in an apples-to-oranges comparison. The result, in turn, is a situation in which marked variability in the amount and design of sex crime laws and policies makes it difficult to arrive at generalizable assessments of impact.

Policy Implications

During the last two decades addressing sexual violence has emerged as a prominent public policy focus across the U.S. Notwithstanding the intense national emphasis on developing ever-new responses to sex crime, scholars have charged that these laws "lack research on effectiveness or have produced less than promising results" (Cohen & Jeglic, 2007, p. 380). The point bears mention when we consider the results of current impact evaluations of prominent sex crime laws. For example, a study exploring whether sex offender registries had any impact on monthly rape rates in ten states found no consistent effect of the law (Vásquez et al., 2008). A more recent examination found no effect of several sex crime reforms (Megan's Laws, sexually violent predator laws, imprisonment, and the elimination of discretionary parole) on reports of forcible rape from 1970 to 2003 (Ackerman et al., 2012). Similar findings have emerged in studies examining community notification laws; extant research "cast[s] doubt on the effectiveness of community notification laws to significantly reduce rates of sexual offending" (Freeman, 2012, p. 559). Other investigations testing the impact of a residence restriction law in Florida (Zandbergen et al., 2010) have also revealed null effects.

In contrast, however, there are two studies that suggest some sex offender policies may have a modest deterrent effect. Specifically, Letourneau, Levenson et al. (2010) found an approximately 11 percent reduction in sex crime arrests (first-time offenses only) in South Carolina following the passage of a registration and notification policy. In addition, a 2005 meta-analysis examining sex offender treatment in several countries found some indirect support for castration laws. In particular, Lösel and Schmucker (2005, p. 135) concluded that "the very low rate of sexual recidivism in castrated offenders suggests that societies should not abandon this approach right away." The study, however, did not examine the effect of any one state's particular castration law *per se*, but rather its use as a treatment for sex offenders in various nations. For this reason, it was unable to control for the effects of current sex crime laws in place in particular areas. Further complicating matters is the fact that, as the current chapter found, substantial variation within these policies exists. Thus, we are left with no clear picture of the likely impacts of the variants of these laws (e.g., residence restriction laws that differ from Florida's).

Drawing on this observation, one policy implication here centers on a "less is more" approach toward addressing sex crime. Given that substantial variability exists in the types of laws states have adopted and in the design of these laws, and because the effects of any one type of law may very well depend of the effects of other laws in place, state legislatures might consider imposing a moratorium on certain sex crime reforms until their various effects have been identified. This line of reasoning derives in part from the recent commitment to evidence-based crime policy and laws that constitute "best practices" in criminal justice. Simply put, if policymakers wish to embrace this movement, establishing an evidence base for evaluating the effects of existing sex offender policies across states is key. In the absence of this empirical foundation potentially created is a situation which may result in policies premised on incorrect assumptions about sex crime and offenders, or laws or variants of laws which bring with them substantial unintended or collateral consequences (see e.g., Barnes, 2011; Levenson, 2011).

It should be emphasized as well that controversy surrounds the costs of these policies. Recently, scholars have questioned the costs states might incur because of proposed federal initiatives. For example, the Sex Offender Registration and Notification Act (SORNA), a provision of the Adam Walsh Child Protection and Safety Act (2006), is designed to standardize states' registration and community notification practices by dividing sex offenders into three tiers based solely on the conviction of offense. A recent review has shown that the costs associated with SORNA implementation (e.g., reclassification, expanded enforcement personnel) "far outweigh" the costs of losing federal funding for not implementing the changes (Freeman & Sandler, 2010, p. 44). Because of the substantial costs associated with the law, states thus far, according to Harris and Lobanov-Rostovsky (2010, p. 219), have adopted a "wait and see" approach to compliance. The absence of uniformity in the implementation of the law presents a situation which could potentially generate yet another source of variability—whereby some states with greater fiscal resources may come into substantial compliance with the law and others, perhaps because the costs of implementing the law exceed the costs of sanctions for non-compliance, may not.

The consequences of this variability are likely to remain salient for many years to come—even in the face of potential policy changes like SORNA and other federal initiatives—and are not readily addressed with a few well-conducted studies. Rather, for the next decade or more, assessments of the diversity of sex crime laws that exist will be greatly needed. Indeed, if future policymaking efforts do not take into account the issues highlighted in this study, then the same identified problems likely will confound efforts to assess the policies being enacted this year, next year, the year thereafter, and so on. This consideration leads to an additional virtue of a moratorium—the possibility of avoiding a vicious cycle in which more and more public tax dollars are expended on policies that will be less and less evaluable.

That said, it appears that sex crime will remain a prominent public policy focus. For example, a study published by the federally funded Center for Sex Offender Management (2008) revealed that when asked to list their top ten public policy concerns, state legislators rated "sex offenders and sexual predators" as their fifth-highest priority. Notably, only "immigration," "homeland security," "budget pressures," and "health insurance" ranked higher (p. 1). Findings from opinion polls indicate that addressing sex crime is also viewed as an important priority among the public (Mears et al., 2008) and that Americans support a variety of measures to deal with it (Beauregard & Lieb, 2011). The problem, however, is that continuing to invest in a range of costly, unproven sex offender laws and policies, described by scholars as "knee-jerk" and "panic-driven" responses (see Meloy, Saleh, & Wolff, 2007, p. 433), seems imprudent and counter to recent criminal justice reforms that have emphasized "best practices" (see, e.g., Wilson & Petersilia, 2011). Two decades ago, the argument might have been that policy innovation was needed, given the limited number of laws and policies in effect that targeted sex crimes. That argument no longer holds true. Many types of sex crime laws now exist, and there is considerable variability in the extent to which states have embraced these efforts. That situation creates a unique opportunity to begin to disentangle the relative effects of various laws and policies. Doing so will be difficult, but it will be all the more difficult, if not impossible, if states continue to create more laws without commensurate attention to developing a research base that supports such efforts.

Chapter Summary

It is clear that rising public concern about sexual victimization, in part, has led to the plethora of sex crime laws adopted by the federal government and states over the last two decades. Although well-intended, many of these reforms have not been systematically evaluated. Thus, the extent to which such laws reduce sexual offending is not fully understood. Complicating evaluation efforts is the variability surrounding the enactment and implementation of sex crime policies across states. Put simply, the considerable variation across states and within the content of laws makes it difficult to determine the impacts of the various reforms in place in the U.S. This chapter examined the variability of measures adopted across states and also, the variation within sex offender reforms. The implications from this analysis suggest that future evaluation studies will need to somehow account for this variation and also, the effects of other sex crime policies in place.

The reading list below highlights scholarship related to criminal justice policy evaluation. In keeping with the goal of understanding sex offender legislation nationally, Chapter 11 outlines recent legal challenges to prominent sex crime policies.

Additional Suggested Readings

Cole, G. F., Smith, C. E., & DeJong, C. (2012). *The American system of criminal justice* (13th ed.). Belmont, CA: Wadsworth/Cengage.

Houston, J. G., Bridgmon, P. B., & Parsons, W. W. (2008). *Criminal justice and the policy process.* Lanham, MD: University Press of America.

La Fond, J. Q. (2005). *Preventing sexual violence: How society should cope with sex offenders.* Washington, D.C.: American Psychological Association.

Logan, W. A. (2008). Sex offender registration and community notification: Past, present, and future. *New England Journal of Criminal & Civic Confinement, 34,* 3–16.

Welsh, W. N., & Harris, P. W. (2010). *Criminal justice policy and planning* (3rd ed.). Newark, NJ: Anderson.

Appendix. State Sex Offender Statutes

Alabama Statutes, Title 13A, Chapter 11
Alabama Statutes, Title 15, Chapter 20
Alaska Statutes Annotated, Title 12
Alaska Statutes Annotated Title 18, Chapter 65
Arizona Revised Statutes Annotated, Title 13, Chapter 38, Article 3
Arizona Revised Statutes Annotated, Title 36, Chapter 37
Arkansas Code Annotated, Title 12, Chapter 12
California Health and Safety Code, Division 2, Chapter 3
California Health and Safety Code, Section 1564
California Penal Code, Part I, Title 9, Chapter 5.5
California Welfare and Institutions Code, Section 6600 et seq.
Colorado Revised Statutes, Title 16, Article 22
Connecticut General Laws, Section 54-251
Delaware Code, Title 11, Chapter 41
Delaware Code, Title 11, Chapter 5

Florida Statutes Annotated, Title XLVI, Chapter 775
Florida Statutes Annotated, Title XLVI, Chapter 794
Florida Statutes Annotated, Title XLVII, Chapter 943
Code of Georgia Annotated, Title 42, Chapter 1, Article 2
Hawaii Penal Code, Chapter 846E
Idaho Code Annotated, Title 18, Chapters 83 and 84
Illinois Compiled Statutes Annotated, Chapter 720, Act 5
Illinois Compiled Statutes Annotated Chapter 725, Act 207
Illinois Compiled Statutes Annotated, Chapter 730, Act 150
Illinois Compiled Statutes Annotated, Chapter 730, Act 152
Annotated Indiana Code, Title 11, Chapter 8
Annotated Indiana Code, Title 35, Chapter 38
Indiana Annotated Code, Title 26, Chapter 2
Indiana Annotated Code, Title 35, Chapter 42
Iowa Statutes Annotated, Title VI, Chapter 229A
Iowa Statutes Annotated, Title XVI, Chapter 692A
Kansas Statutes Annotated 59-29a01
Kansas Statutes Annotated, 22—4901-4910
Kansas Statutes Annotated, 22—4909
Kentucky Revised Statutes, 17.510
Kentucky Revised Statutes, 17.545
Louisiana Revised Statutes, 15:542
Louisiana Revised Statutes, 15:542.1
Maine Revised Statutes, Ch. 15, Title 34-A, Section 11222-27
Maryland Code, Criminal Procedure, Title 11
Massachusetts General Law, Chapter 6, Section 178C et seq.
Massachusetts General Laws, Chapter 123A
Michigan Compiled Laws, Chapter 28
Minnesota Statutes, Chapter 243
Minnesota Statutes, Chapter 244
Minnesota Statutes, Chapter 253B
Mississippi Statutes Annotated, Title 45, Chapter 33
Missouri Revised Statutes, Chapter 566.147
Missouri Revised Statutes, Chapter 589
Missouri Revised Statutes, Chapter 632.483
Missouri Revised Statutes, Chapter 632.513
Montana Code Annotated, Title 46, Chapter 23
Nebraska Revised Statutes, Chapter 29
Nebraska Revised Statutes, Chapter 71
Nevada Revised Statutes, Chapter 179B
Nevada Revised Statutes, Chapter 179D
Nevada Revised Statutes, Chapter 176A.410
Nevada Revised Statutes, Chapter 213.1245
Nevada Revised Statutes, Chapter 213.1255
New Hampshire Revised Statutes, Title 10, Chapter 135-E
New Hampshire Revised Statutes, Title 52, Chapter 651-B
New Jersey Statutes Annotated, Title 2C, Chapter 7
New Jersey Statutes Annotated, Title 30, Chapter 4
New Mexico Statutes Annotated, Chapter 29, Article 11A
New York Statutes Annotated, Correction Law, Chapter 43, Article 6-C
New York Statutes Annotated, Mental Hygiene Law, Chapter 27, Article 10
North Carolina General Statutes, Chapter 14 Article 27A
North Carolina General Statutes, Chapter 14 Article 208.10
North Carolina General Statutes, Chapter 14 Article 208.16

North Dakota Century Code, Chapter 12
North Dakota Century Code, Chapter 12.1-32-15
North Dakota Century Code Chapter 25-03.3
Ohio Revised Code, Title 29, Chapter 2950
Ohio Revised Code, Title 29, Chapter 2950.31
Ohio Revised Code, Title 29, Chapter 2950.10-2950.99
Oklahoma Statutes, Title 57, Chapter 8B
Oregon Revised Statutes, Title 18, Chapter 181
Oregon Revised Statutes, Title 14, Chapter 144
42 Pennsylvania Code, Section 9799.1 et seq.
Rhode Island General Laws, Section 11-37.1-1 et seq.
South Carolina Statutes Annotated, Title 23, Chapter 3, Article 7
South Carolina Statutes Annotated, Title 44, Chapter 48
South Dakota Codified Laws, Title 22, Chapter 22-24B
Tennessee Code Annotated, Title 40, Chapter 39
Texas Code of Criminal Procedure, Chapter 62
Texas Health and Safety Code, Chapter 841
Utah Code, Title 77, Chapter 27
Vermont Statutes Annotated, Title 13, Chapter 167
Annotated Code of Virginia, Title 9.1, Chapter 9
Annotated Code of Virginia, Title 18.2, Chapter 8
Annotated Code of Virginia, Title 37.2, Chapter 9
Revised Code of Washington Annotated, Chapter 9.94A
Revised Code of Washington Annotated, Chapter 9A.44
Revised Code of Washington Annotated, Chapter 71.09
West Virginia Code, Chapter 15, Article 12-2
West Virginia Code, Chapter 15, Article 12-5
West Virginia Code, Chapter 62, Article 12-26
Wisconsin Statutes Annotated, Chapter 301
Wisconsin Statutes Annotated, Chapter 980
Wyoming Statutes Annotated, Title 7, Chapter 19, Article 3

Chapter 11

Legal Challenges to Sex Crime Laws

Chapter Introduction

As previously emphasized, the 1990s marked an unprecedented shift in sex crime policy in the U.S. Since that time, in addition to implementing federal restrictions—namely sex offender registration and community notification laws—states have developed a wide variety of reforms that aim to reduce sexual recidivism by imposing post-incarceration sanctions for sex offenders. To illustrate, most states have enacted residence restriction laws, some have passed chemical castration procedures, civil commitment laws, and other measures. Despite their popularity, these laws have been challenged in the courts on a number of fronts. These legal decisions potentially affect the constitutionality and implementation of sex crime laws. For this reason, having an adequate comprehension of them is important. The goal of this chapter is to analyze U.S. Supreme Court and other rulings regarding sex offender laws over the last two decades. In particular, U.S. Supreme Court majority decisions are presented for the following policies: civil commitment, mandated treatment for sex offenders, registration/community notification policies, child pornography laws, rape shield legislation, statutes of limitations exceptions, capital punishment for sex offenders, and SORNA. The U.S. Supreme Court has not heard challenges to some other policies—particularly, residence restrictions, chemical castration laws, gateway legislation, and Internet bans. For these laws, the chapter looks toward landmark federal and state court challenges.

U.S. Supreme Court Decisions

U.S. Supreme Court decisions reflect the "law of the land." Put differently, U.S. Supreme Court rulings affirm, modify, or overturn legislation (Stolz, 2002). Illustrative of this authority are a series of death penalty cases in the 1970s. For example, in *Furman v. Georgia* (1972), the U.S. Supreme Court ruled that states could no longer permit capital punishment. In part, the decision emphasized that capital punishment was capricious and arbitrary and thus tantamount to "cruel and unusual punishment." In essence, *Furman v. Georgia* (1972) imposed an immediate national moratorium on death sentences that lasted for years. The issue would later be revisited by the Court in a 1976 decision, *Gregg v. Georgia*. In a reversal of the Court's earlier ruling, the *Gregg v. Georgia* (1976) decision enabled states who had revised their capital punishment statutes to resume using the sanction. This example highlights the Court's influence on public policy. Put differently, although the U.S. Supreme Court does not function primarily as a law-making body, its decisions can, and often do, affect the implementation of crime policy. It, for example, has heard recent cases in other arenas such as gun control legislation (*District of Columbia v. Heller*, 2008) and mandatory life sentences for juvenile offenders (*Miller v. Alabama*, 2012).

To be clear, there are limits to the Court's authority. For instance, the Court can only rule on issues inherent to the cases brought before it. That is, it can only grant certiorari to cases requesting judicial review. Thus, U.S. Supreme Court decisions have not necessarily reviewed the constitutionality of all crime laws enacted by states and the federal government. A separate issue involves how U.S. Supreme Court decisions translate into actual policy changes. Although it is true that U.S. Supreme Court decisions constitute the law of the land, there may still be disparities between what its decisions require and how well these requirements are implemented in the criminal justice system. Even so, the larger point worth emphasizing is that U.S. Supreme Court decisions have the potential to affect the constitutionality and implementation of sex crime policy. Under that backdrop, specific U.S. Supreme Court cases decided in the 1990s and 2000s involving sex offender laws are reviewed.

Civil Commitment

Recall from previous chapters that civil commitment procedures allow jurisdictions to detain potentially dangerous offenders even after their prison sentences have passed. Civil commitment can in theory be used to detain virtually any type of offender; however, in recent decades, states have become increasingly active in enacting sex offender specific commitment statutes. Although there is variation across states in the enactment of such laws, the general process involves court proceedings as well as mental health evaluations in determining whether the offender presents evidence of substantial risk of reoffending.

The U.S. Supreme Court has heard three cases involving civil commitment laws. The first decision, *Kansas v. Hendricks* (1997), involved the constitutionality of a Kansas law ("Sexually Violent Predator Act") that permitted the state to indefinitely detain offenders it deemed to be at high risk of reoffending even after their prison sentence expired. In particular, respondent Hendricks argued that the statute violated the due process, double jeopardy, and ex-post facto clauses of the Constitution. The Court rejected all three claims. Instead, it ruled (in a narrow decision, 5 for and 4 against) that the Act outlines civil proceedings, and thus, is not punitive in nature. Additionally, the decision noted that strict procedural safeguards were in place during the commitment process. That is, the Court found that the confinement criterion outlined in the Kansas statute, "mental abnormality or personality disorder" which would impair an offender's level of self-control to resist offending was sufficient to ensure substantive due process. Beyond this broad requirement, however, the Court did not specify the threshold of control that needed to be shown, nor did it set forth requirements about whether states need to evaluate an offender's level of control prior to civil commitment.

In 2002, the U.S. Supreme Court revisited civil commitment in *Kansas v. Crane*. Here, the central question was one left open by their earlier decision. Specifically, it addressed whether the state, in addition to showing evidence of mental abnormality, also has to demonstrate an offender's total lack of volition for civil commitment to ensue. In this particular case, the state of Kansas challenged a Kansas Supreme Court's ruling that a convicted sex offender, Michael Crane, could not be civilly committed because the state did not clearly show that his mental impairment led to total or complete lack of control in his propensity to reoffend. Put differently, the Kansas Supreme Court took the position that the state had to not only demonstrate that the offender had a mental impairment, but also that the offender lacked significant control over his or her dangerous behavior. The U.S. Supreme Court found this "total to complete lack of control" requirement to be an overly broad interpretation of *Kansas v. Hendricks* (1997). Adopting a middle ground however, the Court did acknowledge in its ruling (7 for and 2 against) that states must, at the very least, evaluate an offender's level of control prior to detainment procedures. However, the state need not show the offender has a *total* lack of control in resisting his or her criminal behavior for civil commitment to occur.

In 2010, the Court heard a third case involving civil commitment. In *U.S. v. Comstock*, the issue involved whether the federal government had the authority under the "necessary and proper" clause of the Constitution to civilly commit sexually dangerous persons in federal custody, or those nearing the expiration of federal sentences. A group of sex offenders including Graydon Comstock (the respondent named in the decision) were nearing the completion of their federal sentences for sex crimes. All were certified to be "sexually dangerous persons" by the Attorney General. Lower courts, however, ruled their detainment to be unconstitutional on the grounds that their civil commitment exceeded Congress's constitutional authority. In a reversal of the lower courts (7 for and 2 against), the U.S. Supreme Court ruled that the government had the authority to detain sexually dangerous individuals beyond the expiration of their federal sentences.

To summarize, these cases have affirmed sex offender civil commitment statutes in the U.S. As an extension of the landmark *Kansas v. Hendricks* (1997) decision, *Kansas v. Crane* (2002) requires that states show a potential candidate for civil commitment a) has a mental or personality abnormality, and b) that the disorder affects the extent to which an offender can control his or her criminal behavior. Despite this new mandate, however, the U.S. Supreme Court has not specified that states prove "absolute" lack of control. That standard, per the Court, "would risk barring the civil commitment of highly dangerous persons suffering severe mental abnormalities" (p. 412). Put differently, the Court recognizes the need for civil commitment, but it also outlines additional requirements for states to detain "dangerous persons" beyond the duration of their prison sentences. The Court recognizes as well that the federal government (per *U.S. v. Comstock*, 2010) has the authority to civilly commitment persons who may be at high risk of recommitting sexual offenses upon their release.

Coerced Treatment Policies

Beyond civil commitment procedures, states have also developed policies that mandate treatment for incarcerated offenders. Kansas is one such state. Its treatment program was challenged in a 2002 case, *McKune v. Lile*. Before turning to the U.S. Supreme Court's decision, a brief summary of the policy and case is in order.

In the 1990s, Kansas established the Sexual Abuse Treatment Program (SATP) for incarcerated sex offenders. The program requires that participating inmates complete and sign an "Admission of Responsibility" form, which acknowledges their personal responsibility for the crime in which they have been sentenced. Additionally, inmates must also complete a sexual history form, which details all prior sexual experiences, regardless of whether such activities constitute undetected criminal offenses. The SATP program employs a polygraph examination to verify the accuracy of the offender's sexual history. The information shared by the participating inmates is not privileged. Accordingly, the state can use the information divulged by the inmates participating in the program to advance future criminal proceedings. Kansas also has a mandated reporting law which requires the SATP staff to report undetected offenses involving children to law enforcement. In 1994, months prior to his release, Robert Lile, a convicted sex offender incarcerated in a Kansas prison was informed that he must participate in the SATP. Lile was serving a sentence for kidnapping and rape. Despite his conviction, Lile continued to maintain his innocence claiming that he engaged in consensual sex acts with the victim. If Lile refused to participate in the program, his "privilege status" in the prison would be reduced from Level III to Level I. As a result, he would have a reduction in his visitation rights, earnings from prison jobs, ability to send money to family, canteen expenditures, access to amenities such as a television, and other privileges. He also faced a transfer to a maximum-security unit which would put him in contact with potentially dangerous offenders.

Lile, concerned that his participation in the program would violate his Fifth Amendment protection against self-incrimination, first sought an injunction from the United States District Court for the District of Kansas. The Court sided with Lile. Specifically, it found that because Lile had testified at trial that his sexual intercourse with the victim was consensual, a statement of responsibility for the crime on the "Admission of Guilt" form would subject the respondent to potential perjury charges. The Court further advanced that the loss of prison privileges that the respondent would face for refusing to incriminate himself, constituted coercion in violation of the Fifth Amendment. This decision was affirmed in an appeal by the state to the Court of Appeals for the Tenth Circuit. Kansas then appealed to the U.S. Supreme Court. In a reversal of the lower courts' ruling, the Court ruled (5 for and 4 against) in *McKune v. Lile* (2002) that the sex offender program served a "vital penological purpose" (p. 29). Specifically, the decision recognized that the efficacy of SATP depended on the truthfulness of the participants. It further noted that the coercive nature of the program (in the sense that inmates relinquish privileges for refusal to participate) served to encourage participation, and thus, enhance rehabilitation efforts (pp. 47–48):

> If the State found it was forced to graduate prisoners from its rehabilitation program without knowing what other offenses they may have committed, the integrity of its program would be very much in doubt. If the State found it had to comply by allowing respondent the same perquisites as those who accept counseling, the result would be a dramatic illustration that obduracy has the same rewards as acceptance, and so the program itself would become self-defeating, even hypocritical, in the eyes of those whom it seeks to help. The Fifth Amendment does not require the State to suffer these programmatic disruptions when it seeks to rehabilitate those who are incarcerated for valid, final convictions.

In short, the Court has affirmed the use of mandatory treatment for incarcerated sex offenders. Its decision has rested largely on the belief that such programs are integral to promoting rehabilitation.

Registration/Community Notification Policies

Beyond civil commitment cases, the U.S. Supreme Court has also heard a number of challenges to registry and community notification laws. Recall from our earlier discussions that all 50 states have developed some form of registry and community notification policy. Although variation exists, most states have implemented websites that provide information about convicted and released sex offenders, including their names, addresses, pictures, and other details. Variability also exists in community notification procedures across states. But to generalize, these procedures typically include law enforcement notifying communities about the presence of convicted sex offenders' locations via face to face visits, flyer postings, and e-mail.

Two U.S. Supreme Court decisions centered on the constitutionality of registries and notification laws. Both cases were decided in 2003. The *Smith v. Doe* (2003) decision involved an Alaska registration law ("Sex Offender Registration Act"). The law—enacted in 1994—required any sex offender to register with the state's correctional system or local law enforcement within one business day of entering the state. Specifically, the respondents Doe I and Doe II (two unnamed sex offenders affected by the law) challenged the state's retroactive registration requirement. The offenders were released from prison and completed rehabilitative programs for sex offenders. Although both were convicted of their sex crimes before the Act's passage, respondents were still required to register with the state. As a result, the respondents argued that the law was punitive, and thus violated their Constitutional rights. However, the U.S. Supreme Court disagreed. In its majority opinion (6 for and 3 against), the Court observed that the law outlined civil proceedings and thus served a regulatory, public safety purpose. Under this logic, the law did not violate the ex-post facto clause of the Constitution.

In contrast, the second case, *Connecticut Department of Public Safety v. Doe* (2003) challenged community notification procedures. The respondent, Doe, a convicted sex offender, argued that a Connecticut law that required pictures of all sex offenders and their personal information to be posted on a state website violated his Constitutional rights, specifically, the due process clause of the 14th Amendment because the law did not allow him to establish his low-risk status as a sex offender. Adopting a similar logic evident in prior sex crime cases, the Court, in its unanimous decision ruled that the law did not constitute additional punishment, finding instead that it involved civil proceedings. In particular, the Court argued that the information posted on the website served the best interests of the public.

To conclude, challenges to registry and community notification laws—enacted in some form by all states—have been unsuccessfully challenged in the U.S. Supreme Court. Broadly, the Court has upheld both policies, finding that they serve to enhance public safety. At the same time, across its decisions, the Court views these post-incarceration measures as civil and not additional criminal proceedings.

Child Pornography Laws

Child pornography crimes refer to the manufacturing, distribution, or accessing of images depicting children engaged in sex acts. For example, the creation of child pornography would include an individual who captures sexually explicit images of children. Distribution would encompass acts that aim to dispense the media to third parties. In contrast, accessing such images refers to the downloading of child pornography on the Internet, or receiving pornographic pictures of children. Calculating the number of illegal pornographic images available online is an incredibly difficult task. However, one review found that at any given time more than one million pornographic images of children on the Internet exist, with 200 new images posted daily (Wortley & Smallbone, 2006). Another federal study showed a nearly 83 percent increase in child pornography cases referred for prosecution in 2006 compared to 1994 (U.S. Department of Justice, 2010). As a result, over the last two decades policymakers have enacted laws that aim to increase the criminal penalties for the production and dissemination of child pornography.

One of the first child pornography cases to be heard by the Court in the 1990s was *Osborne v. Ohio* (1990). In the prior decade, Ohio had enacted legislation to prohibit the possession of child pornography. Petitioner Osborne contended that the state law was overly broad. In particular, he claimed that laws banning "mere possession" of child pornography violated the First Amendment. Notably, the U.S. Supreme Court in an earlier decision (*New York v. Ferber*, 1982) found that states could prohibit the *manufacturing* of child pornography. However, prior to *Osborne v. Ohio* (1990), it had not considered the constitutionality of laws that outlaw the *possession* of child pornography. Extending its reasoning from *New York v. Ferber* (1982), the U.S. Supreme Court rejected the petitioner's claims. Rather it found that the law served to protect victims of sex crime; specifically, the decision argued that even "mere possession" of the images causes "double victimization," as evident by the Court's observation (p. 111) that "the materials produced by child pornographers permanently record the victim's abuse ... [its] continued existence causes the child victims continuing harm by haunting the children in years to come."

The Court revisited child pornography legislation in a 2002 case, *Ashcroft v. Free Speech Coalition*. The case centered on the manufacturing and distribution of "virtual" pornography—or, computer-generated images that depict children engaging in sexually explicit behavior. As discussed earlier in the text, in 1996, the federal government enacted the Child Pornography Prevention Act (CPPA). It prohibited the manufacturing and possession of "actual" and virtual child pornography. Thus, at question was whether the government could legally prohibit the sale and distribution of material that did not involve an actual child victim, but rather ones created by computer. The Act however was vague in defining "child pornography." The petitioner, Free Speech Coalition, argued that as written the CPPA could be applied to prohibit a range of media that would under most standards not be considered "pornographic." The U.S. Supreme Court appeared persuaded by this logic. It ruled (6 for and 3 against) that the CPPA was overly broad and thus could potentially criminalize media that on its face were not at all pornographic, such as performances of *Romeo and Juliet*, and highly acclaimed films that appeared to depict minors engaging in sex acts.

In 2008, the U.S. Supreme Court heard one final case related to child pornography, *U.S. v. Williams*. At issue here was whether a related act to the CPPA, PROTECT, violates the Constitution. Specifically, the law (per *Williams*, p. 290) stipulates that, "any person who knowingly advertises, promotes, presents, distributes, or solicits through the mails, or in interstate or foreign commerce by any means, including by computer, any material or purported material in a manner that reflects the belief, or that is intended to cause another to believe, that the material or purported material is, or contains an obscene visual depiction of a minor engaging in sexually explicit conduct; or a visual depiction of an actual minor engaging in sexually explicit conduct, shall be punished ..." Put differently, PROTECT criminalizes the use of virtual pornography if it is used to "pander," that is, promote the impression among others that it is actual child pornography. Respondent Williams argued that PROTECT's statutory definition of pandering is vague and overly broad. The U.S. Supreme Court disagreed in a 7–2 decision. Specifically, it ruled that although the *Free Speech Coalition* decision permits the lawful possession of simulated child pornography under the First Amendment, the act of *advertising* it as actual child pornography to others is not constitutionally protected.

The U.S. Supreme Court has simultaneously upheld laws to criminalize the manufacture and distribution of child pornography and has also drawn limits on the scope of pornography legislation. The *Osborne v. Ohio* (1990) decision clearly highlights that the Court recognizes a need for laws that restrict pornographic media of children. At the same time, the Court has not upheld stricter laws that prohibit even computer-generated pornographic media, finding instead that such measures violate the First Amendment privilege (per *Ashcroft v. Free Speech Coalition*, 2002). Even so, as the Court's logic in *U.S.*

v. Williams (2008) demonstrates, legislation that criminalizes pandering of virtual pornography is constitutional under the law.

Rape Shield Laws

As discussed previously, states implemented rape shield legislation over the last three decades to ensure that victims were afforded certain rights during criminal proceedings. These reforms were multi-pronged. For instance, some forbid defendants from insinuating that the victim's attire or previous sexual history contributed to the offense. Relatedly, rape shield laws also typically prohibit the public naming of sex crime victims. Under this legislation, the media, for instance, could not publicly identify a rape or sexual assault victim.

In 1991, the U.S. Supreme Court heard the case of *Michigan v. Lucas* which involved the question of whether Michigan's rape shield statute violated the First Amendment. In 1979, Michigan enacted a law that restricted defendants from introducing evidence of the victim's prior sexual history. However, a special provision permits defendants to introduce evidence of prior sexual relationships with victims if defendants can demonstrate that it was directly relevant to the defense. The law requires advanced notification of the defense's intent to introduce the evidence to the state within ten days after arraignment. Nolan Lucas, an offender charged with sex offenses, wished to present evidence of his prior sexual relationship with the victim. Because his request was made after the statutorily designated time frame, he was barred from admitting this evidence at trial. Ultimately, after a bench trial he was convicted of multiple counts of sex offenses. Lucas appealed his conviction to the Michigan Court of Appeals. The Court reversed his conviction on grounds that the time period mandated by the state violates the 6th Amendment Clause to confront witnesses. The state then sought relief from the U.S. Supreme Court. In contrast to the appellate court, the U.S. Supreme Court in 1991 ruled that Michigan's rape shield law incorporated a reasonable amount of time for defendants to provide notification. Under this logic, the Court argued that the rape shield provision is not unduly restrictive and therefore does not violate defendants' rights to confront witnesses in a criminal trial. Even more, the Court noted the value of the statute in that it "serves legitimate state interests in protecting against surprise, harassment, and undue delay" (p. 153).

Notably, the Court's rationale underpinning the *Michigan v. Lucas* (1991) decision diverges from two earlier cases heard in the 1970s and 1980s. For instance in 1975 the Court heard the *Cox Broadcasting Corporation v. Cohn* case which challenged a Georgia rape shield law that forbid naming of rape victims even in cases where court documents open to public inspection naming the victim exist. In particular, the case involved the question of whether a news agency could be held liable for civil damages in an instance where a rape victim's name was publicized in violation of state law. The reporter who investigated the case and publicized the victim's name obtained the information from a public court proceeding, which clearly identified the victim in various court documents. In their decision, the Court ruled (8 for and 1 against) that the Georgia law violated the First Amendment. Specifically, it ruled that so long as the government made available identifying information of victims during criminal proceedings, the state may not then punish individuals who publicize that information.

A second case heard in 1989 also involved a state law that prohibited the naming of rape victims. In *Florida Star v. B. J. F* (1975), the petitioner, a newspaper agency, appealed a civil judgment decision won by a rape victim (B. J. F.) whose name the newspaper accidentally published in an article. The *Florida Star* obtained the information from a publicly available police report that inadvertently included the victim's name. Adopting a similar logic as in *Cox Broadcasting Corporation v. Cohn* (1975), the Court ruled (6 for and 3 against) that the Florida law violated the First Amendment. It ordered that the civil judgment decision be reversed. This is not to say that the Court did not see merit in the law. That is, in the *Florida Star v. B. J. F.* (1989) decision (p. 541), it noted, "Our holding today [that Florida's rape shield law violates constitutional protections] is limited. We do not hold that truthful publication is automatically constitutionally protected, or that there is no zone of personal privacy within which the State may protect the individual from intrusion by the press, or even that a State may never punish publication of the name of a victim of a sexual offense." In short then, the Court recognizes that states can pursue rape shield laws in an effort to protect sex crime victims, but it also recognizes that such laws do not extend to instances where information is lawfully obtained by media agencies.

Although both the *Cox Broadcasting Corporation v. Cohn* (1975) and *Florida Star v. B. J. F.* (1989) cases are outside of the focus on more recent Court decisions, they are important for highlighting that the Court places limits on some sex crime policies. In turn, these decisions affect the implementation of prominent laws. Overall though, the Court has upheld the use of rape shield protections. For example, in *Michigan v. Lucas* (1991) the Court upheld the use of legislation that prevents irrelevant and harassing questions to be asked of rape victims by the defense. At the same time, however, it has defined instances where publication of a rape victim's name is permissible — that is, in instances where police agencies or courts make such information publicly available (per *Cox Broadcasting Corporation v. Cohn*, 1975; *Florida Star v. B. J. F.*, 1989).

Statutes of Limitations Laws

In recognition that some victims do not immediately report their assaults to law enforcement, states have implemented laws that extend the statutes of limitations for certain sex crimes in an effort to increase prosecution of sex offenders. For example, in 1993 California enacted legislation that permitted the prosecution of certain sex offenders even in cases where the statutes of limitations for those crimes had passed. In particular, as Jen (2004, p. 728) underscored, the law was narrow in scope applying in cases where a) the victim was less than eighteen years old when the crime occurred, b) the offense involved "substantial" sexual abuse (e.g., penetration of the victim), c) reliable independent sources corroborate the victim's allegations, d) the victim reported the offense to police, and e) prosecution begins within one year of the victim's report to law enforcement.

The law was challenged in 2003 in *Stogner v. California*. The petitioner, Marion Stogner, was indicted by the state for child sexual abuse committed between 1955 and 1973 after his adult daughters came forward with their allegations in 1998. The daughters claimed that the abuse was so frequent that it was not until several years later, as adults, that they realized they were victims of incest. Their father denied ever molesting his children. The state moved forward with prosecuting Stogner for two counts of committing lewd acts on children even though the statute of limitations for those crimes had since passed. Stogner filed several challenges to the charges. In 2003, the U.S. Supreme Court reviewed the case, its only ruling on statutes of limitations exceptions pertaining to sex crime laws. Petitioner Stogner argued to the Court that because the California statute was applied after the statute of limitations for his alleged crimes had expired, it violated the ex-post facto punishment clause of the Constitution. In 2003, the U.S. Supreme Court agreed with the petitioner in *Stogner v. California* (5 for and 4 against) and found that the law was applied retroactively by the state and thus was unconstitutional. In short, the Court does not discount the importance of efforts undertaken by states to increase the prosecution of sex offenders. However, the retroactive application of such legislation is not constitutional. *Stogner v. California* (2003) has forced states to revise their exemptions to statutes of limitations laws for certain sex crimes to ensure they comport with the Court's decision.

Capital Punishment Statutes

The U.S. Supreme Court has also ruled on whether states may impose the death penalty for sex offenders who have sexually abused children. As reviewed earlier, a handful of states—Louisiana, Georgia, Texas, Montana, Oklahoma, and South Carolina—enacted legislation in the 1990s that permitted the execution of offenders who have sexually victimized children. Louisiana enacted one of the strictest laws in 1995. Its version made child rape a capital offense even in cases where the offender had not committed prior sex offenses. This law is in contrast to the other remaining states, with the exception of Georgia, which mandated that the offender be a repeat sex offender to be considered for capital punishment. Georgia's statute applies to offenses where aggravating circumstances are present, including but not limited to a prior conviction.

The question of whether states can enact capital punishment statutes for sex offenders who did not murder their victims was seemingly addressed by the Court decades ago. In *Coker v. Georgia* (1977; 5 for and 4 against), the Court determined that capital punishment for sexual offenses constituted excessive punishment. This case however involved an adult female victim. Indeed, the *Coker v. Georgia* (1977) decision appeared to be narrowly applied to only those instances in which an adult woman was sexually victimized (p. 597): "We do not discount the seriousness of rape as a crime … [but] death is indeed a disproportionate penalty for the crime of raping an *adult* woman" (emphasis added; "adult" woman referenced throughout the majority opinion). As a result, the question of whether states may execute offenders who have sexually victimized children remained open.

Kennedy v. Louisiana, a 2008 case, forced the Court to demarcate the circumstances under which capital punishment could be imposed for sex offenders, if at all. Petitioner Kennedy was convicted of aggravated rape of a child under 12 years old in 2003. The victim, Kennedy's step-daughter, testified that he had sexually battered her and forced her to claim that she had been victimized by neighborhood children. As a result of the rape, the victim suffered severe internal injuries that required emergency surgery. Although the victim initially claimed she had been assaulted by two peers, a police investigation revealed probable cause to try Kennedy for the crime. Given the nature of the crime, the state sought to convict Kennedy under their child rape statute. In appealing the state's conviction to the U.S. Supreme Court, Kennedy claimed that his sentence constituted "cruel and unusual" punishment, and also, that the Court, in *Coker v. Georgia* (1977), had already struck down laws that permit the execution of sex offenders. The Court was persuaded by Kennedy's arguments. In a narrow decision (5 for and 4 against), the Court ruled that capital punishment statutes for sex offenses where victims survived violated the Eighth Amendment. The majority opinion emphasized that although child rape is a heinous crime, laws that permit the execution of child rapists are disproportionate and excessive.

Although *Coker v. Georgia* (1977) and *Kennedy v. Louisiana* (2008) appear to settle the question of capital punishment for sex crimes some policymakers have vowed to develop new child rape laws that permit the execution of sex offenders. For example, as reported in Mancini and Mears (2010, p. 966), shortly after the *Kennedy* ruling Governor Bobby

Jindal declared that the decision reflected "a clear abuse of judicial authority." He further intimated that his Office would "evaluate ways to amend [the state's] statute to maintain death as a penalty for this horrific crime." Despite this rhetoric, however, legal scholars remain doubtful that any such laws would stand up to constitutional challenges given prior case law (see Biskupic, 2008).

SORNA

As mentioned in previous chapters, in 2006 the federal government created legislation—SORNA—designed to standardize and strengthen existing sex offender registry and community notification laws. SORNA requires states to incorporate several provisions. First, it mandates that states adopt a three tier system in assessing offenders' risk of reoffending. Based on this classification system, SORNA mandates specific time periods for offenders to remain on the registry. Thus, offenders with lower risk status register for shorter durations compared to those who are determined to be higher risk. The Act also implements specific sanctions for failure to register. Additionally, per SORNA, all convicted sex offenders must appear on the registry. This provision departs from an earlier practice where states determine which offenders appear on the registries. Finally, the legislation requires that states collect DNA samples from all registrants. Perhaps the most legally contested aspect of SORNA, however, involves the retroactive nature of the law. That is, as written, SORNA applies to offenders who have committed their offenses many years prior to the law's enactment in 2006. Thus, constitutional questions arise as to the retroactive application of SORNA to pre-Act offenders. The U.S. Supreme Court has heard two cases regarding this issue.

Carr v. U.S. (2010) involved petitioner Carr, a sex offender registered in Alabama who moved to Indiana in 2005, prior to the effective date of SORNA. Once in Indiana, Carr did not register as a convicted sex offender. In 2007, he came to the attention of law enforcement after being involved in a physical altercation with another individual. Indiana officers discovered that Carr had not registered with the state, and thus determined he was in violation of SORNA. Federal authorities began criminal proceedings to charge Carr with failing to register, a felony offense per SORNA. Carr filed a motion to the United States District Court for the Northern District of Indiana to dismiss the indictment, claiming that because he moved prior to SORNA's implementation, charging him would amount to ex post facto punishment. The Court denied his motion and Carr entered a conditional guilty plea which resulted in a 30 month prison sentence.

Shortly after his sentence, Carr sought relief from the U.S. Supreme Court. The Court agreed to hear the case. Carr claimed that because his travel to Indiana predates the enactment of SORNA, he should not have to abide by its restrictions. The Court then, had to address two questions. First, can an offender be prosecuted under SORNA even when the defendant's offense and interstate travel predate the law's official implementation? Second, does the ex post fact clause of the Constitution prohibit prosecution under SORNA when the defendant's crime and interstate travel both predate the Act's enactment? In addressing the first question, the Court ruled (6 for and 3 against) that SORNA does not apply to sex offenders whose interstate travel occurred prior to the law's effective date. The Court did not address the second question regarding whether application of the law results in ex post facto punishment.

Two years after the *Carr v. U.S.* (2010) decision, the Court heard a similar case, *Reynolds v. U.S.* (2012). Here, the question at issue was does SORNA require pre-Act offenders to register before the Attorney General "validly specifies" (i.e., officially clarifies) that the Act's registration provisions apply to them? In 2006, after the official enactment of SORNA, there was some confusion regarding whether the legislation applied to offenders with convictions prior to the Act's passage (i.e., pre-Act offenders). Congress delegated the authority to the Attorney General to determine how to apply it to pre-Act offenders. In February 2007, the U.S. Attorney General issued an interim rule that clarified that the Act indeed applied to *all* sex offenders (*Reynolds v. U.S.*, 2012).

Petitioner Reynolds was convicted of a sex crime in 2001 in Missouri. He served four years in a correctional facility and was released in July 2005. In accordance with state law, he registered as a sex offender in Missouri shortly after his release from prison. However, in September 2007, he moved to Pennsylvania without updating his new address with Missouri and without notifying Pennsylvania of his status as a registered sex offender. A federal grand jury indicted him for failing to register and update registration within three business days after moving. Notably, Reynolds conceded that his move occurred after the passage of SORNA and also, after the Attorney General issued the interim rule clarifying that SORNA covered pre-Act offenders. However, he argued that the Attorney General's interim rule was invalid because it violated both the Constitution's "nondelegation" doctrine and the Administrative Procedure Act's (APA) requirement for "good cause" to promulgate a rule without "notice and comment." In short then, Reynolds questioned whether the interim rule issued by the Attorney General was properly implemented. Reynolds's appeals to lower courts upheld the charges against him.

However, in contrast to the lower courts' decisions, the U.S. Supreme Court ruled (7 for and 2 against) that SORNA did not apply to pre-Act offenders who traveled between jurisdictions after SORNA was enacted (July 26, 2006) but before the Attorney General's interim rule became effective (February 28, 2007). It did not however rule directly on the validity of the interim rule. Instead, its ruling focused primarily on the language of SORNA as it relates to pre-Act offenders. It found the provisions of the statute to be sufficiently vague as to warrant varying interpretations of the law. It reversed the decision of the lower courts and mandated that the validity of the interim rule be determined. To be sure, the *Reynolds v. U.S.* (2012) decision does not tackle the constitutionality of registration. The Court has clearly upheld the use of registries and notification in two prior decisions, *Connecticut Department of Public Safety v. Doe* (2003) and *Smith v. Doe* (2003). Instead, *Reynolds v. U.S.* (2012) requires that the validity of the interim rule be evaluated. In the case that the lower courts find the specification to have been properly issued, Pennsylvania can proceed with prosecuting Reynolds for registry violations given that his interstate travel occurred months after the promulgation by the Attorney General. Given the recency of the *Reynolds v. U.S.* (2012) decision, however, these issues have yet to be settled.[1]

Both the *Carr v. U.S.* (2010) and *Reynolds v. U.S.* (2012) decisions addressed whether SORNA may be retroactively applied to pre-Act offenders. Having said that, neither case speaks to the constitutionality of the federal law. Put differently, the U.S. Supreme Court has upheld the use of registry and notification procedures in earlier decisions. Further, it has not ruled on whether SORNA constitutes ex post facto punishment as alleged by the petitioner in *Carr v. U.S.* (2010). Instead, the cases it has ruled on have focused on a relatively narrow provision of the federal Act—its retroactive application to pre-Act offenders. Given that both decisions related to SORNA legislation have been handed down by the U.S. Supreme Court fairly recently, how jurisdictions respond to the retroactive

---

1. One other case, *U.S. v. Juvenile Male* (2011) reversed a Ninth Circuit Court of Appeals decision that invalidated the retroactive application of SORNA to juvenile registrants. However, the U.S. Supreme Court took the unusual route of reversing the Court's ruling without rendering any decision concerning the underlying issues decided by the lower court. As a result, there is little content to analyze for this decision.

challenges remains to be seen. Table 11.1 summarizes prominent U.S. Supreme Court decisions concerning sex crime laws.

Other Judicial Challenges

Notably, the U.S. Supreme Court has not yet heard challenges to some of the other sex crime reforms that currently exist nationally. For example, it has not reviewed the constitutionality of four controversial laws: residence restrictions, chemical castration, gateway legislation, and Internet-related restrictions. Below, case law on these policies is discussed.

Residence Restrictions

Residence restrictions, as described in prior chapters, refer to laws that prohibit sex offenders from living near places where children congregate. Most states have enacted some form of boundary restriction for convicted sex offenders. There is variation within residence boundary statutes. For instance, states differ in the length of buffer zone. Some have adopted relatively small boundaries (e.g., 500 feet). Others, in contrast, have implemented substantially wider restrictions (e.g., 2,000 feet). Complicating matters is that some states allow counties and municipalities to proscribe additional restrictions beyond the state-level boundary. Further still, some states apply the restrictions to all offenders, even those who have not victimized children. Although strong public and legislative approval exists for boundary laws, there have been recent legal challenges to them. These cases have not yet been decided by the U.S. Supreme Court as the Court has denied certiorari to challenges involving residence laws. However, legal scholars emphasize the implications of recent case law involving federal and state courts.

Boundary restrictions have been challenged on several fronts nationally. The highest court decision involving these laws was *Doe v. Miller* (2005), in which a three-judge panel affirmed Iowa's 2,000-feet buffer zone. In this federal case, the courts ruled in favor of Iowa, adopting the U.S. Supreme Court's logic in *Connecticut Department of Public Safety v. Doe* (2003) and *Smith v. Doe* (2003). Specifically, it found that the state has the right to enact public safety measures designed to protect vulnerable populations. The decision also rejected arguments that the law results in ex post facto punishment. Instead, the federal ruling emphasized the civil, regulatory purpose of the law.

Beyond this federal ruling, residence restrictions have also been challenged in state courts. California, for example, has enacted one of the strictest residence restriction laws for sex offenders in the nation. Per Proposition 93, a referendum which California voters approved in 2006, sex offenders must not live within 2,000 feet of schools or parks. A 2010 decision by the California Supreme Court, *In re E. J.*, clarified that this buffer zone applies to all paroled sex offenders (5 for and 2 against), regardless of when they committed their offense. However, in this same case the state Supreme Court stopped short of ruling on the constitutionality of the reform citing insufficient evidence to issue a ruling on that aspect of the law. One year later, four convicted sex offenders living in San Diego and displaced because of the law appealed the 2010 decision in Superior Court. The matter under review was the question left open by the earlier Supreme Court decision — does the law violate constitutional protections? The Superior Court judge held an evidentiary hearing in which experts testified that the law severely restricts the pool of legal housing

Table 11.1. Sex Crime Policies and U.S. Supreme Court Cases

Policy	U.S. Supreme Court Decision(s)
Civil Commitment	Upheld in three separate decisions: *Kansas v. Hendricks* (1997), *Kansas v. Crane* (2002), and *U.S. v. Comstock* (2010). Per *Kansas v. Crane* (2002) states have to clearly demonstrate that an offender's mental disorder limits his or her control of sexual urges and criminal behavior. The Court also affirmed civil commitment by the federal government (*Comstock v. U.S.*, 2010).
Coerced Treatment	Affirmed in *McKune v. Lile* (2002). States have a vested interest in requiring offenders to be forthcoming concerning their prior sexual history and offenses.
Registration/ Notification	Upheld in two separate decisions: *Connecticut Department of Public Safety v. Doe* (2003) and *Smith v. Doe* (2003). Both registries and notification policies serve to enhance public safety. Neither violates constitutional protections given that they include civil, not criminal, proceedings.
Child Pornography Laws	Upheld laws that prohibit the manufacture, distribution, and possession of child pornography (e.g., *Osborne v. Ohio*, 1990). Struck down statutes in *Ashcroft v. Free Speech Coalition* (2002) that restrict the manufacturing and possession of virtual child pornography (except where it is used in a way that suggests it is actual child pornography, *U.S. v. Williams*, 2008). The Court distinguished between "actual" pornography involving children versus images which are computer-generated. In short, it expressed concern that a broad ban on virtual media violates the First Amendment.
Rape Shield Laws	The Court has affirmed the use of rape shield protections. *Michigan v. Lucas* (1991) permits states to enact laws that prevent irrelevant questioning of sex crime victims (e.g., their manner of dress before the offense) during criminal proceedings. However, it has narrowed some provisions of the laws. In two earlier cases, *Florida Star v. B. J. F.* (1989) and *Cox Broadcasting Corporation v. Cohn* (1975) the Court ruled that news agencies may report publicly released information about the identity of sex crime victims. State agencies then are responsible for ensuring any publicly available information about sex crime redact identifying information regarding alleged victims.
Statutes of Limitations Laws	Prohibited laws that extend statutes of limitations for sex offenses retroactively in one case, *Stogner v. California* (2003). Specifically, the ruling found such reforms to constitute ex post facto punishment, and therefore, in violation of constitutional protections.
Capital Punishment Statutes	Outlawed death penalty for sex offenses committed against adults (*Coker v. Georgia*, 1977) and children (*Kennedy v. Louisiana*, 2008). Laws that permit the execution of individuals who have committed sex crimes but have not murdered their victims constitute excessive punishment, and are thus unconstitutional.
SORNA	In a series of cases heard in the 2000s, the Court has limited some aspects of SORNA. Both the *Carr v. U.S.* (2010) and *Reynolds v. U.S.* (2012) decisions limited the retroactive application of some provisions of SORNA. However, neither case directly evaluated the constitutionality of the law.

for sex offenders. The judge ruled in the offenders' favor, finding that the restriction boundaries were unconstitutional and unreasonable provisions of the law. The judge's decision noted that the law does not take into account individual offender's risk of recidivism or the circumstances of previous offenses.

Shortly thereafter, California's Fourth Appellate District Court, in *In re Taylor* (2012) affirmed the ruling noting that the law's "blanket enforcement as a parole condition in San Diego County has been unreasonable and constitutes arbitrary and oppressive official action." The state has since then appealed the decision to the California Supreme Court. *In re Taylor* is not a binding decision given the state's appeal. The state's Supreme Court has yet to rule on whether the residence restrictions are constitutional, but a decision is expected by the end of 2013. In the absence of a U.S. Supreme Court ruling, California Supreme Court's forthcoming decision will settle the matter, at least in that state, once and for all.

Similar challenges have been recently levied against residence restrictions in other states. To illustrate, the Kentucky Supreme Court in 2009 issued a decision (*Commonwealth v. Baker*) that outlawed retroactive application of residence restrictions to sex offenders who committed their crimes prior to the law's enactment in 2006. The Court further advanced the argument that the law, at least as applied retroactively, constituted ex post facto punishment. The *Commonwealth v. Baker* (2009) decision however does not prohibit the state from applying residence restrictions to offenders who committed crimes after the law's enactment. Even so, the state concerned that the decision would negatively affect public safety efforts, immediately appealed the decision to the U.S. Supreme Court. The Court however denied certiorari (*Commonwealth v. Baker*, 2010, cert. denied). One other recent decision includes *State ex rel. White v. Billings* (2008), an Ohio Supreme Court case which denied the application of residence restrictions to offenders who have committed crimes prior to the state's passage of the law. Similar to the *Commonwealth v. Baker* (2009) decision, per *Billings* residence restrictions are still in effect in the state, but do not apply to registrants who committed crimes prior to 2003 (the date of the law's passage).

One final case regarding the retroactive application of residence restrictions concerned a Georgia law. In particular, *Mann v. Georgia Department of Corrections* (2007) refers to a case decided by the Georgia Supreme Court. Here, several issues regarding Georgia's residence restriction were to be decided—particularly, the extent to which offenders had to comply with residence restriction laws once they have bought a home or secured employment. Georgia's law at the time specified that sex offenders not reside or work within 1,000 feet of areas frequented by children. The case involved Anthony Mann, a registered sex offender who in 2002 committed a sex crime and was required to register as a sex offender in the state. In 2003, he purchased a home in Clayton County, Georgia; at the time, the home complied with Georgia's residence restriction (i.e., it was not located within 1,000 feet of a child care facility, church, school, or other area outlined by the law). At around the same time, Mann became a part-owner and operator of a restaurant that also appeared to be in compliance with the statute.

However, soon after, child care facilities were built within 1,000 feet of Mann's home and business. Per the law, Mann's probation officer ordered him to move from his current home and stop working at the restaurant. Mann faced felony charges if he failed to comply with the orders. The Court ruled that forcing Mann to give up his home without providing just compensation was unconstitutional. However, per the Court's decision, the Constitution does not prohibit the employment restrictions set forth by the law. The Court noted that the Georgia statute did not include a "move-to-the-offender" exception that would permit an offender who establishes legal residency or accepts employment in a permissible location to stay there when a new child-related establishment moves nearby (statutes in other states such as Alabama and Iowa include this exception). Barring this exception, the Court reasoned that offenders would be continually at risk of having to move every time a new child-related establishment is built. Concerned about the implications of the *Mann* ruling, the Georgia legislature has revised its residence restriction to comport with the decision (Grubesic, Murray, & Mack, 2011). As a result, residence restrictions are still enforced in the state.

Recently, there have been a series of other cases involving county-level residence restrictions. New Jersey's Supreme Court in *G. H. v. Township of Galloway* (2009) invalidated Cherry Hill Township's buffer zone ordinance that restricted convicted sex offenders from residing within 2,500 feet of a school, park, playground, public library, or daycare center. The Supreme Court's reasoning held that because the state had not yet enacted a residence boundary, counties could not legally require offenders to abide by local level ordinances. The decision does not rule that residence laws are unconstitutional per se, but adopts the logic that a state law preempts county-level law. A similar decision regarding preemption was rendered in a later Pennsylvania case, *Fross et al. v. County of Allegheny* (2010).

Notwithstanding some rulings that limit the reach of boundary laws, residence restrictions have been largely affirmed by federal and state courts. For example, *Doe v. Miller* (2005), a federal case and the highest ranking decision involving residence laws, upheld the constitutionality of them. Some of the provisions of residence laws have been struck down, however. Courts have invalidated the retroactive application of many state residence laws (*Commonwealth v. Baker*, 2009; *Mann v. Georgia Department of Corrections*, 2007; *State ex rel. White v. Billings*, 2008). Not least, the practice of "preemption" or instances where counties in states without statewide buffer zones enact county-level laws has been prohibited (see, *Fross et al. v. County of Allegheny*, 2010; *G. H. v. Township of Galloway*, 2009).

Chemical Castration

Chemical castration statutes represent perhaps the most unique and controversial sex offender reform. It is difficult to identify other criminal sanctions that involve a biological intervention as a mandatory condition of probation or parole. As mentioned earlier, about eight states have permitted the use of chemical castration as part of reentry efforts to prevent recidivism. Typically, chemical castration is reserved for "high-risk" offenders—that is, those with an extensive history of violent sex offending, or with child victims. It is administered via MPA, a drug designed to temper sexual arousal among males. Interestingly, the U.S. Supreme Court has yet to rule on the constitutionality of statutes that mandate chemical castration for sex offenders. What follows is a review of recent state cases involving the law.

Stinneford (2006) in a legal analysis of chemical castration laws in the U.S. identified an "exceedingly sparse" history of recent legal challenges. That assessment rings true today. One case heard in 2005 *Jackson v. State* involved a Florida law that mandates chemical castration for certain offenders, such as those with child victims and prior sex offense histories. The petitioner, Jackson, was ordered to undergo chemical castration after he was certified as a "sexual predator" by the state in January 2004. Per Florida law, predators are required to undergo a medical evaluation within 60 days of sentencing to determine the health implications of MPA. Jackson contended that the state erred in its administration of a medical evaluation. Specifically, the state submitted Jackson to a medical evaluation— which showed no potential medical issues—beyond the statutorily required time frame. The Florida District Court reversed the order mandating chemical castration because of the delay in the evaluation. Thus, the Court did not address whether the sanction as administered was unconstitutional, but rather whether the trial procedure was legally flawed (the appellate court applied a similar logic involving another case, *Houston v. State*, 2003).

Another case, *Bruno v. State* (2003), also challenged a Florida castration law. Specifically at issue was the constitutionality of a plea agreement that required a sex offender to undergo surgical castration for a reduced sentence. Petitioner Bruno was charged with five counts of lewd and lascivious acts. The state proposed two options for a plea bargain. Option one allowed adjudication of all counts and a sentence of nearly 21 years. The second option provided for adjudication of four counts and a 15 year sentence. However, the plea would also require that the offender undergo surgical castration. Bruno selected the latter option. He then appealed the sentence to the District Court. The state conceded that no specific statute authorized castration — either surgical or chemical — for lewd and lascivious offenses. The appellate court ruled in Bruno's favor finding that the state offered an illegal plea bargain to the offender and remanded the case to the lower court. Accordingly, the Court addressed a rather narrow issue related to castration. It did not rule on the constitutionality of the sanction as it is applied in the state, but rather the instances in which castration can be offered as a punishment resulting in reduced prison time.

One final case involved a California decision, *People v. Foster* (2002). The question put forth before the Court involved whether defendants who agree to plea agreements involving chemical castration as a condition of parole reserve the right to challenge that sentence. The offender, Foster, was charged with committing in excess of 30 lewd acts against a girlfriend's child over a six month period. In June 2000, as part of a plea agreement with the state, Foster agreed to plead guilty to five counts of forcible lewd acts upon a child in exchange for a stipulated prison term of 30 years and the dismissal of the remaining counts — five of which carried sentences of 15 years to life in prison. As part of the agreement, Foster was required to affirm that he understood that accepting the sentence precluded him from later appealing his punishment, particularly the provision that upon release he undergo chemical castration. He did so and was sentenced. Even so, he appealed the decision to the California Appellate Court. Foster contended that the portion of the sentence that mandates hormone suppression treatment should be reversed for two reasons. First, he argued that the sanction is grossly disproportionate to his crimes. Second, Foster claimed that the practice of castration violates state and federal constitutional protections against cruel and unusual punishment. The Court affirmed Foster's mandatory chemical castration sanction given that ample evidence existed to indicate he was aware of the repercussions of accepting the plea agreement proposed by the state. As a result, the decision affirms chemical castration as a legal sanction in the state.

Collectively, state courts, albeit in a limited number of cases, have upheld the use of chemical castration for convicted sex offenders. Having said that, limits have been placed on the application of the sanction. That is, at least one state mandates that it may not be given as a sanction in exchange for reduced sentences when statutes do not clearly permit it (*Bruno v. State*, 2003). Even so, chemical castration — practiced by an increasing number of states — has largely withstood constitutional challenges.

Gateway Legislation

As reviewed in previous chapters, some states have implemented preemptive or "gateway" legislation that mandates registration of non-sex offenders to sex offender databases. Under these statutes, offenders who have committed crimes believed to progress to sex offending would be required to submit their information to a sex offender database. Given that only a small handful of states have implemented such laws, the case law in this area is limited. However, one recent Georgia Supreme Court decision illustrates the legal controversies surrounding gateway reforms. In *Rainer v. State of Georgia* (2010), petitioner Rainer challenged a state law that mandated he register as a sex offender after being released from prison in 2006 for robbery and false imprisonment offenses. Specifically, Rainer argued that because the offenses were not sexual in nature, requiring him to register as a convicted sex offender violates several constitutional protections, including the Eighth Amendment against cruel and unusual punishment.

In a 5–2 decision, the Georgia Supreme Court in *Rainer v. State of Georgia* (2010) disagreed. Noting in part that since registration requirements are not punitive (per prior case law) it is not relevant "whether or not one has committed an offense that is 'sexual' in nature before being required to register" (p. 3). At the same time, the Court reasoned that the law serves to protect the best interests of vulnerable populations, such as children: "it is rational to conclude that requiring those who falsely imprison minors ... advances the State's legitimate goal of informing the public for purposes of protecting children from those who would harm them" (*Rainer v. State of Georgia*, 2010, p. 6).

It is difficult to generalize regarding case law and future challenges to gateway legislation given that it is the exception rather than the rule in way of sex crime reforms. Only a small number of states have implemented such laws. As a result, very few challenges to these laws exist. The one case discussed above, *Rainer v. State of Georgia* (2010), indicates that state and appellate courts may continue to view registration requirements as civil proceedings, even when applied to offenders whose crime did not involve sexual violence per se. Accordingly, "cruel and unusual" punishment challenges to such provisions are not likely to be successful. Additionally, SORNA legislation—albeit not yet fully implemented nationally—permits states to include non-sex offenses (such as kidnapping and false detainment crimes) as registerable offenses. As a result, this federal authority given to states means offenders will have greater difficulties in challenging such provisions.

Internet Bans

With the growing recognition that some sex crimes may be facilitated by the Internet, states have experimented with restricting offenders' Internet use. Recall that as mentioned in previous chapters, these laws prohibit sex offenders from visiting certain Internet websites or restricting their access to online social networking sites. Since the implementation of these reforms in the 2000s, offenders have challenged them in state and federal courts. Three recent cases deserve mention.

An Indiana case, *Doe v. Marion County Prosecutor* (2013), examined the constitutionality of a state law that prohibits sex offenders from knowingly using a social networking site, an instant messaging service, or chat room program. The law applies broadly to all sex offenders who are required to register under Indiana law. It makes little distinction regarding factors related to the offense such as the age of the victim, the manner in which the crime was committed, or the time since the offense was committed. As written, the statute provides an exemption for statutory rape offenses where the victim and offender are close in age.

Plaintiff-Appellant Doe, a registered sex offender, was convicted of child exploitation in 2000. He was released from prison in 2003. Per Indiana law, he was required to register as a sex offender. Doe was also required to abide by the state's Internet ban. He challenged this provision on the grounds that it violated the First Amendment. The United States Court of Appeals for the Seventh Circuit reviewed the case in 2013. It issued a ruling in favor of the offender. Specifically, the decision emphasized that the law unduly restricts free speech. It noted for instance that "there is no disagreement that illicit communication comprises a minuscule subset of the universe of social network activity ... [accordingly] the Indiana law targets substantially more activity than the evil it seeks to redress" (*Doe v. Marion County Prosecutor*, 2013, p. 10). The Court however intimates that revised statutes could pass Constitutional muster as evident by their closing remarks; specifically laws that restrict the First Amendment "require narrow tailoring ... subsequent Indiana statutes may well meet this requirement, but the blanket ban on social media in this case regrettably does not" (p. 20). Given the recency of the case, is not known whether the state will appeal the decision.

A second case concerning challenges to Internet restrictions involved a Louisiana statute. In *Doe v. Jindal* (2012), a group of registered sex offenders challenged a state law that banned sex offenders who had committed crimes against juveniles from using or accessing social networking sites, chat rooms, and peer-to-peer networks in the U.S. District Court for the Middle District of Louisiana. The penalties for a first-time offense include fines and potentially felony charges. Repeat offenses carry additional fines and up to a 20 year prison sentence. Although the law seemingly covers all use, it does permit offenders to seek special permission to use or access certain online services from probation/parole officers or the courts. Even so, the plaintiffs in the case critiqued the statute as being overly broad. They allege that as written it has the potential to outlaw all Internet use. For example, the law prohibits offenders from searching employment message boards. At the same time, it potentially limits offenders from accessing news websites that might also include a peer-to-peer or social networking component (e.g., by allowing "comments" to be posted by registered users/guests). As a result, the plaintiffs argued that the statute violates the First Amendment. In defense of the law, the state contended that such regulations are necessary to ensure public safety. Additionally, the state emphasized that the law outlines procedures for obtaining exemptions to the restriction, and so, provides for exceptions where appropriate. Not least, the state argued that it incorporated a regulation to the law that provided further guidance in fulfilling the obligations of the statute. Despite these safeguards, the Court ruled that the law was overly broad and an infringement on offenders' First Amendment right to free speech. In particular, it pointed to the ambiguity in the statute, particularly in defining the specific types of use that are prohibited (e.g., "chat room" per the Court's opinion is only vaguely defined by the state). The Court's decision, however, emphasizes that a more tailored law—one that does not impose a broad ban on Internet use—would likely pass constitutional muster. Notably, Louisiana has since revised the law to comport with the court's ruling (Onishi, 2012).

One final decision, rendered by the United States District Court for the District of Nebraska, *Doe v. State of Nebraska* (2012), ruled on Nebraska legislation that prohibits sex offenders from accessing and using certain Internet websites. Here again, the challenges centered on whether Internet restrictions unduly infringe on offenders' constitutional rights. Specifically, Nebraska law sets forth several requirements related to offender Internet use. It mandates that offenders disclose content that they have posted to Internet blogs and websites. Offenders must also consent to searches of their computers and monitoring of their Internet history. Finally, the statute prohibits certain sex offenders (e.g., those who have committed sex offenses against minors, kidnapping offenses) from accessing and using social networking web sites, instant messaging programs, or chat room services that also allow permit minors' use of the services. The law applies equally to offenders currently under community corrections supervision and those offenders who are no longer under probation or parole. For first-time violations, offenders face misdemeanor charges; repeat crimes carry felony punishment. A group of registered sex offenders affected by the law argued that it amounted to ex post facto punishment, infringed on the First Amendment, and constituted illegal search and seizure by the state. The Court issued a decision in support of these arguments. It ruled that the state can no longer require that offenders submit their posts on blogs and Internet websites. Additionally, the decision precludes the state from requesting consent from offenders to search their Internet history or to monitor their Internet use. Moreover, Nebraska is not permitted to restrict offenders from accessing social networking sites that might also be frequented by minors. State lawmakers have vowed to review the legislation to identify areas that could be revised to comply with the Court's decision (Pilger, 2012).

What are the implications of this case law? Overall, these three decisions indicate that broad Internet bans may not pass appellate review. Indeed, the legal concerns appear to center around the following issues: statutes that are not narrowly tailored, use ambiguous definitions, and unfairly infringe on offenders' constitutional rights, particularly the First Amendment. Table 11.2 reviews Internet ban case law as well as prominent federal and state cases involving residence restrictions, chemical castration laws, and gateway legislation.

Table 11.2. Sex Crime Policies and Federal/State Court Cases

Policy	Court Decision(s)
Residence Restrictions	The only federal decision affirmed residence boundaries in Iowa (*Doe v. Miller*, 2005). A California decision (*In re Taylor*, 2012) found the state residence law to be unconstitutional. California has appealed the decision to the California Supreme Court. The Kentucky Supreme Court has upheld the use of residence boundaries, but forbids the retroactive application of them (*Commonwealth v. Baker*, 2009). The Ohio Supreme Court and the Georgia Supreme Court issued similar rulings in earlier cases, *State ex rel. White v. Billings* (2008) and *Mann v. Georgia Department of Corrections* (2007), respectively. Preemptive laws, or boundaries set forth by counties and not states, have been struck down in New Jersey (*G. H. v. Township of Galloway*, 2009) and Pennsylvania (*Fross et al. v County of Allegheny*, 2010).
Chemical Castration	Two state cases struck down chemical castration due to errors in trial procedure, but not because of constitutional questions regarding the sanction—*Jackson v. State* (2005) and *Houston v. State* (2003). One Florida case, *Bruno v. State* (2003), invalidated the offering of surgical castration as a punishment where no specific state statute authorizing its use existed. A California decision, *People v. Foster* (2002), affirmed plea bargains that include mandatory chemical castration in exchange for reduced prison time, so long as offenders knowingly consent to the sentence.
Gateway Legislation	Only one state case has heard challenges to laws that mandate sex offender registration for offenders who have not yet committed a sex crime. Per *Rainer v. State of Georgia* (2010), gateway laws are constitutional given that registries comprise civil and not punitive sanctions, and are designed to protect vulnerable populations from sexual victimization.
Internet Bans	Three recent cases have limited the breadth of Internet restrictions for convicted sex offenders. *Doe v. Marion County Prosecutor* (2013) invalidated an Indiana law that prohibited registered offenders from accessing several Internet websites and social networking sites because it targets lawful use of the Internet. A decision involving a Louisiana statute (*Doe v. Jindal*, 2012) similarly found the state law to be vague and excessively broad, and thus unconstitutional. Since then, Louisiana has introduced revised legislation that comports with the decision. The ruling rendered in *Doe v. State of Nebraska* (2012) favored the plaintiffs, convicted sex offenders covered by the state's Internet ban, who challenged its constitutionality. The ruling will force Nebraska to revisit their statute.

Chapter Summary

Given the proliferation of sex crime legislation in the U.S. over the last two decades, understanding how the courts have ruled on the constitutionality of these reforms is critical. When focusing on U.S. Supreme Court decisions, it is apparent that most sex crime laws have passed recent constitutional challenges. The Supreme Court has upheld the controversial use of civil commitment, finding that is serves to protect the public while providing for civil procedures and due process. Registry and notification laws, and with some exceptions, SORNA legislation—which aims to strengthen and standardize state registry and notification procedures—have been affirmed by the U.S. Supreme Court. Indeed, across many decisions involving challenges to these laws, the Court has emphasized that such policies are not designed to punish offenders ex post facto, but rather serve to enhance public safety. Mandatory sex offender treatment, as well, has been upheld to be constitutional by the Court. In contrast, the Supreme Court has prohibited policies it has evaluated as unconstitutional: laws restricting the possession of virtual child pornography, retroactively enforced statutes of limitations exceptions, capital punishment, and retroactive components of SORNA. The U.S. Supreme Court has not heard challenges to other controversial laws such as residence restrictions, chemical castration, gateway legislation, and Internet restrictions. Here, state and federal courts have issued decisions. However, because these rulings have been mixed and may be superseded at any time by higher courts, it is more difficult to generalize about the impact of them. This point notwithstanding, what remains clear is that legal decisions affect the implementation and existence of such laws. The reading list below includes some scholarship centered on sex crime policy and legal challenges. Chapter 12 concludes the text by highlighting future issues of sex crime policy and reform.

Additional Suggested Readings

Carpenter, C. L., & Beverlin, A. E. (2012). The evolution of unconstitutionality in sex offender registration laws. *Hastings Law Journal, 63*, 1071–1134.

Janus, E. S. (2013). Preventive detention of sex offenders: The American experience versus international human rights norms. *Behavioral Sciences and the Law, 31*, 328–343.

Shepard, R. (2011). Does the punishment fit the crime? Applying Eighth Amendment proportionality analysis to Georgia's sex offender registration statute and residency and employment restrictions for juvenile offenders. *Georgia State University Law Review, 28*, 529–557.

Wright, R. G. (Ed.). (2009). *Sex offender laws: Failed policies, new directions.* New York: Springer.

Yung, C. (2009). One of these laws is not like the others: Why the federal sex offender registration and notification act raises new constitutional questions. *Harvard Journal on Legislation, 46*, 369–424.

Chapter 12

The Future of Sex Crime Policy

Chapter Introduction

As the preceding chapters of this book have highlighted, sex offending has been prioritized as an important public policy concern. Looking toward the future, what are some of the issues sex offender policies should confront to effectively reduce sex crime? Admittedly, without the aid of a crystal ball, there is little way to guarantee that any proposed policy response would substantially reduce sex crime. Even so, the goal of this chapter is to highlight three sex crime policy efforts that may go a long way toward the development of "best practices" in criminal justice. First, a continued focus on practices to increase reporting among victims is needed. Only a minority of all sex offenses are ever reported to law enforcement. In turn, most offenders are not held accountable for their crimes and are free to reoffend, and, tragically, victims do not receive the justice that they deserve. Second, in conjunction with greater reporting efforts, an equal emphasis should be placed on treatment and reentry interventions for sex offenders. Most sex offenders will be released from our nation's prisons and jails and so it is imperative that they are given the tools needed to successfully reenter society. Third, and finally, there should be greater recognition that not all sex crimes are "created equal." This is by way of saying that some offenders pose a substantially greater risk to reoffend than others. Given this, policymakers might consider restricting registration to better divert scarce criminal justice resources toward punishing the worst of the worst offenders, rather than "widening the net" to include those who have not yet committed a sex offense and low level juvenile offenders. To be sure, the homogeneity belief has in large part contributed to the perpetuation of various myths about sex offenders. Yet, as has been a common theme of the text, wide heterogeneity exists across sex offenses and within sex offenders. In turn, any evidence-based approach would need to account for these differences. The chapter ends with a brief restatement of the goal of the text and concluding comments. We turn now to the first policy recommendation.

Increase Reporting

Unquestionably, individuals who commit sex offenses are deserving of punishment. Nearly all sex crime statutes—even for lower-level non-contact sex crimes—specify a period of incarceration. However, offenders cannot be held accountable if their crimes go undetected by law enforcement. All too often, this occurs. Compared to other serious crimes, as the preceding chapters have shown, sex offenses involving children and adults are underreported nationally. In response, states have incorporated several measures to increase reporting both among minors and adults. Mandatory reporting laws, for instance, require certain individuals, such as physicians and social workers, to report suspicions of child sexual abuse. Additionally, various reforms aimed at increasing reporting among adults, with the creation of rape shield laws, for example, have been developed and implemented nationally. These reforms, with a special emphasis on how they might impact reporting in the future, are now discussed.

Mandatory Reporting Laws for Child Sexual Abuse

As mentioned previously, nearly all states have incorporated some type of mandated reporting law. Typically, these statutes require the following professionals to report any suspicions of abuse against minors, including sexual victimization: social workers; teachers, principals, and other school personnel; medical doctors, nurses, and other health-care workers; counselors, therapists, and other mental health professionals; child care providers; medical examiners or coroners; and, law enforcement officers. In the wake of high profile scandals involving allegations of sexual abuse within universities, some states have expanded their laws to include all university staff as professional mandated reporters (Administration for Children and Families, 2012). For example, Florida's new statute requires any university employee to report suspected cases of child abuse or face third-degree felony charges and a $5,000 fine. Institutions found in violation of the law are also liable for fines by the state (Florida Council Against Sexual Violence, 2013). Some states do not explicitly define mandated reporters, but instead designate any resident as a reporter. New Jersey and Wyoming are two such states (Administration for Children and Families, 2012). To protect reporters, all states have procedures to ensure the confidentiality of the reporter. Some for instance permit the reports to be submitted anonymously. Other states require reporters to identify themselves, but pledge to keep their identities confidential. Additionally, states typically incorporate "good faith" provisions to protect reporters from liability in cases where abuse is not substantiated (Administration for Children and Families, 2012).

How might these laws impact sex crime reporting in the future? Again, it is difficult to predict the effects of any one proposed policy initiative. Most people cannot understand why one would neglect to report cases of suspected abuse. The simple answer is that many factors—such as fear of being wrong and disbelief—might deter individuals from disclosing their suspicions to law enforcement. Thus, from a deterrence standpoint, the laws may increase reporting in cases where the abuse is suspected by a third person given that non-disclosure subjects people to penalties such as imprisonment and fines. However, mandatory reporting laws are unlikely to impact the reporting of crimes where only the victim and perpetrator are aware of the abuse. Because "tougher" versions of mandatory reporting laws, such as the one in Florida, have only recently been implemented, it is not clear whether they will more effectively increase reporting to a greater extent than earlier versions of the law.

Efforts to Increase Reporting among Adults

Nationally, there have also been efforts to increase reporting among adults. As reviewed earlier, over the last three decades, states have revised their rape statutes, penalizing a broader array of unwanted sexual behavior, incorporated policies within police departments to ensure victims are treated fairly, and devised rape shield laws that prevent "victim blaming" in court (Baumer, 2004). In line with these innovations, rape crisis and victim advocacy centers have been created to assist victims of sex crimes (Page, 2010). With few exceptions, research indicates that these reforms have had a positive impact on reporting. On average, rape reporting among adult victims age 12 and older has increased. In their analysis, Lonsway and Archambault (2012) relayed that reporting, as measured by the NCVS, increased by about nine percent over the last decade, from 32 percent in 1995 to 41 percent in 2008 (see also Clay-Warner & Burt, 2005). Even so, rape remains one of the most underreported crimes in the U.S. As a result, perhaps what is needed to increase reporting to an even greater extent in the future is a continued or larger "dose" of these legal reforms.

At the same time, focusing reporting efforts on high-risk populations may also encourage increased reporting among victims. Research finds that approximately one in four women attending colleges or universities will be a victim of a sex crime (Fisher et al., 2000). Fisher and her colleagues (2000), analyzing results from the NCWSV survey, uncovered that nearly 95 percent of college students do not report their victimizations to authorities. Recognizing that sex crime on campus is substantially underreported, colleges and universities have implemented policies designed to increase reporting. Many of these have focused on victim advocacy and educational programs to create better awareness of reporting procedures (Tamborra & Narchet, 2011). There is evidence, albeit tentative, that these policies may have had a positive effect on reporting among college students. The NWS-R administered some years after the NCWSV survey found nearly double the rate of reporting that Fisher and colleagues did in their 2000 study. Kilpatrick et al. (2007) estimated that 12 percent of adult females attending colleges or universities in the U.S. reported their victimization to law enforcement in 2006. Ideally, future research will systematically evaluate whether in fact these policies are associated with a significant increase in reporting among victims using similar instruments administered annually.

Most recently, Congress has focused on understanding the nature and extent of rape in another institution—the U.S. military—in an effort to increase reporting of sex crime. Current statistics indicate sex crimes are prevalent offenses in the military; even so, they are frequently unreported or insufficiently investigated. In a recent report, the Department of Defense (2011) estimated that annually, 19,000 sex assaults occur in the U.S. military. This number translates into 4.4 percent of women and 0.9 percent of men experiencing unwanted sexual contact. Comparing anonymous survey data with official reports, the government estimates that, on average, only 14 percent of these crimes are reported to military officials. Notably, this estimate is even lower than reporting rates for sexual victimization in the general population (Hart & Rennison, 2003; Langton et al., 2012; finding approximately 33 percent of all sex crimes are reported to law enforcement during any given year). Several proposals have been developed by the Department of Defense to increase the reporting of sex offenses and apprehension of sex offenders in the U.S. military. The Department of Defense has established these policy initiatives to increase reporting in its 2011 marketing campaign, "Hurts one. Affects all" (Department of Defense, 2011). For example, the military has contracted with non-profit victim advocacy centers to develop a special emergency hotline for victims. It has also increased its educational efforts regarding reporting procedures (Department of Defense, 2011). However, some lawmakers have criticized these initiatives arguing that the military has not done enough to encourage reporting of sexual assault (Steinhauer, 2013). As a result, the U.S. Congress has proposed additional procedures to enhance reporting among victims of sex crime, such as replacing the current system of reporting which requires that victims report sexual assault to their superior officer via the "chain of command" (Steinhauer, 2013). The impact of these initiatives on reporting rates in the U.S. military has not yet been rigorously evaluated by researchers. To the extent that these reforms have similar effects as other reporting reforms in the general population, there is reason to be cautiously optimistic

Table 12.1. Future Policy Considerations: Reporting Efforts

Policy Consideration	Reasons for Focus
Increase Reporting for Offenses Involving Children	• Only a small minority of sex offenses are reported to law enforcement. • As a result, offenders are not apprehended for their offenses, and so are free to recommit crime. • Mandatory reporting laws may go far to increase reports of sexual abuse, but only for cases where others are aware of the abuse. • Future research is needed to fully understand the impact of such measures on reporting behavior.
Increase Reporting for Offenses Involving Adults/Special Populations	• Rape reforms enacted in the last few decades are associated with an increase in the reporting of rapes involving adults. • Even so, most sex crimes committed against adults are never reported to law enforcement. • Future reporting efforts should focus on special populations—such as college students and those serving in the military—that may be particularly vulnerable to sexual victimization, but not likely to report it.

that they will have the desired effect of increasing reporting of sex crimes that occur in the military.

Collectively, what do these findings suggest as a policy recommendation? A continuation and larger "dose" of these reforms is perhaps needed to increase reporting rates. One function of law is to express moral outrage about unacceptable behavior. Thus, it may be that sustained reporting reforms—in addition to having an actual impact on the reporting of sexual victimization—also lead to larger sociocultural changes—whereby abuse against children is not ignored. Additionally, such reforms may result in "victim blaming" becoming less entrenched in society. Finally, greater efforts undertaken to increase reporting in organizations and institutions like colleges/universities and the military might also send the message that sex crimes that occur in any context will not be tolerated. Table 12.1 briefly summarizes these reporting considerations. The second policy recommendation is discussed below.

Treatment and Reentry Strategies

Treatment Interventions

As highlighted in prior chapters, the question of what "works" for treating sex offenders is a controversial one. It is true that many treatment interventions currently exist and that some are more effective than others. It is equally true that some offenders will not benefit from treatment. Having said that, recent meta-analyses have concluded that treated sex offenders fare better than offenders who receive no treatment. For this reason, greater investment into treatment oriented strategies for combating sex offending is worthy of consideration in the future. Below, promising approaches are reviewed.

In recent meta-analyses, cognitive behavioral therapy and medical/hormonal interventions have been evaluated to be the two most effective treatments for sex offenders (see e.g., Lösel & Schmucker, 2005). Cognitive behavioral therapy aims to first identify distorted thinking of offenders. Recall as discussed in Chapter 4 that some sex offenders experience "cognitive distortions" or erroneous beliefs employed to justify their offenses. For example, some offenders may adopt the view that their crimes were not really harmful to victims, or that victims secretly wanted the offense to occur. Once these distortions are identified, cognitive behavioral interventions assist with helping the offender learn new cognitive skills, or ways to think about their actions. Additionally, as Cullen and Gendreau (2000) note in their review, some offenders have minimal interpersonal skills that enable them to conform to societal norms. Given these deficits, effective cognitive behavioral treatments also assist offenders with the following: (1) define the problems that led them into conflict with authorities, (2) select goals, (3) generate new alternative prosocial solutions, and then (4) implement these solutions (Cullen & Gendreau, 2000, p. 146). In short then, cognitive behavioral therapy centers on assisting offenders with thinking differently about their actions and responding to stimuli in a prosocial fashion.

Overall, research has found cognitive behavioral therapy to reduce sexual recidivism more effectively than other psychological interventions. In a seminal meta-analysis, Lösel and Schmucker (2005) analyzed results from 69 treatment studies. They identified seven broad categories of treatment, five of which were considered psychosocial interventions — cognitive-behavioral, classic behavioral, insight-oriented, therapeutic community, and "other" psychological treatment. Offenders who received cognitive behavioral therapy were significantly less likely to sexually reoffend compared to non-treated offenders and those who received other types of treatment. More recent studies have replicated these results. For example, Hanson et al. (2009) in a large-scale meta-analysis (n=23 studies) demonstrated that treatment based on "risk-need-responsivity," or RNR, such as cognitive behavioral programs performed the best in reducing sexual recidivism (see also, Schmucker & Lösel, 2008 in their meta-analysis).

Some researchers have called for advancing cognitive behavioral therapy programs by incorporating the "good lives model" into treatment (Willis, Yates, Gannon, & Ward, 2012). Under this model which draws on concepts from psychological, sociological, biological, and anthropological research, offenders, like all individuals place emphasis on "certain states of mind, personal characteristics, and experiences" (Willis et al., 2012, p. 125); these are defined as "primary human goods." In a series of articles, Ward and his colleagues (see e.g., Ward & Gannon, 2003; Ward, Yates, & Willis, 2012) have proposed 11 types of primary goods: 1) "life" (healthy living and functioning), 2) "knowledge," 3) "excellence in play" (e.g., enjoyment in sports), 4) "excellence in work" (personal fulfillment in professional occupation), 5) "excellence in agency" (i.e., autonomy and self-directedness), 6) "inner peace" (i.e., freedom from emotional turmoil and stress), 7) "relatedness" (such as intimate, family, and friend relationships), 8) "community," 9) "spirituality" (in the broad sense of finding meaning and purpose in life), 10) "happiness," and 11) "creativity."

Per the model, "instrumental" or "secondary goods" refer to the means of satisfying primary goods. Put differently, secondary goods represent specific actions individuals engage in to achieve their primary goods — or, the concrete actions through which primary goods are achieved. To illustrate, the primary good of spirituality might be achieved through pursuing religion. In contrast, the primary good of autonomy might be achieved through securing stable housing.

However, offenders, unlike those who are not criminally involved, have "criminogenic needs" (i.e., dynamic risk factors) that present challenges toward achieving primary goods in the legally permissible ways described in the above example. Willis and colleagues (2012, pp. 125–126) explain how these concepts relate to treatment:

> The GLM [good lives model] assumes that all humans fashion their lives around their core values and follow some sort of (often implicit) good life plan (GLP), however rudimentary. Offending relates either directly or indirectly to the pursuit of primary goods and is considered to result from flaws in an individual's GLP. Importantly, these flaws relate to problems with secondary goods—the activities/means individuals use to achieve primary goods—and not the primary goods themselves (citations omitted).

Treatment centers on addressing these "flaws," and thus establishing appropriate options for achieving primary goods. Specifically, four types of flaws, not necessarily mutually exclusive, have been identified. Willis and colleagues (2012, p. 126) describe them as follows. The first flaw is "use of inappropriate or harmful means to obtain primary goods." Illustrative of this flaw would be an individual who sexually assaults another to achieve the primary good of relatedness. A second flaw is "lack of scope in a good lives plan" (i.e., as described above, a good lives plan refers to the set of methods/techniques used to achieve primary goods). Specifically, this flaw refers to situations in which individuals neglect some goods and overly focus on others. For example, an individual might devote a disproportionate amount of time engaged in activities to fulfill the good of excellence in play, but neglect other goods such as excellence in work. A third flaw occurs when an individual experiences conflict between valued primary goods and/or in the secondary goods (the "means") used to obtain primary goods. Willis et al. (2012, p. 126), shares the following example, "Attempting to secure autonomy by dominating a partner (itself a problem with means), for example, conflicts with satisfying the good of relatedness through the same relationship." The fourth and final flaw outlined in the model relates to the absence of personal/internal or external capabilities to satisfy primary goods. For example, a lack of personal/internal capabilities refers to an individual not having certain skills to achieve primary goods, such as the skills necessary to secure excellence in work. The absence of external capabilities include factors in the environment, such as lacking prosocial intimates or friends needed to fulfill the primary good of relatedness.

In short, as Ward and colleagues have explained (Ward & Gannon, 2006, p. 80; see also, Ward & Stewart, 2003) "by focusing on providing offenders with the necessary internal and external conditions (e.g., skills, values, opportunities, and social supports) for meeting their human needs in more adaptive ways, the assumption is that they will be less likely to harm others or themselves." How do these concepts relate to cognitive behavioral therapy? The good lives model represents a theoretical framework for treating sex offenders ("what to do in treatment") whereas cognitive behavioral therapy informs "how" to do so (Willis et al., 2012, p. 124). Given its novelty, good lives-based interventions have yet to be systematically evaluated as successful tools to treat sex offenders. Thus, future research is needed to assess whether good lives-based approaches enhance sex offender rehabilitation.

Cognitive behavioral therapy is one of the most effective tools for treating sex offenders. The extent to which it can be strengthened by applying the good lives model remains to be seen, but the approach—grounded in encouraging offenders to take a stake in their treatment—appears promising, and one that will likely be explored and examined in the future.

Hormonal Treatment

The use of hormonal treatments, most notably, chemical castration, has also been recognized as an effective treatment for reducing reoffending among sex offenders compared to other types of treatment efforts, with some caveats. That is, although recent reviews indicate significant positive effects of hormonal intervention on recidivism, there is strong concern that methodological shortcomings limit the generalizability of such impacts. As reviewed earlier, chemical castration involves administering anti-androgen drugs such as MPA that significantly reduce sexual urges among male sex offenders. There is no counterpart treatment for females.

Lösel and Schmucker's (2005) meta-analysis of treatment effects is once again instructive. In their study of nearly 70 studies that collectively examined 22,181 offenders, offenders exposed to organic treatment—specifically, surgical castration and hormonal interventions—had significantly reduced odds of sexual recidivism compared to controls. In particular, surgical castration evinced the strongest effect of any treatment examined in the meta-analysis. A later review included these same studies but better controlled for confounding factors. Here again in this more sophisticated analysis, surgical castration and hormonal treatment exhibited the strongest effects on desistance compared to other treatments (Schmucker & Lösel, 2008).

One other review concluded that anti-androgen treatment combined with selective serotonin reuptake inhibitor treatment (SSRIs) may be the most effective combination to treat deviant sexual behavior in sex offenders with paraphilic disorders (Garcia, Garcia, Assumpção, & Thibaut, 2013). Thus, the study poses a host of implications for more effective use of chemical castration in the future.

There are of course caveats to these conclusions. First, hormonal interventions are typically combined with other forms of treatment (Schmucker & Lösel, 2008). Thus, it is difficult to assess the extent to which purely hormonal treatment affects recidivism vis-à-vis other interventions. Relatedly, future investigation is needed to determine the impacts of chemical castration treatment using randomly derived samples. Currently, offenders may either opt to undergo chemical castration as part of a treatment program, or they are required to do so as a condition of release. Thus, extant evaluation studies have tested the impacts of castration on potentially biased samples. Rice and Harris (2011) recommend that ideally impact evaluations use randomly derived samples of offenders and blind research designs to test the effects of castration on recidivism. In their view, this would go a long way in ensuring any significant effect of castration is due to actual impacts and not to other effects. For example, by randomly selecting participants to either the "treatment" or "control" group, evaluations can better account for "self-selection" effects—whereby significant initial differences between the two groups impact results, and not the treatment itself. A double blind research design (where neither researchers nor participants are aware of who is in the treatment versus control group) ensures that any observed effects are due to an actual impact of the treatment and not to "placebo" effects—or instances where offenders knowingly undergoing treatment alter their behavior, and so any effects are due to that behavioral change and not the actual intervention (Rice & Harris, 2011).

A separate caveat involves ethical concerns regarding castration as a treatment or punishment. A multitude of ethical issues concerning the treatment have been identified. Indeed, some view chemical castration as unconstitutional when it is used as a condition of release (Simpson, 2006). Others emphasize that offenders undergoing chemical castration may develop health conditions in the future, such as increased risk for breathing difficulties, migraine headaches, gastrointestinal problems, diabetes, hypertension, and thrombosis, which may potentially lead to cardiac arrest (Appel, 2012). For these reasons, some scholars caution against the use of chemical castration for sex offenders (Stinneford, 2006).

The use of medical interventions for treating sex offenders brings with it a host of questions and concerns. There is a clear need for systematic research centered on understanding the impacts of chemical castration. At the same time, preliminary findings indicate that chemical castration may be a promising tool in the sex offender treatment arsenal. Accordingly, the following observation made by Schmucker and Lösel (2008, p. 16) is noteworthy, "[O]ne can only say that abandoning this approach without closer inspection may not be in the best interest of society nor the most serious sex offenders ... it is necessary to collect more solid knowledge on circumstances and modes that may prove such a treatment to be reasonable."

Reentry Strategies

A separate issue involves reentry. Nearly 90 percent of offenders, including those who have committed sex crimes, will return to communities after incarceration (Hughes & Wilson, 2002; Washington Department of Corrections, 2013). Recognizing the reentry needs of ex-offenders, in 2007, the U.S. Congress created a first-of-its-kind reentry law, the Second Chance Act. The law authorizes nearly $200 million to states and local government for the creation of specific programs that assist released offenders with transitional needs — such as providing job training and placement, transitional housing, and other services. However, sex offenders are specifically excluded from the legislation (Willis, Levenson, & Ward, 2010). Indeed, beyond programs funded by the Second Chance Act, sex offenders are often not permitted from enrolling in state-level reentry initiatives (see e.g., Duwe, 2013, p. 372 discussing that a prior sex offense served as "exclusionary" criteria for a reentry program in Minnesota; see also, S. X. Zhang, Roberts, & Callanan relaying that the California reentry program they evaluated excluded convicted sex offenders, p. 556).

This exclusion is striking because reentry interventions have been shown to enhance successful sex offender reintegration, albeit in a small body of research. Using a quasi-experimental design, Bouffard and Bergeron (2006) evaluated the efficacy of a reentry program on recidivism among offenders (including sex offenders) in North Dakota. The program was tailored to address offenders' unique needs through a series of assessments made prior to release. Generally, the program assisted offenders with developing job skills, finding suitable housing, and improving their health issues. On average, offenders who received the services, compared to controls were 60 percent less likely to reoffend over a 17 month period.

One other program created in Minnesota, "Circles of Support and Accountability" (Mn-COSA), was recently evaluated by Duwe (2013). Grounded in the restorative justice model and COSA programs in Canada, the MnCOSA was one of the first of its kind to be implemented in the U.S. Its mission is to improve offender outcomes, particularly the reduction of recidivism, by providing newly released offenders with "circles," or groups of community volunteers who meet with the offender and support him/her during the transition to the community. In the program evaluated by Duwe (2013), offenders convicted of a prior sex offense and nearing completion of their prison sentence were assigned to either an experimental (i.e., participated in MnCOSA) or control (i.e., did not participate in the program) group. Experimental designs are typically considered the "gold standard" in evaluation research because they ensure any differences between the experimental and control groups are due to random chance and not underlying differences. Thus, any perceived benefit of the program should be due solely to the intervention and not the result of other factors. Overall, Duwe's (2013) results indicate that participation in MnCOSA significantly reduced the likelihood of new rearrests, technical violation revocations, and reincarcerations. Additionally, a cost-benefit analysis of the program was conducted. Findings suggest that the use of MnCOSA for select sex offenders results in a savings of close to $12,000 per participant. To be sure, as Duwe (2013) has noted, future studies using longer follow-up periods and larger samples will need to carefully measure the effects of COSA programs in other settings. Even so, his study is one of the first to demonstrate the potential of COSA interventions to reduce sex offending in the U.S.

Given these promising results, some scholars have argued that other reentry services, such as those offered under the national Second Chance Act, should apply to sex offenders (Willis et al., 2010). They point to research showing sex offenders have additional reentry needs exacerbated by the collateral consequences of sex crime laws. Sex offenders experience what Travis (2005) has termed "invisible punishment." For instance, per federal law, released sex offenders are subject to registry and community notification requirements. Additionally, depending on the state, offenders may also be required to abide by residence and employment restrictions. Recent evaluations suggest that the reentry needs of sex offenders are greater than those of non-sex offenders. To illustrate, residence restrictions—enacted by a majority of states—limit the availability of legal housing for sex offenders. As a result, affected offenders have experienced displacement (Burchfield & Mingus, 2008). Barnes and his colleagues (2009) analyzed the impact of boundary restrictions on sex offenders' ability to find housing in South Carolina. Their results indicate that longer residence boundaries beyond 1,000 feet—in effect in some places and frequently being considered by a number of states and counties—significantly diminish access to legally permissible housing for sex offenders. Socia (2011) demonstrated that residence restriction laws hold the potential to displace sex offenders to rural areas where access to social supports, treatment, and public transportation is limited. In a separate analysis, Levenson and Cotter (2005a) evaluated the extent to which registered sex offenders living in Florida are displaced once they establish residency. Their study did not focus on residence restrictions per se, but whether external factors were associated with housing difficulties. Over one-third of the sample reported having to relocate because either a landlord found out about their registration status (15 percent) or because neighbors complained about them (20 percent).

Concomitantly, convicted sex offenders report having difficulties securing employment given their registered sex offender status (Tewksbury & Lees, 2006). For example, one study examining sex offender experiences in Kentucky found that a significant proportion have experienced employment difficulties, such as loss of job (43 percent) or denial of promotion at work (23 percent; Tewksbury, 2005; see also Levenson, D'Amora, & Hern, 2007 finding similar results). A separate investigation evaluated the collateral consequences of Internet restrictions for sex offenders in New Jersey. Approximately 4 in 10 offenders reported that the most significant loss was difficulty finding and applying for employment (Tewksbury & Zgoba, 2010).

Beyond housing and employment difficulties, nearly half of all registrants will experience physical or verbal harassment from the public, and approximately one in ten will be victims of actual physical violence (Mercado, Alvarez, & Levenson, 2008). In Levenson and Cotter's (2005a) analysis of sex offenders living in Florida (n=183), 33 percent of registrants reported being threatened or harassed by neighbors, 5 percent were physically assaulted or injured because of their status, and 21 percent reported property damage in retaliation for being a sex offender. Harassment in some instances has extended to registrants' family members and associates. Levenson and Cotter (2005a) relayed that 19 percent of the sex offenders in their sample reported that someone living with them has been threatened, harassed, or assaulted by the public due to their registrant status.

There is the growing concern that unintended effects go beyond merely making life difficult for sex offenders. A larger reentry literature has identified homelessness as a significant predictor of future offending (Roman & Travis, 2004). Employment instability has been linked to sex offender recidivism (Hanson & Morton-Bourgon, 2004). Few studies have evaluated the direct impact of experiencing harassment on future sex offending, but some have demonstrated that a loss of social support reduces desistance from crime (Hanson & A. J. R. Harris, 1998, 2001). Results from Levenson and Cotter's (2005a, p. 58) survey of convicted sex offenders indicate that registration may entice offenders to recidivate. In that study, most offenders agreed that the collateral consequences of registration "interferes with my recovery" (71 percent), and that they had "less hope for the future now that I will be a registered sex offender for life" (72 percent). And finally, nearly half of the sample endorsed the view that "no one believes I can change so why even try?"

Given these potentially criminogenic impacts, one policy recommendation is to develop reentry services that better address the transitional needs of sex offenders. This means focusing federal efforts on providing additional reentry services, not fewer, to sex offenders in an effort to mitigate the collateral consequences of sex crime laws. As written, the Second Chance Act is not explicit about the logic to exclude sex offenders. It may be that the decision to exclude such offenders stems from the belief that they are not "rehabilitatable" and so, current efforts exclude them. Or, perhaps, there is concern that the public will not support such efforts. It is true as Mancini (in press) demonstrated, that the public—stakeholders in criminal justice policy—have expressed little concern about some of the collateral consequences of popular laws despite their potentially negative effects on public safety. Even so, on balance research indicates sex offenders can be effectively treated (Hanson et al., 2009), and that most will desist from sex crime after their initial offense (Piquero et al., 2012). Despite this well established empirical finding, media accounts tend to perpetuate myths about sex offending (Galeste et al., 2012), such as the view that all sex offenders are predatory and homicidal, and so, the public is presented with a rather distorted portrait of the reality of sex offending. Accordingly, Meloy, Curtis, and Boatwright's (2013, p. 449) recommendation is on-point, "scholars and academic institutions could prioritize and become more savvy at 'marketing' their scientific outcomes ... researchers need to disseminate findings beyond the relatively small and isolated academic community that is the typical consumer ... [a]nd we need to make this information understandable, interesting, and relevant to society much the same way that new health information, published in scholarly medical journals, is currently considered 'newsworthy...'" Under this logic, the challenge thus lies in developing new efforts to effectively educate the American public and lawmakers about the unintended effects of prominent sex offender laws and promising advances to rectify and address them. Table 12.2 outlines treatment and reentry strategies discussed here. The third and final section examines considerations related to restricting sex offender registration for certain offenders.

Registration Restrictions

Since its initial inception in the mid-1990s, sex offender registries have expanded to include a wide range of offenders. As noted previously, some states mandate that offenders with no sex crime convictions preemptively register. Additionally, juvenile offenders who have committed non-contact sex crimes appear beside those who have been convicted of violent and predatory sex offenses. This expansion clearly highlights the increased concern about sex offending, and those factors that presumably might contribute to it (e.g., prior

Table 12.2. Future Policy Considerations: Treatment and Reentry Interventions

Policy Consideration	Reasons for Focus
Pursue Effective Treatment for Sex Offenders	• Cognitive behavioral treatment and hormonal interventions are two of the most effective sex offender treatments. • Both types of treatment have strengths and drawbacks. • Greater research examining them is needed. • Even so, they remain among the two most empirically validated approaches and thus should be considered for sex offender management.
Reentry Strategies	• Most offenders, including sex offenders, will be released from prison and will return to the community. • Because specific post-incarceration laws exist solely for sex offenders (registration, notification, residence restrictions), they face additional reentry challenges. • However, federal reentry legislation specifically precludes sex offenders from receiving reentry interventions. • Promising reentry programs exist. • Since sex offender reentry is compounded by "invisible punishment," greater reentry efforts should be considered.

burglary convictions). However, there is the concern that "widening the net" may have unintended consequences that diminish any potential deterrent effects of sex crime laws. Below, I argue that the final policy recommendation to "narrow the net," might be considered to better allocate resources to address the most serious sex crimes. In particular, I discuss gateway legislation and restricted registration for certain offenses committed by juveniles.

Further Examine the Impacts of Gateway Legislation

First, the logic underlying the proposal to extend registration to non-sex offenders, "gateway legislation," should be subjected to careful empirical analysis before any such laws are widely implemented. As early as 2003, Sample and Bray observed that the preemptive laws being considered in some states which mandate registration of those who have committed burglary offenses may be misguided. The researchers question whether predicate legislation is evidence-based given that in their study only a tiny fraction (2 percent) of those who committed burglary offenses went on to commit a sex-related offense.

Instead, concerns have mounted regarding the potential for labeling to occur as a result of such efforts. That is, offenders convicted of non-sex crimes who are preemptively required to register as sex offenders might in fact amplify their offending to fit their new role of registered sex offender (see generally, Winick, 1998). Relatedly, other scholars have pointed to the increased collateral consequences — as discussed above — that might follow, and in turn, might contribute to increased sexual recidivism. Finally, including ever-more offenders, per Tewksbury and Jennings (2010, p. 580), "produces unnecessarily large lists of individuals … the sheer length [of which] is likely to lead the public to feel both unnecessarily unsafe and that there are simply too many sex offenders in their communities of which they need to be aware." Even so, as Sample and Bray's (2003) analysis indicates gateway legislation is being pursued by some states. At the same time, SORNA—federal legislation designed to standardize registries and notification systems—includes provisions that mandate the addition of certain non-sex crimes to registerable offenses (e.g., kidnap/false imprisonment offenses). Discussed previously in Chapter 11, these laws—including one in Georgia—have met with little judicial challenge, and so, it may be that an increasing number of states implement them in the future. However, the disadvantages of this approach, in the form of labeling, collateral consequences, and the substantial increase in the number of offenders who will now appear on the registry (see e.g., Tewksbury & Jennings, 2010) might very well outweigh any perceived benefit. At the same time, it is unclear how many offenders—currently registered nationally—are affected by gateway legislation. Accordingly, future efforts that evaluate the possible impact of these new measures should be pursued prior to the national implementation of them.

Decriminalization of Certain Juvenile Sex Crimes

In addition to a greater examination of the impact of gateway offense legislation, there should be consideration of "Romeo and Juliet" exemptions, which exclude registration for statutory rape offenders where the victim and offender are close in age. Although the exact extent of the number of registered statutory rape offenders nationally is unknown, one study reported that up to 2,000 teens appeared on the Illinois state registry in 2011 (Beck & Boys, in press). These crimes would otherwise not be criminalized less the relatively small difference in age between offender and victim (Cocca, 2004).

Scholars have outlined reasons for why states have "gotten tough" on statutory rape offenders in recent years. For instance, federal legislation enacted in the mid-1990s encouraged states to reduce teen pregnancy by implementing tougher sanctions for statutory rape in an attempt to decrease reliance on welfare benefits for unwed teen mothers (Koon-Magnin, Kreager, & Ruback, 2010). Beck and Boys (in press, p. 2) explain the detrimental effects of such efforts, "through the application of statutory rape laws, states, at best, may merely be transferring social costs from one government entity (aid for dependent children) to another (corrections) … using this strategy may not reduce teen pregnancy and may be creating an additional tax burden through the increased correctional costs of criminalizing teen romances." At the same time, mandatory registration for statutory rape offenders has the potential to "dilute" the registry. As Tewksbury and Jennings (2010) have noted in their study, registries with large numbers of offenders—such as non-violent statutory rape offenders—may overwhelm the public in their prevention efforts and unnecessarily perpetuate fear regarding one's actual risk of sexual victimization.

Recognizing these potential unintended effects, some states have implemented "Romeo and Juliet" exemptions to statutory rape statutes. Recall as discussed in Chapter 1 that Georgia was one of the first states to do so. The laws are designed to decriminalize acts in cases where consensual sexual activity occurs between two young people. The federal government includes a provision in SORNA that does not require states to implement registry procedures for statutory rape offenders (particularly when "consensual" sexual activity occurs between a victim who is at least 13 years old and an offender who is no more than four years older than the victim). However, this is far from being standard practice as most states have not sufficiently enacted provisions of SORNA and also because the law does not mandate that states include exemptions.

Relatedly, there are other crimes committed by juveniles which often involve consensual relationships. As previous chapters have reviewed "sexting" offenses can carry with them child pornography charges. One study reported that despite the potential for criminal sanctions, sexting is not atypical among teens (Temple et al., 2012). It found that nearly 30 percent of high school students have sent sexually explicit images of themselves to others. Additionally, 31 percent of students admitted requesting a "sext" from another student. Not least, the study also revealed that most students—60 percent—had been solicited by their peers to share a nude image.

Perhaps recognizing that "sexting" offenses differ from other child pornography crimes, some states—but not all—have begun to move toward introducing legislation that would decriminalize these acts (Wolak & Finkelhor, 2011). However, some states have retained tough child pornography laws and have prosecuted teens under them—even in cases of sexting—perhaps in an effort to deter minors from taking part in sexting, and to avoid the harms of such acts (Lampe, 2013), such as the potential for exploitation. Prosecutions for sexting crimes under existing child pornography statutes typically trigger registration requirements, even for juveniles. And so, the same net widening problem evident for statutory rape offenses arises here. Policymakers thus might want to consider the strengths and drawbacks of applying registration to juveniles who have committed offenses that involve either consensual acts or behaviors that appear to be acceptable in the teenage community. This is not to suggest that some sexting acts—particularly where images are distributed without consent of the creator—are undeserving of punishment, but rather that applying sex offender registration to such cases carries with it a number of unintended effects that should be further explored. Table 12.3 briefly reviews registration restrictions. The text concludes in the final section.

Table 12.3. Future Policy Considerations: Registration Restrictions

Policy Consideration	Reasons for Focus
Greater Examination of Gateway Legislation	• Predicate legislation is being considered by states nationally. • It is unclear the extent to which non-sex offenders appear on registries. • Extending registries to non-sex offenders may have negative effects such as net-widening, and specifically, labeling, collateral consequences, and the potential for registries to be "diluted." • Thus, a greater examination of the effects of these laws is needed before they are implemented nationally.
Decriminalize Certain Sex Crimes Committed by Juveniles	• Juveniles who have committed statutory rape offenses and "sexting" crimes appear on sex offender registries alongside predatory and violent adult offenders. • The number of statutory rape offenders is unkown nationally; prevalence statistics for sexting offenses indicate that nearly 60 percent of teens have either sent or solicited sexually explicit images. • Scholars have argued that these offenses are distinct from sex offenses involving adult offenders and non-consenting victims. • Thus, one policy recommendation is to reconsider registration for acts that appear relatively acceptable among teens.

Concluding Comments

The text has taken a critical look at the nature, extent, and causes of sexual offending, societal reactions to sexual deviance, and the numerous policy responses developed to prevent sex crime. Its goal was to highlight the complex issues surrounding the sex offender debate. It has argued that moving beyond simplistic perceptions of sex crime and offenders is needed for policies built on solid empirical ground. On the one hand, the preceding chapters indicate cause for pessimism regarding sex crime and sex offender laws, particularly the extent to which they continue to be shaped by overly simplistic misperceptions of sex offending. But it also—as this last chapter shows—can be viewed as a cause for optimism in the future. If anything, the greater attention to sexual violence in the form of sex crime laws highlights the premium we have placed on the rights and dignity of all Americans, particularly for vulnerable populations such as children. Without question, the issue has united lawmakers, policymakers, and the general public in a quest to ensure greater accountability of sex offenders and to develop better prevention efforts to enhance public safety. In the same way that this drive has contributed to well-intentioned, but flawed policies, it can also direct evidence-based laws that better address and prevent a very serious crime that impacts all of society. Accomplishing this goal, however, requires the start of earnest discussions and debates that account for the full spectrum of complex issues related to sex offending and our responses to reduce it.

Bibliography

Abel, G. G., Becker, J. V., & Skinner, L. J. (1980). Aggressive behavior and sex. *Psychiatric Clinics of North America, 3,* 133-151.

Abel, G. G., Gore, D. K., Holland, C. L., Camp, N., Becker, J. V., & Rathner, B. A. (1989). The measurement of the cognitive distortions of child molesters. *Annals of Sex Research, 2,* 135-153.

Abel, G. G., Mittleman, M. S., & Becker, J. V. (1985). Sexual offenders: Results of assessment and recommendations for treatment. In M. R. Ben-Aron, S. J. Huckle, & C. D. Webster (Eds.), *Clinical criminology: The assessment and treatment of criminal behavior* (pp. 191-205). Toronto: M & M Graphic Ltd.

Abracen, J., & Looman, J. (2006). Evaluation of civil commitment criteria in a high risk sample of sexual offenders. *Journal of Sexual Offender Civil Commitment: Science and the Law, 1,* 124-140.

Abrahamsen, D. (1960). *The psychology of crime.* New York: Columbia University Press.

Ackerman, A. R., Sacks, M., & Greenberg, D. F. (2012). Legislation targeting sex offenders: Are recent policies effective in reducing rape? *Justice Quarterly, 29,* 858-887.

Adam Walsh Child Protection and Safety Act, Public Law 109-248 (2006).

Addington, L. A., & Rennison, C. M. (2008). Rape co-occurrence: Do additional crimes affect victim reporting and police clearance of rape? *Journal of Quantitative Criminology, 24,* 205-226.

Administration for Children and Families. (2012). *Mandatory reporters of child abuse and neglect.* Washington, D.C.: Author.

Ahlmeyer, S., English, K., & Simons, D. (1999). *The impact of polygraphy on admissions of crossover offending behavior in adult sexual offenders.* Presentation at the Association for the Treatment of Sexual Abusers 18th Annual Research and Treatment Conference, Lake Buena Vista, FL.

Ahlmeyer, S., Heil, P., McKee, B., & English, K. (2000). The impact of polygraphy on admissions of victims and offenses in adult sexual offenders. *Sexual Abuse: A Journal of Research and Treatment, 12,* 123-138.

Aigner, M., Eher, R., Fruehwald, S., Frottier, P., Gutierrez-Lobos, K., & Dwyer, S. M. (2000). Brain abnormalities and violent behavior. *Journal of Psychology & Human Sexuality, 11,* 57-64.

Akers, R. L. (1985). *Deviant behavior: A social learning approach.* Belmont, CA: Wadsworth/Cengage.

Akers, R. L., & Sellers, C. (2004). *Criminological theories: Introduction, evaluation, and application* (4th ed.). Los Angeles: Roxbury.

Alder, C. (1985). Exploration of self-reported sexually aggressive behavior. *Crime & Delinquency, 31,* 306-331.

Alexy, E. M., Burgess, A. W., & Baker, T. (2005). Internet offenders: Traders, travelers, and combination trader-travelers. *Journal of Interpersonal Violence, 20*, 804-812.

Allen, M., D'Alessio, D., & Emmers-Sommer, T. M. (2000). Reactions of criminal sexual offenders to pornography: A meta-analytic summary. In M. Roloff (Ed.), *Communication yearbook 22* (pp. 139-169). Thousand Oaks, CA: Sage.

Alvarez, K. M., Donohue, B., Kenny, M. C., Cavanagh, N., & Romero, V. (2005). The process and consequences of reporting child maltreatment: A brief overview for professionals in the mental health field. *Aggression and Violent Behavior, 10*, 311-331.

American Psychiatric Association. (2000). *Diagnostic and statistical manual of mental disorders* (4th ed.). Washington, D.C.: Author.

Anderson, A. L., Evans, M. K., & Sample, L. L. (2009). Who accesses the sex offender registries? A look at legislative intent and citizen action in Nebraska. *Criminal Justice Studies, 22*, 313-329.

Anderson, A. L., & Sample, L. L. (2008). Public awareness and action resulting from sex offender community notification laws. *Criminal Justice Policy Review, 19*, 371-396.

Appel, J. M. (2012). Castration anxiety: Physicians, "Do no harm," and chemical sterilization laws. *Journal of Bioethical Inquiry, 9*, 85-91.

Appelbaum, P., Saleh, F. M., Grudzinskas, A. J., Bradford, J. M., & Brodsky, D. J. (Eds.). (2009). *Sex offenders: Identification, risk assessment, treatment, and legal issues.* New York: Oxford University Press.

Applegate, B. K., Cullen, F. T., & Fisher, B. S. (2002). Public views toward crime and correctional policies: Is there a gender gap? *Journal of Criminal Justice, 30*, 89-100.

Araji, S. (1997). *Sexually aggressive children: Coming to understand them.* Thousand Oaks, CA: Sage.

Archer, R. P., Buffington-Vollum, J. K., Stredny, R. V., & Handel, R. W. (2006). A survey of psychological test use patterns among forensic psychologists. *Journal of Personality Assessment, 87*, 84-94.

Armstrong, G. S., & Freeman, B. C. (2011). Examining GPS monitoring alerts triggered by sex offenders: The divergence of legislative goals and practical application in community corrections. *Journal of Criminal Justice, 39*, 175-182.

Aromaki, A. S., Lindman, R. E., & Eriksson, C. J. P. (2002). Testosterone, sexuality, and antisocial personality in rapists and child molesters: A pilot study. *Psychiatry Research, 110*, 239-247.

Avrahamian, K. A. (1998). A critical perspective: Do "Megan's Laws" really shield children from sex-predators? *Journal of Juvenile Law, 19*, 301-317.

Babchishin, K. M., Blais, J., & Helmus, L. M. (2012). Do static risk factors predict differently for Aboriginal sex offenders? A multi-site comparison using the original and revised Static-99 and Static-2002 scales. *Canadian Journal of Criminology and Criminal Justice, 54*, 1-43.

Bachman, R. (1993). Predicting the reporting of rape victimizations: Have rape reforms made a difference? *Criminal Justice and Behavior, 20*, 254-270.

Bachman, R. (1998). The factors related to rape reporting behavior and arrest: New evidence from the National Crime Victimization Survey. *Criminal Justice and Behavior, 25*, 8- 29.

Bachman, R., & Saltzman, L. E. (1995). *Violence against women: Estimates from the redesigned survey.* Washington, D.C.: Bureau of Justice Statistics.

Bain, J., Langevin, R., Hucker, S., Dickey, R., Wright, P., & Schonberg, C. (1988). Sex hormones in pedophiles: I baseline values of six hormones; II the gonadotropin releasing hormone test. *Annals of Sex Research, 1*, 443-454.

Baker, K. K. (1997). Once a rapist? Motivational evidence and relevancy in rape law. *Harvard Law Review, 110*, 563-623.

Bandy, R. (2011). Measuring the impact of sex offender notification on community adoption of protective behaviors. *Criminology & Public Policy, 10*, 237-263.

Barnes, J. C. (2011). Place a moratorium on the passage of sex offender residence restriction laws. *Criminology & Public Policy, 10*, 401-409.

Barnes, J. C., Dukes, T., Tewksbury, R., & De Troye, T. M. (2009). Analyzing the impact of a statewide residence restriction law on South Carolina sex offenders. *Criminal Justice Policy Review, 20*, 21-43.

Barnett-Ryan, C. (2007). Introduction to the Uniform Crime Reporting Program. In J. P. Lynch & L. A. Addington (Eds.), *Understanding crime incidence statistics: Revisiting the divergence of the NCVS and the UCR* (pp. 55-92). New York: Cambridge University Press.

Baumer, E. P. (2004). *Temporal variation in the likelihood of police notification by victims of rapes, 1973-2000.* Washington, D.C.: U.S. Department of Justice.

Baumer, E. P., Felson, R. B., & Messner, S. F. (2003). Changes in police notification for rape, 1973-2000. *Criminology, 41*, 841-873.

Baumer, E. P., Messner, S. F., & Rosenfeld, R. (2003). Explaining spatial variation in support for capital punishment: A multilevel analysis. *American Journal of Sociology, 108*, 844-875.

Bauserman, R. (1996). Sexual aggression and pornography: A review of correlational research. *Basic and Applied Social Psychology, 18*, 405-428.

Beauregard, E., & Lieb, R. (2011). Sex offenders and sex offender policy. In J. Q. Wilson & J. Petersilia (Eds.), *Crime and public policy* (2nd ed., pp. 345-367). New York: Oxford University Press.

Beck, A. J., & Shipley, B. E. (1989). *Recidivism of prisoners released in 1983.* Washington, D.C.: Bureau of Justice Statistics.

Beck, V. S., & Boys, S. (in press). Romeo & Juliet: Star-crossed lovers or sex offenders? *Criminal Justice Policy Review.*

Beck, V. S., Clingermayer, J., Ramsey, R. J., & Travis, L. F. (2004). Community response to sex offenders. *Journal of Psychiatry & Law, 32*, 141-168.

Beck, V. S., & Travis, L. F. (2004). Sex offender notification and protective behavior. *Violence and Victims, 19*, 289-302.

Beck, V. S., & Travis, L. F. (2005). Sex offender notification: An exploratory assessment of state variation in notification processes. *Journal of Criminal Justice, 34*, 51-55.

Beckett, K., & Western, B. (2001). Governing social marginality: Welfare, incarceration, and the transformation of state policy. *Punishment and Society, 3*, 43-59.

Beech, A. R., Parrett, N., Ward, T., & Fisher, D. (2009). Assessing female sexual offenders' motivations and cognitions: An exploratory study. *Psychology, Crime, & Law, 15*, 201-216.

Belknap, J. (2007). *The invisible woman: Gender, crime, and justice* (3rd ed.). Belmont, CA: Wadsworth/Cengage.

Belluck, P. (2012, August 20). Health experts dismiss assertions on rape. *New York Times*, p. A13.

Ben-Veniste, R. (1971). *Pornography and sex crime: The Danish experience.* Technical reports of the Commission on Obscenity and Pornography (no. 7). Washington, D.C.: U.S. Government Printing Office.

Birgden, A., & Cucolo, H. (2011). The treatment of sex offenders: Evidence, ethics, and human rights. *Sexual Abuse: A Journal of Research and Treatment, 23*, 295-313.

Biskupic, J. (2008, June 26). Justices reject death penalty for child rapists: Court limits use of capital punishment. *USA Today*, p. A4.

Black, M. C., Basile, K. C., Breiding, M. J., Smith, S. G., Walters, M. L., Merrick, M. T., Chen, J., & Stevens, M. R. (2011). *The National Intimate Partner and Sexual Violence Survey (NISVS): 2010 summary report.* Atlanta: National Center for Injury Prevention and Control, Centers for Disease Control and Prevention.

Blalock, H. M. (1967). *Toward a theory of minority-group relations.* New York: Capricorn Books.

Blanchard, R., Cantor, J. M., & Robichaud, L. K. (2006). Biological factors in the development of sexual deviance and aggression in males. In H. E. Barbaree & W. L. Marshall (Eds.), *The juvenile sex offender* (2nd ed., pp. 77-104). New York: Guilford.

Blanchard, R., Kolla, N. J., Cantor, J. M., Klassen, P. E., Dickey, R., Kuban, M. E., & Blak, T. (2007). IQ, handedness, and pedophilia in adult male patients stratified by referral source. *Sexual Abuse: A Journal of Research and Treatment, 19*, 285-309.

Blecker, E. T., & Murnen, S. K. (2005). Fraternity membership, the display of degrading sexual images of women, and rape myth acceptance. *Sex Roles, 53*, 487-493.

Block, S. (2006). *Rape and sexual power in early America.* Chapel Hill: University of North Carolina Press.

Blood, P., Watson, L., & Stageberg, P. (2008). *State legislation, monitoring report: FY 2007.* Des Moines: Iowa Department of Human Rights.

Blumstein, A., & Wallman, J. (Eds.). (2006). *The crime drop in America* (2nd ed.). New York: Cambridge University Press.

Boccaccini, M. T., Murrie, D. C., Caperton, J. D., & Hawes, S. W. (2009). Field validity of the STATIC-99 and MnSOST-R among sex offenders evaluated for civil commitment as sexually violent predators. *Psychology, Public Policy, and Law, 15*, 278-314.

Bogaert, A. (2001). Handedness, criminality, and sexual offending. *Neuropsychologia, 39*, 465-469.

Bohner, G., Reinhard, M. A., Rutz, S., Sturm, S., Kerschbaum, B., & Effler, D. (1998). Rape myths as neutralizing cognitions: Evidence for a causal impact of anti-victim attitudes on men's self-reported likelihood of raping. *European Journal of Social Psychology, 28*, 257-268.

Bonnar-Kidd, K. K. (2010). Sexual offender laws and prevention of sexual violence or recidivism. *American Journal of Public Health, 100*, 412-419.

Bouffard, J. A., & Bergeron, L. E. (2007). Reentry works: The implementation and effectiveness of a serious and violent offender reentry initiative. *Journal of Offender Rehabilitation, 44*, 1-29.

Bouffard, L. A. (2010). Exploring the utility of entitlement in understanding sexual aggression. *Journal of Criminal Justice, 38*, 870-879.

Bourke, M. L., & Hernandez, A. E. (2009). The "Butner Study" redux: A report of the incidence of hands-on child victimization by child pornography offenders. *Journal of Family Violence, 24,* 183-191.

Braet, C., Tanghe, A., Decaluwé, V., Moens, E., & Rosseel, Y. (2004). Inpatient treatment for children with obesity: Weight loss, psychological well-being, and eating behavior. *Journal of Pediatric Psychology, 29,* 519-529.

Brannon, Y. N., Levenson, J. S., Fortney, T., & Baker, J. N. (2007). Attitudes about community notification: A comparison of sexual offenders and the non-offending public. *Sexual Abuse: A Journal of Research and Treatment, 19,* 369-379.

Brecklin, L. R. (2007). Evaluation outcomes of self-defense training for women: A review. *Aggression and Violent Behavior, 13,* 60-76.

Brecklin, L. R., & Forde, D. R. (2001). A meta-analysis of rape education programs. *Violence and Victims, 16,* 303-321.

Brecklin, L. R., & Ullman, S. E. (2005). Self-defense or assertiveness training and women's responses to sexual attacks. *Journal of Interpersonal Violence, 20,* 738-762.

Brown, S. (1999). Public attitudes toward the treatment of sex offenders. *Legal and Criminological Psychology, 4,* 239-252.

Brownmiller, S. (1975). *Against our will.* New York: Simon and Schuster.

Bufkin, J., & Eschholz, S. (2000). Images of sex and rape: A content analysis of popular film. *Violence Against Women, 6,* 1317-1344.

Burchfield, K. B. (2011). Residence restrictions. *Criminology & Public Policy, 10,* 411-419.

Burchfield, K. B., & Mingus, W. (2008). Not in my neighborhood: Assessing registered sex offenders' experiences with local social capital and social control. *Criminal Justice and Behavior, 35,* 356-374.

Bureau of Justice Statistics. (2012). *Survey methodology for criminal victimization in the United States.* Washington, D.C.: Author.

Bureau of Justice Statistics. (2013). *National Crime Victimization Survey Victimization analysis tool.* Washington, D.C.: Author.

Burt, M. R. (1980). Cultural myths and supports for rape. *Journal of Personality and Social Psychology, 38,* 217-230.

Burton, D., Miller, D., & Shill, C. T. (2002). A social learning theory comparison of the sexual victimization of adolescent sexual offenders and non-sexual offending male delinquents. *Child Abuse and Neglect, 26,* 893-907.

Burton, D., Nesmith, A., & Badten, L. (1997). Clinicians' views of sexually aggressive children: A theoretical exploration. *Child Abuse and Neglect, 21,* 157-170.

Button, D. M., Tewksbury, R., Mustaine, E. E., & Payne, B. K. (2013). Factors contributing to perceptions about policies regarding the electronic monitoring of sex offenders: The role of demographic characteristics, victimization experiences, and social disorganization. *International Journal of Offender Therapy and Comparative Criminology, 57,* 25-54.

Campus Sex Crimes Prevention Act (CSCPA), Public Law 106-386 (2000).

Cantor, J. M., Blanchard, R., Robichaud, L. K., & Christensen, B. K. (2005). Quantitative reanalysis of aggregate data on IQ in sexual offenders. *Psychological Bulletin, 131,* 555-568.

Cantor, J. M., Klassen, P. E., Dickey, R., Christensen, B. K., Kuban, M. E., Blak, T., Williams, N. S., & Blanchard, R. (2005). Handedness in pedophilia and hebephilia. *Archives of Sexual Behavior, 34*, 447-459.

Caputo, A. A., & Brodsky, S. L. (2004). Citizen coping with community notification of released sex offenders. *Behavioral Sciences & the Law, 22*, 239-252.

Carpenter, C. L. (2010). Legislative epidemics: A cautionary tale of criminal laws that have swept the country. *Buffalo Law Review, 58*, 1-67.

Carson, E. A., & Sabol, W. J. (2012). *Prisoners in 2011*. Washington, D.C.: Bureau of Justice Statistics.

Center for Sex Offender Management. (1999). *Sex offender registration: Policy overview and comprehensive practices*. Silver Spring, MD: Author.

Center for Sex Offender Management. (2007). *Female sex offenders*. Silver Spring, MD: Author.

Center for Sex Offender Management. (2008). *Legislative trends in sex offender management*. Silver Spring, MD: Author.

Chaffin, M., Letourneau, E. J., & Silovsky, J. F. (2002). Adults, adolescents, and children who sexually abuse children: A developmental perspective. In J. E. B. Myers, L. Berliner, J. Briere, C. T. Hendrix, C. Jenny,. & T. A. Reid (Eds.), *The APSAC handbook on child maltreatment* (2nd ed., pp. 205-232). Thousand Oaks, CA: Sage.

Chaffin, M., Levenson, J., Letourneau, E. J., & Stern, P. (2009). How safe are trick-or-treaters? An analysis of child sex crime rates on Halloween. *Sexual Abuse: A Journal of Research and Treatment, 21*, 363-374.

Child Pornography Prevention Act (CPPA), Public Law 104-208 (1996).

Chiricos, T., Padgett, K., Bratton, J., Pickett, J. T., & Gertz, M. (2012). Racial threat and opposition to the re-enfranchisement of ex-felons. *International Journal of Criminology and Sociology 1*, 13-28.

Christopher, R. L., & Christopher, K. H. (2012). The paradox of statutory rape. *Indiana Law Journal, 87*, 506-549.

Chu, M. C., Ng, K., Fong, J., & Teoh, J. (2012). Assessing youth who sexually offended: The predictive validity of the ERASOR, J-SOAP-II, and the YLS/CMI in a non-western context. *Sexual Abuse: A Journal of Research and Treatment, 24*, 153-174.

Church, W., Sun, F., & Li, X. (2011). Attitudes toward the treatment of sex offenders: A SEM analysis. *Journal of Forensic Social Work, 1*, 82-95.

Clay-Warner, J., & Burt, C. H. (2005). Rape reporting after reforms: Have times really changed? *Violence Against Women, 11*, 150-176.

Cocca, C. E. (2004). *Jailbait: The politics of statutory rape laws in the United States*. Albany, NY: SUNY Press.

Cohen, M., & Jeglic, E. L. (2007). Sex offender legislation in the United States: What do we know? *International Journal of Offender Therapy and Comparative Criminology, 51*, 369-383.

Cohen, M. A., Rust, R. T., Steen, S., & Tidd, S. T. (2004). Willingness-to-pay for crime control programs. *Criminology, 42*, 89-110.

Cohn, A. M., Zinzow, H. M., Resnick, H. S., & Kilpatrick, D. G. (2013). Correlates of reasons for not reporting rape to police: Results from a national telephone household probability sample of women with forcible or drug-or-alcohol facilitated/incapacitated rape. *Journal of Interpersonal Violence, 28*, 455-473.

Cole, S. A. (2000). From the sexual psychopath statute to "Megan's Law": Psychiatric knowledge in the diagnosis, treatment, and adjudication of sex criminals in New Jersey, 1949-1999. *Journal of the History of Medicine, 55*, 292-314.

Colorado Department of Corrections. (2002). *Lifetime supervision of sex offenders: Annual report.* Denver: Author.

Colorado Department of Public Safety. (2004). *Report on safety issues raised by living arrangements for and location of sex offenders in the community.* Denver: Sex Offender Management Board.

Comartin, E., Kernsmith, P., & Kernsmith, R. (2009). Sanctions for sex offenders: Fear and public policy. *Journal of Offender Rehabilitation, 48*, 605-619.

Comartin, E., Kernsmith, R., & Kernsmith, P. (2013). "Sexting" and sex offender registration: Do age, gender, and sexual orientation matter? *Deviant Behavior, 34*, 38-52.

Cooper, C. L., Murphy, W. D., & Haynes, M. R. (1996). Characteristics of abused and nonabused adolescent sexual offenders. *Sexual Abuse: A Journal of Research and Treatment, 8*, 105-119.

Cortoni, F., Hanson, R. K., & Coache, M. . (2010). The recidivism rates of female sexual offenders are low: A meta-analysis. *Sexual Abuse: A Journal of Research and Treatment, 22*, 387-401.

Council of State Governments. (2010). *Sex offender management policy in the states: Strengthening policy and practice.* Lexington, KY: Author.

Craig, L. A., & Beech, A. R. (2010). Towards a guide to best practice in conducting actuarial risk assessments with sex offenders. *Aggression and Violent Behavior, 15*, 278-293.

Craig, L. A., Browne, K., & Beech, A. (2008). *Assessing risk in sex offenders.* New York: Wiley.

Craissati, J. (2004). *Managing high-risk sex offenders in the community: A psychological approach.* New York: Routledge.

Craun, S. W. (2010). Evaluating awareness of registered sex offenders in the neighborhood. *Crime & Delinquency, 56*, 414-435.

Craun, S. W., & Theriot, M. T. (2009). Misperceptions of sex offender perpetration considering the impact of sex offender registration. *Journal of Interpersonal Violence, 24*, 2057-2072.

Crompton, L. (1976). Homosexuals and the death penalty in colonial America. *Journal of Homosexuality, 1*, 277-293.

Cullen, F. T., Fisher, B. S., & Applegate, B. K. (2000). Public opinion about punishment and corrections. *Crime and Justice, 27*, 1-79.

Cullen, F. T., & Gendreau, P. (2000). Assessing correctional rehabilitation: Policy, practice, and prospects. *Criminal Justice, 3*, 109-175.

Currivan, D. B., Nyman, A. L., Turner, C. F., & Biener, L. (2004). Does telephone audio computer-assisted self-interviewing improve the accuracy of prevalence estimates of youth smoking? Evidence from the UMass Tobacco Study. *Public Opinion Quarterly, 68*, 542-564.

D'Amato, A. (2006). *Porn up, rape down.* Public Law and Legal Theory Research Paper Series. Chicago: Northwestern University School of Law.

D'Avella, J. H. D. (2006). Death row for child rape? Cruel and unusual punishment under the Roper-Atkins 'evolving standard of decency' framework. *Cornell Law Review, 92,* 129-156.

Department of Defense. (2011). *Department of Defense annual report on sexual assault in the military.* Washington, D.C.: Author.

Devlin, R. (2005). "Acting out the Oedipal wish": Father-daughter incest and the sexuality of adolescent girls in the United States, 1941-1965. *Journal of Social History, 38,* 609-633.

Ditton, P. M. (1999). *Mental health and treatment of inmates and probationers.* Washington, D.C.: Bureau of Justice Statistics.

Doble, J. (2002). Attitudes to punishment in the U.S. Punitive and liberal opinions. In J. V. Roberts & M. Hough (Eds.), *Changing attitudes to punishment: Public opinion, crime, and justice* (pp. 148-162). Cullompton: Willan.

Donnerstein, E. (1984). Pornography: Its effect on violence against women. In N. Malamuth & E. Donnerstein (Eds.), *Pornography and sexual aggression* (pp. 53-81). Orlando: Academic Press, Inc.

Doren, D. M. (1998). Recidivism base rates, predictions of sex offender recidivism, and the "sexual predator" commitment laws. *Behavioral Sciences and the Law, 16,* 97-114.

Doren, D. M. (Ed.). (2002). *Evaluating sex offenders: A manual for civil commitments and beyond.* Thousand Oaks, CA: Sage.

Doren, D. M. (2007). *A critique of Hart, Michie, and Cooke: The precision of actuarial risk instruments.* Unpublished manuscript.

Douard, J. (2008). Sex offender as scapegoat: The monstrous other within. *New York Law School Law Review, 53,* 31-52.

Dreznick, M. T. (2003). Heterosocial competence of rapists and child molesters: A meta-analysis. *The Journal of Sex Research, 40,* 170-178.

Du Mont, J., Miller, K., & Myhr, T. L. (2003). The role of "real rape" and "real victim" stereotypes in the police reporting practices of sexually assaulted women. *Violence Against Women, 9,* 466-486.

Durling, C. (2006). Never going home: Does it make us safer? Does it make sense? Sex offenders, residence restrictions, and reforming risk management law. *Journal of Criminal Law & Criminology, 97,* 317-364.

Duwe, G. (2013). Can Circles of Support and Accountability (COSA) work in the United States? Preliminary results from a randomized experiment in Minnesota. *Sexual Abuse: A Journal of Research and Treatment, 25,* 143-165.

Duwe, G., & Donnay, W. (2008). The impact of Megan's Law on sex offender recidivism: The Minnesota experience. *Criminology, 46,* 411-446.

Duwe, G., & Freske, P. J. (2012). Using logistic regression modeling to predict sexual recidivism: The Minnesota Sex Offender Screening Tool-3 (MnSOST-3). *Sexual Abuse: A Journal of Research and Treatment, 24,* 350-377.

Edwards, W., & Hensley, C. (2001). Contextualizing sex offender management legislation and policy: Evaluating the problem of latent consequences in community notification laws. *International Journal of Offender Therapy and Comparative Criminology, 45,* 83-101.

Eher, R., Matthes, A., Schilling, F., Haubner-MacLean, T., & Rettenberger, M. (2012). Dynamic risk assessment in sexual offenders using Stable-2000 and the Stable-2007: An investigation of predictive and incremental validity. *Sexual Abuse: A Journal of Research and Treatment, 24,* 5-28.

Eligon, J., & Schwirtz, M. (2012, August 19). Senate candidate provokes ire with "legitimate rape" comment. *New York Times,* p. A13.

Epperson, D. L., Kaul, J. D., Huot, S., Goldman, R., & Alexander, W. (2003). *Minnesota Sex Offender Screening Tool-Revised (MnSOST-R) technical paper: Development, validation, and recommended risk level cut scores.* St. Paul, MN: Minnesota Department of Corrections.

Epperson, D. L., Kaul, J. D., Huot, S., Goldman, R., Hesselton, D., & Alexander, W. (2005). *Minnesota Sex Offender Screening Tool-Revised (MnSOST-R) scoring guidelines-updated.* St. Paul, MN: Minnesota Department of Corrections.

Erikson, K. T. (1966). *Wayward puritans: A study in the sociology of deviance.* New York: Wiley.

Faggiani, D., Kubu, B., & Rantala, R. (2005). *Facilitating the implementation of incident-based data systems.* Washington, D.C.: Police Executive Research Forum.

Faller, K. C. (1987). Women who sexually abuse children. *Violence and Victims, 2,* 263-276.

Federal Bureau of Investigation. (2000). *National Incident-Based Reporting System Volume 1: Data collection guidelines.* Washington, D.C.: Author.

Federal Bureau of Investigation. (2004). *Uniform Crime Reporting handbook, 2004.* Washington, D.C.: Author.

Federal Bureau of Investigation. (2010a). *Crime in the United States, 2009.* Washington, D.C.: Author.

Federal Bureau of Investigation. (2010b). *Summary of the Uniform Crime Reporting (UCR) Program.* Washington, D.C.: Author.

Federal Bureau of Investigation. (2012). *Uniform Crime Reporting offense definitions.* Washington, D.C.: Author.

Federal Bureau of Investigation. (2013). *Uniform Crime Reports data tool.* Washington, D.C.: Author.

Feild, H. S. (1978). Attitudes toward rape: A comparative analysis of police, rapists, crisis counselors, and citizens. *Journal of Personality and Social Psychology, 36,* 156-179.

Finckenauer, J. O. (1988). Public support for the death penalty: Retribution as just deserts or retribution as revenge? *Justice Quarterly, 5,* 81-100.

Finkelhor, D., & Dziuba-Leatherman, J. (1995). Victimization prevention programs: A national survey of children's exposure and reactions. *Child Abuse & Neglect, 19,* 129-139.

Finkelhor, D., & Jones, L. M. (2004). *Explanations for the decline in child sexual abuse cases.* Washington, D.C.: U.S. Department of Justice.

Finkelhor, D., & Jones, L. M. (2006). Why have child maltreatment and child victimization declined? *Journal of Social Issues, 62,* 685-716.

Finkelhor, D., & Jones, L. M. (2012). *Have sexual abuse and physical abuse declined since the 1990s?* Durham, NH: Crimes Against Children Research Center.

Finkelhor, D., & Ormrod, R. K. (2000). *Kidnapping of juveniles: Patterns from NIBRS.* Washington, D.C.: U.S. Department of Justice.

Finkelhor, D., & Ormrod, R. K. (2001). *Offenders incarcerated for crimes against juveniles.* Washington, D.C.: U.S. Department of Justice.

Finkelhor, D., & Ormrod, R. K. (2004). *Child pornography: Patterns from NIBRS.* Washington, D.C.: U.S. Department of Justice.

Finkelhor, D., Ormrod, R. K., & Chaffin, M. (2009). *Juveniles who commit sex offenses against minors.* Washington, D.C.: Office of Juvenile Justice and Delinquency Prevention.

Finkelhor, D., Ormrod, R. K., Turner, H. A., & Hamby, S. L. (2011). School, police, and medical authority involvement with children who have experienced victimization. *Archives of Pediatrics & Adolescent Medicine, 165,* 9-15.

Finkelhor, D., Turner, H. A., & Hamby, S. L. (2011). *Questions and answers about the National Survey of Children's Exposure to Violence.* Washington, D.C.: U.S. Department of Justice.

Finkelhor, Turner, H. A., Ormrod, R. K., & Hamby, S. L. (2010). Trends in childhood violence and abuse exposure: Evidence from two national surveys. *Archives of Pediatrics & Adolescent Medicine, 164,* 238-242.

Finkelhor, D., Turner, H. A., Ormrod, R. K., Hamby, S. L., & Kracke, K. (2009). *Children's exposure to violence: A comprehensive national survey.* Washington, D.C.: U.S. Department of Justice.

Finkelhor, D., Turner, H. A., Shattuck, A., Hamby, S. L. (in press). Violence, crime, and abuse exposure in a national sample of children and youth. *Pediatrics.*

Finkelhor, D., & Yllo, K. (1985). *License to rape: Sexual abuse of wives.* New York: Holt, Rinehart, and Winston.

Fisher, B. S., & Cullen, F. T., (2000). Measuring the sexual victimization of women: Evolution, current controversies, and future research. *Criminal Justice, 4,* 317-390.

Fisher, B. S., Cullen, F. T., & Turner, M. G. (2000). *The sexual victimization of college women.* Washington, D.C.: U.S. Department of Justice.

Fisher, B. S., Daigle, L. E., Cullen, F. T., & Turner, M. G. (2000). Acknowledging sexual victimization as rape: Results from a national level study. *Justice Quarterly, 20,* 401-440.

Fitch, W. L. (1998). Sex offender commitment in the United States. *The Journal of Forensic Psychiatry, 9,* 237-240.

Fitzgibbon, D. W. M. (2007). Risk analysis and the new practitioner: Myth or reality? *Punishment & Society, 9,* 87-97.

Flood, M. (2009). The harms of pornography exposure among children and young people. *Child Abuse Review, 18,* 384-400.

Florida Council Against Sexual Violence. (2013). *Florida's new mandatory reporting law.* Tallahassee, FL: Author.

Florida Department of Children and Families. (2011). *Florida sexual violence benchbook.* Tallahassee, FL: Author.

Fortney, T., Levenson, J. S., Brannon, Y., & Baker, J. N. (2007). Myths and facts about sexual offenders: Implications for treatment and public policy. *Sexual Offender Treatment, 2,* 1-17.

Frank, B. (1931). Mental level as a factor in crime. *Journal of Juvenile Research, 15*, 192-197.

Freedman, E. B. (1987). "Uncontrolled desires": The response to the sexual psychopath, 1920-1960. *Journal of American History, 74*, 83-106.

Freeman, N. J. (2012). The public safety impact of community notification laws: Rearrest of convicted sex offenders. *Crime & Delinquency, 58*, 539-564.

Freeman, N. J., & Sandler, J. C. (2010). The Adam Walsh Act: A false sense of security or an effective public policy initiative? *Criminal Justice Policy Review, 21*, 31-49.

Freske, P. J. (2012). *Minnesota Sex Offender Screening Tool-3.1 (MnSOST-3.1) coding rules.* St. Paul, MN: Minnesota Department of Corrections.

Fuselier, D. A., Durham, R. L., & Wurtele, S. K. (2002). The child sexual abuser: Perceptions of college students and professionals. *Sexual Abuse: A Journal of Research and Treatment, 14*, 267-276.

Galeste, M. A., Fradella, H. F., & Vogel, B. (2012). Sex offender myths in print media: Separating fact from fiction in U.S. newspapers. *Western Criminology Review, 13*, 4-24.

Gallagher, C. A., Wilson, D. B., Hirschfield, P., Coggeshall, M. B., & MacKenzie, D. L. (1999). Quantitative review of the effects of sex offender treatment on sexual reoffending. *Corrections Management Quarterly, 3*, 19-29.

Garcia, F. D., Delavenne, H. G., Assumpç o, A. F. A., & Thibaut, F. (2013). Pharmacologic treatment of sex offenders with paraphilic disorder. *Current Psychiatry Report, 15*, 1-6.

Garland, R. J., & Dougher, M. J. (1990). The abused/abuser hypothesis of child sexual abuse: A critical review of theory and research. In J. Feierman (Ed.), *Pedophilia: Biosocial dimensions* (pp. 488-509). New York: Springer-Verlag.

Gavey, N. (2005). *Just sex? The cultural scaffolding of rape.* New York: Routledge.

Geraghty, S. (2007). Challenging the banishment of registered sex offenders from the state of Georgia: A practitioner's perspective. *Harvard Civil Rights-Civil Liberties Law Review, 42*, 513-529.

Gibb, W. T. (1894). Indecent assault upon children. In A. M. Hamilton & L. Godkin (Eds.), *System of legal medicine* (pp. 649-657). New York: E. B. Treat.

Gibson, L. E., & Leitenberg, H. (2000). Child sexual abuse prevention programs: Do they decrease the occurrence of child sexual abuse? *Child Abuse & Neglect, 24*, 1115-1125.

Gilbert, N. (1992). Realities and mythologies of rape. *Society, 29*, 4-10.

Gilbert, N. (1997). Advocacy research exaggerates rape statistics. In M. R. Walsh (Ed.), *Women, men, and gender: Ongoing debates* (pp. 236-242). New Haven: Yale University Press.

Giltay, E. J., & Gooren, L. J. G. (2009). Potential side effects of androgen deprivation treatment in sex offenders. *Journal of American Academy of Psychiatry and the Law, 37*, 53-58.

Giotakos, O., Markianos, M., Vaidakis, N., & Christodoulou, G. N. (2003). Aggression, impulsivity, plasma sex hormones, and biogenic amine turnover in a forensic population of rapists. *Journal of Sex & Marital Therapy, 29*, 215-225.

Godbeer, R. (1995). Discourse, intercourse, and desire in colonial New England. *William and Mary Quarterly, 52*, 259-286.

Golan, M., & Crow, S. (2004). Parents are key players in the prevention and treatment of weight-related problems. *Nutrition Reviews, 62*, 39-50.

Goodwill, A., & Allison, L. J. (2007). When is profiling possible? Offense planning and aggression as moderators in predicting offender age from victim age in stranger rape. *Behavioral Sciences & the Law, 25,* 823-840.

Gottschalk, M. (2008). Hiding in plain sight: American politics and the carceral state. *Annual Review of Political Science, 11,* 235-260.

Gould, S. J. (1996). *The mismeasure of man.* New York: WW Norton & Company.

Gray, A., Busconi, A., Houchens, P., & Pithers, W. D. (1997). Children with sexual behavior problems and their caregivers: Demographics, functioning, and clinical patterns. *Sexual Abuse: A Journal of Research and Treatment, 9,* 267-290.

Greenberg, D. F., & West, V. (2001). State prison populations and their growth, 1971-1991. *Criminology, 39,* 615-654.

Greenfeld, L. A. (1997). *Sex offenses and offenders: An analysis of data on rape and sexual assault.* Washington, D.C.: Bureau of Justice Statistics.

Griset, P. L. (2002). New sentencing laws follow old patterns: A Florida case study. *Journal of Criminal Justice, 30,* 287-301.

Groth, A. N. (1979). *Men who rape: The psychology of the offender.* New York: Plenum Press.

Groth, A. N. (1982). The incest offender. In S. M. Sgroi (Ed.), *Handbook of clinical intervention in child sexual abuse* (pp. 215-239). Lexington, MA: Heath & Co.

Groth, A. N., & Birnbaum, H. (1978). Adult sexual orientation and attraction to underage persons. *Archives of Sexual Behavior, 7,* 175-181.

Groth, A. N., Burgess, A. W., & Holmstrom, L. L. (1977). Rape: Power, anger, and sexuality. *American Journal of Psychiatry, 134,* 1239-1243.

Grubesic, T. H., Murray, A. T., & Mack, E. A. (2011). Sex offenders, residence restrictions, housing, and urban morphology: A review and synthesis. *Cityscape: A Journal of Policy Development and Research, 13,* 7-31.

Hald, G. M., Malamuth, N. M., & Yuen, C. (2010). Pornography and attitudes supporting violence against women: Revisiting the relationship in nonexperimental studies. *Aggressive Behavior, 36,* 14-20.

Hanson, R. K., Bourgon, G., Helmus, L. M., & Hodgson, S. (2009). The principles of effective correctional treatment also apply to sexual offenders: A meta-analysis. *Criminal Justice and Behavior, 36,* 865-891.

Hanson, R. K., & Bussière, M. T. (1998). Predicting relapse: A meta-analysis of sexual offender recidivism studies. *Journal of Consulting and Clinical Psychology, 66,* 348-362.

Hanson, R. K., Gizzarelli, R., & Scott, H. (1994). The attitudes of incest offenders: Sexual entitlement and acceptance of sex with children. *Criminal Justice and Behavior, 21,* 187-202.

Hanson, R. K., & Harris, A. J. R. (1998). *Dynamic predictors of sexual recidivism.* Ottawa: Department of the Solicitor General of Canada.

Hanson, R. K., & Harris, A. J. R. (2000). Where should we intervene? Dynamic predictors of sexual offense recidivism. *Criminal Justice and Behavior, 27,* 6-35.

Hanson, R. K., & Harris, A. J. R. (2001). A structured approach to evaluating change among sexual offenders. *Sexual Abuse: A Journal of Research and Treatment, 13,* 105-122.

Hanson, R. K., Harris, A. J. R., Scott, T., & Helmus, L. M. (2007). *Assessing the risk of sexual offenders on community supervision: The Dynamic Supervision Project.* Ottawa: Public Safety Canada.

Hanson, R. K., & Morton-Bourgon, K. E. (2004). *Predictors of sexual recidivism: An updated meta-analysis.* Ottawa: Public Safety and Emergency Preparedness Canada.

Hanson, R. K., & Morton-Bourgon, K. E. (2005). The characteristics of persistent sexual offenders: A meta-analysis of recidivism studies. *Journal of Consulting and Clinical Psychology, 73,* 1154-1163.

Hanson, R. K., & Morton-Bourgon, K. E. (2009). The accuracy of recidivism risk assessments for sexual offenders: A meta-analysis of 118 prediction studies. *Psychological Assessment, 21,* 1-21.

Hanson, R. K., & Scott, H. (1996). Social networks of sex offenders. *Psychology, Crime, & Law, 2,* 249-258.

Hanson, R. K., & Thornton, D. (2000). Improving risk assessments for sex offenders: A comparison of three actuarial scales. *Law and Human Behavior, 24,* 119-136.

Hanson, R. K., & Thornton, D. (2003). *Notes on the development of Static-2002.* Ottawa: Department of the Solicitor General of Canada.

Harrington, C., & Neilson, T. (2009). *A review of research on sexual violence in audio-visual media.* Wellington, NZ: Office of Film and Literature Classification.

Harris, A. J., & Lobanov-Rostovsky, C. (2010). Implementing the Adam Walsh Act's sex offender registration and notification provisions: A survey of the states. *Criminal Justice Policy Review, 21,* 202-222.

Harris, A. J., & Lurigio, A. J. (2010). Introduction to special issue on sex offenses and offenders: Toward evidence-based public policy. *Criminal Justice and Behavior, 3,* 477-481.

Harris, A. J. R., & Hanson, R. K. (2004). *Sex offender recidivism: A simple question* (No. 2004-03). Ottawa: Public Safety and Emergency Preparedness Canada.

Harris, A. J. R., & Hanson, R. K. (2010). Clinical, actuarial and dynamic risk assessment of sexual offenders: Why do things keep changing? *Journal of Sexual Aggression, 16,* 296-310.

Harris, A. J. R., Phenix, A., Thornton, D., & Hanson, R. K. (2003). *Static 99: Coding rules revised 2003.* Ottawa: Solicitor General Canada.

Harris, D. A., Knight, R. A., Smallbone, S., & Dennison, S. (2011). Postrelease specialization and versatility in sexual offenders referred for civil commitment. *Sexual Abuse: A Journal of Research and Treatment, 23,* 243-259.

Hart, S. D., Michie, C., & Cooke, D. J. (2007). Precision of actuarial risk assessment instruments: Evaluating the "margins of error" of group v. individual predictions of violence. *British Journal of Psychiatry, 190,* 60-65.

Hart, T., & Rennison, C. (2003). *Reporting crime to the police, 1992-2000.* Washington, D.C.: Bureau of Justice Statistics.

Hattem, T. (2000). *Survey of sexual assault survivors* (Report No. 2000-4e). Ottawa: Department of Justice Canada.

Hayashino, D. S., Wurtele, S. K., & Klebe, K. J. (1995). Child molesters: An examination of cognitive factors. *Journal of Interpersonal Violence, 10,* 106-116.

Hazelwood, R. R., & Warren, J. I. (2000). The sexually violent offender: Impulsive or ritualistic? *Aggression and Violent Behavior, 5*, 267-279.

Helmus, L. M., & Hanson, R. K. (2007). Predictive validity of the Static-99 and Static-2002 for sex offenders on community supervision. *Sexual Offender Treatment, 2*, 1-14.

Helmus, L. M., Thornton, D., Hanson, R. K., & Babchishin, K. M. (2012). Improving the predictive accuracy of Static-99 and Static-2002 with older sex offenders: Revised age weights. *Sexual Abuse: A Journal of Research and Treatment, 24*, 64-101.

Hendricks, S. E, Fitzpatrick, D. F., Hartmann, K., Quaife, M. A., Stratbucker, R. A., & Graber, B. (1988). Brain structure and function in sexual molesters of children and adolescents. *Journal of Clinical Psychiatry, 49*, 108-112.

Hendrix, K. (1991, July 9). Defining controversy: Professor raises furor by claiming date rape statistics are inflated. *Los Angeles Times*, p. 1.

Hill, M. S., & Fischer, A. R. (2001). Does entitlement mediate the link between masculinity and rape-related variables? *Journal of Counseling Psychology, 48*, 39-50.

Hinduja, S., & Patchin, J. W. (2012). *School climate 2.0: Preventing cyberbullying and sexting one classroom at a time*. Thousand Oaks, CA: Sage.

Hirschfield, P. J., & Piquero, A. R. (2010). Normalization and legitimation: Modeling stigmatizing attitudes toward ex-offenders. *Criminology, 48*, 27-55.

Holmes, R. M., & Holmes, S. T. (1996). *Profiling violent crimes: An investigative tool*. Thousand Oaks, CA: Sage.

Holmes, S. T., & Holmes, R. M. (2009). *Sex crimes: Patterns and behavior* (3rd ed.). Thousand Oaks, CA: Sage.

Howitt, D., & Sheldon, K. (2007). The role of cognitive distortions in pedophilic offending: Internet and contact offenders compared. *Psychology, Crime, & Law, 13*, 469-486.

Hucker, S., Langevin, R., Dickey, R., Handy, L., Chambers, J., Wright, S., Bain, J., & Wortzman, G. (1988). Cerebral damage and dysfunction in sexually aggressive men. *Sexual Abuse: A Journal of Research and Treatment, 1*, 33-47.

Hucker, S., Langevin, R., Wortzman, G., Bain, J., Handy, L., Chambers, J., & Wright, S. (1986). Neuropsychological impairment in pedophiles. *Canadian Journal of Behavioral Science, 18*, 440-448.

Hughes, T., & Wilson, D. J. (2002). *Reentry trends in the United States*. Washington, D.C.: U.S. Department of Justice.

Humbach, J. A. (2010). "Sexting" and the First Amendment. *Hastings Constitutional Law Quarterly, 37*, 433-485.

Jackson, R., Schneider, J., & Travia, T. (2010). *SOCCPN annual survey of sexual offender civil commitment programs*. Presentation at the Sexual Offender Civil Commitment Programs Network, Phoenix, AZ.

Jacob Wetterling Crimes Against Children and Sexually Violent Offender Registration Act, Public Law 103-322 (1994).

Jacobs, J. E., Hashima, P. Y., & Kenning, M. (1995). Children's perceptions of the risk of sexual abuse. *Child Abuse & Neglect, 19*, 1443-1456.

Janus, E. S., & Prentky, R. A. (2003). Forensic use of actuarial risk assessment with sex offenders: Accuracy, admissibility, and accountability. *American Criminal Law Review, 40*, 1443-1499.

Jen, A. (2004). *Stogner v. California*: A collision between the ex post facto clause and California's interest in protecting child sex abuse victims. *Journal of Criminal Law and Criminology, 94*, 723-760.

Jenkins, P. (1998). *Moral panic: Changing concepts of the child molester in modern America.* New Haven, CT: Yale University Press.

Jenkins, P. (2001). *Beyond tolerance: Child pornography on the Internet* (2nd ed.). New York: NYU Press.

Jespersen, A. F., Lalumière, M. L., & Seto, M. C. (2009). Sexual abuse history among adult sex offenders and non-sex offenders: A meta-analysis. *Child Abuse & Neglect, 33*, 179-192.

Jessica Lunsford Act, H. R. 1505, 109th Cong., 1st Sess. (2005).

Jimmy Ryce Involuntary Civil Commitment for Sexually Violent Predators' Treatment and Care Act, Florida Statute 394.912 (1998).

Johnson, J. D., Adams, M. S., Ashburn, L., & Reed, W. (1995). Differential gender effects of exposure to rap music on African American adolescents' acceptance of teen dating violence. *Sex Roles, 33*, 597-605.

Justice Research and Statistics Association. (2012). *Status of NIBRS in the states.* Washington, D.C.: Author.

Kafka, M. P., & Hennen, J. (2002). A DSM-IV Axis I comorbidity study of males (n=120) with paraphilias and paraphilia-related disorders. *Sexual Abuse: A Journal of Research and Treatment, 14*, 349-366.

Kalof, L. (1999). The effects of gender and music video imagery on sexual attitudes. *Journal of Social Psychology, 139*, 378-385.

Kanin, E. J. (1967). Reference groups and sex conduct norm violations. *Sociological Quarterly, 8*, 495-504.

Katz-Schiavone, S., Levenson, J. S., & Ackerman, A. R. (2008). Myths and facts about sexual violence: Public perceptions and implications for prevention. *Journal of Criminal Justice and Popular Culture, 15*, 291-311.

Kempe, R., & Kempe, C. H. (1978). *Child abuse.* Cambridge, MA: Harvard University Press.

Kernsmith, P. D., Comartin, E., Craun, S. W., & Kernsmith, R. M. (2009). The relationship between sex offender registry utilization and awareness. *Sexual Abuse: A Journal of Research and Treatment, 21*, 181-193.

Kernsmith, P. D., Craun, S. W., & Foster, J. (2009). Public attitudes toward sexual offenders and sex offender registration. *Journal of Child Sexual Abuse, 18*, 290-301.

Kesler, K. (2002). Is a feminist stance in support of prostitution possible? An exploration of current trends. *Sexualities, 5*, 219-235.

Kilpatrick, D. G., Edmunds, C. N., & Seymour, A. K. (1992). *Rape in America: A report to the nation.* Arlington, VA: National Victim Center.

Kilpatrick, D. G., Resnick, H. S., Ruggiero, K. J., Conoscenti, L. M., & McCauley, J. (2007). *Drug-facilitated, incapacitated, and forcible rape: A national study.* Charleston, SC: Medical University of South Carolina, National Crime Victims Research & Treatment Center.

Kingston, D. A., Fedoroff, P., Firestone, P., Curry, S., & Bradford, J. M. (2008). Pornography use and sexual aggression: The impact of frequency and type of pornography use on recidivism among sexual offenders. *Aggressive Behavior, 34*, 341-351.

Kirby, S. L., & Wintrup, G. (2002). Running the gauntlet: An examination of initiation/ hazing and sexual abuse in sport. *Journal of Sexual Aggression, 8,* 49-68.

Kleban, H., & Jeglic, E. (2012). Dispelling the myths: Can psychoeducation change public attitudes towards sex offenders? *Journal of Sexual Aggression, 18,* 179-193.

Knight, R. A. (1999). Validation of a typology for rapists. *Journal of Interpersonal Violence, 14,* 303-330.

Knight, R. A., & Prentky, R. A. (1990). Classifying sexual offenders: The development and corroboration of taxonomic models. In W. L. Marshall, D. R. Laws, & H. E. Barbaree (Eds.), *Handbook of sexual assault: Issues, theories, and treatment of the offender* (pp. 23-53). New York: Plenum.

Knight, R. A., & Prentky, R. A. (1993). Exploring characteristics for classifying juvenile sex offenders. In H. E. Barbaree, W. L. Marshall, & S. M. Hudson (Eds.), *The juvenile sex offender* (pp. 45-83). New York: Guilford.

Knight, R. A., & Thornton, D. (2007). *Evaluating and improving risk assessment schemes for sexual recidivism: A long-term follow-up of convicted sexual offenders.* Washington, D.C.: National Institute of Justice.

Ko, S. F., & Cosden, M. A. (2001). Do elementary school-based child abuse prevention programs work? A high school follow-up. *Psychology in the Schools, 38,* 57-66.

Koon-Magnin, S., Kreager, D. A., & Ruback, R. B. (2010). Partner age differences, educational contexts and adolescent female sexual activity. *Perspectives on Sexual and Reproductive Health, 42,* 206-213.

Koss, M. P. (1985). The hidden rape victim: Personality, attitudinal, and situational characteristics. *Psychology of Women Quarterly, 9,* 193-212.

Koss, M. P., Leonard, K. E., Beezley, D. A., & Oros, C. J. (1985). Nonstranger sexual aggression: A discriminant analysis of psychological characteristics of nondetected offenders. *Sex Roles, 12,* 981-992.

Kruttschnitt, C., Uggen, C., & Shelton, K. (2000). Predictors of desistance among sex offenders: The interaction of formal and informal social controls. *Justice Quarterly, 17,* 61-87.

Kutchinsky, B. (1973). The effect of easy availability of pornography on the incidence of sex crimes: The Danish experience. *Journal of Social Issues, 29,* 163-181.

La Fond, J. Q. (1998). The costs of enacting a sexual predator law. *Psychology, Public Policy, and Law, 4,* 468-504.

Lam, A., Mitchell, J., & Seto, M. C. (2010). Lay perceptions of child pornography offenders. *Canadian Journal of Criminology and Criminal Justice, 52,* 173-201.

Lampe, J. R. (2013). A victimless sex crime: The case for decriminalizing consensual teen sexting. *University of Michigan Journal of Law Reform, 46,* 703-737.

Lancaster, R. N. (2011a, August 20). Sex offenders: The last pariahs. *New York Times,* p. SR6.

Lancaster, R. N. (2011b). *Sex panic and the punitive state.* Berkeley: University of California Press.

Langan, P. A., Schmitt, E. L., & Durose, M. R. (2003). *Recidivism of sex offenders released from prison in 1994.* Washington, D.C.: Bureau of Justice Statistics.

Langevin, R. (2009). Neuropsychological findings in sex offenders. In F. M. Saleh, A. Grudzinskas, J. M. Bradford, & D. J. Brodsky (Eds.), *Sex offenders: Identification, risk assessment, treatment, and legal issues,* (pp. 27-35). New York: Oxford University Press.

Langevin, R., Ben-Aron, M. H., Wright, P., & Marchese, V., & Handy, L. (1988). The sex killer. *Sexual Abuse: A Journal of Research and Treatment, 1,* 263-301.

Langevin, R., Wortzman, G., Wright, P., & Handy, L. (1989). Studies of brain damage and dysfunction in sex offenders. *Sexual Abuse: A Journal of Research and Treatment, 2,* 163-179.

Långström, N. (2004). Accuracy of actuarial procedures for assessment of sexual offender recidivism risk may vary across ethnicity. *Sexual Abuse: A Journal of Research and Treatment, 16,* 107-120.

Langton, L., Berzofsky, M., Krebs, C. P., & Smiley-McDonald, H. (2012). *Victimizations not reported to the police, 2006-2010.* Washington, D.C.: Bureau of Justice Statistics.

Lanning, K. V. (2001). *Child molesters: A behavioral analysis* (4th ed.). Alexandria, VA: National Center for Missing and Exploited Children.

Leon, C. S. (2011a). *Sex fiends, perverts, and pedophiles: Understanding sex crime policy in America.* New York: NYU Press.

Leon, C. S. (2011b). The contexts and politics of evidence-based sex offender policy. *Criminology & Public Policy, 10,* 421-430.

Letourneau, E. J., Bandyopadhyay, D., Armstrong, K. S., & Sinha, D. (2010). Do sex offender registration and notification requirements deter juvenile sex crimes? *Criminal Justice and Behavior, 37,* 553-569.

Letourneau, E. J., Levenson, J. S., Bandyopadhyay, D., Armstrong, K. S., & Sinha, D. (2010). Effects of South Carolina's sex offender registration and notification policy on deterrence of adult sex crimes. *Criminal Justice and Behavior, 37,* 537-552.

Levenson, J. S. (2004). Sexual predator civil commitment: A comparison of selected and released offenders. *International Journal of Offender Therapy and Comparative Criminology, 48,* 638-648.

Levenson, J. S. (2011). Sex offender policies in an era of zero tolerance: What does effectiveness really mean? *Criminology & Public Policy, 10,* 229-233.

Levenson, J. S., Brannon, Y. N., Fortney, T., & Baker, J. (2007). Public perceptions about sex offenders and community protection policies. *Analyses of Social Issues and Public Policy, 7,* 137-161.

Levenson, J. S., & Cotter, L. P. (2005a). The effect of Megan's Law on sex offender reintegration. *Journal of Contemporary Criminal Justice, 21,* 49-66.

Levenson, J. S., & Cotter, L. P. (2005b). The impact of sex offender residence restrictions: 1,000 feet from danger or one step from absurd? *International Journal of Offender Therapy and Comparative Criminology, 49,* 168-178.

Levenson, J. S., & D'Amora, D. A. (2007). Social policies designed to prevent sexual violence: The emperor's new clothes? *Criminal Justice Policy Review, 18,* 168-199.

Levenson, J. S., D'Amora, D. A., & Hern, A. (2007). Megan's Law and its impact on community reentry for sex offenders. *Behavioral Sciences & the Law, 25,* 587-602.

Levenson, J. S., & Harris, A. J. (2012). 100,000 sex offenders missing . . . or are they? De-construction of an urban legend. *Criminal Justice Policy Review, 23*, 375-386.

Levenson, J. S., Letourneau, E. J., Armstrong, K., & Zgoba, K. M. (2010). Failure to register as a sex offender: Is it associated with recidivism? *Justice Quarterly, 27*, 305-331.

Levenson, J. S., & Morin, J. W. (2008). Factors predicting selection of sexually violent predators for civil commitment. *International Journal of Offender Therapy and Comparative Criminology, 50*, 609-629.

Levenson, J. S., Shields, R. T., & Singleton, D. (in press). Collateral punishments and sentencing policy: Perceptions of residence restrictions for sex offenders and drunk drivers. *Criminal Justice Policy Review.*

Lieb, R., Quinsey, V., & Berliner, L. (1998). Sexual predators and social policy. *Crime and Justice, 23*, 43-114.

Lilly, J. R., Cullen, F. T., & Ball, R. A. (2007). *Criminological theory: Context and consequences* (4th ed.). Thousand Oaks, CA: Sage.

Lindsey, D. (2004). *The child welfare system* (2nd ed.). New York: Oxford University Press.

Linz, D. G., Donnerstein, E., & Penrod, S. (1988). Effects of long-term exposure to violent and sexually degrading depictions of women. *Journal of Personality and Social Psychology, 55*, 758-768.

Lippman, M. (2010). *Contemporary criminal law: Concepts, cases, and controversies* (2nd ed.). Thousand Oaks, CA: Sage.

Lipsey, M., Petrie, C., Weisburd, D., & Gottfredson, D. (2006). Improving evaluation of anti-crime programs: Summary of a national research council report. *Journal of Experimental Criminology, 2*, 271-307.

Lipton, D., Martinson, R., & Wilks, J. (1975). *The effectiveness of correctional treatment: A survey of treatment evaluation studies.* New York: Praeger.

Lisak, D. (2011). Understanding the predatory nature of sexual violence. *Sexual Assault Report, 14*, 49-64.

Loewy, A. H. (2005). Statutory rape in a post *Lawrence v. Texas* world. *Southern Methodist University Law Review, 58*, 77-101.

Logan, W. A. (2003). Jacob's legacy: Sex offender registration and community notification laws, practice, and procedure in Minnesota. *William and Mary Law Review, 29*, 1287-1342.

Logan, W. A. (2008). Criminal justice federalism and national sex offender policy. *Ohio State Journal of Criminal Law, 6*, 51-122.

Logan, W. A. (2011). Prospects for the international migration of U.S. sex offender registration and community notification laws. *International Journal of Law and Psychiatry, 34*, 233-238.

Lonsway, K. A., & Archambault, J. (2012). The "justice gap" for sexual assault cases: Future directions for research and reform. *Violence Against Women, 18*, 145-168.

Lonsway, K. A., Banyard, V. L., Berkowitz, A. D., Gidycz, C. A., Katz, J. T., Koss, M. P., Schewe, P. A., & Ullman, S. E. (2009). *Rape prevention and risk reduction: Review of the research literature for practitioners.* Atlanta: Centers for Disease Control.

Lonsway, K. A., & Fitzgerald, L. F. (1994). Rape myths: In review. *Psychology of Women Quarterly, 18*, 133-164.

Looman, J., Gauthier, C., & Boer, D. (2001). Replication of the Massachusetts Treatment Center child molester typology in a Canadian sample. *Journal of Interpersonal Violence, 16*, 753-767.

Lösel, F., & Schmucker, M. (2005). The effectiveness of treatment for sexual offenders: A comprehensive meta-analysis. *Journal of Experimental Criminology, 1*, 117-146.

Lucken, K., & Latina, J. (2002). Sex offender civil commitment laws: Medicalizing deviant sexual behavior. *Barry Law Review, 3*, 15-38.

Lussier, P., Bouchard, M., & Beauregard, E. (2011). Patterns of criminal achievement in sexual offending: Unraveling the "successful" sex offender. *Journal of Criminal Justice, 39*, 433-444.

Lussier, P., & Mathesius, J. (2012). Criminal achievement, criminal career initiation, and detection avoidance: The onset of successful sex offending. *Journal of Crime and Justice, 35*, 376-394.

Lynch, M. (2002). Pedophiles and cyber-predators as contaminating forces: The language of disgust, pollution, and boundary invasions in federal debates on sex offender legislation. *Law & Social Inquiry, 27*, 529-557.

Maguire, M., & Singer, J. K. (2011). A false sense of security: Moral panic driven sex offender legislation. *Critical Criminology, 19*, 301-312.

Maletzky, B. M., & Steinhauser, C. (2002). A 25-year follow-up of cognitive/behavioral therapy with 7,275 sexual offenders. *Behavior Modification, 26*, 123-147.

Mancini, C. (in press). Examining factors that predict public concern about the collateral consequences of sex crime policy. *Criminal Justice Policy Review*.

Mancini, C., Barnes, J. C., & Mears, D. P. (2013). It varies from state to state: An examination of sex crime laws nationally. *Criminal Justice Policy Review, 24*, 166-198.

Mancini, C., & Mears, D. P. (2010). To execute or not to execute? Examining public support for capital punishment of sex offenders. *Journal of Criminal Justice, 38*, 959-968.

Mancini, C., Reckdenwald, A., & Beauregard, E. (2012). Pornographic exposure over the life course and the severity of sexual offenses: Imitation and cathartic effects. *Journal of Criminal Justice, 40*, 21-30.

Mancini, C., Shields, R. T., Mears, D. P., & Beaver, K. M. (2010). Sex offender residence restriction laws: Parental perceptions and public policy. *Journal of Criminal Justice, 38*, 1022-1030.

Manza, J., Brooks, C., & Uggen, C. (2004). Public attitudes toward felon disenfranchisement in the United States. *Public Opinion Quarterly, 68*, 275-286.

Mardorossian, C. (2002). Toward a newfeminist theory of rape. *Signs: Journal of Women in Culture and Society, 27*, 743-755.

Marolla, J. A., & Scully, D. (1986). Attitudes toward women, violence, and rape: A comparison of convicted rapists and other felons. *Deviant Behavior, 7*, 337-355.

Marques, J. K., Day, D. M., & Nelson, C. (1994). Effects of cognitive-behavioral treatment on sex offender recidivism: Preliminary results of a longitudinal study. *Criminal Justice and Behavior, 21*, 28-54.

Marques, J. K., Nelson, C., & West, M. A. (1994). The relationship between treatment goals and recidivism among child molesters. *Behavior Research & Therapy, 32*, 577-588.

Marshall, W. L., & Barbaree, H. E. (1990). Cognitive-behavioral treatment programs. In W. L. Marshall, D. R. Laws, & H. E. Barbaree (Eds.), *Handbook of sexual assault: Issues, theories, and treatment of the offender* (pp. 363-385). New York: Plenum Press.

Martinez, R., Flores, J., & Rosenfeld, B. (2007). Validity of the Juvenile Sex Offender Assessment Protocol-II (J-SOAP-II) in a sample of urban minority youth. *Criminal Justice and Behavior, 34*, 1284-1295.

Martinson, R. (1974). What works? Questions and answers about prison reform. *The Public Interest, 35*, 22-54.

Maruna, S., & Mann, R. (2006). Fundamental attribution errors? Re-thinking cognitive distortions. *Legal and Criminological Psychology, 11*, 155-177.

Marziano, V., Ward, T., Beech, A., & Pattison, P. (2006). Identification of five fundamental implicit theories underlying cognitive distortions in child abusers: A preliminary study. *Psychology, Crime, & Law, 12*, 97-105.

Mathews, R., Hunter, J. A., & Vuz, J. (1997). Juvenile female sexual offenders: Clinical characteristics and treatment issues. *Sexual Abuse: A Journal of Research and Treatment, 9*, 187-199.

Mathews, R., Matthews, J., & Speltz, K. (1989). *Female sexual offenders: An exploratory study*. Brandon, VT: The Safer Society Press.

Matson, S., & Lieb, R. (1996). *Sex offender community notification: A review of laws in 32 states*. Olympia, WA: Washington State Institute for Public Policy.

McCabe, M. P., & Wauchope, M. (2005). Behavioral characteristics of men accused of rape: Evidence for different types of rapists. *Archives of Sexual Behavior, 34*, 241-253.

McCorkle, R. C. (1993). Research note: Punish and rehabilitate? Public attitudes toward six common crimes. *Crime & Delinquency, 39*, 240-252.

McDaniel, P. (1993). Self-defense training and women's fear of crime. *Women Studies International Forum, 16*, 37-45.

McGrath, R. J., Cumming, G. F., Burchard, B. L., Zeoli, S., & Ellerby, L. (2010). *Current practices and emerging trends in sexual abuser management*. Brandon, VT: Safer Society Press.

McLaughlin, J. F. (2000). *Cyber child sex offender typology*. Keene, NH: Keene Police Department.

McLawsen, J. E., Scalora, M. J., & Darrow, C. (2012). Civilly committed sex offenders: A description and interstate comparison of populations. *Psychology, Public Policy, and Law, 18*, 453-476.

McLean, N., Griffin, S., Toney, K., & Hardeman, W. (2003). Family involvement in weight control, weight maintenance, and weight-loss interventions: A systematic review of randomized trials. *International Journal of Obesity, 27*, 987-1005.

McMahon-Howard, J. (2011). Does the controversy matter? Comparing the causal determinants of the adoption of controversial and noncontroversial rape law reforms. *Law & Society Review, 45*, 401-434.

Mears, D. P. (2010). *American criminal justice policy: An evaluation approach to increasing accountability and effectiveness*. New York: Cambridge University Press.

Mears, D. P., & Barnes, J. C. (2010). Toward a systematic foundation for identifying evidence-based criminal justice sanctions and their relative effectiveness. *Journal of Criminal Justice, 38,* 702-710.

Mears, D. P., Mancini, C., Gertz, M., & Bratton, J. (2008). Sex crimes, children, and pornography: Public views and public policy. *Crime & Delinquency, 54,* 532-559.

Megan's Law, Public Law 104-145 (1996).

Meijer, E. H., Verschuere, B., Merckelbach, H. L., & Crombez, G. (2008). Sex offender management using the polygraph: A critical review. *International Journal of Law and Psychiatry, 31,* 423-429.

Meloy, M. L., Curtis, K. M., & Boatwright, J. (2013). The sponsors of sex offender bills speak up: Policymakers' perceptions of sex offenders, sex crimes, and sex offender legislation. *Criminal Justice and Behavior, 40,* 438-452.

Meloy, M. L., Miller, S. L., & Curtis, K. M. (2008). Making sense out of nonsense: The deconstruction of state-level sex offender residence restrictions. *American Journal of Criminal Justice, 33,* 209-222.

Meloy, M. L., Saleh, Y., & Wolff, N. (2007). Sex offender laws in America: Can panic-driven legislation ever create safer societies? *Criminal Justice Studies, 20,* 423-443.

Mendez, M. F., Chow, T., Ringman. J., Twitchell, G., & Hinkin, C. H. (2000). Pedophilia and temporal lobe disturbances. *Journal of Neuropsychiatry & Clinical Neuroscience, 12,* 71-76.

Mercado, C. C, Alvarez, S., & Levenson, J. (2008). The impact of specialized sex offender legislation on community reentry. *Sexual Abuse: A Journal of Research and Treatment, 20,* 188-205.

Messner, S. F., Baumer, E. P., & Rosenfeld, R. (2006). Distrust of government, the vigilante tradition, and support for capital punishment. *Law & Society Review, 40,* 559-590.

Meyer, W. J., & Cole, C. M. (1997). Physical and chemical castration of sex offenders: A review. *Journal of Offender Rehabilitation, 25,* 1-18.

Miccio-Fonseca, L. C. (2000). Adult and adolescent female sex offenders: Experiences compared to other female and male sex offenders. *Journal of Psychology and Human Sexuality, 11,* 75-88.

Miccio-Fonseca, L. C., & Rasmussen, L. A. (2011). A concise review on validated risk assessment tools for sexually abusive youth. *Sexual Offender Treatment, 6,* 1-13.

Milburn, M. A., Mather, R., & Conrad, S. D. (2000). The effects of viewing R-rated movie scenes that objectify women on perceptions of date rape. *Sex Roles, 43,* 645-664.

Minnesota Department of Corrections. (2003). *Level three sex offenders residential placement issues.* St. Paul, MN: Author.

Minugh, K. (2012, October 2). Prop. 35 backers say human-trafficking measure is needed; foes argue it's badly flawed. *The Sacramento Bee,* p. 1A.

Moon, M. M., Wright, J. P., Cullen, F. T., & Pealer, J. A. (2000). Putting kids to death: Specifying public support for juvenile capital punishment. *Justice Quarterly, 17,* 663-684.

Muehlenhard C. L., & Linton M. A. (1987). Date rape and sexual aggression dating situations: Incidence and risk factors. *Journal of Counseling Psychology, 34,* 186-196.

Murnen, S. K., & Kohlman, M. H. (2007). Athletic participation, fraternity membership, and sexual aggression among college men: A meta-analytic review. *Sex Roles, 57*, 145-157.

Murphy, W. D. (1990). Assessment and modification of cognitive distortions in sex offenders. In W. L. Marshall, D. R. Laws, & H. E. Barbaree (Eds.), *Handbook of sexual assault* (pp. 331-342). New York: Plenum Press.

Murphy, W. D., Coleman, E. M., & Haynes, M. R. (1986). Factors related to coercive sexual behavior in a nonclinical sample of males. *Violence and Victims, 1*, 255-278.

Mustaine, E., & Tewksbury, R. (2002). Sexual assault of college women: A feminist routine activities analysis. *Criminal Justice Review, 27*, 89-123.

Myers, W. C. (2002). Juvenile sexual homicide. New York: Academic Press.

Nash, M. (1999). *Police, probation, and protecting the public*. London, UK: Blackstone.

Nathan, P., & Ward, T. (2002). Female sex offenders: Clinical and demographic features. *Journal of Sexual Aggression, 8*, 5-21.

National Center for Missing and Exploited Children. (2012). *Map of registered sex offenders in the United States*. Alexandria, VA: Author.

National Center for Prosecution of Child Abuse. (2012). *Statutes of limitations for prosecution of offenses against children*. Alexandria, VA: Author.

National Conference of State Legislatures. (2003). *State statutes regarding lifetime community supervision of sex offenders*. Denver: Author.

National Conference of State Legislatures. (2008a). *Laws requiring sex offender notation on driver's license*. Denver: Author.

National Conference of State Legislatures. (2008b). *Sex offender chemical treatment (castration) laws July 2008 update*. Denver: Author.

Neumann, S. (2006). Gang rape: Examining peer support and alcohol in fraternities. In E. W. Hickey (Ed.), *Sex crimes and paraphilia* (pp. 397-407). Upper Saddle River, NJ: Pearson/Prentice Hall.

Neville, H. A., & Pugh, A. O. (1997). General and culture specific factors influencing African American women's reporting patterns and perceived social support following sexual assault: An exploratory investigation. *Violence Against Women, 3*, 361-381.

Nieto, M. (2004). *Community treatment and supervision of sex offenders: How it's done across the country and in California*. Sacramento, CA: California Research Bureau.

Nobles, M. R., Levenson, J. S., & Youstin, T. J. (2012). Effectiveness of residence restrictions in preventing sex offense recidivism. *Crime & Delinquency, 58*, 491-513.

O'Brien, M., & Bera, W. H. (1986). Adolescent sexual offenders: A descriptive typology. *Preventing Sexual Abuse: A Newsletter of the National Family Life Education Network, 1*, 2-4.

Olver, M. E., & Barlow, A. A. (2010). Public attitudes toward sex offenders and their relationship to personality traits and demographic characteristics. *Behavioral Sciences & the Law, 28*, 832-849.

Onishi, N. (2012, November, 18). Suit says new law violates sex offenders' rights online. *New York Times*, p. A20.

Page, A. D. (2010). True colors: Police officers and rape myth acceptance. *Feminist Criminology, 5*, 315-334.

Pam Lychner Sexual Offender Tracking and Identification Act, Public Law 104-236 (1996).

Paolucci E. O., Genuis, M. L, & Violato, C. (2001). A meta-analysis of the published research on the effects of child sexual abuse. *Journal of Psychology, 135*, 17-36.

Payne, B. K., & DeMichele, M. T. (2010). Electronic supervision for sex offenders: Implications for work load, supervision goals, versatility, and policymaking. *Journal of Criminal Justice, 38*, 276-281.

Payne, B. K., Tewksbury, R., & Mustaine, E. E. (2010). Attitudes about rehabilitating sex offenders: Demographic, victimization, and community-level influences. *Journal of Criminal Justice, 38*, 580-588.

Petrunik, M. G. (2002). Managing unacceptable risk: Sex offenders, community response, and social policy in the United States and Canada. *International Journal of Offender Therapy and Comparative Criminology, 46*, 483-511.

Pew Research Center. (2012). *Assessing the representativeness of public opinion surveys.* Washington, D.C.: Author.

Phenix, A., Doren, D., Helmus, L. M., Hanson, R. K., & Thornton, D. (2008). *Coding rules for Static-2002.* Ottawa: Public Safety Canada.

Phillips, D. M. (1998). *Community notification as viewed by Washington's citizens.* Olympia, WA: Washington State Institute for Public Policy.

Pickett, J. T., Mears, D. P., Stewart, E. A., & Gertz, M. (in press). Security at the expense of liberty: A test of predictions deriving from the culture of control thesis. *Crime & Delinquency.*

Pilger, L. (2012, October 12). Judge overturns parts of Nebraska sex offender law. *Lincoln Journal Star*, p. A1.

Piquero, A. R., Farrington, D. P., Jennings, W. G., Diamond, B., & Craig, J. (2012). Sex offenders and sex offending in the Cambridge study in delinquent development: Prevalence, frequency, specialization, recidivism, and (dis)continuity over the life-course. *Journal of Crime and Justice, 35*, 412-426.

Planty, M., Langton, L., Krebs, C., Berzofsky, M., & Smiley-McDonald, H. (2013). *Female victims of sexual violence, 1994-2010.* Washington, D.C.: Bureau of Justice Statistics.

Polizzi, D. M., MacKenzie, D. L., & Hickman, L. J. (1999). What works in adult sex offender treatment? A review of prison-and non-prison-based treatment programs. *International Journal of Offender Therapy and Comparative Criminology, 43*, 357-374.

Pratt, T. C., Cullen, F. T., Blevins, K. R., Daigle, L. E., & Madensen, T. D. (2006). The empirical status of deterrence theory: A meta-analysis. *Taking Stock: The Status of Criminological Theory, 15*, 367-395.

Prentky, R. A., Harris, B., Frizzell, K., & Righthand, S. (2000). An actuarial procedure for assessing risk with juvenile sex offenders. *Sexual Abuse: A Journal of Research and Treatment, 12*, 71-93.

Prentky, R. A., & Righthand, S. (2003). *Juvenile Sex Offender Assessment Protocol-II (J-SOAP-II) manual.* Bridgewater, MA: Justice Resource Institute.

Proctor, J. L., Badzinski, D. M., & Johnson, M. (2002). The impact of media on knowledge and perceptions of Megan's Law. *Criminal Justice Policy Review, 13*, 356-379.

Prosecutorial Remedies and Tools Against the Exploitation of Children Today Act (PROTECT), Public Law 108-21 (2003).

Quinn, J. F., Forsyth, C., & Mullen-Quinn, C. (2004). Societal reaction to sex offenders: A review of the origins and results of the myths surrounding their crimes and treatment amenability. *Deviant Behavior, 25*, 215-232.

Quinsey, V. L., Khanna, A., & Malcolm, P. B. (1998). A retrospective evaluation of the Regional Treatment Center Sex Offender Treatment Program. *Journal of Interpersonal Violence, 13*, 621-644.

Rada, R. T., Laws, D. R., & Kellner, R. (1976). Plasma testosterone levels in the rapist. *Psychosomatic Medicine, 38*, 257-268.

Radeloff, C., & Carnes, E. (2009). Sex offenders, mandatory HIV testing, and intentional transmission. In R. G. Wright, *Sex offender laws: Failed policies, new directions* (pp. 159-209). New York: Springer.

Rajlic, G., & Gretton, H. M. (2010). An examination of two sexual recidivism risk measures in adolescent offenders. *Criminal Justice and Behavior, 37*, 1066-1085.

Rand, M., & Catalano, S. (2006). *Criminal victimization, 2006.* Washington, D.C.: Bureau of Justice Statistics.

Rantala, R. R. (2000). *Effects of NIBRS on crime statistics.* Washington, D.C.: Bureau of Justice Statistics.

Rapaport, W., & Lieberman, D. (1956). The sexual psychopath in California. *California Medicine, 85*, 232-234.

Redlich, A. D. (2001). Community notification: Perceptions of its effectiveness in preventing child sexual abuse. *Journal of Child Sexual Abuse, 10*, 91-116.

Reid, S. L, Wilson, N. J., & Boer, D. P. (2010). Application of the Massachusetts Treatment Center Revised Rapist Typology to New Zealand high-risk rapists: A pilot study. *Sexual Abuse in Australia and New Zealand, 2*, 77-84.

Reilly, M., Lott, B., Caldwell, D., & DeLuca, L. (1992). Tolerance for sexual harassment related to self-reported sexual victimization. *Gender and Society, 6*, 122-138.

Reitzel, L. R., & Carbonell, J. L. (2006). The effectiveness of sexual offender treatment for juveniles as measured by recidivism: A meta-analysis. *Sexual Abuse: A Journal of Research and Treatment, 18*, 401-421.

Rice, M. E., & Harris, G. T. (2011). Is androgen deprivation therapy effective in the treatment of sex offenders? *Psychology, Public Policy, and Law, 17*, 315-332.

Rich, P. (2009). *Juvenile sexual offenders: A comprehensive guide to risk evaluation.* New York: Wiley.

Roberts, J. V., & Grossman, M. (1994). Changing definitions of sexual assault: An analysis of police statistics. In J. V. Roberts & R. M. Mohr (Eds.), *Confronting sexual assault: A decade of legal and social change* (pp. 57-83). Toronto: University of Toronto Press.

Rodriguez, R. (2010). The sex offender under the bridge: Has Megan's Law run amok? *Rutgers Law Review, 62*, 1023-1061.

Rogers, D. L., & Ferguson, C. J. (2011). Punishment and rehabilitation attitudes toward sex offenders versus nonsexual offenders. *Journal of Aggression, Maltreatment, & Trauma, 20*, 395-414.

Rogers, L. (2007). *The SMART Office: Open for business.* Washington, D.C.: U.S. Department of Justice.

Rogers, P., Hirst, L., & Davies, M. (2011). An investigation into the effect of respondent gender, victim age, and perpetrator treatment on public attitudes towards sex offenders, sex offender treatment, and sex offender rehabilitation. *Journal of Offender Rehabilitation, 50*, 511-530.

Roiphe, K. (1993). *The morning after: Sex, fear, and feminism on campus.* Boston: Little, Brown and Company.

Roman, C. G. & Travis, J. (2004). *Taking stock: Housing, homelessness, and prisoner reentry.* Washington, D.C.: Urban Institute.

Rossi, P. H., Freeman, H. E., & Lipsey, M. W. (2004). *Evaluation: A systematic approach,* (7th ed.). Thousand Oaks, CA: Sage.

Rozee, P., & Koss, M. (2001). Rape: A century of resistance. *Psychology of Women Quarterly, 25*, 295-311.

Russell, D. E. H. (1993). *Against pornography: The evidence of harm.* Berkeley: Russell Publishing.

Sacco, L. (2002). Sanitized for your protection: Medical discourse and the denial of incest in the United States, 1890-1940. *Journal of Women's History, 14*, 80-104.

Sahlstrom, K. J., & Jeglic, E. L. (2008). Factors affecting attitudes toward juvenile sex offenders. *Journal of Child Sexual Abuse, 17*, 180-196.

Salerno, J. M., Najdowski, C. J., Stevenson, M. C., Wiley, T. R., Bottoms, B. L., Vaca, R., & Pimentel, P. S. (2010). Psychological mechanisms underlying support for juvenile sex offender registry laws: Prototypes, moral outrage, and perceived threat. *Behavioral Sciences & the Law, 28*, 58-83.

Salter, A. (2003). *Predators: Pedophiles, rapists, and other sex offenders: Who they are, how they operate, and how we can protect ourselves and our children.* New York: Basic Books.

Sample, L. L. (2011). The need to debate the fate of sex offender community notification laws. *Criminology & Public Policy, 10*, 265-274.

Sample, L. L., & Bray, T. M. (2003). Are sex offenders dangerous? *Criminology & Public Policy, 3*, 59-82.

Sample, L. L., & Bray, T. M. (2006). Are sex offenders different? An examination of rearrest patterns. *Criminal Justice Policy Review, 17*, 83-102.

Sample, L. L., Evans, M. K., & Anderson, A. L. (2011). Sex offender community notification laws: Are their effects symbolic or instrumental in nature? *Criminal Justice Policy Review, 22*, 27-49.

Sample, L. L., & Kadleck, C. (2008). Sex offender laws: Legislators' accounts of the need for policy. *Criminal Justice Policy Review, 19*, 40-62.

Sandler, J. C., & Freeman, N. J. (2007). Typology of female sex offenders: A test of Vandiver and Kercher. *Sexual Abuse: A Journal of Research and Treatment, 19*, 73-89.

Sandler, J. C., Freeman, N. J., & Socia, K. M. (2008). Does a watched pot boil? A time-series analysis of New York State's sex offender registration and notification law. *Psychology, Public Policy, and Law, 14*, 284-302.

Schiavone, S. K., & Jeglic, E. L. (2009). Public perception of sex offender social policies and the impact on sex offenders. *International Journal of Offender Therapy and Comparative Criminology, 53*, 679-695.

Schiltz, K., Witzel, J., Northoff, G., Zierhut, K., Gubka, U., Fellmann, H., Kaufmann, J., Tempelmann, C., Wiebking, C., & Bogerts, B. (2007). Brain pathology in pedophilic offenders: Evidence of volume reduction in the right amygdala and related diencephalic structures. *Archives of General Psychiatry, 64,* 737-746.

Schmucker, M., & Lösel, F. (2008). Does sexual offender treatment work? A systematic review of outcome evaluations. *Psicotherma, 20,* 10-19.

Schwartz, M. D., & DeKeseredy, W. S. (1997). *Sexual assault on the college campus: The role of male peer support.* Thousand Oaks, CA: Sage.

Schwartz, M. D., DeKeseredy, W. S., Tait, D., & Alvi, S. (2001). Male peer support and a feminist routine activities theory: Understanding sexual assault on the college campus. *Justice Quarterly, 18,* 623- 650.

Schwartz, M. D., & Nogrady, C. A. (1996). Fraternity membership, rape myths, and sexual aggression on a college campus. *Violence Against Women, 2,* 148-162.

Scott, C. L., & del Busto, E. (2009). Chemical and surgical castration. In R. G. Wright (Ed.), *Sex offender laws: Failed policies, new directions* (pp. 291-338). New York: Springer.

Scott, C. L., & Holmberg, T. (2003). Castration of sex offenders: Prisoners' rights vs. public safety. *Journal of the American Academy of Psychiatry and Law, 31,* 502-509.

Second Chance Act, Public Law 110-199 (2007).

Seim, H. C., & Dwyer, M. (1988). Evaluation of serum testosterone and luteinizing hormone levels in sex offenders. *Family Practice Research Journal, 7,* 175-180.

Seto, M. C., Hanson, R. K., & Babchishin, K. M. (2011). Contact sexual offending by men with online sexual offenses. *Sexual Abuse: A Journal of Research and Treatment, 23,* 124-145.

Seto, M. C., & Lalumière, M. L. (2010). What is so special about male adolescent sexual offending? A review and test of explanations through meta-analysis. *Psychological Bulletin, 136,* 526-575.

Siegel, L. (2010). *Criminology: Theories, patterns, and typologies* (10th ed.). Belmont, CA: Wadsworth/Cengage.

Simon, L., Sales, B., Kazniac, A., & Kahn, A. (1992). Characteristics of child molesters: Implications for the fixated-regressed dichotomy. *Journal of Interpersonal Violence, 7,* 211-225.

Simpson, T. (2006). "If your hand causes you to sin …": Florida's chemical castration statute misses the mark. *Florida State University Law Review, 34,* 1221-1246.

Skuse, D., Bentovim, A., Hodges, J., Stevenson, J., Andreou, C., Lanyado, M., New, M., Williams, B., & McMillan, D. (1998). Risk factors for development of sexually abusive behavior in sexually victimized adolescent boys: Cross-sectional study. *British Medical Journal, 317,* 175-179.

Smith, D. W., Letourneau, E. J., Saunders, B. E., Kilpatrick, D. G., Resnick, H. S., & Best, C. L. (2000). Delay in disclosure of childhood rape: Results from a national survey. *Child Abuse and Neglect, 24,* 273-287.

Snyder, H. N., & Sickmund, M. (2006). *Juvenile offenders and victims: 2006 national report.* Washington, D.C.: Office of Juvenile Justice and Delinquency Prevention.

Socia, K. M. (2011). The policy implications of residence restrictions on sex offender housing in Upstate NY. *Criminology & Public Policy, 10,* 351-389.

Socia, K. M. (2012). The efficacy of county-level sex offender residence restrictions in New York. *Crime & Delinquency, 58*, 612-641.

Soothill, K. (2010). Sex offender recidivism. *Crime and Justice, 39*, 145-211.

Sorensen, J., & Stemen, D. (2002). The effect of state sentencing policies on incarceration rates. *Crime & Delinquency, 48*, 456-475.

Soss, J., Langbein, L., & Metelko, A. R. (2003). Why do White Americans support the death penalty? *Journal of Politics, 65*, 397-421.

Spalding, L. H. (1998). Florida's 1997 chemical castration law: A return to the dark ages. *Florida State University Law Review, 25*, 117-139.

Stack, S. (2000). Support for the death penalty: A gender-specific model. *Sex Roles: A Journal of Research, 43*, 163-179.

Stankiewicz, J. M., & Rosselli, F. (2008). Women as sex objects and victims in print advertisements. *Sex Roles, 57*, 579-589.

Steinhauer, J. (2013, March 14). Veterans testify on rapes and scant hope of justice. *New York Times*, p. A24.

Stemen, D., & Rengifo, A. F. (2002). Policies and imprisonment: The impact of structured sentencing and determinate sentencing on state incarceration rates, 1978-2004. *Justice Quarterly, 28*, 174-201.

Stermac, L. E., & Segal, Z. V. (1989). Adult sexual contact with children: An examination of the cognitive factors. *Behavior Therapy, 20*, 573-584.

Stevenson, M. C., Sorenson, K. M., Smith, A. C., Sekely, A., & Dzwairo, R. A. (2009). Effects of defendant and victim race on perceptions of juvenile sex offenders. *Behavioral Sciences & the Law, 27*, 957-979.

Stewart, M. W., Dobbin, S. A., & Gatowski, S. I. (1996). "Real rapes" and "real victims": The shared reliance on common cultural definitions of rape. *Feminist Legal Studies, 4*, 159- 177.

Stinneford, J. (2006). Incapacitation through maiming: Chemical castration, the Eighth Amendment, and the denial of human dignity. *University of St. Thomas Law Journal, 3*, 559-599.

Stolz, B. A. (2002). *Criminal justice policy making: Federal roles and processes.* Westport, CT: Praeger.

Strossen, N. (1993). A feminist critique of "the" feminist critique of pornography. *Virginia Law Review, 79*, 1099-1190.

Studer, L. H., Aylwin, S., & Reddon, J. R. (2005). Testosterone, sexual offense recidivism, and treatment effect among adult male sex offenders. *Sexual Abuse: A Journal of Research and Treatment, 17*, 171-181.

Suarez, E., & Gadalla, T. M. (2010). Stop blaming the victim: A meta-analysis on rape myths. *Journal of Interpersonal Violence, 25*, 2010-2035.

Sutherland, E. H. (1947). *Principles of criminology* (4th ed.). Philadelphia: Lippincott.

Sutherland, E. H. (1950). The sexual psychopathy laws. *Journal of Criminal Law and Criminology, 40*, 543-554.

Syed, F., & Williams, S. (1996). *Case studies of female sex offenders in the Correctional Service of Canada.* Ottawa: Correctional Service Canada.

Sykes, G. M., & Matza, D. (1957). Techniques of neutralization: A theory of delinquency. *American Sociological Review, 22,* 664-670.

Tabachnick, J., & Klein, A. (2011). *A reasoned approach: Reshaping sex offender policy to prevent child sexual abuse.* Beaverton, OR: Association for the Treatment of Sexual Abusers.

Tajalli, H., De Soto, W., & Dozier, A. (in press). Determinants of punitive attitudes of college students toward criminal offenders. *Journal of Criminal Justice Education.*

Tamborra, T. L., & Narchet, F. M. (2011). A university sexual misconduct policy: Prioritizing student victims' voices. *Crime Prevention & Community Safety, 13,* 16-33.

Temple, J. R., Paul, J. A., van den Berg, P., Le, V. D., McElhany, A., & Temple, B. W. (2012). Teen sexting and its association with sexual behaviors. *Archives of Pediatrics & Adolescent Medicine, 166,* 828-833.

Terry, K. J. (2005). *Sexual offenses and offenders: Theory, practice, and policy.* Belmont, CA: Wadsworth/Cengage.

Terry, K. J. (2011). What is smart sex offender policy? *Criminology & Public Policy, 10,* 275-282.

Terry, K. J., & Ackerman, A. R. (2008). A brief history of major sex offender laws. In R. G. Wright (Ed.), *Sex offender laws: Failed policies, new directions* (pp. 65-98). New York: Springer.

Terry, K. J., & Furlong, J. (2006). *Sex offender registration and community notification: A "Megan's Law" Sourcebook* (2nd ed.). Kingston, NJ: Civic Research Institute.

Terry, K. J., & Tallon, J. (2004). *Child sexual abuse: A review of the literature. The nature and scope of the problem of sexual abuse of minors by priests and deacons, 1950 2002.* Washington, D.C.: United States Conference of Catholic Bishops.

Tewksbury, R. (2002). Validity and utility of the Kentucky sex offender registry. *Federal Probation, 66,* 21-26.

Tewksbury, R. (2005). Collateral consequences of sex offender registration. *Journal of Contemporary Criminal Justice, 21,* 67-81.

Tewksbury, R. (2007). Effects of sexual assaults on men: Physical, mental, and sexual consequences. *International Journal of Men's Health, 6,* 22-35.

Tewksbury, R., & Jennings, W. G. (2010). Assessing the impact of sex offender registration and community notification on sex-offending trajectories. *Criminal Justice and Behavior, 37,* 570-582.

Tewksbury, R., & Lees, M. (2006). Perceptions of sex offender registration: Collateral consequences and community experiences. *Sociological Spectrum, 26,* 309-334.

Tewksbury, R., & Levenson, J. S. (2007). When evidence is ignored: Residential restrictions for sex offenders. *Corrections Today, 69,* 54-57.

Tewksbury, R., & Zgoba, K. M. (2010). Perceptions and coping with punishment: How registered sex offenders respond to stress, Internet restrictions, and the collateral consequences of registration. *International Journal of Offender Therapy and Comparative Criminology, 54,* 537-551.

Thornton, D. (2002). Constructing and testing a framework for dynamic risk assessment. *Sexual Abuse: A Journal of Research and Treatment, 14,* 139-153.

Tier, R., & Coy, K. (1997). Approaches to sexual predators: Community notification and civil commitment. *New England Journal on Criminal and Civil Commitment, 23*, 405-426.

Tjaden, P., & Thoennes, N. (2000). *Full report of the prevalence, incidence, and consequences of violence against women: Findings from the National Violence Against Women Survey.* Washington, D.C.: U.S. Department of Justice.

Tourangeau, R., & Yan, T. (2007). Sensitive questions in surveys. *Psychological Bulletin, 133*, 859-883.

Travis, J. (2005). *But they all come back: Facing the challenges of prisoner reentry.* Washington, D.C.: Urban Institute.

Truman, J. L., & Planty, M. (2012). *Criminal victimization, 2011.* Washington, D.C.: Bureau of Justice Statistics.

Turner, C. F., Villarroel, M. A., Rogers, S. M., Eggleston, E., Ganapathi, L., Roman, A. M, & Al-Tayyib, A. A. (2002). Reducing bias in telephone survey estimates of the prevalence of drug use: A randomized trial of Telephone Audio-CASI. *Addictions, 100*, 1432-1444.

Turner, M., & Turner, T. (1994). *Female adolescent sexual abusers: An exploratory study of mother-daughter dynamics with implications for treatment.* Brandon, VT: The Safer Society Press.

U.S. Census Bureau. (2003). *National Crime Victimization Survey interviewing manual for field representatives.* Washington, D.C.: Author.

U.S. Census Bureau. (2012). *National Crime Victimization Survey.* Washington, D.C.: Author.

U.S. Census Bureau. (2013). *State and county quick facts.* Washington, D.C.: Author.

U.S. Department of Justice. (2010). *The national strategy for child exploitation, prevention, and interdiction: A report to Congress.* Washington, D.C.: Author.

U.S. Department of Justice. (2012). *Dru Sjodin National Sex Offender Public Website.* Available online: http://www.nsopw.gov.

U.S. General Accounting Office. (1996). *Cycle of sexual abuse: Research inconclusive about whether child victims become adult abusers.* Washington, D.C.: Author.

U.S. Government Accountability Office. (2008). *Factors that could affect the successful implementation of driver's license-related processes to encourage registration and enhance monitoring.* Washington, D.C.: Author.

Vandiver, D. M. (2006). Female sex offenders. In R. D. M. Anulty & M. M. Burnette (Eds.), *Sex and Sexuality* (Vol. 3, pp. 47-80). Westport, CT: Praeger.

Vandiver, D. M., & Kercher, G. (2004). Offender and victim characteristics of registered female sexual offenders in Texas: A proposed typology of female sexual offenders. *Sexual Abuse: A Journal of Research and Treatment, 16*, 121-137.

Vásquez, B. E., Maddan, S., & Walker, J. T. (2008). The influence of sex offender registration and notification laws in the United States: A time-series analysis. *Crime & Delinquency, 54*, 175-192.

Velázquez, T. (2008). *The pursuit of safety: Sex offender policy in the United States.* New York: Vera Institute of Justice.

Veysey, B. M., & Zgoba, K. M. (2010). Sex offenses and offenders reconsidered: An investigation of characteristics and correlates over time. *Criminal Justice and Behavior, 37*, 583-595.

Vick, J., McRoy, R., & Matthews, B. M. (2002). Young female sex offenders: Assessment and treatment issues. *Journal of Child Sexual Abuse, 11*, 1-23.

Viljoen, J. L., Elkovitch, N., Scalora, M. J., & Ullman, D. (2009). Assessment of reoffense risk in adolescents who have committed sexual offenses: Predictive validity of the ERASOR, PCL: YV, YLS/CMI, and Static-99. *Criminal Justice and Behavior, 36*, 981-1000.

Viljoen, J. L., Mordell, S., & Beneteau, J. L. (2012). Prediction of adolescent sexual re-offending: A meta-analysis of the J-SOAP-II, ERASOR, J-SORRAT-II, and Static-99. *Law and Human Behavior, 36*, 423-438.

Viljoen, J. L., Scalora, M., Cuadra, L., Bader, S., Chavez, V., Ullman, D., & Lawrence, L. (2008). Assessing risk for violence in adolescents who have sexually offended: A comparison of the J-SOAP-II, J-SORRAT-II, and SAVRY. *Criminal Justice and Behavior, 35*, 5-23.

Vogel, B. L., & Vogel, R. E. (2003). The age of death: Appraising public opinion of juvenile capital punishment. *Journal of Criminal Justice, 31*, 169-183.

Walker, J. T. (2007). Eliminate residency restrictions for sex offenders. *Criminology & Public Policy, 6*, 863-870.

Ward, T., & Beech, A. R. (2004). The etiology of risk: A preliminary model. *Sexual Abuse: A Journal of Research and Treatment, 16*, 271-284.

Ward, T., & Beech, A. R. (2006). An integrated theory of sexual offending. *Aggression and Violent Behavior, 11*, 44-63.

Ward, T., & Gannon, T. A. (2006). Rehabilitation, etiology, and self-regulation: The comprehensive Good Lives Model of treatment for sexual offenders. *Aggression and Violent Behavior, 11*, 77-94.

Ward, T., Hudson, S. M., Johnston, L., & Marshall, W. L. (1997). Cognitive distortions in sex offenders: An integrative review. *Clinical Psychology Review, 17*, 479-507.

Ward, T., & Keenan, T. (1999). Child molesters' implicit theories. *Journal of Interpersonal Violence, 14*, 821-838.

Ward, T., & Stewart, C. A. (2003). The treatment of sex offenders: Risk management and Good Lives. *Professional Psychology: Research and Practice, 34*, 353-360.

Ward, T., Yates, P. M., & Willis, G. M. (2012). The Good Lives Model and the Risk Need Responsivity Model: A critical response to Andrews, Bonta, and Wormith (2011). *Criminal Justice and Behavior, 39*, 94-110.

Washington Department of Corrections. (2012). *Civil commitment of sexually violent predators.* Olympia, Washington: Author.

Washington Department of Corrections. (2013). *Sex offender treatment in prison.* Olympia, Washington: Author.

Webber, D. (1997). HIV/AIDS in the workplace. In D. W. Webber (Ed.), *AIDS and the law*, (3rd ed., pp. 97-176). New York: Wiley.

Weekes, J. R., Pelletier, G., & Beaudette, D. (1995). Correctional officers: How do they perceive sex offenders? *International Journal of Offender Therapy and Comparative Criminology, 39*, 55-61.

Weiss, K. G. (2010). Male sexual victimization: Examining men's experiences of rape and sexual assault. *Men and Masculinities, 12*, 275-298.

Weitzer, R. (2009). Sociology of sex work. *Annual Review of Sociology, 35,* 213-234.

Widom, C. S. (1989). Child abuse, neglect, and violent criminal behavior. *Criminology, 27,* 251-272.

Wiehe, V. R., & Richards, A. L. (1995). *Intimate betrayal. Understanding and responding to the trauma of acquaintance rape.* Thousand Oaks, CA: Sage.

Willis, G. M., Levenson, J. S., & Ward, T. (2010). Desistance and attitudes towards sex offenders: Facilitation or hindrance? *Journal of Family Violence, 25,* 545-556.

Willis, G. M., Yates, P. M., Gannon, T. A., & Ward, T. (2012). How to integrate the Good Lives Model into treatment programs for sexual offending: An introduction and overview. *Sexual Abuse: A Journal of Research and Treatment, 25,* 123-142.

Wilson, J. Q., & Petersilia, J. (Eds.). (2011). *Crime and public policy* (2nd ed.). New York: Oxford.

Wilson, K. M., Abel, G. G., Coyne, B., & Rouleau, J. (1991). Sex guilt and paraphilic sexual arousal. *Journal of Interpersonal Violence, 6,* 520-525.

Wilson, R. J., McWhinnie, A., Picheca, J. E., Prinzo, M., & Cortoni, F. (2007). Circles of Support and Accountability: Engaging community volunteers in the management of high-risk sexual offenders. *Howard Journal of Criminal Justice, 46,* 1-15.

Winick, B. J. (1998). Sex offender law in the 1990s: A therapeutic jurisprudence analysis. *Psychology, Public Policy, and Law, 4,* 505-570.

Wolak, J., & Finkelhor, D. (2011). *Sexting: A typology.* Durham, NH: Crimes Against Children Research Center.

Wolak, J., Mitchell, K., & Finkelhor, D. (2007). Unwanted and wanted exposure to online pornography in a national sample of youth Internet users. *Pediatrics, 119,* 247-257.

Worling, J. R. (2001). Personality-based typology of adolescent male sexual offenders: Differences in recidivism rates, victim-selection characteristics, and personal victimization histories. *Sexual Abuse: A Journal of Research and Treatment, 13,* 149-166.

Worling, J. R. (2004). The Estimate of Risk of Adolescent Sexual Offense Recidivism (ERASOR): Preliminary psychometric data. *Sexual Abuse: A Journal of Research and Treatment, 16,* 235-254.

Worling, J. R., Bookalam, D., & Litteljohn, A. (2012). Prospective validity of the Estimate of Risk of Adolescent Sexual Offense Recidivism (ERASOR). *Sexual Abuse: A Journal of Research and Treatment, 24,* 203-223.

Worling, J. R., & Curwen, T. (2001). Estimate of Risk of Adolescent Sexual Offense Recidivism (Version 2.0: The "ERASOR"). In M. C. Calder (Ed.), *Juveniles and children who sexually abuse: Frameworks for assessment* (pp. 372-397). Dorset, UK: Russell House Publishing.

Wortley, R., & Smallbone, S. (2006). *Child pornography on the Internet.* Washington, D.C.: Office of Community Oriented Policing Services.

Wright, R. G. (2008). Sex offender post-incarceration sanctions: Are there any limits? *New England Journal of Criminal & Civil Confinement, 34,* 17-50.

Wright, R. G. (Ed.). (2009). *Sex offender laws: Failed policies, new directions.* New York: Springer.

Yeudall, L. T., & Fromm-Auch, D. (1979). Neuropsychological impairments in various psychopathological populations. In J. Gruzelier & P. Flor-Henry (Eds.), *Hemisphere asymmetries of function in psychopathology* (pp. 5-13). New York: Elsevier.

Yildirim, B., & Derksen, J. J. L. (2012). A review on the relationship between testosterone and the interpersonal/affective facet of psychopathy. *Psychiatric Review, 197,* 181-198.

Zandbergen, P. A., Levenson, J. S., & Hart, T. C. (2010). Residential proximity to schools and daycares: An empirical analysis of sex offense recidivism. *Criminal Justice and Behavior, 37,* 482-502.

Zevitz, R. G. (2006). Sex offender community notification: Its role in recidivism and offender reintegration. *Criminal Justice Studies, 19,* 193-208.

Zevitz, R. G., & Farkas, M. A. (2000). Sex offender community notification: Managing high-risk criminals or exacting further vengeance? *Behavioral Sciences & the Law, 18,* 375-391.

Zgoba, K. M. (2011). Residence restriction buffer zones and the banishment of sex offenders. *Criminology & Public Policy, 10,* 391-400.

Zgoba, K. M., Witt, P., Dalessandro, M., & Veysey, B. (2008). *Megan's Law: Assessing the practical and monetary efficacy.* Washington, D.C.: U.S. Department of Justice.

Zhang, X. (2010). Charging children with child pornography: Using the legal system to handle the problem of "sexting." *Computer Law & Security Review, 26,* 251-259.

Zhang, S. X., Roberts, R. E., & Callanan, V. J. (2006). Preventing parolees from returning to prison through community-based reintegration. *Crime & Delinquency, 52,* 551-571.

Zilney, L. J., & Zilney, L. A. (2009). *Perverts and predators: The making of sexual offending laws.* Lanham, MD: Rowman and Littlefield.

Legal Cases Cited

Ashcroft v. Free Speech Coalition, 535 U.S. 234 (2002).

Bruno v. State, 837 So.2d 521, 522 (Fla. 1st Dist. App. 2003).

Carr v. U.S., 560 U.S. _____ (2010).

Coker v. Georgia, 433 U.S. 584 (1977).

Commonwealth v. Baker, 295 S.W.3d 437 (Ky. 2009).

Commonwealth v. Baker, 295 S.W.3d 437 (Ky. 2009), cert. denied, 562 U.S. _____ (U.S. Oct. 4, 2010) (No. 09-10615).

Connecticut Department of Public Safety v. Doe, 538 U.S. 1 (2003).

Cox Broadcasting Corporation v. Cohn, 420 U.S. 469 (1975).

District of Columbia v. Heller, 554 U.S. 570 (2008).

Doe v. Jindal, 853 F.Supp.2d 596 (2012).

Doe v. Marion County Prosecutor, 705 F.3d 694 (2013).

Doe v. Miller, 405 F.3d 700 (8th Cir. 2005).

Doe v. State of Nebraska, Nos. 8:09CV456, 4:10CV3266, 4:10CV3005 (United States District Court, D. Nebraska, 2012).

Florida Star v. B. J. F., 491 U.S. 524 (1989).

Fross v. County of Allegheny, 20 A.3d 1193 (Pa. 2011).

Furman v. Georgia, 408 U.S. 238 (1972).

G. H. v. Township of Galloway, 971 A.2d 401 (N.J. 2009).

Gregg v. Georgia, 428 U.S. 153 (1976).

Houston v. State, 852 So.2d 425, 428 (Fla. 5th Dist. App. 2003).

In re E. J., 47 Cal. 4th 1258 (Cal. 2010).

In re Taylor, 209 Cal. 4th 210 (Cal. 2012).

Jackson v. State, 907 So.2d 696 (Fla. 4th Dist. App. 2005).

Kansas v. Crane, 534 U.S. 407 (2002).

Kansas v. Hendricks, 521 U.S. 346 (1997).

Kennedy v. Louisiana, 554 U.S. 407 (2008).

Lessard v. Schmidt, 414 U.S. 473 (1974).

Mann v. Georgia Department of Corrections, 653 S.E.2d 740 (Ga. 2007).

McKune v. Lile, 536 U.S. 24 (2002).

Michigan v. Lucas, 500 U.S. 145 (1991).

Miller v. Alabama, 567 U.S. ____ (2012).

Miranda v. Arizona, 384 U.S. 436 (1966).

New York v. Ferber, 458 U.S. 747 (1982).

Osborne v. Ohio, 495 U.S. 103 (1990).

People v. Foster, 101 Cal. App. 4th 247, 249 (Ca. 2002).

Rainer v. State of Georgia, 690 S.E. 2d 827 (Ga. 2010).

Reynolds v. U.S., 565 U. S. ____ (2012).

Smith v. Doe, 538 U.S. 84 (2003).

Specht v. Patterson, 386 U.S. 605 (1967).

State ex rel. White v. Billings, 117 Ohio St. 3d 536 (Oh. 2008).

Stogner v. California, 539 U.S. 607 (2003).

U.S. v. Comstock, 560 U.S. 126 (2010).

U.S. v. Juvenile Male, 564 U.S. ____ (2011).

U.S. v. Williams, 553 U.S. 285 (2008).

Wilson v. State, 652 S.E. 2d 501, 282 Ga. 520 (2007).

Index